Adam's
Shŏtŏkan
Karate Books

The Basia Lerman
Karate Research Foundation

EMERALD
LAW GROUP

I0153040

ADAM'S KARATE DICTIONARY

A PROFESSIONAL GLOSSARY OF SHOTOKAN TERMS

ADAM DOBRZYŃSKI

Adam's Shotokan Karate Books
The Basia Lerman Karate Research Foundation
Published in the United States
by Adam Dobrzyński at Emerald Law Group, 280 N Oak St, Ukiah, CA 95482

e-mail: adamd⌧mscc.huji.ac.il

Front cover: The Chinese ancestor of Shōtōkan's symbol (p. 249). Western Han dynasty (206 BCE–9 CE), China // Earthenware (Ceramics) // "Roof tile end with tiger" Gallery 207 **The Metropolitan Museum of Art** NYC.
Back cover: Kankū // Naomi Kaempfer // oil on paper // Belgium 2023.

Adam's Karate Dictionary: A Professional Glossary of Shotokan Terms
ISBN Paperback: 978-1-7363447-2-9
ISBN Hardcover: 978-1-7363447-3-6

First Edition 2023

Library of Congress Cataloging-in-Publication Data
Dobrzynski, Adam.
Adam's Karate Dictionary: A Professional Glossary of Shotokan Terms / Adam Dobrzynski.
p. cm. - (martial arts)
Includes Bibliographical References and Index
Library of Congress Control Number: 2023946348

Tables of Contents

Chapters

Chapters and Subchapters

Dedicated to the Lerman family, for their unconditional love, as well as their kind help and support which enabled this book to be published.

Special Thanks

Editte Lerman, Esq.

Barbara Lerman

Joseph Lerman

Mickey Topaz

Julek Dobrzyński

Naomi Kaempfer

Bobby Bamgboye, WSKF, Nigeria

Joel Ibanga, WSKF, Nigeria

Sophie Le Bas, FSK, France

Patrick Schoeffer, FSK, France

Maria Anette Pavlović, Kase-ha, Sweden

Caroline Antgren, Kase-ha, Sweden

Denis Sopovic, Kase-ha, Sweden

Angela Babin, SKA, USA

Yael Magnes, SKA, USA

Iris Platt, SKA, USA

Gal Papkin, SOD, Israel

Omer Mienis, SOD, Israel

Ohad Shahar, SOD, Israel

Shlomi Ofir

Like us
facebook.com/KarateBooks

Text us (SMS)
Author's SMS

WhatsApp us
Author's WhatsApp

Email us
Author's mailbox

Sign up for a yearly mail!
groups.google.com/g/
shotokanyearlymail

Visit our bookshop!
amazon.com/stores/Adam-
Dobrzynski/author/B08W6QKR4G

Shop Now!

Donate to the project!
paypal.me/KarateBooks

Presentation

Karate jargon is integral to everyday practice. Without solid understanding of the Karate vocabulary, it is easy to fall into technical and conceptual errors. The purpose of this Shotokan dictionary is to bring the reader closer to the Karate terminology we so often use, but so rarely explore. This book can be described as a Japanese-English Shotokan dictionary, as well as a heavy-duty professional glossary of Karate terms related to Funakoshi styles. It can also be defined as a Shotokan encyclopedia or as a Karate lexicon, which focuses on the linguistic aspects of Karate phrases. Through the language, we dive into Karate itself. Although planned for senior Karate instructors, absolute beginners may also benefit from this Karate wordlist.

As for its content, the main goal – naturally – is to translate from "Karate language" to English. The book offers various English definitions of the Japanese technical terms, making it a powerful Japanese-English dictionary of the terms used in Karate. Sometimes the Karate meaning does not overlap with the general meaning of a word. If the common, or general, Japanese translation of a Karate term may be relevant, we bring it as well.

It was Seneca who said: "If one does not know to which port one is sailing, no wind is favorable". If we were to achieve a high standard of execution, we cannot afford not to understand – literally - the Karate commands. A clear understanding of the Karate terms is indispensable. Breaking down Karate expressions into their building blocks, does seem to achieve a deeper understanding of them. This Karate glossary puts a special emphasis on the important Kanji, including thorough Kanji-analysis and relevant cross-references. Deep meanings of important Shotokan expressions are sought, and their links to other Karate words are drawn. In our opinion, the references are this book's greatest virtue, and we urge our dear readers to be diligent and to follow them – especially when it comes to the Kanji that compose the value.

A large part of this Shotokan glossary is devoted to pronunciation issues. This Karate wordbook presents different Kanji readings, which may be very important in the case of several terms that have a common Kanji. Critical phenomena in Japanese phonology, such as the rendaku rules, are addressed too.

Besides transliterations of Japanese and Chinese into the Latin alphabet (romanization, Rōmaji), the advanced user will find logographic Kanji and syllabic Kana. Often, alternative writings are presented, so the reader can make better use of other sources – especially Japanese sources.

Introduction

During a Gasshuku (合宿) (training camp) that took place in Israel in 2022, Yaniv Murciano Sensei was correcting his disciples' Kankū-dai. Talking about the finishing double kick, he asked everyone what Nidan-geri means. Whan the practitioners said that it means a double kick, the Sensei's response was: "so You should kick twice, not once". Indeed, Nidan-geri (p. 184) is not Tobi-geri (p. 246). The former is less about flying. The name reminds us to perform the technique better.

Our words affect our insights, and our perceptions determine the words we are using. FUNAKOSHI Sensei and other masters had profound knowledge, not only of the Chinese classics[1] and the Japanese culture, but also of the Japanese language[2]. The names that we use in our Karate trainings were not chosen lightly nor accidentally. As for us, those names have great significance. "What's in a name? That which we call a rose by any other name would smell as sweet", says Juliet in William Shakespeare's Romeo and Juliet. In Karate's case, we humbly prefer Confucius's[3] approach. In the words of the Chinese philosopher Feng Youlan (1895 – 1990)[4]:

> Every name possesses its own definition, which designates that which makes the thing to which the name is applied be that thing and no other. In other words, the name is that thing's essence or concept. What is pointed out by the definition of the name 'ruler,' for example, is that essence which makes a ruler a ruler. In the phrase: 'Let the ruler be ruler,' etc., the first word, 'ruler,' refers to ruler as a material actuality, while the second 'ruler' is the name and concept of the ideal ruler.

Take the example of the name Jitte (p. 111). If a day comes, when they debate about how many hand movements there are in the opening of the Kata, the name of the Kata will be there to help. Some are going to realize, that there are Ten Hands - meaning ten palm strikes - up to the first Kiai; this understanding will derive from the name of the Kata. Some of the ten hand strikes are simultaneous. So, the right answer, they will hopefully conclude, is three.

But why Japanese, one asks; You can say Double Kick or Ten Hands in any language. First, it is a tradition. Second, we feel connected to something bigger than our Dōjō[5]. And indeed, in mutual training, correspondence, etc., we can communicate well with people that do not speak our language. The Japanese parts of our Karate-pidgin are a common ground. But most importantly, studies show that language influences the way we think[6].

The Chinese philosopher Dong Zhongshu (179-104 BC) used etymology as a hermeneutic tool[7]:

> The present generation is ignorant about human nature, giving various teachings about it. Why do they not try to examine the name "nature"? Does not the name "nature" (xìng 性) mean "birth" (shēng 生)? The capacity that one naturally has at birth is what is called the "nature". The nature is one's mere potential.

Accordingly, if we want to understand what it means to be a warrior, we should look at the Kanji for warrior. That is what the Chinese King Zhuāng of Chǔ (7th century B.C.) did. The Kanji for warrior is 武 (p. 45). If one looks carefully, one can see that this Compound Logogram is composed of the Radical 止 (p. 272) which could mean to stop – just as in our yame {{止め}} (p. 271), and from the Stem 戈 (dagger-axe). We should never look at the command Yame in the same way again. Putting an end to violence is indeed the highest level of the art of war; that was the King's conclusion, based on the Logogram[8,9]. For us, the language and the Sino-Japanese Logograms are indispensable for understanding Karate, from technique to spirit.

Lists of Figures

List of Sensei Demonstrations next to Values

Height 1.5''

List of Large Images

Height 3''

List of QR Codes (Video)

Height 0.5"

List of Scripts (Heigh up to 0.5")

List of Anatomy Images

List of Other Figures

Keys and Remarks

Abbreviations

Ch. Chinese

Comp. Compound Logogram/s *(p. 287)*

E. Eastern name order – family name, given name

ea Eastern

Freq. Frequency

Hir. Hiragana (p. 99)

His. Historical

Jp. Japanese

Jp. simp. Japanese Simplified Character

Kat. Katakana (p. 136)

ky Kyūjitai (Traditional Character)

Ok. Okinawan (Ryukyuan)

pol Transcription to Polish

sh Shinjitai (Simplified Character)

simp. Simplified Character (ˈShin-ji-ˈtai)

Str. Strokes *(p. 295)*

trad. Traditional Character (Kyū-ji-ˈtai)

var. Kanji Variants - abbreviated forms

W. Western name order - given name, family name

Symbols

ˈ Stress mark (before stressed syllable)

ⓘ Characteristics

⚏ Components *(p. 287)*

✖ Composition, graphical components *(p. 287)*, decomposition

✤ Example

☞ Go to

⊙ Hiragana (p. 99)

✎ Kanji (p. 127)

📖 Meaning

♦ Persons

🔔 Phonological alert

🌏 Places

✛ Radical *(p. 292)* or semantic component

👄 Readings

👌 Research

🎋 Schools

👁 See ,related terms, see also

📚 Sources - books

Keys and Remarks

✂ This dictionary's jargon: terminology that is either used only in this dictionary or may have different meaning in other sources or contexts.

🐞 Verb

💧 Warning, alert, alarm

📖! Imperative mood

📖!🕴 Imperative mood – intransitive

📖!🍸 Imperative mood – transitive

🖌🐞☛ Kanji and/or verb

👁⸛ Group of terms

🖌🖌 Alternatives or see also

👁↻ Antonyms (139-an)

🐚📖 Chinese (pinyin)

🚫💧 End of warning, alert, alarm

⌛📖 Examples of common translations

👁✉ Including terms (examples)

🐞☠ Irregular verb

✿📖 Japanese

🖌✍ Kanji notes

🖐📖 Karate term

🐚⸡ Kung Fu Terminology

💧ᴀᴀ Not necessarily correct, ordinary, or literal meaning

📖✍ Notes and examples

✿⸡ Other Martial Arts Terminology

👁⏩ See noun form (derived words) – nominalization or gerund

👁⏪ See verb (derives from)

⌛☉ Usually or often written using Hiʼra-ga-ʼna (p. 99)

⌛⬤ Usually or often written using Kaʼta-ka-na (p. 136)

🐞✍ Verb notes

📖◑ Imperative mood - verb pair

👁◑ See verb pair

👁◑◐ See verb pair (double-intransitive)

①, ②, ③ Karate term (meanings)

❶, ❷, ❸ Meanings other than Karate terms

👁✚ See also

👁= Synonyms

👁≈ Coordinate terms

🐞①◖ Kami ichidan verb *(p. 290)*

🐞①◗ Shimo ichidan verb *(p. 294)*

🐞⑤ Godan verb *(p. 289)*

🐞⑤⚱ Irregular godan verb

👁∞ Related terms

≋**M** 1922, 1925, 1935 and/or 1958 editions of FUNAKOSH's main book.

≋**N** FUNAKOSHI's **Karate-Dō Nyūmon** translated by Teramoto (1988).

🜚 Pronunciation

[] Silent letter

=✂ Synonyms in this dictionary

● 0kinawan

we Western

𝕎 Word - Kanji plus something: A Word or a Compound Word *(p. 288)*.

形 Kata

形形形 Kata group

手 Upper limb strike & anatomy

技 Technique

技技技 Technique group

投技 Throwing Technique (Nage-waza)

立 Stance

足 Lower Limb Strike & Anatomy

Subscript Round Brackets

Cautioning in advance

💣 This term has different meanings.

💣 This term has alternative spellings, using different Kanji.

💣 This term is not related to…

💣 Not to be confused with…

💣 Do not confuse:…

0 – Basic Reference

(000-it)*INCLUDING TERMS (EXAMPLES)* 👁✉: Reference to terms that include the current term.

(001-REF-rom)A ☞ B: Reference to the main term.

(002-REF-hi)A ☞ B: Reference to the Hiragana (p. 99) used in main term.

(003-REF-kat)A ☞ B: Reference to the Katakana (p. 136) used in main term.

(009-REF-kan)A ☞ B: Reference to the Kanji (p. 127) used in main term.

10 – Reference to Building Blocks

(011-k1)*KANJI 1* ☞: The first Chinese Logogram *(p. 286)* included in the term.

(011-k1-s1)*KANJI 1 SPELLING 1* ☞:

(011-k1-s2)*KANJI 1 SPELLING 2* ☞:

(012-k2)*KANJI 2* ☞: The second Chinese Logogram *(p. 286)* included in the term.

(013-k3)*KANJI 3* ☞: The third Chinese Logogram *(p. 286)* included in the term.

(014-k4)*KANJI 4* ☞: The fourth Chinese Logogram *(p. 286)* included in the term.

(015-w1)*WORD 1* ^W_W ☞: The first Word or Compound Word *(p. 288)* included in the term. The first Kanji plus something.

(016-w2)*WORD 2* ^W_W ☞: The second Word or Compound Word *(p. 288)* included in the term. The second Kanji plus something.

(017-w3)*WORD 3* ^W_W ☞: The third Word or Compound Word *(p. 288)* included in the term. The third Kanji plus something.

(018-imp)*IMPERATIVE FORM OF* ! ☞: The Imperative Form of.

(018-te)*TE FORM OF* ! ☞: The Conjunctive Form of.

(019-nom)*NOMINAL FORM (NOUN FORM) OF* ! ☞: The Nominal Form (noun form) of.

(019-ste)*STEM FORM OF* ! ☞: The Stem Form of.

20 – Term topic

(020-re)*RESEARCH* &: Value for Karate researchers or related to Karate research.

(021-rb)*RESEARCH (FOR BOOKS)*: Value related to Karate books.

(025-sch)*SCHOOLS* ⚒: Value related to Karate branches.

(028-pl)*PLACES* 🌐: Value related to geographical locations.

(029-pe)*PERSONS* ⛄: Value related to Karateka.

30 - Stances

(030-st)*STANCE* ⊥: Stances.

(031-ms)*FUNAKOSHI MAIN BOOK - STANCES* ❤**MS**: Stances in 1922, 1925, 1935 and/or 1958 editions of FUNAKOSH's main book.

(032-ns)*FUNAKOSHI NYUMON TERAMOTO - STANCES* ⊜**NS**: Stances in FUNAKO-SHI's **Karate-Dō Nyūmon** translated by Teramoto (1988).

40 - Limbs

(040-ul)*UPPER LIMB STRIKE & ANATOMY* 手: Upper limb strikes and/or anatomy.

(041-mu)*FUNAKOSHI MAIN BOOK - UPPER LIMB* ⊜**MUL**: Upper limb strikes and/or anatomy in 1922, 1925, 1935 and/or 1958 editions of FUNAKOSH's main book.

(042-nu)*FUNAKOSHI NYUMON TERAMOTO – UPPER LIMB* ⊜**NUL**: Upper limb strikes and/or anatomy in FUNAKOSHI's **Karate-Dō Nyūmon** translated by Teramoto (1988).

(045-ll)*LOWER LIMB STRIKE & ANATOMY* 足: Lower limb strikes and/or anatomy.

(046-ml)*FUNAKOSHI MAIN BOOK - LOWER LIMB* ⊜**MLL**: Lower limb strikes and/or anatomy in 1922, 1925, 1935 and/or 1958 editions of FUNAKOSH's main book.

(047-nl)*FUNAKOSHI NYUMON TERAMOTO – LOWER LIMB* ⊜**NLL**: Lower limb strikes and/or anatomy in FUNAKOSHI's **Karate-Dō Nyūmon** translated by Teramoto (1988).

50 - Techniques

(050-tg)*TECHNIQUE GROUP* 技技技: Group of Karate techniques.

(051-te)*TECHNIQUE* 技: Karate techniques.

(055-tt)*THROWING TECHNIQUE* 投技: Karate throwing techniques.

(056-mt)*FUNAKOSHI MAIN BOOK - THROWING TECHNIQUES* ⊜**MTT**: Karate throwing techniques in 1922, 1925, 1935 and/or 1958 editions of FUNAKOSH's main book.

60 - Kata

(060-kg)*KATA GROUP* 形形形: Group of Shotokan Kata.

(061-ka)*KATA* 形: Shotokan Kata.

(062-mk)*FUNAKOSHI MAIN BOOK - KATA* 🐢**MK**: Shotokan Kata in 1922, 1925, 1935 and/or 1958 editions of FUNAKOSH's main book.

(068-me)*FUNAKOSHI MAIN BOOK - ENBUSEN* 🐢**MEN**: Kata performance line in 1922, 1925, 1935 and/or 1958 editions of FUNAKOSH's main book.

70 - Other topics and meaning

(070-kt)*KARATE MEANING* ✋📖: Meaning in the Karate sense of the term.

(071-dl)🔴✳ ᴬᴬ *DOJO LANGUAGE* 🏺📖: Meaning in the Dōjō (or at least some Dōjō) sense of the term. Sometimes mistakenly used.

(077-jg)*JAPANESE* ⚙📖: Meaning in the general sense of the term.

(078-mg)*FUNAKOSHI MAIN BOOK – GENERALLY* 🐢**MG**: Other topics in 1922, 1925, 1935 and/or 1958 editions of FUNAKOSH's main book.

(079-ng)*FUNAKOSHI NYUMON TERAMOTO - GENERALLY* 🐢**NG**: Other topics in FU-NAKOSHI's **Karate-Dō Nyūmon** translated by Teramoto (1988).

80-90 - Notes

(089-no)*NOTES AND EXAMPLES* 📖✍: Elaborations about the term.

(090-te)*TELL YOUR STUDENTS* 📖☺: Recommended elaborations for Karate students.

(095-3t)*THE THREE TEACHINGS* **3**🔔: Confucianism, Dàoism, Buddhism.

120-140 – Reference to related terms

(133-sy)*SYNONYMS* 👁=: Reference to term/s with the same meaning.

(133-gr-sy)*GROUP* 👁❨❩ The following terms are synonyms: List of synonyms that the term belongs to.

(134-re)*RELATED TERMS* 👁∞: Reference to closely related term/s.

(134-gr-re)*GROUP* 👁❨❩ The following terms are related: : List of related terms that the term belongs to.

(135-ge)*GERUND* 👁 ▸▸: Reference to a noun that equals the Stem Form (Conjunctive Form) of the current value.

(138-co)*COORDINATE TERMS* 👁≈ : Reference to coordinate term/s.

(136-se)*SEE ALSO* 👁✛ : Reference to remotely related term/s.

(139-an)*ANTONYMS* 👁↺: Reference to term/s with the opposite meaning.

180 – Chinese and Okinawan (mainly transliteration)

(185-ch)*CHINESE (PINYIN)* 👁📖: Transliteration from Chinese, and sometimes notes or translation.

(186-cs)*CHINESE SIMPLIFIED* 👁📖: Transliteration from Chinese (simplified characters).

(187-ct)*CHINESE TRADITIONAL* 👁📖: Transliteration from Chinese (traditional characters).

(189-ok)*OKINAWAN* ◕: Transliteration from Okinawan.

(190-kf)*KUNG FU TERMINOLOGY* 👁⌇ : Kung Fu Terminology.

(191-ot)*OTHER MARTIAL ARTS TERMINOLOGY* ✿⌇ : Other Martial Arts Terminology.

200 – The Kanji is not the main writing

(203-hi)⧖☉: The Hiragana script (p. 99) is more popular than the Kanji script.

(206-kata)⧖⭘: The Katakana script (p. 136) is more popular than the Kanji script.

210 – Japanese writing

(211-1): First way to write the term in Japanese.

(211-al)*ALTERNATIVES OR SEE ALSO* ✐✐:Alternative writings and/or other Kanji worth noting.

(211-sh-1) (simp.): Simplified Kanji.

(211-sh-2) (simp.): Another version of the simplified Kanji.

(211-ky-1) (trad.): Traditional Kanji.

(211-var): Variations of the Kanji.

(211-ka+hi): Writing that uses both Kanji and Hiragana (p. 99).

(211-ka+hiAlt): Alternative writing that uses both Kanji and Hiragana (p. 99).

(212-2): Second way to write the term in Japanese.

(213-3) : Third way to write the term in Japanese.

(214-4) : Forth way to write the term in Japanese.

(215-5) : Fifth way to write the term in Japanese.

(216-ea): Eastern way to write a name.

(216-ea-2): Another Eastern way to write a name.

(217-we): Western way to write a name.

(217-we-2): Another Western way to write a name.

250 – Kana Writing

(250-hi): The way to write the term in Hiragana (p. 99).

(250-hi-Alt): Another way to write the term in Hiragana (p. 99).

(256-kat): The way to write the term in Katakana (p. 136).

270 - Tōkyō pronunciation

(275-tō):Tōkyō pronunciation.

(275-tō-Alt):Tōkyō pronunciation with **alternative** Hiragana spelling (another reading).

(276-tō2):Another Tōkyō pronunciation with the **same** Hiragana spelling (same reading).

280 – Polish transliteration

(280-po)Transliteration to Polish. The Polish Alphabet was chosen because of its ability to convey the correct pronunciation.

300 – 320 – Kanji Analysis

(302-kn)*KANJI NOTES* ✐ ✍:Notes about the Kanji.

(313-ka)*KANJI* ✐: Analysis of the Kanji.

(313k-cn)Components ⬚: The Kanji's components *(p. 287)*.

(313k-ra)Radical ✛: The Kanji's radical *(p. 292)*. If a character *(p. 286)* is itself a radical, it is its own radical.

(313k-cs)Composition ✴: The Kanji's composition.

(313k-re)Readings (examples) ✊: Examples of the Kanji's readings (in a Kanji analysis paragraph).

(325-kr)*KANJI READINGS* 🖊🗨: Examples of the Kanji's readings (outside a Kanji analysis paragraph).

400 – Meaningful Hiragana

(409-no)*HIRAGANA* ☉: The particle ˈNo (の).

(409-ka)*HIRAGANA* ☉: The particle ˈKa (か).

(409-o)*HIRAGANA* ☉: The prefix ˈO (お～).

460 - Characteristics

(466-cha)*CHARACTERISTICS* ⓘ: The number of Kanji and the number of Hiragana (p. 99) that the term contains.

480 – 490 – Phonetic phenomena

(480-hb)**H⤳b** 🔔: Possible ˈRen-daku related to unvoiced consonant /H/ (becoming ~/b/ as a suffix).

(481-hp)**H⤳p** 🔔 : Possible ˈRen-daku related to unvoiced consonant /H/ (becoming ~/p/ as a suffix).

(482-kg)**K⤳g** 🔔 : Possible ˈRen-daku related to unvoiced consonant /K/.

(483-td)**T⤳d** 🔔 : Possible ˈRen-daku related to unvoiced consonant /T/.

(484-tsz)**Ts⤳z** 🔔 : Possible ˈRen-daku related to unvoiced consonant /Ts/.

(491-npmp)**/n/p** 🗨 **[m]p** 🔔: Realization of moraic nasal ん when preceding /p/.

(492-nbmb)**/n/b** 🗨 **[m]b** 🔔: Realization of moraic nasal ん when preceding /b/.

(493-g)**G** 🔔 🗨 : Possible Nasalization of /g/ - Bidakuon (鼻濁音).

600 – Verb form table

(600-vt): Table of forms.

610 - References to pairs

(610-In-Tr)*VERB PAIR* 👁◑: References to the transitive part and the intransitive part of a verb pair (two parts).

(611-1Tr2In)*VERB PAIRS (INTRANSITIVE X2)* 👁 ◖▌▌: References to parts of two pairs that share the same transitive part (three parts).

650 - Imperative mood in a double pair (4 parts)

700 – Verb forms, translation, and notes

(705-gv)*GODAN VERB* 🐾⑤: The terminal form (u form, plain form, dictionary form, informal form, attributive form) and the polite form (formal form) or the masu form (i form, stem form, conjunctive form, continuative form) of a Godan group verb (Five-grade verb, Class-5 verb).

(705.1-ir)*IRREGULAR GODAN VERB* 🐾⑤☠: The terminal form (u form, plain form, dictionary form, informal form, attributive form) and the polite form (formal form) or the masu form (i form, stem form, conjunctive form, continuative form) of an irregular Godan group verb.

(711-ka)*KAMI ICHIDAN VERB* 🐾①♉: The terminal form (u form, plain form, dictionary form, informal form, attributive form) and the polite form (formal form) or the masu form (i form, stem form, conjunctive form, continuative form) of a Kami Ichidan (upper monograde) subgroup verb.

(711-sh)*SHIMO ICHIDAN VERB* 🐾①♉ : The terminal form (u form, plain form, dictionary form, informal form, attributive form) and the polite form (formal form) or the masu form (i form, stem form, conjunctive form, continuative form) of a Shimo Ichidan (lower monograde) subgroup verb.

(730-vt)*VERB TRANSLATION* 🐾📖: Examples of the verb's translations.

(731-vn)*VERB NOTES* 🐾✍: Notes about the verb.

800 - Tags

(800-tag)*TAGS* 💻: Tags that could be assigned to the value.

810 – Categories of transitive and intransitive verbs

(810-vpTr)**VERB PAIR – TRANSITIVE PART**: Indicates that this value is the transitive (active or causative) part of a Japanese transitive-intransitive (active-mediopassive) verb pair. Example: "He rotated his arm at the end of the thrust" – a verb which takes a direct object (the arm in this case).

_(811-vpIn)**VERB PAIR – INTRANSITIVE PART**: Indicates that this value is the intransitive (mediopassive) part of a Japanese transitive-intransitive (active-mediopassive) verb pair. Example: "He rotated at the sound of Kaite" – a self-move verb.

_(812-vpIn-1)**VERB PAIR – INTRANSITIVE PART 1**: In a double-passive pair.

_(813-vpIn-2)**VERB PAIR – INTRANSITIVE PART 2**: In a double-passive pair.

830 – Categories of Kanji and importance

_(830-ik)**IMPORTANT KANJI**: Indicates that the value is an important Kanji (for Karate).

_(833-kan)**KANJI**: Indicates that the value is a not very important Kanji (for Karate).

_(838-su)**SUPER-TERM**: Indicates that the value is very important (for Karate).

Bibliographic Abbreviations

1922/1922 original 船越義珍『琉球拳法 唐手』（大正 11 年）[Funakoshi Gichin **Ryūkyū Kenpō Tō-te** (1922)].

1925 Ishida Gichin Funakoshi **To-Te Jitsu** (Shingo Ishida trns., 1994).

1925 Teramoto Gichin Funakoshi **Karate Jutsu – the Original Teachings of Master Funakoshi** (John Teramoto trans., 2001).

1935 Ohshima Gichin Funakoshi **Karate-Dō Kyōhan: The Master Text** (Tsutomu Ohshima trans., 1973).

1935 Suzuki-Johnston Gichin Funakoshi **Karate Dō Kyōhan: Master Text for the Way of the Empty-Hand** (Harumi Suzuki-Johnston trans., 2nd ed. 2012).

1973 Gichin Funakoshi **Karate-Dō Kyōhan: The Master Text** (Tsutomu Ohshima trans., 1973).

Funakoshi Nyūmon Teramoto Gichin Funakoshi **Karate-Dō Nyūmon: The Master Introductory Text** (John Teramoto trans., 1988).

Technical Remarks

It is impossible to include all the words we use in Karate in a dictionary. If, for instance, You do not find the word Age-uke, look for "Age" and for "Uke". We tried to put an emphasis on the building blocks.

For the reader's convenience, we did not follow the common referencing rules as to repeated references. Instead, all footnotes provide full citations.

Special Values

Recommended Values

Ashi-foot {足}, p. 37

baribari {{ばりばり}}, p. 42

Bu-warrior {武}, p. 45

Dai-big {大}, p. 56

fumikiri {{踏み切り}}, p. 65

hangetsudachi {{半月立ち}}, p. 84

hiraken {{平拳}}, p. 99

Iri-entering {入}, p. 107

jitte {{十手}}, p. 111

kankūgamae {{観空構え}}, p. 128

Kata-type {型}, p. 133

katawaguruma {{片輪車}}, p. 137

kiai {{気合}}, p. 144

Ki-energy {気}, p. 142

kime {{決め}}, p. 146

komanage {{独楽投げ}}, p. 152

Ma-space {間}, p. 159

Moto-origin {元}, p. 173

Obi-belt {帯}, p. 187

oizuki {{追い突き}}, p. 188

seiryūtō {{青龍刀}}, p. 206

shōreiryū {{昭霊流}}, p. 218

shōrin {{少林}}, p. 218

taikyoku {{太極}}, p. 230

tanden {{丹田}}, p. 232

Tatsu-to stand {立}, p. 234

Ten-heaven {天}, p. 240

Tennokata {{天の形}}, p. 241

tettsui {{鉄槌}}, p. 245

tokkōzuki {{特攻突き}}, p. 247

Tora-tiger {虎}, p. 249

torite {{捕手}}, p. 250

Tsubame-swallow {燕}, p. 256

Tsuku-to thrust {突}, p. 255

Ukeru-to receive {受}, p. 263

Uma-horse {馬}, p. 264

yamadachi {{山立ち}}, p. 269

Yama-mountain {山}, p. 268

yamazuki {{山突き}}, p. 270

List of Commands

Command	Part of speech	Form	of the Verb	Verb's Group	Verb's Pair

Special Values

hajime {{ 始 め}}, p. 81	Noun	Stem*	Hajimeru-to begin {始}, p. 82	Shimo Ichidan **Transitive** ~eru	hajimaru {{始まる}}, p. 80
kaette {{返っ て}}, p. 119	Verb	~te (Conjunctive)	Kaeru-to return {返}, p. 118	Godan Intransitive ~ru (v. su)	kaesu {{ 返 す}}, p. 119
kamaete {{構 えて}}, p. 125	Verb	~te (Conjunctive)	Kamaeru-to prepare {構}, p. 124	Shimo Ichidan **Transitive** ~eru	No pair
maware (p. 168)	Verb	Imperative	Mawaru-to turn {回}, p. 165	Godan Intransitive ~ru (v. su)	mawasu {{回 す}}, p. 167
mawatte {{回 って}}, p. 168	Verb	~te (Conjunctive)	Mawaru-to turn {回}, p. 165	Godan Intransitive ~ru (v. su)	mawasu {{回 す}}, p. 167
mokusō {{黙 想}}, p. 171	Noun (Multi-kanji)	-	-	-	-
naore {{ 直 れ}}, p. 180	Verb	Imperative	Naoru-to be fixed {直}, p. 181	Godan Intransitive ~ru (v. su)	naosu {{ 直 す}}, p. 182
Naotte (p. 180)	Verb	Imperative	Naoru-to be fixed {直}, p. 181	Godan Intransitive ~ru (v. su)	naosu {{ 直 す}}, p. 182
Rei-thanks { 礼}, p. 196	Noun	-	-	-	-
yame {{ 止 め}}, p. 271	Verb	Imperative	Yamu-to stop {止}, p. 272	Godan Intransitive ~mu	yameru {{止 める }}, p. 271
yame {{ 止 め}}, p. 271	Noun	Stem	yameru {{ 止 める}}, p. 271	Shimo Ichidan **Transitive** (~eru)	Yamu-to stop {止}, p. 272
yasume {{ 休	Verb	Imperative	Yasumu-to	Godan Intransitive ~mu	yasumaru

め}}, **p. 274**			rest {休}, p. 276		{{休まる}}, p. 274 yasumeru {{休める}}, p. 275
yasume {{**休め**}}, **p. 274**	Noun	Stem	yasumeru {{休める}}, p. 275	Shimo Ichidan **Transitive** (~eru)	Yasumu-to rest {休}, p. 276 yasumaru {{休まる}}, p. 274
Yasumi (**p. 274**)	Noun	Stem	Yasumu-to rest {休}, p. 276	Godan Intransitive ~mu	yasumaru {{休まる}}, p. 274 yasumeru {{休める}}, p. 275
yōi {{**用意**}}, **p. 277**	Noun (Multi-kanji)	-	-	-	-

*And one of the Kun readings of the Kanji.

Large Images

Script 1 - Oracle Bone Script

Script 2 - Bronze Script

After You get familiar with the Pictogrammatic Radical Uma-horse {馬} (p. 264), will You be able to spot the Horse Radical in this ancient Oracle Bone Script? Hint: the horse is vertical.

Another hint: The three-line mane.

After learning them, try to spot the following Characters: Iri-entering {入} (p. 107), Mon-gate {門} (p. 172), Tatsu-to stand {立} (p. 234), Dai-big {大} (p. 56), and the Component Tsuki-moon {月} (p. 253) – a Component of 霸.

Big 1 – Irimi / Adam Dobrzyński

See: irimi {{入り身}}, p. 107; tennomon {{天の門}}, p. 243; tokkōzuki {{特攻突き}}, p. 247

Big 2 – Yamadachi by Pavlović Sensei

See: yamadachi {{山立ち}}, p. 269; Yama-mountain {山}, p. 268

Maria Anette Pavlović of Sweden Kase-ha.

Photographer: Denis Sopovic.

The shape of the Kanji, which depicts three mountains, is the shape of the posture. The forearms, too, are heavy as mountains.

"Know that a person needs to cross a very, very narrow bridge, and what is essential is that one should not be overcome by fear."[10]

(Nachman of Bracław)

Big 3 – Hangetsudachi by Bamgboye Sensei

See hangetsudachi {{半月立ち}}, p. 84

Big 4 – Osaeuke by Bamgboye Sensei

See osaeuke {{押え受け}}, p. 191

Big 5 – Jūjiuke by Bamgboye Sensei

See jūjiuke {{十字受け}}, p. 116

Bobby Bamgboye of Nigeria WSKF. Photographer: Joel Ibanga.

Big 6 – Oizuki by Le Bas Sensei

See oizuki {{追い突き}}, p. 188

Big 7 – Heian nidan by Le Bas Sensei

See: heiannidan {{平安二段}}, p. 92; haiwanuke {{背腕受け}}, p. 79

Big 8 – Yōi by Le Bas Sensei (Warrior, Yame and stopping violence)

See: yame {{止め}}, p. 271; Bu-warrior {武}, p. 45; heikodachi {{平行立ち}}, p. 95; yōi {{用意}}, p. 277

Sophie Le Bas of France Shōtōkan. Photographer: Patrick Schoeffer

Values

A term that consists of one Kanji only, is followed by the Chinese Logogram put in round brackets.

The terms are sorted **by column 1 ignoring diacritics (ˈ).**

The order may differ from the common order, due to spacing and special characters.

For instance:

"Kaˈkato ˈOtosh[i] Geˈri" comes before "Kaˈkato-geˈri", although Kakato-**g**eri should come before Kakato-**o**toshi-geri.

"Ts[u]ˈku" comes before "Tsuˈbame", although Tsu**b**ame should come before Tsu**k**u.

1. Aˈge

(000-it)*INCLUDING TERMS (EXAMPLES)*

👁✉ ageuke {{上げ受け}}, p. 30; agezuki {{上げ突き}}, p. 31; keage {{蹴上げ}}, p. 139

(011-k1)*KANJI 1* ☞ Ue-top {上}, p. 262

(077-jg)*GENERAL MEANING (EXAMPLES)* ☼📖 *noun* ❶ Rise

#age {{上げ}}##

(211-1)上げ

(212-2)揚げ

(250-hi)あげ (hir.)

(466-cha)*CHARACTERISTICS* ① A Two-character, which consists of 1 Chinese Logograms and 1 Hiˈra-ga-ˈna Characters

(015-w1)*WORD 1* ^W_W ☞ age {{上げ}}, p. 30

(016-w2)*WORD 2* ^W_W ☞ uke {{受け}}, p. 262

(070-kt)*KARATE MEANING* ✋📖 *noun phrase* ① Rising block, upward block, upper block

(185-ch)*CHINESE (PINYIN)* ☯📖 **Shàng shòu**

#ageuke {{上げ受け}}##

(211-1)上げ受け　(212-2)上げ受

(250-hi)あげうけ (hir.)

(466-cha)*CHARACTERISTICS* ① A Four-character, which consists of 2 Chinese Logograms and 2 Hiˈra-ga-ˈna Characters.

2. Aˈge Uˈke

(800-tag)*TAGS* 🖳 #age-uke, age uke

(838-su)**SUPER-TERM**

3.   A˙ge Zu˙ki

(015-w1)*WORD 1* ᵂ⁄ᵂ ☛ age {{上げ}}, p. 30

(016-w2)*WORD 2* ᵂ ☛ tsuki {{突き}}, p. 253

(070-kt)*KARATE MEANING* ✋📖 *noun phrase* ① Rising thrust

(185-ch)*CHINESE (PINYIN)* ☯📖 ***Shàng tú***

(211-sh-2)上げ突き (simp.)

#agezuki {{上げ突き}}##

(211-ky-1)上げ突き (trad.)

(250-hi)あげづき (hir.)

(280-po)pol:AGEDZYKI

(466-cha)*CHARACTERISTICS* ① A Four-character, which consists of 2 Chinese Logograms and 2 Hi˙ra-ga-ˈna Characters.

(800-tag)*TAGS* 🖳 #age-zuki, age zuki, #agetsuki, #agezki, #agetski

4.   A˙geru

(000-it)*INCLUDING TERMS (EXAMPLES)* 👁✉ keageru {{蹴上げる}}, p. 139

(077-jg)*GENERAL MEANING (EXAMPLES)* ☼📖 *verb* ❶ To raise, to elevate ❷ To give.

#ageru {{上げる}}##

(011-k1)*KANJI 1* ☛ Ue-top {上}, p. 262

(211-1)上げる

(250-hi)あげる (hir.)

(275-tō)あ│げ│る [àgérú]

5.   ˈAi-uˈchi

(015-w1)*WORD 1* ᵂ⁄ᵂ ☛ uchi {{打ち}}, p. 258

(070-kt)*KARATE MEANING* ✋📖 *noun* ① Clash, simultaneous mutual strike, simultaneously striking one another ② Tie, draw.

(185-ch)*CHINESE (PINYIN)* ☯📖 ***Xiāng dǎ***

#aiuchi {{相打ち}}##

(211-1)相打ち (250-hi)あいうち (hir.)

(466-cha)*CHARACTERISTICS* ① A Three-character, which consists of 2 Chinese Logograms and 1 Hi˙ra-ga-ˈna Characters.

(800-tag)*TAGS* 🖳 #ai-uchi, ai uchi

6.   ˈAka (赤)

(000-it)*INCLUDING TERMS (EXAMPLES)* 👁✉ akai {{赤い}}, p. 32; akanokachi {{赤の勝ち}}, p. 32

(077-jg)*GENERAL MEANING (EXAMPLES)* ✿📖 *noun* ❶ Red (noun) #Aka-red {赤}##

(185-ch)*CHINESE (PINYIN)* ☯📖 ***Chì***

(211-1)赤

(250-hi)あか (hir.) (275-tō)あ|か [áˈkà]

(833-kan)**KANJI**

7. ˈAka no Kaˈchi

(011-k1)*KANJI 1* ☛ Aka-red {赤}, p. 32

(112-w1)*WORD 1* W W ☛ kachi {{勝ち}}, p. 117

(070-kt)*KARATE MEANING* ✋📖 *phrase* ① Red is the winner, red wins.

(185-ch)*CHINESE (PINYIN)* ☯📖 ***Chì sheng***

(211-1)赤の勝ち

(250-hi)あかのかち (hir.)

#akanokachi {{赤の勝ち}}##

(256-kat)アカノカチ (kat.)

(J99no)*HIRAGANA* ☉ The particle ˈNo (の) is a genitive case marker, which indicates possession: of, -'s.

(466-cha)*CHARACTERISTICS* ⓘ A Four-character, which consists of 2 Chinese Logograms and 2 Hiˈra-ga-ˈna Characters.

(800-tag)*TAGS* 💻 #akano-kachi, akano kachi, aka-no-kachi, aka no kachi

8. Aˈkai

(011-k1)*KANJI 1* ☛ Aka-red {赤}, p. 32

(077-jg)*GENERAL MEANING (EXAMPLES)* ✿📖 *adjective* ❶ Red (adjective)

(211-1)赤い

(250-hi)あかい (hir.)

#akai {{赤い}}##

(275-tō)あ|かい [àkáí]

(466-cha)*CHARACTERISTICS* ⓘ A Two-character, which consists of 1 Chinese Logograms and 1 Hiˈra-ga-ˈna Characters.

9. ˈAki (昭)

(000-it)*INCLUDING TERMS (EXAMPLES)* 👁✉ shōreiryū {{昭霊流}}, p. 218; shōwa {{昭和}}, p. 221

(077-jg)*GENERAL MEANING (EXAMPLES)* ✿📖 *adjective* ❶ Bright, shining ❷ Clear.

(185-ch)*CHINESE (PINYIN)* ☯📖 ***zhāo***

#Aki-bright {昭}##

(211-1)昭 (250-hi)あき (hir.)

(325-kr)*KANJI READINGS* 🖉🐾 Go-on: しょう (shō). Kan-on: しょう

(shō). Kun: あきらか (akiraka, 昭らか). Nanori: あき (aki).

(833-kan)**KANJI**

10. ˈAn (安)

(000-it)*INCLUDING TERMS (EXAMPLES)*

👁✉ asatoankō {{安里 安恒}}, p. 36; heian {{平安}}, p. 90; ito-suankō {{糸洲 安恒}}, p. 108

(077-jg)*GENERAL MEANING (EXAMPLES)* ☼📖 *adjective* ❶ Calm, peaceful, quiet

(089-no)*NOTES AND EXAMPLES* 📖✍

Yaˈsui (安い) means cheap.

(133-sy)*SYNONYMS* 👁= Hira-calm { 平}, p. 98

(185-ch)*CHINESE (PINYIN)* 👁📖 *ān* as in *píng'ān* (平安)[11] and as in *tiān'ānmén* (天安門).

(211-al)*ALTERNATIVES OR SEE ALSO*

✍✍ 侒, 安, 㛧, 㢾, 安い, やすい, 廉い

#An-calm {安}##

(211-1)安

(250-hi)あん (hir.)

(256-kat)アン (kat.)

(302-kn)*KANJI NOTES* ✍✍ It may depict a woman[12] under a roof – meaning in a house[13]

(313-ka)*KANJI* ✍ The Compound Ideogram ˈAn-calm (安). (313k-cn)**Components** ⚎ [宀 | 女]. (313k-ra)**Radical** ✛ 宀 roof. (313k-cs)**Composition** ⚒ Top: 宀, bottom: 女. (313k-re)**Readings (examples)** 🗣 Go-on: あん (an). Kan-on: あん (an). Kun: やすい (yasui, 安い).

(830-ik)**IMPORTANT KANJI**

11. Aˈnata

(012-k2)*KANJI* 2 ☞ Kata-direction {方 }, p. 135

(077-jg)*GENERAL MEANING (EXAMPLES)* ☼📖 *pronoun* ❶ You, second-person pronoun (polite)

(203-hi)⌛☉ (250-hi)あなた (hir.)

(211-1)貴方 (212-2)貴女 (to a female)

#anata {{貴方}}##

(213-3)貴男 (to a male)

(275-tō)あ[な]た [ànáˈtà]

(466-cha)*CHARACTERISTICS* ① A Three-character, which consists of 0 Chinese Logograms and 3 Hiˈra-gaˈna Characters

12. ˈAo (青)

(000-it)*INCLUDING TERMS (EXAMPLES)*

◉ ✉ seiryū {{青龍}}, p. 205

(077-jg)*GENERAL MEANING (EXAMPLES)* ☼ 📖 *noun* ❶ Blue (noun) ❷ Green (noun) ❸ East[14] ❹ Young[15] (prefix)

(185-ch)*CHINESE (PINYIN)* ☯ 📖 *Qīng*

(211-1)青 (212-2)青 (Hist.)

(250-hi)あお (hir.)

(833-kan)**KANJI**

#Ao-blue {青}##

(275-tō)あお [áˈò]

(313-ka)*KANJI* 🖊 The Compound Ideogrammatic Radical (Radical 174) ˈAo-blue (青). (313k-cn)**Components** 🖧 [生｜丹]. (313k-cs)**Composition** ⚒ Top: 𰀄 , bottom: 月 . (313k-re)**Readings (examples)** 👊 Kan-on: せい (ˈSei). Kun: あお (ˈAo). Nanori: お (ˈO).

13. Aˈoi

(011-k1)*KANJI 1* ☛ Ao-blue {青}, p. 34

(077-jg)*GENERAL MEANING (EXAMPLES)* ☼ 📖 *adjective* ❶ Blue (adjective)

(211-1)青い (212-2)青い (Hist.)

(250-hi)あおい (hir.)

#aoi {{青い}}##

(275-tō)あおい [àóˈ ì]

(466-cha)*CHARACTERISTICS* ⓘ A Two-character, which consists of 1 Chinese Logograms and 1 Hiˈra-ga-ˈna Characters.

14. ˈAri

(000-it)*INCLUDING TERMS (EXAMPLES)*

◉ ✉ wazaari {{技有り}}, p. 268

(011-k1)*KANJI 1* ☛ Yū-existence {有}, p. 282

(077-jg)*GENERAL MEANING (EXAMPLES)* ☼ 📖 *noun* ❶ Existing now *adjectival noun* ❷ Acceptable, passible, OK, alright.

(203-hi)⌛☉

#ari {{有り}}##

(250-hi)あり (hir.)

(211-1)有

(212-2)在 り

(089-no)*NOTES AND EXAMPLES* 📖✍ Derives from the verb ˈAru (有る).

(466-cha)*CHARACTERISTICS* ⓘ A Two-character, which consists of 0 Chinese Logograms and 2 Hiˈra-ga-ˈna Characters

15. Aˈri-gaˈtō

(011-k1)*KANJI 1* ☛ Yū-existence {有}, p. 282

(077-jg)*GENERAL MEANING (EXAMPLES)* ✿📖 *interjection* ❶ Thanks (casual)

(134-re)*RELATED TERMS* 👁∞ dōmo {{どうも}}, p. 59

(203-hi)⌛☉ (250-hi)ありがとう (hir.)

(211-1)有難う

#arigato {{有難う}}##

(212-2)有り難う

(275-tō)あり|がとー [àríˈgàtòò]

(466-cha)*CHARACTERISTICS* ⓘ A Five-character, which consists of 0 Chinese Logograms and 5 Hiˈra-gaˈna Characters.

(800-tag)*TAGS* 💻 #ari-gato, ari gato

(838-su)**SUPER-TERM**

16. Ariˈ-gaˈtō-go-zaiˈmas[u]

(011-k1)*KANJI 1* ☛ Yū-existence {有}, p. 282

(014-k4)*KANJI 4* ☛ Za-seat {座}, p. 283

(077-jg)*GENERAL MEANING (EXAMPLES)* ✿📖 *interjection* ❶ Thank You (polite, present tense)

(203-hi)⌛☉

(250-hi)ありがとうございます (hir.)

(211-1)有難う御座います

(212-2)有難うございま

#arigatogozaimasu {{有難う御座います}}##

(213-3)有り難う御座います

(214-4)有り難ございます

(466-cha)*CHARACTERISTICS* ⓘ A Ten-character, which consists of 0 Chinese Logograms and 10 Hiˈra-gaˈna Characters.

(800-tag)*TAGS* 💻 #ari-gato-go-zaimasu, arigato gozaimasu, arigatogozaimas, arigato gozaimas

(838-su)**SUPER-TERM**

17. Aˈri-gaˈtō-go-zaiˈmash[i]ta

(011-k1)*KANJI 1* ☛ Yū-existence {有}, p. 282

(014-k4)*KANJI 4* ☛ Za-seat {座}, p. 283

(077-jg)*GENERAL MEANING (EXAMPLES)* ✿📖 *interjection* ❶ Thank You (polite, past tense)

(203-hi)⌛☉

(250-hi)ありがとうございました (hir.)

(211-1)有難う御座いました

(212-2)有難うございました

ˈAru (Yū) - Aˈshi (足)

(213-3)有り難ございました

#arigatogozaimashita {{ 有難う御

座いました}}##

(214-4)有り難う御座いました

(466-cha)*CHARACTERISTICS* ⓘ An

Eleven-character, which consists of

0 Chinese Logograms and 11 Hiˈra-

ga-ˈna Characters.

(800-tag)*TAGS* 💻 #ari-gato-go-

zaimashita, arigato gozaimashita,

arigatogozaimashta, arigato gozai-

mashta

(838-su)**SUPER-TERM**

18. ˈAru (Yū)

(001-REF-rom)ˈAru ☞ Yū-existence {

有}, p. 282

(203-hi)⧗⊙ (002-REF-hi)ある ☞ ゆう

#Aru (Yū)##

(009-REF-kan)有る ☞ 有

(275-tō)あ る [áˈrù]

19. A-ˈSATO ˈAn-kō

(011-k1)*KANJI 1* ☛ An-calm {安}, p.

33

(013-k3)*KANJI 3* ☛ An-calm {安}, p.

33

(029-pe)*PERSONS* 👥 A-ˈSATO ˈAn-kō

(ˈShu-ri - ˈNa-ha, 1827 – 1906) was

a famous Okinawan Kaˈra-te-ka. A

student of Maˈtsu-mura (p. 165).

One of the two main teachers of

Fuˈna-koˈshi (p. 67).

(185-ch)*CHINESE (PINYIN)* ☯📖 *Ānlǐ*

ānhéng

#asatoankō {{安里 安恒}}##

(216-ea)安里 安恒 (E.)

(217-we)安恒 安里 (W.)

(466-cha)*CHARACTERISTICS* ⓘ A Four-

character, which consists of 2 Chi-

nese Logograms and 2 Hiˈra-ga-ˈna

Characters.

(800-tag)*TAGS* 💻 #ankoazato, anko

asato, anko azato, #azato yasutsune,

#a-sato, #asatoanko

20. Aˈshi (足)

(000-it)*INCLUDING TERMS (EXAMPLES)*

👁✉ ashibarai {{足払い}}, p. 38;

ashisabaki {{足捌き}}, p. 37; ash-

imoto {{足元}}, p. 38; ashiwaza {{

足技}}, p. 39; ashiyubi {{足指}},

p. 39; chūsokukotsu {{中足骨}}, p.

55; maeashi {{ 前足 }}, p. 161;

nakaashi (中足), p. 178; nekoashi

{{猫足}}, p. 182; sokutō {{足刀}},

p. 223; yoriashi {{寄り足}}, p. 281

(077-jg)*GENERAL MEANING (EXAMPLES)* ☼ 📖 *noun* ❶ Foot ❷ Leg (脚, 肢)

(185-ch)*CHINESE (PINYIN)* ☯📖 *zú*

(211-1)足

(211-var)𧾷 (left)

(212-2)脚

(250-hi)あし (hir.)

(275-tō)あ し [àshí˙]

#Ashi-foot {足}##

(731-vn)*VERB NOTES* 🐢✍ The ˈGo-dan Verb Taˈru (足る) and the Kaˈmi-ˈichi-dan Verb Taˈriru (足りる) mean to be enough[16], to be sufficient[17], to satisfy, to fulfill. Just like the foot, which is adequate to support[18] our entire body. That teaches us something about the importance of the foot in Kaˈra-te.

(313-ka)*KANJI* ✐ The Pictogrammatic Radical (Radical 157) Aˈshi-foot (足). (313k-cn)**Components** 🕸 No components - a Simple Logogram. (313k-cs)**Composition** ⚒ Top: 口, bottom: 龰. (313k-re)**Readings (examples)** ✊ Go-on: す (su); そく

A̍ shi ˈSabaki - A̍ shi-ˈbarai (Soˈku). Kan-on: しゅ (shu). Kun: あし (A̍shi); たる (taru, 足る).

(830-ik)**IMPORTANT KANJI**

21. Aˈshi ˈSabaki

(011-k1)*KANJI 1* ☛ Ashi-foot {足}, p. 37

(015-w1)*WORD 1* 𝕎 ☛ sabaki {{捌き}}, p. 198

(070-kt)*KARATE MEANING* AKA ˈUn Soˈku (運足) ✋📖 *noun phrase* ① Footwork, foot movements

(185-ch)*CHINESE (PINYIN)* ☯📖 *Zú bā*

#ashisabaki {{足捌き}}##

(211-1)足捌き (212-2)足さばき

(250-hi)あしさばき (hir.)

(466-cha)*CHARACTERISTICS* ⓘ A Three-character, which consists of 2 Chinese Logograms and 1 Hiˈra-ga-ˈna Characters.

(800-tag)*TAGS* ⌨ #ashi-sabaki, ashi sabaki

22. Aˈshi-ˈbarai

(011-k1)*KANJI 1* ☛ Ashi-foot {足}, p. 37

(012-k2)*KANJI 2* ☛ harai {{払い}}, p. 87

(070-kt)*KARATE MEANING* ✋📖 *noun* ① Foot sweep

(077-jg)*GENERAL MEANING (EXAMPLES)* ☼📖 *noun* ❶ Tripping up

(185-ch)*CHINESE (PINYIN)* ☯📖 ***Zú fǎn***

#ashibarai {{足払い}}##

(211-1)足払い

(250-hi)あしばらい (hir.)

(466-cha)*CHARACTERISTICS* ⓘ A

Three-character, which consists of 2 Chinese Logograms and 1 Hiˈra-ga-ˈna Characters.

(800-tag)*TAGS* 💻 #ashi-barai, ashi barai

23. Ashi-gatana (sokutō)

(001-REF-rom)Ashi-gatana ☞ sokutō {{足刀}}, p. 223

#ashigatana (sokutō)##

(800-tag)*TAGS* 💻 #ashi-gatana, ashi gatana, ashikatana, ashi-katana, ashi katana

24. Aˈshi-geˈri

(011-k1)*KANJI 1* ☞ Ashi-foot {足}, p. 37

(016-w2)*WORD 2* Ⱳ ☞ keri {{蹴り}}, p. 140

(070-kt)*KARATE MEANING* ✋📖 *noun*

① The Kicks

(133-sy)*SYNONYMS* 👁= ashiwaza {{足技}}, p. 39; keriwaza {{蹴り技}}, p. 141

(185-ch)*CHINESE (PINYIN)* ☯📖 ***Zúcù***

#ashigeri {{足蹴り}}##

(211-1)足蹴り (212-2)足蹴

(250-hi)あしげり (hir.)

(466-cha)*CHARACTERISTICS* ⓘ A

Three-character, which consists of 2 Chinese Logograms and 1 Hiˈra-ga-ˈna Characters.

(800-tag)*TAGS* 💻 #ashi-geri, ashi geri, ashikeri

25. Aˈshi-ˈmoto

(011-k1)*KANJI 1* ☞ Ashi-foot {足}, p. 37

(012-k2)*KANJI 2* ☞ Moto-origin {元}, p. 173

(020-re)*RESEARCH* ⌔ *noun* ❶ Step, pace ❷ Way of walking, gait.

(185-ch)*CHINESE (PINYIN)* ☯📖 ***Zúyuán***

(211-1)足元

(212-2)足もと (213-3)足下

#ashimoto {{足元}}##

(214-4)足許

(250-hi)あしもと (hir.)

(275-tō)あ し も と [àshímóˈtò]

(466-cha)*CHARACTERISTICS* ⓘ A Two-character, which consists of 2 Chinese Logograms and 0 Hiˈra-ga-ˈna Characters.

(800-tag)*TAGS* ⌨ #ashi-moto, ashi moto

26. Aˈshi-waˈza

(011-k1)*KANJI 1* ☞ Ashi-foot {足}, p. 37

(012-k2)*KANJI 2* ☞ Waza-technique {技}, p. 267

(070-kt)*KARATE MEANING* ✋📖 *noun* ① Foot techniques

(133-sy)*SYNONYMS* 👁= ashigeri {{足蹴り}}, p. 38; keriwaza {{蹴り技}}, p. 141

#ashiwaza {{足技}}##

(185-ch)*CHINESE (PINYIN)* 👅📖 *Zújì*

(211-1)足技

(250-hi)あしわざ (hir.)

(466-cha)*CHARACTERISTICS* ⓘ A Two-character, which consists of 2 Chinese Logograms and 0 Hiˈra-ga-ˈna Characters.

(800-tag)*TAGS* ⌨ #ashi-waza, ashi waza

27. Aˈshi-yuˈbi

(011-k1)*KANJI 1* ☞ Ashi-foot {足}, p. 37

(012-k2)*KANJI 2* ☞ Yubi-finger {指}, p. 282

(077-jg)*GENERAL MEANING (EXAMPLES)* ☼📖 *noun* ① Toe, one of the digits of the foot

(133-sy)*SYNONYMS* 👁= Ato-toe {趾}, p. 40

(139-an)*ANTONYMS* 👁↺ ˈTe-yuˈbi (手指)

(185-ch)*CHINESE (PINYIN)* 👅📖 *Zú zhǐ*

#ashiyubi {{足指}}##

(211-1)足指

(212-2)足の指

(213-3)趾

(250-hi)あしゆび (hir.)

(466-cha)*CHARACTERISTICS* ⓘ A Two-character, which consists of 2 Chinese Logograms and 0 Hiˈra-ga-ˈna Characters.

(800-tag)*TAGS* ⌨ #ashi-yubi, ashiyubi, #ashiubi

28. Aˈtama (頭)

(000-it)*INCLUDING TERMS (EXAMPLES)* 👁✉ hizagashira {{膝頭}}, p. 100

ˈAto (趾) – ˈAto 後

(077-jg)*GENERAL MEANING (EXAMPLES)* ⚙📖 *noun* ❶ Head

(185-ch)*CHINESE (PINYIN)* 🌑📖 *tóu*

(211-1)頭

(275-tō)あたま [àtámá⁺]

(276-tō2)あたま [àtá⁺mà]

(302-kn)*KANJI NOTES* ✎✍ Contains 16 strokes.

#Atama-head {頭}##

(250-hi)あたま (hir.)

(313-ka)*KANJI* ✎ The Phono-semantic Compound Logogram Aˈtama-head (頭). (313k-cn)**Components** ⛬ [phonetic 豆 | semantic 頁]. (313k-ra)**Radical** ✛ 頁 page. (313k-cs)**Composition** ⚒ Left: 豆, right: 頁. (313k-re)**Readings (examples)** 🗣 Kun: あたま (atama); かしら (kaˈshira) [kàshírá⁺].

(830-ik)**IMPORTANT KANJI**

29. ˈAto (趾)

(000-it)*INCLUDING TERMS (EXAMPLES)* 👁✉ koshi {{虎趾}}, p. 155

(077-jg)*GENERAL MEANING (EXAMPLES)* ⚙📖 *noun* ❶ Toe

(133-sy)*SYNONYMS* 👁 = ashiyubi {{足指}}, p. 39

(185-ch)*CHINESE (PINYIN)* 🌑📖 *zhǐ*

(211-1)趾 (250-hi)あと (hir.)

#Ato-toe {趾}##

(211-al)*ALTERNATIVES OR SEE ALSO* ✎✎ 足指, 足の指

(325-kr)*KANJI READINGS* ✎🗣 Go-on: し (shi). Kan-on: し (shi). Kun: あしゆび (ashiyubi, 趾); あと (ato, 趾); もと (moto).

(833-kan)**KANJI**

30. ˈAtode

(011-k1)*KANJI 1* ☛ Ato-behind {後}, p. 41

(077-jg)*GENERAL MEANING (EXAMPLES)* ⚙📖 *adverb* ❶ Later, afterwards

#atode {{後で}}##

(211-1)後で

(250-hi)あとで (hir.)

(800-tag)*TAGS* 🖳 #ato-de, ato de

31. ˈAto 後

(000-it)*INCLUDING TERMS (EXAMPLES)* 👁✉ atode {{後で}}, p. 40; kōkutsu {{後屈}}, p. 150; saigo {{

最後}}, p. 199; ushirogeri {{後ろ蹴り}}, p. 265

(077-jg)GENERAL MEANING (EXAMPLES) ☼📖 *noun* ❶ Behind, back, rear

(139-an)ANTONYMS 👁↺ Mae-front {前}, p. 160

(185-ch)CHINESE (PINYIN) ☯📖 ***hòu***

(211-1)後

#Ato-behind {後}##

(250-hi)あと (hir.)

(275-tō)あと [á⁺tò]

(313-ka)KANJI 🖋 The Compound Ideogram 'Ato-behind (後). (313k-cn)**Components** [彳 | 幺 | 夊][19]. (313k-re)**Readings (examples)** 🗣 Kan-on: こう (kō). Tō-on: ご (go). Kun: あと (ato); うしろ (ushiro) [ùshíró] (後ろ).

(833-kan)**KANJI**

32. 'Au (合)

(000-it)INCLUDING TERMS (EXAMPLES) 👁✉ kiai {{気合}}, p. 144; maai {{間合}}, p. 160

(077-jg)GENERAL MEANING (EXAMPLES) ☼📖 *verb* ❶ To unite, to join, to merge, to come together ❷ To meet, to encounter, to see ❸ To match, to fit, to suit ❹ To agree.

(185-ch)CHINESE (PINYIN) ☯📖 ***hé***

(275-tō)あう [á⁺ù]

(211-1)合 (211-ka+hi)合う

(211-al)ALTERNATIVES OR SEE ALSO 🖋🖋 合い

(250-hi)あう (hir.)

#Au-to unite {合}##

(313-ka)KANJI 🖋 The Compound Ideogram 'Au-to unite (合)[20]. (313k-cn)**Components** [亼 | 口] (313k-ra)**Radical** ✦ 口 mouth (313k-cs)**Composition** ⚒ Top: 亼, bottom: 口 (313k-re)**Readings (examples)** 🗣 Go-on: ごう (gō). Kun: あう (au, 合う). Nanori: かい (kai).

(705-gv)GODAN VERB ⑤ **<u>Terminal Form {u* but not i*-ru or e*-ru}</u>** Au [á⁺ù] (合う), which means to unite. **<u>Polite Form {i*-masu}</u>** Aimas[u] [àímá⁺sù] (合います).

(830-ik)**IMPORTANT KANJI**

33. 'Ban-chi

(021-rb)*RESEARCH (FOR BOOKS)* 📖

noun ❶ House number, address (book's details)

#banchi##

(211-1)番地

(185-ch)*CHINESE (PINYIN)* 🌑📖 *Fānde*

34. Baˈrai (harai)

(001-REF-rom)Baˈrai ☞ harai {{払い}}, p. 87

(002-REF-hi)ばらい ☞ はらい

#barai (harai)##

(275-tō)ば ら い [bàráˈì]

(885-tag)*TAGS* 💻 #baray

35. Baˈribaˈri

(070-kt)*KARATE MEANING* ✋📖 *noun*

① Continuous punches alternating hands.

(077-jg)*GENERAL MEANING (EXAMPLES)* ⚙📖 *noun* ❶ Tearing, ripping *adverb* ❷ Vigorously, energetically, actively.

(466-cha)*CHARACTERISTICS* ① A Four-character, which consists of 0 Chinese Logograms and 4 Hiˈra-ga-ˈna Characters

#baribari {{ばりばり}}##

(089-no)*NOTES AND EXAMPLES* 📖✍

An onomatopoeic word. An anec-dote for the gamers among the readers: In The King of Fighters video game, the technique is called Vulcan Punch; AKA Rush Hits or Rush Hit.

(250-hi)ばりばり (hir.) (256-kat)バリバリ (kat.)

(800-tag)*TAGS* 💻 #bari-bari, bari bari

36. Bas-ˈsai

💣 Do not confuse: Tsuranuku-to pierce {貫}, p. 257 as in nukite {{貫手}}, p. 185 with Nuku-to extract {抜}, p. 186 as in bassai {{拔塞}}, p. 43 and as in Iai-do's Nuˈki-ts[u]ˈke (抜き付け)!

(000-it)*INCLUDING TERMS (EXAMPLES)* 👁✉ bassaidai {{拔塞大}}, p. 44; bassaigamae {{拔塞構え}}, p. 43

(011-k1)*KANJI 1* ☞ Nuku-to extract {抜}, p. 186

(012-k2)*KANJI 2* ☞ Sai-fortress {塞}, p. 199

(060-kg)*KATA GROUP* 形形形 **AKA** Pas-ˈsai (パッサイ), Patsai, Penetrating a Fortress, To Penetrate a Fortress **Style** Shōrin (少林) **Number of Kata** Two

(089-no) *NOTES AND EXAMPLES* 📖✎ In Ōshima Dōjō - for instance - the name refers specifically to Bas-ˈsai-ˈdai (抜塞大), since the small Kata is not practiced.

(185-ch) *CHINESE (PINYIN)* 🌐📖 ***Básāi*** #bassai {{抜塞}}##

(062-mk) *FUNAKOSHI MAIN BOOK – KATA* 🔰**MK 1922 original** 6 (list beginning), 51 (list Enbusen), 242. **1925 Ishida** 20 (list beginning), 58 (list Enbusen), 248. **1925 Teramoto** 26 (list beginning), 52 (list Enbusen), 150. **1935 Suzuki-Johnston** 9 (list styles), 33 (list names), 40 (list Enbusen), 72. **1935 Ohshima** 8-9 (list styles), 36 (list names), 87.

(189-ok) *OKINAWAN* ⚫ Pas-ˈsai

(211-sh-1) 抜塞 (simp.)

(211-sh-2) 拔塞 (simp.)

(211-ky-1) 拔塞 (trad.)

(250-hi) ばっさい (hir.)

(256-kat) バッサイ (kat.)

(275-tō) ば っ さ い [bàssái]

(466-cha) *CHARACTERISTICS* ① A Two-character, which consists of 2 Chi-

Bas-ˈsai ˈGamae - Bas-ˈsai ˈGamae nese Logograms and 0 Hiˈra-ga-ˈna Characters.

(800-tag) *TAGS* 💻 #bas-sai, bas sai, #basai

(838-su) **SUPER-TERM**

37. Bas-ˈsai ˈGamae

(015-w1) *WORD 1* ᵂᵂ ☞ bassai {{抜塞}}, p. 43

(016-w2) *WORD 2* ᵂᵂ ☞ kamae {{構え}}, p. 123

(070-kt) *KARATE MEANING* ✋📖 *noun phrase* ① Bas-ˈsai-ˈdai's (抜塞大) standby position.

(482-kg) **K↻g** 🔔 Due to the ˈRen-daku laws, the unvoiced consonant /K/ may get a Dak[u]-ˈten (゛) and become ~/g/ as a suffix. Example 🖊 Keˈri (けり) turns into Maˈe-geˈri (まえげり).

(185-ch) *CHINESE (PINYIN)* 🌐📖 ***Básāi gòu***

(800-tag) *TAGS* 💻 #bassai-gamae, bassai gamae #bassaigamae {{抜塞構え}}##

Masters 1 – Bassai-gamae by Bamgboye Sensei
List of Sensei Demonstrations next to Values, p. 10
Bobby Bamgboye of Nigeria WSKF demonstrates Bassai-gamae. Photographer: Joel Ibanga.

(211-sh-1)抜塞構え (simp.)

(250-hi)ばっさいがまえ (hir.)

(256-kat)バッサイガマエ (kat.)

(466-cha)*CHARACTERISTICS* ① A Four-character, which consists of 3 Chinese Logograms and 1 Hiˈra-ga-ˈna Characters.

38. Bas-ˈsai-ˈdai

(015-w1)*WORD 1* ☝ bassai {{抜塞}}, p. 43

(013-k3)*KANJI 3* ☝ Dai-big {大}, p. 56

(061-ka)*KATA* 形 **AKA** Passai dai, Major Bassai, Major Passai, Bassai Shodan, Passai Shodan, Bassai, Passai (パッサイ), Patsai, Penetrating a Fortress big, To Penetrate a Fortress big **Style** Shōrin (少林) **Group** Bas-ˈsai (抜塞). **Enbusen** ˈTe[i]-ji-ˈgata (丁字形) - 丁 Shape. **Number of** movements (approximately) Once 43 (1922, 1925), later 42 (1935, 1958).

(089-no)*NOTES AND EXAMPLES* 📖✍ In Ōshima Dōjō - for instance - the Kata is called simply Bas-ˈsai, since the small Kata is not practiced.

(185-ch)*CHINESE (PINYIN)* 💬📖 *Bá sāi dà*

(211-sh-1)拔塞大 (simp.)

#bassaidai {{抜塞大}}##

(062-mk)*FUNAKOSHI MAIN BOOK - KATA*

📖**MK 1922 original** 6 (list beginning), 51 (list Enbusen), 242. **1925 Ishida** 20 (list beginning), 58 (list Enbusen), 248. **1925 Teramoto** 26 (list beginning), 52 (list Enbusen), 150. **1935 Suzuki-Johnston** 9 (list styles), 33 (list names), 40 (list Enbusen), 72. **1935 Ohshima** 8-9 (list styles), 36 (list names), 87.

(211-sh-2)拔塞大 (simp.)

(211-ky-1)拔塞大 (trad.)

(250-hi)ばっさいだい (hir.)

(256-kat)バッサイダイ (kat.)

(466-cha)*CHARACTERISTICS* ① A Three-character, which consists of 3

Chinese Logograms and 0 Hiˈra-ga-ˈna Characters.

(800-tag)*TAGS* 🖥 #bassai-dai, bassai dai, bas-sai dai

(838-su)**SUPER-TERM**

39. ˈBō (棒)

(077-jg)*GENERAL MEANING (EXAMPLES)* ☼📖 *noun* ❶ Rod, pole, staff, stick, cane

(185-ch)*CHINESE (PINYIN)* ☻📖 ***Bàng***

(203-hi)⌛☉ (250-hi)ぼう (hir.)

#Bō-rod {棒}##

(211-1)棒

(275-tō)ぼ— [bɔ́ó]

(800-tag)*TAGS* 🖥 #bo, bou, boh, boo

(833-kan)**KANJI**

40. ˈBon (Hon)

(001-REF-rom)ˈBon ☞ Hon-source {本}, p. 102

#Bon (Hon)##

(002-REF-hi)ぼん ☞ ほん

41. ˈBu (武)

List of large photos - p. 10

(000-it)*INCLUDING TERMS (EXAMPLES)*

👁✉ budō {{武道}}, p. 46 ; bujutsu {{武術}}, p. 47; bukyōsha {{武侠社}}, p. 47; bushi {{武士}}, p. 48; enbu {{演武}}, p. 61; enbusen {{演武線}}, p. 61

(077-jg)*GENERAL MEANING (EXAMPLES)* ☼📖 *noun* ❶ Warrior, military officer, military man ❷ Military, military force, military power ❸ Martial Arts, military arts, art of war, strategy, tactics ❹ Courage, bravery, valor ❺ Battle, war.

(078-mg)*FUNAKOSHI MAIN BOOK - GENERALLY* 🏴**MG** 1922 original 273 **1925 Ishida** We did not find **1925 Teramoto** 174 **1935 Suzuki-Johnston** 259 **1935 Ohshima** 274

(133-gr-sy)*GROUP* 👁😵 The following terms are synonyms: Samurai-warrior {侍}, p. 201; Bu-warrior {武}, p. 45; Shi-warrior {士}, p. 211; bushi {{武士}}, p. 48.

(136-se)*SEE ALSO* 👁➕ Yamu-to stop {止}, p. 272

#Bu-warrior {武}##

(185-ch)*CHINESE (PINYIN)* ☻📖 ***wǔ*** - as in as in *wǔshù* (武術).

(211-1)武

(250-hi)ぶ (hir.)

(275-tō)ぶ [bú⁺]

(302-kn)*KANJI NOTES* ✐ ✎ Pay attention to the Radical (Yamu-to stop {止}, p. 272), which could mean to stop – in this case to stop the dagger-axe (戈). Putting an end to violence is indeed the highest level of the art of war. King Zhuāng of Chǔ (7th century B.C.) came to that conclusion based on this very Logogram (武)[21]:止戈為武[22].

(313-ka)*KANJI* ✐ The Compound Ideogram ˈBu-warrior (武). (313k-cn)**Components** ⛬ [戈 blade | 止 foot, to walk, to stop]. (313k-ra)**Radical** ⊹ 止 stop. (313k-cs)**Composition** 弌 一 弋 止. (313k-re)**Readings (examples)** 🎋 Go-on: む (mu). Kan-on: ぶ (bu). Kun: たけ (take); たけし (takeshi, 武し).

(830-ik)**IMPORTANT KANJI**

42. ˈBu-dō

(011-k1)*KANJI 1* ☛ Bu-warrior {武}, p. 45

(012-k2)*KANJI 2* ☛ Dō-way{道}, p. 57

(077-jg)*GENERAL MEANING (EXAMPLES)* ✿📖 *noun* ❶ Modern Japanese Martial Arts ❷ Japanese Martial Arts ❸ Martial Arts.

(089-no)*NOTES AND EXAMPLES* 📖✎ Bu-ˈdō-ka (武道家) is a martial artist.

(000-it)*INCLUDING TERMS (EXAMPLES)* 👁✉ budōkan {{武道館}}, p. 47 #budō {{武道}}##

(185-ch)*CHINESE (PINYIN)* 🗨📖 ***wǔdào***

(211-1)武道

(250-hi)ぶどう (hir.)

(275-tō) ぶ どー [bú⁺dòò]

(466-cha)*CHARACTERISTICS* ⓘ A Two-character, which consists of 2 Chinese Logograms and 0 Hiˈra-ga-ˈna Characters.

(800-tag)*TAGS* ⌨ #budo, budou, bu-do, bu do, #budoka

43. Bu-ˈdō-kan

(015-w1)*WORD 1* ᵂ⁄ᵂ ☛ budō {{武道}}, p. 46

(013-k3)*KANJI 3* ☛ Kan-hall {館}, p. 126

(077-jg)*GENERAL MEANING (EXAMPLES)* ✿📖 *noun* ❶ Martial arts stadium

(134-re)*RELATED TERMS* 👁∞ dōjō {{道場}}, p. 58

(185-ch)*CHINESE (PINYIN)* ☯📖 ***Wǔdào guǎn***

#budōkan {{武道館}}##

(211-1)武道館

(250-hi)ぶどーかん (hir.)

(275-tō)ぶ|ど|ーかん [bùdóˈòkàn]

(466-cha)*CHARACTERISTICS* ⓘ A Three-character, which consists of 3 Chinese Logograms and 0 Hiˈra-ga-ˈna Characters.

(800-tag)*TAGS* 💻 #budokan, budo-kan, budo kan, budoukan, budohkan, budookan

44. ˈBu-jutsu

(011-k1)*KANJI 1* ☞ Bu-warrior {武}, p. 45

(012-k2)*KANJI 2* ☞ Jutsu-art {術}, p. 116

(077-jg)*GENERAL MEANING (EXAMPLES)* ⚙📖 *noun* ❶ Japanese Martial Arts ❷ Martial Arts ❸ *wǔshù*

(185-ch)*CHINESE (PINYIN)* ☯📖 ***wǔshù*** noun ❶ Chinese Martial Arts, *gōngfu* (功夫) ❷ Martial Art

#bujutsu {{武術}}##

(211-1)武術

(250-hi)ぶじゅつ (hir.)

(280-po)pol:BUDZIUCY

(466-cha)*CHARACTERISTICS* ⓘ A Two-character, which consists of 2 Chinese Logograms and 0 Hiˈra-ga-ˈna Characters.

(800-tag)*TAGS* 💻 #bujitsu, bu-jutsu, bu-jitsu, bu jutsu, bu jitsu

45. Bu-ˈkyō-sha

(011-k1)*KANJI 1* ☞ Bu-warrior {武}, p. 45

(021-rb)*RESEARCH (FOR BOOKS)* ✍ *name* ❶ The name of a Tōkyō publishing house in the first half of the 20th century that apparently specialized in sport books, as well as other genres for youngsters such as adventure, crime, and mystery[23]. The publisher of FUˈNA-KOSHI's (p. 67) 1922 edition.

#bukyōsha {{武侠社}}##

(211-1)武侠社

(212-2)武侠社

(466-cha)*CHARACTERISTICS* ⓘ A Three-character, which consists of 3 Chinese Logograms and 0 Hiˈra-ga-ˈna Characters.

(800-tag)*TAGS* 💻 #bukyosha, #bukiosha, bu-kyo-sha

46. Buˈn-kai

(070-kt)*KARATE MEANING* ✋📖 *noun*

① Kata practical analysis, putting to combat use.

(077-jg)*GENERAL MEANING (EXAMPLES)* ☼📖 *noun* ❶ Disassembly, breaking down, dismantling ❷ Analysis.

(134-re)*RELATED TERMS* 👁∞ ōyō {{応用}}, p. 194

(185-ch)*CHINESE (PINYIN)* ☯📖 **Fēnjiě**

#bunkai {{分解}}##

(211-1)分解 (250-hi)ぶんかい (hir.)

(275-tō)ぶんかい [bùńkáí]

(280-po)pol:BYNKAJ

(466-cha)*CHARACTERISTICS* ⓘ A Two-character, which consists of 2 Chinese Logograms and 0 Hiˈra-ga-ˈna Characters.

(800-tag)*TAGS* 💻 #bun-kai, bunkai

47. ˈBu-shi

(000-it)*INCLUDING TERMS (EXAMPLES)* 👁✉ bushidō {{武士道}}, p. 49

(011-k1)*KANJI 1* ☛ Bu-warrior {武}, p. 45

(012-k2)*KANJI 2* ☛ Shi-warrior {士}, p. 211

(133-gr-sy)*GROUP* 👁🫂 The following terms are synonyms: Samurai-warrior {侍}, p. 201; Bu-warrior {武}, p. 45; Shi-warrior {士}, p. 211; bushi {{武士}}, p. 48

#bushi {{武士}}##

(077-jg)*GENERAL MEANING (EXAMPLES)* ☼📖 *noun* ❶ Warrior, samurai.

(185-ch)*CHINESE (PINYIN)* ☯📖 **Wǔshì**

(211-1)武士 412-hi)ぶし (hir.)

(275-tō)ぶし [búˈshì]

(466-cha)*CHARACTERISTICS* ⓘ A Two-character, which consists of 2 Chinese Logograms and 0 Hiˈra-ga-ˈna Characters.

(800-tag)*TAGS* 💻 #bu-shi, bu shi

48. Bu-ˈshi-dō

(015-w1)*WORD 1* ☛ bushi {{武士}}, p. 48

(013-k3)*KANJI 3* ☛ Dō-way{道}, p. 57

(077-jg)*GENERAL MEANING (EXAMPLES)* ☼📖 *noun* ❶ Way of the samurai, way of the warrior, ethical code of the samurai, samurai code of chivalry

(185-ch)*CHINESE (PINYIN)* ☯📖

Wǔshìdào

#bushidō {{武士道}}##

(211-1)武士道

(250-hi)ぶしどう (hir.)

(275-tō)ぶしどー [bùshí˧dòò]

(466-cha)*CHARACTERISTICS* ⓘ A Three-character, which consists of 3 Chinese Logograms and 0 Hiˈra-ga-ˈna Characters.

(800-tag)*TAGS* 💻 #bushido, bu-shi-do, bu shi do, bushi do

49. Byˈō-bu

(000-it)*INCLUDING TERMS (EXAMPLES)* 👁✉ byōbudaoshi {{屏風倒し}}, p. 49

(077-jg)*GENERAL MEANING (EXAMPLES)* ⚙📖 *noun* ❶ Folding screen.

(185-ch)*CHINESE (PINYIN)* ☯📖

Píngfēng

(211-1)屏風 (250-hi)びょうぶ (hir.)

(256-kat)ビョウブ (kat.)

#byōbu {{屏風}}##

(275-tō)びょ─ぶ [byòóbú]

(280-po)pol:BJOOBY

(466-cha)*CHARACTERISTICS* ⓘ A Two-character, which consists of 2 Chi-

---

By ̍ō-bu - By ̍ō-bu- ̍daoshi

nese Logograms and 0 Hiˈra-ga-ˈna Characters.

(800-tag)*TAGS* 💻 #byobu, byo-bu, byo bu, #biobu

50. Byˈō-bu-ˈdaoshi

(015-w1)*WORD 1* ☞ byōbu {{屏風}}, p. 49

(055-tt)*THROWING TECHNIQUE* 投技

AKA Folding-screen Topple, To Topple a Folding Screen, Toppling of a Folding Screen

(089-no)*NOTES AND EXAMPLES* 📖✎

Byˈō-bu-ˈdaoshi includes a reverse kick. In Jū-dō the technique is called Ō-ˈsoto-gaˈri (大外刈).

(185-ch)*CHINESE (PINYIN)* ☯📖

Píngfēng dǎo

(211-1)屏風倒し

(250-hi)びょうぶだおし (hir.)

#byōbudaoshi {{屏風倒し}}##

(056-mt)*FUNAKOSHI MAIN BOOK - THROWING TECHNIQUES* 📚**MTT**

1922 original Does not appear **1925 Ishida** Does not appear **1925 Teramoto** Does not appear **1935 Suzuki-Johnston** 192-193 (Byōbu-daoshi). **1935 Ohshima** 227-228 (Byōbudaoshi).

(466-cha)*CHARACTERISTICS* ⓘ A Four-character, which consists of 3 Chinese Logograms and 1 Hiˈra-ga-ˈna Characters.

(800-tag)*TAGS* 🖥 #byobudaoshi, #biobudaoshi

51. Ch[i]ˈkara (力)

(077-jg)*GENERAL MEANING (EXAMPLES)* ⚙📖 *noun* ❶ Power, force, strength ❷ Vigor, energy ❸ Capability, ability

(211-1)力

#Chikara-power {力}##

(250-hi)ちから (hir.)

(275-tō) ち|から| [chɨkárá⁺]

(833-kan)**KANJI**

52. ˈChin (ikusa)

(001-REF-rom)ˈChin ☞ Ikusa-war {戦}, p. 105

#chin (ikusa)##

(002-REF-hi)ちん ☞ いくさ

53. ˈChin-tō (gankaku)

(001-REF-rom)ˈChin-tō ☞ gankaku {{岩鶴}}, p. 68

(002-REF-hi)ちんとう ☞ がんかく

(009-REF-kan)鎮東 ☞ 岩鶴

#chintō (gankaku)##

(256-kat)チントウ (kat.)

(185-ch)*CHINESE (PINYIN)* ☯📖

zhèndōng

(800-tag)*TAGS* 🖥 #chinto, chin-to, chin to, #chintou

54. ˈChō (丁)

(000-it)*INCLUDING TERMS (EXAMPLES)*

👁✉ chōji {{丁字}}, p. 51

(077-jg)*GENERAL MEANING (EXAMPLES)* ⚙📖 *noun* ❶ Street, town ❷ Even number ❸ 4th in rank

(185-ch)*CHINESE (PINYIN)* ☯📖 *ding*

(211-1)丁 (250-hi)ちょう (hir.)

(275-tō) ちょ|ー| [chó⁺ò]

(302-kn)*KANJI NOTES* ✎✍ We use this Logogram for its shape (T-shape) and not its meaning.

#Chō-street {丁}##

(313-ka)*KANJI* ✎ The Pictogram ˈChō-street (丁). (313k-cn)**Components** 🖧 No components - a Simple Logogram (313k-ra)**Radical** ✦ 一 one (313k-cs)**Composition** ✗ Top: 一, bottom: 亅

(313k-re)**Readings (examples)** 🎙 Go-on: ちょう (chō). Kan-on: てい (tei).

(800-tag)*TAGS* 🖥 #cho 1, chou 1, choo 1, chou 1

(830-ik)**IMPORTANT KANJI**

55. ˈCho (著)

(000-it)*INCLUDING TERMS (EXAMPLES)*

👁 ✉ chosaku {{著作}}, p. 53

(021-rb)*RESEARCH (FOR BOOKS)* 🔍 *suffix (~cho)* ❶ Written by, author.

(185-ch)*CHINESE (PINYIN)* 🔊📖 *Zhe*

(211-1)著

#Cho-author {著}##

(089-no)*NOTES AND EXAMPLES* 📖✎

Examples: 船越義珍 著 (富名腰義珍 著) means written by FUNAKO-SHI Gichin. 江上 は 著書 means EGAMI is the author.

(833-kan)**KANJI**

56. ˈChō-ji

(000-it)*INCLUDING TERMS (EXAMPLES)*

👁 ✉ teijidachi {{丁字立ち}}, p. 235; teijigata {{丁字形}}, p. 236

(011-k1)*KANJI 1* ☛ Chō-street {丁}, p. 50

(012-k2)*KANJI 2* ☛ Ji-character {字}, p. 109

(185-ch)*CHINESE (PINYIN)* 🔊📖 *dīngzì*

(211-1)丁字

(250-hi)ちょうじ (hir.)

#chōji {{丁字}}##

(077-jg)*GENERAL MEANING (EXAMPLES)* ☼📖 *noun, adjective* ❶ Letter T, character 丁 ❷ T-shaped, 丁 shaped (丁字形), T shape

(466-cha)*CHARACTERISTICS* ⓘ A Two-character, which consists of 2 Chinese Logograms and 0 Hiˈra-ga-ˈna Characters.

(800-tag)*TAGS* 🖥 #choji, #teiji, #teijikei

57. ˈChō-ji ˈDachi (teijidachi)

(001-REF-rom)ˈChō-ji ˈDachi ☞ teijidachi {{丁字立ち}}, p. 235

(250-hi)ちょうじだち (hir.)

#chōjidachi (teijidachi)##

(800-tag)*TAGS* 🖥 #chojidachi, chojidachi, choji dachi

58. ˈChō-ji-ˈgata (teijigata)

(001-REF-rom)ˈChō-ji-ˈgata ☞ teijigata {{丁字形}}, p. 236

(250-hi)ちょうじがた (hir.)

#chōjigata (teijigata)##

(800-tag)*TAGS* 🖥 #chojigata, chojigata, choji gata, #chojikata, #choji kata

59. Choˈku-zuˈki

(011-k1)*KANJI 1* ☛ Naoru-to be fixed {直}, p. 181

(015-w1)*WORD 1* W/W ☛ tsuki {{突き}}, p. 253

(070-kt)*KARATE MEANING* ✋📖 AKA Jika-zuki（じかづき), Choki-zuki, Kara-zuki *noun* ① Direct thrust, any straight punch, including Oizuki and Gyakuzuki ② Stationary straight punch, straight punching executed from a fixed stance.

(089-no)*NOTES AND EXAMPLES* 📖✎ Appears in Bassai Dai, in Kankū Dai, and in Enpi.

(466-cha)*CHARACTERISTICS* ⓘ A Three-character, which consists of 2 Chinese Logograms and 1 Hiˈra-gaˈna Characters.

#chokuzuki {{直突き}}##

Masters 2 - Chokuzuki by Bamgboye Sensei
List of Sensei Demonstrations next to Values, p. 10
Bobby Bamgboye of Nigeria WSKF demonstrates Choku-zuki. Photographer: Joel Ibanga.

(185-ch)*CHINESE (PINYIN)* ☯📖 ***Zhí tū***

(211-1)直突き

(212-2)直突

(250-hi)ちょくづき (hir.)

(280-po)pol:CZOKYDZYKI

(800-tag)*TAGS* 🖥 #chokizuki, choki-tsuki, #jikazuki, jika-zuki, jika-tsuki, #karazuki, kara-tsuki

60. Cho-ˈsak[u]-ken

(000-it)*INCLUDING TERMS (EXAMPLES)* 👁✉ chosakukenshoyū {{著作權所有}}, p. 53

(015-w1)*WORD 1* W/W ☛ chosaku {{著作}}, p. 53

(021-rb)*RESEARCH (FOR BOOKS)* ✍ *noun* ❶ Copyright

(211-1)著作権

#chosakuken {{著作権}}##

(250-hi)ちょさくけん (hir.)

(275-tō)ちょ さ く けん [chòsákʉˈkèn]

(466-cha)*CHARACTERISTICS* ⓘ A Three-character, which consists of 3 Chinese Logograms and 0 Hiˈra-gaˈna Characters.

(800-tag)*TAGS* 🖥 #chosaku-ken

61. Cho-ˈsak[u]-ken Sho-ˈyū

(015-w1)*WORD 1* $\frac{W}{W}$ ☛ chosakuken {{著作権}}, p. 52

(104-k5)*KANJI 5* ☛ Yū-existence {有},

p. 282

(021-rb)*RESEARCH (FOR BOOKS)* ✍

noun phrase ❶ Copyright owner

(211-1)著作権所有

(250-hi)ちょさくけんしょゆう (hir.)

#chosakukenshoyū {{著作権所有}}##

(466-cha)*CHARACTERISTICS* ⓘ A Five-character, which consists of 5 Chinese Logograms and 0 Hiˈra-ga-ˈna Characters.

(800-tag)*TAGS* ⌨ #chosakukenshoyu, chosakuken-shoyu, chosakuken shoyu, chosakuken shoyū

62. Cho-ˈsak[u]-sha

(015-w1)*WORD 1* $\frac{W}{W}$ ☛ chosaku {{著作}}, p. 53

(021-rb)*RESEARCH (FOR BOOKS)* ✍

noun ❶ Author, writer

(211-1)著作者

(250-hi)ちょさくしゃ (hir.)

#chosakusha##

(466-cha)*CHARACTERISTICS* ⓘ A Three-character, which consists of 3

Chinese Logograms and 0 Hiˈra-ga-ˈna Characters.

(800-tag)*TAGS* ⌨ #chosaku-sha, chosaku sha, chosaksha

63. Cho-ˈsaku

(000-it)*INCLUDING TERMS (EXAMPLES)*

👁✉ chosakuken {{著作権}}, p. 52

(011-k1)*KANJI 1* ☛ Cho-author {著}, p. 51

(021-rb)*RESEARCH (FOR BOOKS)* ✍

noun ❶ Book, writing

#chosaku {{著作}}##

(185-ch)*CHINESE (PINYIN)* 🔊📖 *Zhùzuò*

(211-1)著作 (250-hi)ちょさく (hir.)

(466-cha)*CHARACTERISTICS* ⓘ A Two-character, which consists of 2 Chinese Logograms and 0 Hiˈra-ga-ˈna Characters

64. ˈCho-sha

(011-k1)*KANJI 1* ☛ Cho-author {著}, p. 51

(021-rb)*RESEARCH (FOR BOOKS)* ✍

noun ❶ Author, writer

(211-1)著者 (250-hi)ちょしゃ (hir.)

(275-tō) ちょ しゃ [chóˈshà]

#chosha##

ˈChū (Naka) - Chū-ˈsok[u]-ˈkotsu

(466-cha)*CHARACTERISTICS* ⓘ A Two-character, which consists of 2 Chinese Logograms and 0 Hiˈra-ga-ˈna Characters.

(800-tag)*TAGS* 🖥 #chosha, cho-sha, sho sha

65. ˈChū (Naka)

(001-REF-rom)ˈChū ☞ Naka-middle {中}, p. 178

(002-REF-hi)ちゅう ☞ なか

#chū (Naka)##

(275-tō) ┌──┐ ちゅ│う [chú⁺ù] └──┘

(800-tag)*TAGS* 🖥 #chu, chuu, chuh

66. ˈChū-aˈshi (nakaashi)

(001-REF-rom)ˈChū-aˈshi ☞ nakaashi (中足), p. 178

(002-REF-hi)ちゅうあし ☞ なかあし

#chūashi (nakaashi)##

(800-tag)*TAGS* 🖥 #chuashi, chū-ashi, chu-ashi, chu ashi

67. ˈChū-dan

(011-k1)*KANJI 1* ☞ Naka-middle {中}, p. 178

(012-k2)*KANJI 2* ☞ Dan-level {段}, p. 56

(070-kt)*KARATE MEANING* ✋📖 *noun*

① Middle body, middle section, central section, solar plexus, chest

(185-ch)*CHINESE (PINYIN)* ☯📖 ***zhōng-duàn***

#chūdan {{中段}}##

(211-1)中段 (250-hi)ちゅうだん (hir.)

(466-cha)*CHARACTERISTICS* ⓘ A Two-character, which consists of 2 Chinese Logograms and 0 Hiˈra-ga-ˈna Characters.

(800-tag)*TAGS* 🖥 #chudan, chu-dan, chu dan, chuudan

(838-su)**SUPER-TERM**

68. ˈChū-kō (nakadaka)

(001-REF-rom)ˈChū-kō ☞ nakadaka {{中高}}, p. 179

(002-REF-hi)ちゅうこう ☞ なかだか

#chūkō (nakadaka)##

(250-hi)ちゅうこう (hir.)

(800-tag)*TAGS* 🖥 #chuko, chu-ko, chu ko, chuukoo, chuhkoh

69. Chū-ˈsok[u]-ˈkotsu

(011-k1)*KANJI 1* ☞ Naka-middle {中}, p. 178

(012-k2)*KANJI 2* ☞ Ashi-foot {足}, p. 37

(077-jg)*GENERAL MEANING (EXAMPLES)* ⚙📖 *noun* ❶ Metatarsal bones, metatarsus, the long bones of the foot.

(211-1)中足骨

(250-hi)ちゅうそくこつ (hir.)

(250-hi-Alt)ちゅうそっこつ (hir.)

#chūsokukotsu {{中足骨}}##

(280-po)pol:CIUSOKKOCY

(275-tō) ち ゅ │う そ│ っ こ つ

[chùúsóˈkkòtsù]

(466-cha)CHARACTERISTICS ⓘ A
Three-character, which consists of 3 Chinese Logograms and 0 Hiˈra-ga-ˈna Characters.

(800-tag)TAGS 🖥 #chusokukotsu, chu-soku-kotsu, chu soku kotsu chusok-kotsu, chu-sok-kotsu, chu sok kotsu

70. ˈChū-soˈku (nakaashi)

(001-REF-rom)ˈChū-soˈku ☞ nakaashi (中足), p. 178

(800-tag)TAGS 🖥 #chusoku, chū-soku, chu-soku, chu soku

(002-REF-hi)ちゅうそく ☞ なかあし

(256-kat)チュウソク (kat.)

#chūsoku (nakaashi)##

(133-sy)SYNONYMS 👁= The follow-ing can mean ball of the foot: chūsoku (nakaashi), p. 55; Jō-soku-tei (上足底); koshi {{虎趾}}, p. 155; nakaashi (中足), p. 178;

ˈChū-soˈku (nakaashi) - ˈDai (大) maeashi {{前足}}, p. 161; Zen-soku (前足).

71. Daˈchi (tachi)

(001-REF-rom)Daˈchi ☞ tachi {{立ち}}, p. 228

#dachi (tachi)##

(250-hi)だち (hir.)

72. ˈDai (大)

Script 3 - Big-dai Spring and Autumn Bronze Inscriptions

(000-it)INCLUDING TERMS (EXAMPLES)
👁✉ bassaidai {{抜塞大}}, p. 44; kankūdai {{観空大}}, p. 129; ōkī {{大きい}}, p. 189; taisho {{大正}}, p. 230.

(077-jg)GENERAL MEANING (EXAM-PLES) ☼📖 adjective ❶ Big, large

(302-kn)KANJI NOTES ✎✍ It depicts a man (人) stretching out his limbs[24] (some say just the arms) as far as possible. The extension of the limbs became literally the very symbol of big. We should feel big, extended[25], in every position and in every movement we perform. Can You recognize the Logogram in the an-cient Chinese script on page 28? By the way, 木 (not 大) is the Character for wood.

#Dai-big {大}##

(139-an)*ANTONYMS* 👁️↻ Shō-small { 小}, p. 215

(185-ch)*CHINESE (PINYIN)* 🌐📖 ***dà, dài***

(211-1)大 (250-hi)だい (hir.)

(275-tō)だ̲い̲ [dáˈì]

(313-ka)*KANJI* 🖉 The Pictogrammatic Radical (Radical 37) ˈDai-big (大). (313k-cn)**Components** 🖧 No components - a Simple Logogram. (313k-ra)**Radical** ✛ 大 big. (313k-cs)**Composition** 🖎 Merging of 一 and 人. (313k-re)**Readings (examples)** 🕬 Go-on: だ (da); だい (dai). Kan-on: た (ta); たい (tai). Kun: おお (ō, 大) – as in Ō-ˈsoto-gaˈri (大外刈), which means large outer reap; おおきい (ōkii, 大きい).

(885-tag)*TAGS* 🖥️ #tai, day

(830-ik)**IMPORTANT KANJI**

73. ˈDaka (Taka)

(001-REF-rom)ˈDaka ☞ Taka-quantity { 高}, p. 231

#Daka (Taka)##

(002-REF-hi)だか ☞ たか

74. Dama (Tama)

(001-REF-rom)Dama ☞ Tama-ball {玉}, p. 231

#Dama (Tama)##

(002-REF-hi)だま ☞ たま

75. ˈDan (段)

(000-it)*INCLUDING TERMS (EXAMPLES)* 👁️✉ chūdan {{中段}}, p. 54; gedan {{下段}}, p. 69; godan {{五段}}, p. 71; hachidan {{八段}}, p. 77; jōdan {{上段}}, p. 114; jūdan {{十段}}, p. 115; nidan {{二段}}, p. 184; sandan {{三段}}, p. 204; shodan {{初段}}, p. 217; yodan {{四段}}, p. 277.

(077-jg)*GENERAL MEANING (EXAMPLES)* ⚙📖 *noun, suffix* ❶ Level, rank, grade, ~th rank; ~th degree black belt ❷ Step ❸ Stair.

(185-ch)*CHINESE (PINYIN)* 🌐📖 ***duàn***

#Dan-level {段}##

(089-no)*NOTES AND EXAMPLES* 📖🖉 ˈDan-dan (段々) means gradually.

(211-1)段

(250-hi)だん (hir.) (256-kat)ダン (kat.)

(313-ka)*KANJI* 🖉 The Phone-semantic Compound Ideogram[26] ˈDan-level (

段). (313k-cn)**Components** 🖧 [耑 | 殳]. (313k-ra)**Radical** ✦ 殳 weapon. (313k-re)**Readings (examples)** 🗣 Go-on: だん (dan). Kan-on: たん (tan).

(830-ik)**IMPORTANT KANJI**

(838-su)**SUPER-TERM**

76. 'Dō (動)

(000-it)*INCLUDING TERMS (EXAMPLES)*

👁✉ fudō {{不動}}, p. 64; fudōdachi {{不動立ち}}, p. 64

(077-jg)*GENERAL MEANING (EXAMPLES)* ☼📖 *noun* ❶ Motion, move ❷ Change, shift, shake.

#Dō-motion {動}##

(211-1)動

(250-hi)どう (hir.)

(256-kat) ドウ (kat.)

(800-tag)*TAGS* 💻 #do motion

(833-kan)**KANJI**

77. 'Dō (道)

(000-it)*INCLUDING TERMS (EXAMPLES)*

👁✉ budō {{武道}}, p. 46; bushidō {{武士道}}, p. 49; dōjō {{道場}}, p. 58; karatedō {{空手道}}, p. 132

(077-jg)*GENERAL MEANING (EXAMPLES)* ☼📖 *noun* ❶ Way, road, path ❷ Dàoism - the cosmological philosophy or religion called *Dǎo* (or Tao) ❸ Way of living, proper conduct, moral principles, morals, the way ❹ Teachings, dogma ❺ Journey ❻ Course, road (to something) ❼ Method, means.

(185-ch)*CHINESE (PINYIN)* ☯📖 ***dào*** – as in Dàoism.

(211-1)道

#Dō-way{道}##

(250-hi)どう (hir.)

(275-tō)[ど]ー [dó˺ò]

(313-ka)*KANJI* 🖋 The Phono-semantic Compound Logogram 'Dō-way (道). (313k-cn)**Components** 🖧 [semantic 辵 | phonetic 首]. (313k-ra)**Radical** ✦ 辶 辵辶 walk. (313k-cs)**Composition** ⚒ Bottom-left: 辶, top-right: 首. (313k-re)**Readings (examples)** 🗣 Go-on: どう (dō). Kan-on: とう (tō). Kun: みち (michi). Nanori: さ (sa); じ (ji); ど (do); みつ (mitsu).

(800-tag)*TAGS* 💻 #do way

(830-ik)**IMPORTANT KANJI**

78. Do-'ji-ga'ta

(011-k1)*KANJI 1* ☛ Tsuchi-earth {土}, p. 251

(012-k2)*KANJI 2* ☞ Ji-character {字}, p. 109

(013-k3)*KANJI 3* ☞ Kata-shape {形}, p. 134

(070-kt)*KARATE MEANING* ✋📖 *noun*
① Plus-Minus Pattern, Plus-minus Shape, Character-do Pattern, Character-shi Pattern, 土 Pattern, 土 Character Figure, ± Shape, T and Plus Shapes Combined, ˈShi-ji-ˈgata

(068-me)*FUNAKOSHI MAIN BOOK - ENBUSEN* ⚡**MEN** **1922 original** 51 **1925 Ishida** 58-59 **1925 Teramoto** 52 **1935 Suzuki-Johnston** 40 **1935 Ohshima** 41

(134-re)*RELATED TERMS* 👁∞ enbusen {{演武線}}, p. 61

#dojigata {{土字形}}##

(211-1)土字形

(211-al)*ALTERNATIVES OR SEE ALSO*
✒✑ 士字形, 土字型

(250-hi)どじがた (hir.)

(466-cha)*CHARACTERISTICS* ① A Three-character, which consists of 3 Chinese Logograms and 0 Hiˈra-ga-ˈna Characters.

(482-kg)**Kɔg** 🔔 Due to the ˈRendaku laws, the unvoiced consonant /K/ may get a Dak[u]-ˈten (゙) and become ~/g/ as a suffix. Example ↲ Keˈri (けり) turns into Maˈe-geˈri (まえげり).

(800-tag)*TAGS* 💻 #dojigata, doji-gata, doji gata, #shijigata, #tsuchijigata, #dojikata

79. ˈDō-jō

(011-k1)*KANJI 1* ☞ Dō-way{道}, p. 57

(077-jg)*GENERAL MEANING (EXAMPLES)* ☼📖 *noun* ❶ Dojo, training hall for martial arts, place for deep thinking or learning (like meditation)

(134-re)*RELATED TERMS* 👁∞ budōkan {{武道館}}, p. 47

(185-ch)*CHINESE (PINYIN)* ☯📖
dàochǎng, dàocháng

(211-1)道場

#dōjō {{道場}}##

(250-hi)どうじょう (hir.)

(275-tō)ど゙ーじょー [dóˈòjòò]

(276-tō2)ど゙ーじょー [dòójóó]

(466-cha)*CHARACTERISTICS* ① A Two-character, which consists of 2 Chi-

nese Logograms and 0 Hiˈra-ga-ˈna Characters.

(800-tag)*TAGS* 🖥 #dojo, do-jo, do jo

(838-su)**SUPER-TERM**

80. ˈDōmo

(077-jg)*GENERAL MEANING (EXAMPLES)* ⚙📖 *adverb* ❶ Very much *interjection* ❷ Thanks (very casual) ❸ Hello, goodbye, greetings

(134-re)*RELATED TERMS* 👁∞ arigato {{有難う}}, p. 35

(203-hi)⏳⊙ (250-hi)どうも (hir.)

#dōmo {{どうも}}##

(275-tō) |ど|―も [dóˈòmò]

(466-cha)*CHARACTERISTICS* ⓘ A Three-character, which consists of 0 Chinese Logograms and 3 Hiˈra-ga-ˈna Characters.

(800-tag)*TAGS* 🖥 #domo, doumo, doomo

81. ˈDōmo Aˈri-gaˈtō

(011-k1)*KANJI* 𝟷 ☞ Yū-existence {有}, p. 282

(077-jg)*GENERAL MEANING (EXAMPLES)* ⚙📖 *interjection* ❶ Thanks a lot (casual).

(203-hi)⏳⊙

(250-hi)どうもありがとう (hir.)

(211-1)どうも有難う

#dōmoarigatō {{ どうも 有難 う}}##

(212-2)どうも有り難う

(466-cha)*CHARACTERISTICS* ⓘ An Eight-character, which consists of 0 Chinese Logograms and 8 Hiˈra-ga-ˈna Characters.

(800-tag)*TAGS* 🖥 #domoarigato, domo-ari-gato, domo ari gato, domo ariga-to

(838-su)**SUPER-TERM**

82. ˈDōmo Aˈri-gaˈtō-go-zaiˈmas[u]

(011-k1)*KANJI* 𝟷 ☞ Yū-existence {有}, p. 282

(077-jg)*GENERAL MEANING (EXAMPLES)* ⚙📖 *expression* ❶ Thank You very much (polite, present tense)

(203-hi)⏳⊙ (250-hi)どうもありがとう ございます (hir.)

(211-1)どうも有難う御座います

(212-2)どうも有難うございます

(213-3)どうも有り難う御座います

#domoarigatogozaimasu##

(214-4)どうも有り難ございます

(466-cha)*CHARACTERISTICS* ⓘ A Thir-teen-character, which consists of 0 Chinese Logograms and 13 Hiˈra-gaˈna Characters.

(800-tag)*TAGS* 🖥 #dōmo arigatō gozaimasu, domo ari-gato go-zaimasu, domoarigato gozaimasu, domo arigato gozaimas, domo ari gato gozaimas

(838-su)**SUPER-TERM**

83. ˈDōmo Aˈri-gaˈtō-go-zaiˈmash[i]ta

(011-k1)*KANJI 1* ☛ Yū-existence {有}, p. 282

(077-jg)*GENERAL MEANING (EXAM-PLES)* ✿📖 *interjection* ❶ Thank You very much (polite, past tense)

(250-hi)どうもありがとうございました (hir.)

(211-1)どうも有難う御座いました

(212-2)どうも有難うございました

(213-3)どうも有り難ございました

(214-4)どうも有り難う御座いました

#domoarigatogozaimashita##

(203-hi)⌛☉

(466-cha)*CHARACTERISTICS* ⓘ A Four-teen-character, which consists of 0 Chinese Logograms and 14 Hiˈra-gaˈna Characters.

(800-tag)*TAGS* 🖥 #dōmo arigatō gozaimashita, domo ari-gato go-zaimashita, domo arigato go-zaimashita, domo arigatogozaimashta, domoarigato gozaimashta

(838-su)**SUPER-TERM**

84. ˈEm-pi (enpi)

(001-REF-rom)ˈEm-pi ☞ enpi {{燕飛}}, p. 63

#empi (enpi)##

(800-tag)*TAGS* 🖥 #empi, em-pi, em pi

85. ˈEn (演)

(000-it)*INCLUDING TERMS (EXAMPLES)*

👁✉ enbu {{演武}}, p. 61

(211-1)演 (250-hi)えん (hir.)

#En-performance {演}##

(077-jg)*GENERAL MEANING (EXAM-PLES)* ✿📖 *noun* ❶ Performance

(833-kan)**KANJI**

86. ˈEn-bu

(000-it)*INCLUDING TERMS (EXAMPLES)*

👁✉ enbusen {{演武線}}, p. 61

(011-k1)*KANJI 1* ☛ En-performance {演}, p. 60

(012-k2)*KANJI 2* ☛ Bu-warrior {武}, p. 45

(077-jg)*GENERAL MEANING (EXAMPLES)* ☼📖 *noun* ❶ Martial arts training ❷ Martial arts demonstration ❸ Military exercises, military drills

#enbu {{演武}}##

(185-ch)*CHINESE (PINYIN)* 👁📖 ***yǎnwǔ***

(211-1)演武

(250-hi)えんぶ (hir.)

(280-po)pol:EMBY

(466-cha)*CHARACTERISTICS* ⓘ A Two-character, which consists of 2 Chinese Logograms and 0 Hiˈra-ga-ˈna Characters.

(800-tag)*TAGS* 💻 #enbu, en-bu, en bu

87. ˈEn-bu-sen

(015-w1)*WORD 1* ᵂ☞ enbu {{演武}}, p. 61

(013-k3)*KANJI 3* ☞ Sen-line {線}, p. 207

(070-kt)*KARATE MEANING* ✋📖 *noun* ① Performance line, line of movement, demonstration line, fighting position lines ② Kata's line of movement ③ Starting point of a Kata.

(078-mg)*FUNAKOSHI MAIN BOOK - GENERALLY* 🌀**MG** 1922 original 50-51. **1925 Ishida** 58-59. **1925 Teramoto** 52. **1935 Suzuki-Johnston** 40-41. **1935 Ohshima** 41.

(133-sy)*SYNONYMS* 👁= K[i]-ˈten (起点)

(211-1)演武線

(250-hi)えんぶせん (hir.)

#enbusen {{演武線}}##

(280-po)pol:EMBUSEN

(466-cha)*CHARACTERISTICS* ⓘ A Three-character, which consists of 3 Chinese Logograms and 0 Hiˈra-ga-ˈna Characters.

(492-nbmb)**/n/b** 🔊 **[m]b** 🔔 The moraic nasal ん is realized as [m] when preceding /b/. Example 🔔 ˈSan-bon (さんぼん) is pronounced [ˈSambon]. In such cases, we recommend Karate researchers to look for both spellings (Sanbon and Sambon, for instance) in every search, due to different Romanization systems.

(800-tag)*TAGS* 💻 #enbusen, en-bu-sen, en bu sen

88. ˈEn-pi 1

(011-k1)*KANJI 1* ☞ Saru-monkey {猿}, p. 204

(012-k2)*KANJI 2* ☞ Hi-elbow {臂}, p. 97

(070-kt)*KARATE MEANING* 🖐📖 *noun* ① Elbow, Monkey-elbow ② Elbow strike, Elbow Attack

(077-jg)*GENERAL MEANING (EXAMPLES)* ⚙📖 *noun* ❶ Sharp elbow, monkey-like elbow, long and thin elbow, long and protruding elbow

(041-mu)*FUNAKOSHI MAIN BOOK - UPPER LIMB* 📖**MUL** **1922 original** 41 (list), 45. **1925 Ishida** 54 (list), 55. **1925 Teramoto** 46 (list), 49. **1935 Suzuki-Johnston** 24 (list), 24. **1935 Ohshima** 21 (list), 21.

(042-nu)*FUNAKOSHI NYUMON TERAMOTO - UPPER LIMB* 📖**NUL** 55

#enpi {{猿臂}}##

(211-1)猿臂 (250-hi)えんぴ (hir.)

(280-po)pol:EMPI

(466-cha)*CHARACTERISTICS* ① A Two-character, which consists of 2 Chinese Logograms and 0 Hiˈra-ga-ˈna Characters.

(491-npmp)**/n/p** 🔊 **[m]p** 🔈 The moraic nasal ん is realized as [m] when preceding /p/. Example ⚡ ˈEn-pi (

えんぴ) is pronounced [ˈEm-pi]. In such cases, we recommend Karate researchers to look for both spellings (Enpi and Empi, for instance) in every search, due to different Romanization systems.

(800-tag)*TAGS* 💻 #enpi 1, en-pi 1, en pi 1

(838-su)**SUPER-TERM**

89. ˈEn-pi 2

(011-k1)*KANJI 1* ☞ Tsubame-swallow {燕}, p. 256

(012-k2)*KANJI 2* ☞ Tobu-to fly {飛}, p. 246

(061-ka)*KATA* 形 **AKA** Empi, Wanshu, Wanshū (ワンシュー), Wang Shu, Yun Bi, Swallow Flying, Flying Swallow **Style** Once Shōrei (昭霊) (1922, 1925), later Shōrin (少林) (1935, 1958) **Group** None **Enbusen** ˈTe[i]-ji-ˈgata (丁字形) - 丁 Shape. **Number of movements (approximately)** Once 40 (1922, 1925), later 37 (1935, 1958)

(062-mk)*FUNAKOSHI MAIN BOOK - KATA* 📖**MK** **1922 original** 7 (list beginning), 248. **1925 Ishida** 20 (list beginning), 255. **1925 Teramoto** 26 (list beginning), 154. **1935 Suzuki-Johnston** 9 (list styles), 33 (list names), 40 (list Enbusen), 125. **1935 Ohshima** 8-9 (list styles), 36 (list names), 167.

(185-ch)*CHINESE (PINYIN)* 👁📖 *yànfēi* #enpi {{燕飛}}##

(211-1)燕飛 (250-hi)えんぴ (hir.)

(280-po)pol:EMPI

(466-cha)*CHARACTERISTICS* ⓘ A Two-character, which consists of 2 Chinese Logograms and 0 Hiˈra-ga-ˈna Characters.

(481-hp)**H⊃p** 🔔 Due to the ˈRen-daku laws, the unvoiced consonant /H/ may get a Han-dak[u]-ten (゜) and become ~/p/ as a suffix. Example ↳ ˈHon (ほん) turns into ˈIp-pon (いっぽん).

(491-npmp)**/n/p** 👂 **[m]p** 🔔 The moraic nasal ん is realized as [m] when preceding /p/. Example ↳ ˈEn-pi (えんぴ) is pronounced [ˈEm-pi]. In such cases, we recommend Karate researchers to look for both spellings (Enpi and Empi, for instance) in every search, due to different Romanization systems.

(800-tag)*TAGS* 🖥 #enpi 2, en-pi 2, en pi 2

(838-su)**SUPER-TERM**

90. F[u]ˈto (太)

(000-it)*INCLUDING TERMS (EXAMPLES)* 👁✉ taikyoku {{太極}}, p. 230

(077-jg)*GENERAL MEANING (EXAMPLES)* ⚙📖 *adjective* ❶ Great, grand ❷ Fat

(185-ch)*CHINESE (PINYIN)* 👁📖 *tài* as in *tàijí* (Tai chi) (太极)[27] and as in *Tài chōng* (Taichong) (太冲) - LR-3 acupuncture point[28]

(211-1)太 (211-al)*ALTERNATIVES OR SEE ALSO* ✎✎ 夳

(250-hi)ふと (hir.) #Futo-great {太}##

(275-tō)ふと [fɯ̀tó]

(280-po)pol:FTO

(302-kn)*KANJI NOTES* ✎✎ Contains 4 strokes.

(325-kr)*KANJI READINGS* ✎🗣 Go-on: たい (tai). Kan-on: たい (tai). Kan'yō-on: た (ta); だ (da); だい (dai). Kun: ふと (futo). Nanori: おお (ō).

(800-tag)*TAGS* 🖥 #futo

(833-kan)**KANJI**

91. ˈFu (不)

(000-it)*INCLUDING TERMS (EXAMPLES)*

👁✉ fudō {{不動}}, p. 64

(077-jg)*GENERAL MEANING (EXAMPLES)* ☼📖 *prefix* ❶ un~, non~, negative prefix

#Fu-un~ {不}##

(211-1)不 (250-hi)ふ (hir.)

(325-kr)*KANJI READINGS* ✏🗣 Go-on: ふ (fu); ほち (hochi). Kan-on: ふう (fū).

(833-kan)**KANJI**

92. Fu-ˈdō

(000-it)*INCLUDING TERMS (EXAMPLES)*

👁✉ fudōdachi {{不動立ち}}, p. 64

(011-k1)*KANJI 1* ☛ Fu-un~ {不}, p. 64

(012-k2)*KANJI 2* ☛ Dō-motion {動}, p. 57

(077-jg)*GENERAL MEANING (EXAMPLES)* ☼📖 *noun* ❶ Immobility, motionlessness, unshakability, firmness

#fudō {{不動}}##

(185-ch)*CHINESE (PINYIN)* 👌📖 **bùdòng**

(211-1)不動 (250-hi)ふどう (hir.)

(466-cha)*CHARACTERISTICS* ⓘ A Two-character, which consists of 2 Chinese Logograms and 0 Hiˈra-ga-ˈna Characters.

(800-tag)*TAGS* 💻 #fudo, fu-do, fu do

93. Fu-ˈdō-daˈchi

(015-w1)*WORD 1* ᵂ/ᵂ ☛ fudō {{不動}}, p. 64

(016-w2)*WORD 2* ᵂ/ᵂ ☛ tachi {{立ち}}, p. 228

(030-st)*STANCE* 立 **AKA** Sōchindachi (壮鎮立ち), Immovable Stance, Unshakable Stance, Rooted Stance **Category** Low sidewise stances

(031-ms)*FUNAKOSHI MAIN BOOK - STANCES* 📓**MS** 1922 **original** Does not appear. 1925 **Ishida** Does not appear. 1925 **Teramoto** Does not appear. 1935 **Suzuki-Johnston** Does not appear. 1935 **Ohshima** 19 and note 1, 20.

(032-ns)*FUNAKOSHI NYUMON TERAMOTO - STANCES* 📓**NS** 59 (list), 60

#fudōdachi {{不動立ち}}##

(211-1)不動立ち

(212-2)不動立

(250-hi)ふどうだち (hir.)

(466-cha)*CHARACTERISTICS* ⓘ A Four-character, which consists of 3 Chinese Logograms and 1 Hiˈra-ga-ˈna Characters.

(483-td)**T⟳d** ⌂ Due to the ˈRen-daku laws, the unvoiced consonant /T/ may get a Dak[u]-ˈten (゛) and become ~/d/ as a suffix. Example ↰ ˈTachi (たち) turns into Ki-ˈba Daˈchi (きばだち).

(800-tag)*TAGS* 💻 #fudodachi, fudo-dachi, fudo dachi, fudoudachi, fudoodachi

(838-su)**SUPER-TERM**

94. Fuˈmi-kiˈri

(011-k1)*KANJI 1* ☞ Fumu-to step on {踏}, p. 66

(016-w2)*WORD 2* ^W_W ☞ kiri {{切り}}, p. 147

(070-kt)*KARATE MEANING* ✋📖 AKA Fumikiri-geri *noun* ① Stomping cutting kick, cutting kick, stamping sidekick, stamping cut, sickle kick, step through kick.

(077-jg)*GENERAL MEANING (EXAMPLES)* ☼📖 *noun* ❶ Railroad crossing.

(134-re)*RELATED TERMS* 👁∞ kansetsugeri {{関節蹴り}}, p. 130; fumikomi {{踏み込み}}, p. 66

(211-1)踏切 (212-2)踏切り

(213-3)踏み切 (214-4)踏み切り

(250-hi)ふみきり (hir.)

(466-cha)*CHARACTERISTICS* ⓘ A Two-character, which consists of 2 Chinese Logograms and 0 Hiˈra-ga-ˈna Characters.

#fumikiri {{踏み切り}}##

Masters 3 - Fumikiri by Pavlović Sensei
List of Sensei Demonstrations next to Values, p. 10
Maria Anette Pavlović and Caroline Antgren of Sweden Kase-ha demonstrate Fumi-kiri. Photographer: Denis Sopovic.

(089-no)*NOTES AND EXAMPLES* 📖✍

There is a wide variety of interpretations of this term. According to some, Fumikiri is a low kick that uses the blade of the foot in a cutting manner, for instance to injure the opponent's patellar tendon. Another common version is stepping

Fuˈmi-koˈmi - Fuˈmu (踏)

on the adversary's foot. Indeed, Fumikiri can be used to disbalance the opponent[29].

(275-tō)ふ⃞みきり⃞[fùmíkírí]

(800-tag)*TAGS* 💻 #fumi-kiri, fumi kiri

95. Fuˈmi-koˈmi

(011-k1)*KANJI 1* ☞ Fumu-to step on { 踏}, p. 66

(015-w1)*WORD 1* W꜊W ☞ komi {{込み}}, p. 153

(070-kt)*KARATE MEANING* ✋📖 AKA Fumikomi-geri *noun* ① Stamping kick, trampling kick.

(077-jg)*GENERAL MEANING (EXAMPLES)* ✿📖 *noun* ❶ Stepping into, breaking into, rushing into ❷ Going into dealing fully.

(211-1)踏み込み (212-2)踏込
#fumikomi {{踏み込み}}##

(250-hi)ふみこみ (hir.)

(134-re)*RELATED TERMS* 👁∞ kansetsugeri {{関節蹴り}}, p. 130; fumikiri {{踏み切り}}, p. 65

(466-cha)*CHARACTERISTICS* ⓘ A Four-character, which consists of 2 Chinese Logograms and 2 Hiˈra-ga-ˈna Characters.

(800-tag)*TAGS* 💻 #fumikomi, fumi-komi, fumi komi

(838-su)**SUPER-TERM**

96. Fuˈmu (踏)

(000-it)*INCLUDING TERMS (EXAMPLES)*
👁✉ fumikiri {{踏み切り}}, p. 65; fumikomi {{踏み込み}}, p. 66

(077-jg)*GENERAL MEANING (EXAMPLES)* ✿📖 *verb* ❶ To step on, to tread on, to trample on ❷ To experience, to undergo, to go through.

(185-ch)*CHINESE (PINYIN)* 👁📖 *tà, tā*

(211-1)踏

(705-gv)*GODAN VERB* 🏍⑤ **Terminal Form** {u* ●꙳ but not i*-ru or e*-ru} Fuˈmu [fùmú] (踏む), which means to step on. **Polite Form** {i*-masu} Fuˈmimas[u] [fùmímá꜀sù] (踏みます).

#Fumu-to step on {踏}##

(250-hi)ふむ (hir.)

(280-po)pol:FYMY

(275-tō)ふ⃥む [fùmú]

(313-ka)*KANJI* ✐ The Phono-semantic Compound Logogram Fuˈmu-to step on (踏). (313k-cn)**Components** 🖧 [semantic 足 | phonetic 沓]. (313kra)**Radical** ✦ 足 ⻊ foot. (313k-cs)**Composition** ⚒ Left: ⻊, right: 沓. (313k-re)**Readings (examples)** Go-on: とう (tō). Kan-on: とう (tō). Kun: ふむ (fumu, 踏む); ふまえる (fumaeru, 踏まえる).

(830-ik)**IMPORTANT KANJI**

97. FU'NA-KOSHI 'Gi-chin

(029-pe)PERSONS FU'NA-KOSHI 'Gi-chin ('Shu-ri November 10, 1868 – Tō-kyō April 26, 1957) was a famous Okinawan Ka'ra-te-ka, considered by many the father of modern Ka'ra-te. A student of Ma'tsu-mura (p. 165), and a principal disciple of I'to-su (p. 108) and of A-'sato (p. 36). One of the pioneers who brought Ka'ra-te from O'ki-'nawa to Mainland Japan. The founder of 'Shō-tō-kan-'ryū (松濤館流).

(134-re)RELATED TERMS shōtō {{松濤}}, p. 220

#funakoshigichin {{船越 義珍}}##

(185-ch)CHINESE (PINYIN)

Chuányuè Yì zhēn

(216-ea)船越 義珍 (216-ea-2)富名腰 義珍

(217-we)義珍 船越 (217-we-2)義珍 富名腰

(466-cha)CHARACTERISTICS ⓘ A Four-character, which consists of 2 Chinese Logograms and 2 Hi'ra-ga-'na Characters.

(800-tag)TAGS #gichin funakoshi, gi-chin funa-koshi, gi chin funa koshi, #funakoshi, funa-koshi

(838-su)**SUPER-TERM**

98. Gai-wan-u'ke (sotoudeuke)

(001-REF-rom)Gai-wan-u'ke ☞ sotoudeuke {{外腕受け}}, p. 226

(002-REF-hi)がいわんうけ ☞ そとうでうけ

#gaiwanuke (sotoudeuke)##

(250-hi)がいわんうけ (hir.)

(800-tag)TAGS #gaiwan-uke, gai-wan-uke, gai wan uke

99. Ga'mae (kamae)

(001-REF-rom)Ga'mae ☞ kamae {{構え}}, p. 123

#gamae (kamae)##

(002-REF-hi)がまえ ☞ かまえ

100. 'Gan-kaku

(011-k1)*KANJI* 1 ☛ Iwa-rock {岩}, p. 108

(012-k2)*KANJI* 2 ☛ Tsuru-crane {鶴}, p. 258

(061-ka)*KATA* 形 **AKA** Chintō (チントウ), Chinto, Crane on a Rock **Style** Once Shōrei (昭霊) (1922), later Shōrin (少林) (1925, 1935, 1958) **Group** None **Enbusen** Iˈchi-ji-ˈgata (一字形) - 一 Shape **Number of movements (approximately)** Once 44 (1922, 1925), later 42 (1935, 1958)

(211-1)岩鶴 (250-hi)がんかく (hir.)

(256-kat)ガンカク (kat.)

(280-po)pol:GANKAKY

(838-su)**SUPER-TERM**

#gankaku {{岩鶴}}##

(062-mk)*FUNAKOSHI MAIN BOOK - KATA*

📖**MK 1922 original** 7 (list beginning), 51 (list Enbusen), 255. **1925 Ishida** 20 (list beginning), 58 (list Enbusen), 264. **1925 Teramoto** 26 (list beginning), 52 (list Enbusen), 159. **1935 Suzuki-Johnston** 9 (list styles), 33 (list names), 40-41 (list Enbusen), 131. **1935 Ohshima** 8-9 (list styles), 36 (list names), 177.

(466-cha)*CHARACTERISTICS* ⓘ A Two-character, which consists of 2 Chinese Logograms and 0 Hiˈra-ga-ˈna Characters.

(800-tag)*TAGS* 💻 #gankaku, gan-kaku, gan kaku

101.Gaˈshira (Atama)

(001-REF-rom)Gaˈshira ☞ Atama-head {頭}, p. 40

#Gashira (Atama)##

(002-REF-hi)がしら ☞ あたま

(275-tō)が し ら [gàshírá⁺]

102.Gaˈta (Kata)

(001-REF-rom)Gaˈta-shape ☞ Kata-shape {形}, p. 134

#Gata (Kata)##

(250-hi)がた (hir.) (275-tō)が た [gàtá⁺]

103.Ge-ˈdan

(000-it)*INCLUDING TERMS (EXAMPLES)*

👁️✉️ gedanbarai {{下段払い}}, p. 69

(011-k1)*KANJI* 1 ☛ Shimo-bottom {下}, p. 213

(012-k2)*KANJI* 2 ☛ Dan-level {段}, p. 56

(070-kt)*KARATE MEANING* ✋📖 *noun*

① Lower body.

(211-1)下段 (250-hi)げだん (hir.)

#gedan {{下段}}##

(077-jg)GENERAL MEANING (EXAMPLES) ☼📖 noun ❶ Lower section, lower level, lower step.

(466-cha)CHARACTERISTICS ⓘ A Two-character, which consists of 2 Chinese Logograms and 0 Hiˈra-ga-ˈna Characters.

(800-tag)TAGS 💻 #gedan, ge-dan, ge dan

(838-su)**SUPER-TERM**

104.Ge-ˈdan-ˈbarai

(015-w1)WORD 1 ᵂ/ᵂ ☞ gedan {{下段}}, p. 69

(016-w2)WORD 2 ᵂ/ᵂ ☞ harai {{払い}}, p. 87

(070-kt)KARATE MEANING ✋📖 noun ① Downward block, low block, lower-level sweep.

(466-cha)CHARACTERISTICS ⓘ A Four-character, which consists of 3 Chinese Logograms and 1 Hiˈra-ga-ˈna Characters.

#gedanbarai {{下段払い}}##

(211-1)**下段払い**

(250-hi)**げだんばらい** (hir.)

(480-hb)**H↻b** 🔔 Due to the ˈRen-daku laws, the unvoiced consonant

Ge-ˈdan-ˈbarai - ˈGen-ki

/H/ may get a Dak[u]-ˈten (゛) and become ~/b/ as a suffix. Example ↴ ˈHon (ほん) turns into ˈSan-bon (さんぼん).

(800-tag)TAGS 💻 #gedanbarai, gedan-barai, gedan barai

(838-su)**SUPER-TERM**

105.ˈGen-ki

(000-it)INCLUDING TERMS (EXAMPLES) 👁✉ genkidesuka {{元気ですか}}, p. 70

(011-k1)KANJI 1 ☞ Moto-origin {元}, p. 173

(012-k2)KANJI 2 ☞ Ki-energy {気}, p. 142

(077-jg)GENERAL MEANING (EXAMPLES) ☼📖 adjective ❶ Healthy, well ❷ Energetic, lively, vigorous, vital noun ❸ Health greeting ❹ How are You? (casual)

(211-1)**元気** (250-hi)**げんき** (hir.)

(275-tō)**げ**んき [géˈǹkì]

#genki {{元気}}##

(185-ch)CHINESE (PINYIN) 🌐📖 *yuánqì* (also 原気)

(095-3t)THE THREE TEACHINGS **3**🔥 In Traditional Chinese Medicine: innate *qì*, prenatal *qì*, innate energy, original energy, hereditary energy, source *qì*, primordial *qì*, primum energy[30].

(466-cha)*CHARACTERISTICS* ⓘ A Two-character, which consists of 2 Chinese Logograms and 0 Hiˈra-ga-ˈna Characters.

(800-tag)*TAGS* 🖥 #genki, gen-ki, gen ki, #yuanqi

106. ˈGen-kides[u]ˈka?

(015-w1)*WORD 1* Ⓦ ☞ genki {{元気}}, p. 69

(077-jg)*GENERAL MEANING (EXAMPLES)* ✿📖 *phrase* ❶ How are You? how are You doing? Are You well?

(211-1)元気ですか

(250-hi)げんきですか (hir.)

#genkidesuka {{元気ですか}}##

(466-cha)*CHARACTERISTICS* ⓘ A Five-character, which consists of 2 Chinese Logograms and 3 Hiˈra-ga-ˈna Characters.

(409-ka)*HIRAGANA* ☉ The particle ˈKa (か) is a question denominator.

107. Geˈri (keri)

(001-REF-rom)Geˈri ☞ keri {{蹴り}}, p. 140

#geri (keri)##

(250-hi)げり (hir.)

108. ˈGetsu (Tsuki)

(001-REF-rom)ˈGetsu ☞ Tsuki-moon {月}, p. 253

#Getsu (Tsuki)##

(002-REF-hi)げつ ☞ つき

(280-po)pol:GECY

109. ˈGi (Tsuku)

(001-REF-rom)Giˈ ☞ Tsuku-to wear {着}, p. 254

#Gi (Tsuku)##

(002-REF-hi)ぎ ☞ つく

110. ˈGo (五)

(000-it)*INCLUDING TERMS (EXAMPLES)* 👁✉ godan {{五段}}, p. 71; gohon {{五本}}, p. 71; gokyū {{五級}}, p. 72

(185-ch)*CHINESE (PINYIN)* 🐼📖 *wǔ* as in *wǔxíng* (五行)[31]

(211-1)五

#Go-five {五}##

(077-jg)*GENERAL MEANING (EXAMPLES)* ✿📖 *noun* ❶ Five

(250-hi)ご (hir.)

(800-tag)*TAGS* 🖥 #5

(833-kan)**KANJI**

(838-su)**SUPER-TERM**

111. ˈGo-dan

(000-it) *INCLUDING TERMS (EXAMPLES)* 👁✉ heiangodan {{平安五段}}, p. 91

(011-k1) *KANJI 1* ☛ Go-five {五}, p. 70

(012-k2) *KANJI 2* ☛ Dan-level {段}, p. 56

(070-kt) *KARATE MEANING* ✋📖 *noun* ① Fifth Level ② Fifth dan, Fifth degree black belt ③ Five.

(077-jg) *GENERAL MEANING (EXAMPLES)* ✿📖 *noun* ❶ Level five, fifth rank, fifth-degree, fifth grade.
#godan {{五段}}##

(211-1) 五段

(250-hi) ごだん (hir.)

(256-kat) ゴダン (kat.)

(466-cha) *CHARACTERISTICS* ⓘ A Two-character, which consists of 2 Chinese Logograms and 0 Hiˈra-ga-ˈna Characters.

(800-tag) *TAGS* 💻 #godan, go-dan, go dan

(838-su) **SUPER-TERM**

112. ˈGo-hon

(000-it) *INCLUDING TERMS (EXAMPLES)* 👁✉ gohonkumite {{五本組手}}, p. 71

(011-k1) *KANJI 1* ☛ Go-five {五}, p. 70

(012-k2) *KANJI 2* ☛ Hon-source {本}, p. 102

(077-jg) *GENERAL MEANING (EXAMPLES)* ✿📖 *counter* ❶ Five long slender cylindrical objects (bananas, bottles, pens, trees, buses).
#gohon {{五本}}##

(211-1) 五本

(250-hi) ごほん (hir.)

(256-kat) ゴホン (kat.)

(466-cha) *CHARACTERISTICS* ⓘ A Two-character, which consists of 2 Chinese Logograms and 0 Hiˈra-ga-ˈna Characters.

(800-tag) *TAGS* 💻 #gohon, go-hon, go hon

113. Go-ˈhon-ˈkumi-te

(015-w1) *WORD 1* ʷ/ʷ ☛ gohon {{五本}}, p. 71

(016-w2) *WORD 2* ʷ/ʷ ☛ kumite {{組手}}, p. 157

(070-kt) *KARATE MEANING* ✋📖 *noun* ① Five-time sparring, five step sparring.

(211-1) 五本組手
#gohonkumite {{五本組手}}##

(250-hi) ごほんくみて (hir.)

(466-cha)*CHARACTERISTICS* ⓘ A Four-character, which consists of 4 Chinese Logograms and 0 Hiˈra-ga-ˈna Characters.

(800-tag)*TAGS* 🖥 #gohonkumite, gohon-kumite, gohon kumite, #gohongumite

114.Go-ˈkyū

(011-k1)*KANJI 1* ☛ Go-five {五}, p. 70

(012-k2)*KANJI 2* ☛ Kyū-rank {級}, p. 158

(070-kt)*KARATE MEANING* ✋📖 *adjective* ① Fifth ˈKyū

(077-jg)*GENERAL MEANING (EXAMPLES)* ⚙📖 *adjective* ❶ Fifth-degree, level-five, fifth-class, 5th grade.

(185-ch)*CHINESE (PINYIN)* ☻📖 ***wǔjí*** #gokyū {{五級}}##

(211-1)五級 (250-hi)ごきゅう (hir.)

(280-po)pol:GOKJUU

(466-cha)*CHARACTERISTICS* ⓘ A Two-character, which consists of 2 Chinese Logograms and 0 Hiˈra-ga-ˈna Characters.

(800-tag)*TAGS* 🖥 #gokyu, go-kyu, go kyu, #gokiu, gokyuu, gokyuh

115.Go-ˈshin

(012-k2)*KANJI 2* ☛ Mi-body {身}, p. 169

(077-jg)*GENERAL MEANING (EXAMPLES)* ⚙📖 *noun* ❶ Self-defense, self-protection.

(185-ch)*CHINESE (PINYIN)* ☻📖 ***hùshēn***

(211-1)護身 (250-hi)ごしん (hir.) #goshin {{護身}}##

(275-tō)ごしん [gòshín]

(466-cha)*CHARACTERISTICS* ⓘ A Two-character, which consists of 2 Chinese Logograms and 0 Hiˈra-ga-ˈna Characters.

(800-tag)*TAGS* 🖥 #goshin, go-shin, go shin

116.Goˈzaimas[u]

(077-jg)*GENERAL MEANING (EXAMPLES)* ⚙📖 *verb* ❶ To be, to exist, to have (polite)

(089-no)*NOTES AND EXAMPLES* 📖✍ Often used in formal interjections and greeting.

(203-hi)⧗☉ (250-hi)ございます (hir.) #gozaimasu##

(466-cha)*CHARACTERISTICS* ⓘ A Five-character, which consists of 0 Chinese Logograms and 5 Hiˈra-ga-ˈna Characters.

117.Guˈmi-ˈte (kumite)

(001-REF-rom)Guˈmi-ˈte ☞ kumite {{組手}}, p. 157

#gumite (kumite)##

(002-REF-hi)ぐみて☞くみて

118.Gyaˈku (逆)

(000-it)*INCLUDING TERMS (EXAMPLES)* 👁✉ gyakumawashigeri {{逆回し蹴り}}, p. 74; gyakuzuki {{逆突き}}, p. 73; sakatsuchi {{逆槌}}, p. 200

(070-kt)*KARATE MEANING* ✋📖 *adjective* ① Contralateral, heterolateral.

(077-jg)*GENERAL MEANING (EXAMPLES)* ✿📖 *adjective* ❶ Reverse, opposite, contrary

(185-ch)*CHINESE (PINYIN)* 👁📖 *nì*

(211-1)逆 (211-al)*ALTERNATIVES OR SEE ALSO* 𝒜𝒜 屰, 迸.

(250-hi)ぎゃく (hir.) (256-kat)ギャク (kat.)

(275-tō)ぎゃく [gyàkú]

#Gyaku-reverse {逆}##

(280-po)pol:GJAKY

Guˈmi-ˈte (kumite) - Gyaˈku Zuˈki

(313-ka)*KANJI* 🖉 The Phono-semantic Compound Ideogram Gyaˈku-reverse (逆). (313k-cn)**Components** 🗂 [semantic 辶 | phonetic 屰]. (313k-ra)**Radical** ✛ 辶 辵辶 walk. (313k-cs)**Composition** ✄ Bottom-left: 辶, top-right: 屰. (313k-re)**Readings (examples)** 🗣 Go-on: ぎゃく (gyaku). Kan-on: げき (geki). Kun: さか (saka, 逆); さかう (sakau, 逆う).

(800-tag)*TAGS* 🖳 #gyaku, giaku, #gyako

(830-ik)**IMPORTANT KANJI**

(838-su)**SUPER-TERM**

119.Gyaˈku Zuˈki

(011-k1)*KANJI* 1 ☞ Gyaku-reverse {逆}, p. 73

(015-w1)*WORD* 1 ᴡᴡ ☞ tsuki {{突き}}, p. 253

(070-kt)*KARATE MEANING* ✋📖 *noun phrase* ① Contralateral thrust, reverse thrust.

(138-co)*COORDINATE TERMS* 👁≈ oizuki {{追い突き}}, p. 188

(211-1)逆突き (212-2)逆突

#gyakuzuki {{逆突き}}##

(250-hi)ぎゃくづき (hir.)

Gyaˈku-maˈwashi-geˈri - Gˈyō (行)

(280-po)pol:**GJAKUDZYKI**

(466-cha)*CHARACTERISTICS* ⓘ A Three-character, which consists of 2 Chinese Logograms and 1 Hiˈra-ga-ˈna Characters.

(800-tag)*TAGS* 🖥 #gyakuzuki, gyakuzuki, gyaku zuki, #gyakutsuki, #giakuzuki, #guakuzuki

(838-su)**SUPER-TERM**

120.Gyaˈku-maˈwashi-geˈri

(011-k1)*KANJI 1* ☛ Gyaku-reverse {逆}, p. 73

(015-w1)*WORD 1* ⱲⱲ ☛ mawashigeri {{回し蹴り}}, p. 167

(070-kt)*KARATE MEANING* ✋📖 *noun*
① Reverse roundhouse kick. 💧✳ One should not confuse Uˈra Maˈwashi-geˈri (裏回し蹴り) with Gyaˈku-maˈwashi-geˈri (逆回し蹴り), although both are inside-out round kicks. Uˈra Maˈwashi-geˈri involves a strong knee flexion – usually striking with the back of the heel, whereas Gyaˈku-maˈwashi-geˈri involves a strong hip abduction and external rotation – as well as a knee extension.

#gyakumawashigeri {{逆回し蹴り}}##

QR Code 1 - Gyaku-mawashi-geri Fiore Tartaglia (DY0u17LZrEU)
List of QR Codes (Video), p. 11

(211-1)逆回し蹴り

(250-hi)ぎゃくまわしげり (hir.)

(466-cha)*CHARACTERISTICS* ⓘ A Five-character, which consists of 3 Chinese Logograms and 2 Hiˈra-ga-ˈna Characters.

(800-tag)*TAGS* 🖥 #gyakumawashigeri, gyaku-mawashi-geri, gyaku mawashi geri

121.Gˈyō (行)

(000-it)*INCLUDING TERMS (EXAMPLES)* 👁✉ heikō {{平行}}, p. 94

(077-jg)*GENERAL MEANING (EXAMPLES)* ☼📖 *noun* ❶ Line ❷ Row.

(089-no)*NOTES AND EXAMPLES* 📖✎ H[i]-ˈkō-ki [hɨkó⁺òkì] (飛行機) means airplane.

(133-sy)*SYNONYMS* 👁= Sen-line {線}, p. 207

(185-ch)*CHINESE (PINYIN)* 👁📖 ***xíng***[32], ***xìng*** as in *wǔxíng* (五行) *verb* ❶ To walk, to go, to move, to do, to act

noun ❷ Behavior, conduct[33]

#Gyo-line {行}##

(211-1)行

(250-hi)ぎょう (hir.)

(275-tō) ぎょ — [gyóˑò]

(280-po)pol:GJOO

(325-kr)*KANJI READINGS* 🖊️👄 Go-on: ぎょう (gyō); ごう (gō). Kan-on: こう [kóˑò] (kō). Kun: いく (iku, 行く); ゆく (yuku, 行く). Nanori: つら (tsura); ゆき (yuki).

(800-tag)*TAGS* 💻 #gyō, gyoo, gyou, gyoh

(833-kan)**KANJI**

122. ˈH[i]ki-ˈte

💣※ Not to be confused with Iki-te (活手)

(011-k1)*KANJI 1* ☞ Hiku-to pull {引}, p. 76

(012-k2)*KANJI 2* ☞ Te-hand {手}, p. 234

(070-kt)*KARATE MEANING* ✋📖 *noun* ① Pulling hand ② Pulling-in Block, Pulling Hand Block, one of the Hand Blocks

ˈH[i]ki-ˈte - H[i]ˈki-waˈke

(089-no)*NOTES AND EXAMPLES* 📖✍️

The blocking technique can be found in Bassai Dai and in Kankū Dai.

(211-1)引き手 (212-2)引手

(250-hi)ひきて (hir.)

#hikite {{引き手}}##

(078-mg)*FUNAKOSHI MAIN BOOK - GENERALLY* 📘**MG** **1922 original** 20-22, 41 (list), 44. **1925 Ishida** 31-32, 53 (list), 55. **1925 Teramoto** 36-37, 46 (list), 48. **1935 Suzuki-Johnston** 24 (list), 25. **1935 Ohshima** 21 (list), 22.

(466-cha)*CHARACTERISTICS* ⓘ A Three-character, which consists of 2 Chinese Logograms and 1 Hiˈra-gaˈna Characters.

(800-tag)*TAGS* 💻 #hiki-te, hiki te, #hkite

(838-su)**SUPER-TERM**

123. H[i]ˈki-waˈke

(011-k1)*KANJI 1* ☞ Hiku-to pull {引}, p. 76

(077-jg)*GENERAL MEANING (EXAMPLES)* ⚙️📖 *noun* ❶ Draw, tie, no decision.

(211-1)引き分け (212-2)引分け

H[i]ˈku (引) - ˈHa (派)

(250-hi) ひきわけ (hir.)

#hikiwake {{引き分け}}##

(466-cha) *CHARACTERISTICS* ⓘ A Four-character, which consists of 2 Chinese Logograms and 2 Hiˈra-ga-ˈna Characters.

(800-tag) *TAGS* 🖳 #hiki-wake, hiki wake

124. H[i]ˈku (引)

(000-it) *INCLUDING TERMS (EXAMPLES)* 👁✉ hikite {{引き手}}, p. 75; hikiwake {{引き分け}}, p. 76

(077-jg) *GENERAL MEANING (EXAMPLES)* ✿📖 *verb* ❶ To pull ❷ To draw.

(139-an) *ANTONYMS* 👁↻ Osu-to push {押}, p. 192

(185-ch) *CHINESE (PINYIN)* ☯📖 *yǐn*

(211-1) 引

(211-al) *ALTERNATIVES OR SEE ALSO* ✎✎ 牽く, 曳く

(211-ka+hi) 引く

(250-hi) ひく (hir.)

(705-gv) *GODAN VERB* 🏍⑤ **Terminal Form** {u* 💣※ but not i*-ru or e*-ru} H[i]ˈku [hìkú] (引く), which means to pull.

#Hiku-to pull {引}##

(275-tō) ひく [hɨ̀kú]

(302-kn) *KANJI NOTES* ✎✎ It depicts a bow and its string. Contains 4 strokes.

(313-ka) *KANJI* ✎ The Compound Ideogram H[i]ˈku-to pull (引). (313k-cn) **Components** ⛁ [弓 | ｜]. (313k-ra) **Radical** ✛ 弓 bow. (313k-cs) **Composition** ⚒ Left: 弓, right: ｜. (313k-re) **Readings (examples)** 🗣 Go-on: いん (in). Kan-on: いん (in). Kun: ひく (h[i]ˈku, 引く); ひける (hikeru, 引ける). Nanori: のぶ (nobu); ひき (hiki); ひさ (hisa).
Polite Form {i*-masu} Hiˈkimas[u] [hìkímáˈsù] (引きます).

(830-ik) **IMPORTANT KANJI**

(838-su) **SUPER-TERM**

125. ˈHa (派)

(077-jg) *GENERAL MEANING (EXAMPLES)* ✿📖 *noun suffix* ❶ School, faction, wing, group, branch

(211-1) 派

#Ha-school {派}##

(133-sy) *SYNONYMS* 👁＝ Ryū-style {流}, p. 197

(833-kan)**KANJI**

126. ˈHach[i]-ˈkyū

(011-k1)*KANJI 1* ☞ Hachi-eight {八}, p. 77

(012-k2)*KANJI 2* ☞ Kyū-rank {級}, p. 158

(070-kt)*KARATE MEANING* ✋📖 *adjective* ① Eighth ˈKyū.

(077-jg)*GENERAL MEANING (EXAMPLES)* ⚙📖 *adjective* ❶ Eighth - degree, level-eight, eighth-class, 8th grade.

(185-ch)*CHINESE (PINYIN)* 🌐📖 *bājí*

#hachikyu {{八級}}##

(211-1)八級 (250-hi)はちきゅう (hir.)

(280-po)pol:HACZKJUU

(466-cha)*CHARACTERISTICS* ⓘ A Two-character, which consists of 2 Chinese Logograms and 0 Hiˈra-ga-ˈna Characters.

(800-tag)*TAGS* 🖥 #hachikyu, hachi-kyu, hachikyu, #hachikiu, hachikyuu, hachikyuh

127. ˈHachi (八)

(000-it)*INCLUDING TERMS (EXAMPLES)* 👁✉ hachidan {{八段}}, p. 77; hachiji {{八字}}, p. 78; hachikyu {{八級}}, p. 77

(077-jg)*GENERAL MEANING (EXAMPLES)* ⚙📖 *noun* ❶ Eight.

(185-ch)*CHINESE (PINYIN)* 🌐📖 *bā*

#Hachi-eight {八}##

(211-1)八

(250-hi)はち (hir.)

(275-tō)|はち| [háˈchì]

(800-tag)*TAGS* 🖥 #hachi, #8

(833-kan)**KANJI**

(838-su)**SUPER-TERM**

128. Haˈchi-dan

(011-k1)*KANJI 1* ☞ Hachi-eight {八}, p. 77

(012-k2)*KANJI 2* ☞ Dan-level {段}, p. 56

(070-kt)*KARATE MEANING* ✋📖 *noun* ① Eighth degree black belt, eighth Dan.

(077-jg)*GENERAL MEANING (EXAMPLES)* ⚙📖 *noun* ❶ Level eight, eighth rank, eighth degree #hachidan {{八段}}##

(211-1)八段 (250-hi)はちだん (hir.)

(256-kat)ハチダン (kat.)

(466-cha)*CHARACTERISTICS* ⓘ A Two-character, which consists of 2 Chi-

nese Logograms and 0 Hiˈra-ga-ˈna Characters.

(800-tag)*TAGS* 🖥 #hachidan, hachi-dan, hachi dan

129. Haˈchi-ji

(000-it)*INCLUDING TERMS (EXAMPLES)*

👁✉ hachijidachi {{八字立ち}}, p. 78

(011-k1)*KANJI 1* ☞ Hachi-eight {八}, p. 77

(012-k2)*KANJI 2* ☞ Ji-character {字}, p. 109

(077-jg)*GENERAL MEANING (EXAMPLES)* ⚙📖 *noun* ❶ The character 八.

(185-ch)*CHINESE (PINYIN)* 🌐📖 ***bāzì***

#hachiji {{八字}}##

(211-1)八字

(250-hi)はちじ (hir.)

(256-kat)ハチジ (kat.)

(466-cha)*CHARACTERISTICS* ⓘ A Two-character, which consists of 2 Chinese Logograms and 0 Hiˈra-ga-ˈna Characters.

(800-tag)*TAGS* 🖥 #hachiji, hach-iji, hach iji

130. Haˈchi-ji-daˈchi

(015-w1)*WORD 1* 🆆 ☞ hachiji {{八字}}, p. 78

(016-w2)*WORD 2* 🆆 ☞ tachi {{立ち}}, p. 228

(030-st)*STANCE* 立 **AKA** Soto-hachiji-dachi (外八字立ち), Figure-eight Stance, Character-eight Stance, 八 Character Stance, Outward Feet Stance, Open-leg Stance, Natural Stance, Ready Stance, V-stance **Category** High stances

(089-no)*NOTES AND EXAMPLES* 📖✍

The toes are facing outwards.

(031-ms)*FUNAKOSHI MAIN BOOK - STANCES* 🌀**MS** **1922 original** 30 (list), 31, 63. **1925 Ishida** 41 (list), 42, 70. **1925 Teramoto** 40 (list), 40, 58. **1935 Suzuki-Johnston** 22 (list), 22, 43. **1935 Ohshima** 19 (list), 20, 43.

#hachijidachi {{八字立ち}}##

(032-ns)*FUNAKOSHI NYUMON TERAMO-TO - STANCES* 🌀**NS** 59

(211-1)八字立ち

(212-2)八字立

(250-hi)はちじだち (hir.)

(466-cha)*CHARACTERISTICS* ⓘ A Four-character, which consists of 3 Chinese Logograms and 1 Hiˈra-ga-ˈna Characters.

(483-td)**T⊃d** 🔔 Due to the ˈRen-daku laws, the unvoiced consonant /T/ may get a Dak[u]-ˈten (゙) and become ~/d/ as a suffix. Example 🔥 ˈTachi (たち) turns into Ki-ˈba Daˈchi (きばだち).

(800-tag)*TAGS* 💻 #hachijidachi, hachi-ji-dachi, hachiji dachi, hachi-ji-dachi, hachi ji dachi

131. ˈHai

(077-jg)*GENERAL MEANING (EXAMPLES)* ✿📖 *noun, interjection (polite)* ❶ Yes, right, that is correct ❷ Fine! alright! ❸ Understood, got it ❹ Giddy-up.

(136-se)*SEE ALSO* 👁➕ ossu {{押忍}}, p. 192

#hai##

(203-hi)⌛☉

(250-hi)はい (hir.)

(466-cha)*CHARACTERISTICS* ⓘ A Two-character, which consists of 0 Chinese Logograms and 2 Hiˈra-ga-ˈna Characters.

132. Hai ˈWan Uˈke

(011-k1)*KANJI 1* ☛ Se-back {背}, p. 204

(012-k2)*KANJI 2* ☛ Ude-arm {腕}, p. 260

(015-w1)*WORD 1* Ⓦ ☛ uke {{受け}}, p. 262

(070-kt)*KARATE MEANING* 🖐📖 AKA Shuto-barai, when performed with open palms as in the beginning of Kankū-dai *phrase* ① Back-arm Block, block with the extensor[34] aspect (posterior side) of the forearm.

(211-1)背腕受け

(212-2)背腕受

(250-hi)はいわんうけ (hir.)

(466-cha)*CHARACTERISTICS* ⓘ A Four-character, which consists of 3 Chinese Logograms and 1 Hiˈra-ga-ˈna Characters.

#haiwanuke {{背腕受け}}##

Masters 4 - Haiwanuke by Bamgboye Sensei
List of Sensei Demonstrations next to Values, p. 10
List of large photos - p. 10

ˈHai-tō - haˈjimaru

Bobby Bamgboye of Nigeria WSKF demonstrates Haiwan-uke. Photographer: Joel Ibanga.

(089-no)*NOTES AND EXAMPLES* 📖✍

The left hand in the opening move of ˈHe[i]-an-ˈni-dan (平安二段). The term Hai ˈWan Uˈke is often used to describe the entire Square Side Block ("Jōdan Morote Hai-wanuke"). Nevertheless, in our opinion, Hai ˈWan Uˈke is the move performed with the left arm only.

133. ˈHai-tō

(011-k1)*KANJI 1* ☞ Se-back {背}, p. 204

(012-k2)*KANJI 2* ☞ Katana-sword {刀}, p. 136

(070-kt)*KARATE MEANING* ✋📖 AKA Hai-te *noun* ① Reverse Knife-hand, Reverse Hand Sword, Reverse Handsword, Back Sword, Sword Back, Ridge Hand. Performed with the radial (lateral) aspect of the palm.

(139-an)*ANTONYMS* 👁↻ shutō {{手刀}}, p. 210

#haitō {{背刀}}##

Anatomy 1 - Haito

(211-1)背刀

(250-hi)はいとう (hir.)

(466-cha)*CHARACTERISTICS* ① A Two-character, which consists of 2 Chinese Logograms and 0 Hiˈra-ga-ˈna Characters.

(800-tag)*TAGS* 💻 #haito, hai-to, hai to, haitou, haitoo, haitoh

134. haˈjimaru

(011-k1)*KANJI 1* ☞ Hajimeru-to begin {始}, p. 82

(077-jg)*GENERAL MEANING (EXAMPLES)* ✿📖 *verb (intransitive)* ❶ To begin, to start.

(466-cha)*CHARACTERISTICS* ① A Three-character, which consists of 1 Chinese Logograms and 2 Hiˈra-ga-ˈna Characters.

(211-1)始まる (250-hi)はじまる (hir.)

(256-kat)ハジマル (kat.)

(275-tō)はじまる [hàjímárú]

(811-vpln)**VERB PAIR – INTRANSITIVE PART**

#hajimaru {{始まる}}##

(600-vt)**Form**   **Godan Intransitive**

~aru

Terminal	hàjímárú
Plain ~te Request	hàjímátté
Polite ~te Request	hàjímátté kuda˙sai
Plain Imperative	hàjímáré
Stem	hàjímárí
Polite Imperative	ha˙jimari na˙sai
Formal	hàjímárímá⁺s[ù]

See

List of Commands, p. 25

(610-In-Tr)*VERB PAIR* ◉◖◗ The Intransitive Verb is hajimaru {{始まる}}, p. 80. The Transitive verb is Hajimeru-to begin {始}, p. 82.

135.ha˙jime

(000-it)*INCLUDING TERMS (EXAMPLES)*

◉✉ hajimemashō {{始めましょう}}, p. 82

(019-nom)*NOMINAL FORM (NOUN FORM) OF* ❗☛ Hajimeru-to begin {始}, p. 82

(070-kt)*KARATE MEANING* ✋📖 *verb (imperative mood)* ① Begin! start! get started!

See

List of Commands, p. 25

(077-jg)*GENERAL MEANING (EXAMPLES)* ⚙📖 *noun, adverb* ❶ Beginning, start, origin[35].

(090-te)*TELL YOUR STUDENTS* 📖☺

Ha˙jime is also a Japanese given name, and sometimes even a surname.

(134-re)*RELATED TERMS* ◉∞ Hatsu-first {初}, p. 88

(139-an)*ANTONYMS* ◉↺ yame {{止め}}, p. 271

#hajime {{始め}}##

(134-gr-re)*GROUP* ◉(ᵔᴥᵔ) The following terms are related: hajime {{始め}}, p. 81; kamae {{構え}}, p. 123; kamaete {{構えて}}, p. 125; naore {{直れ}}, p. 180; yame {{止め}}, p. 271; yasume {{休め}}, p. 274; yōi {{用意}}, p. 277.

(211-1)始め (212-2)初め

(250-hi)はじめ (hir.)

(275-tō)は じめ [hàjímé]

(466-cha)*CHARACTERISTICS* ① A Two-character, which consists of 1 Chinese Logograms and 1 Hi˙ra-ga-˙na Characters.

(610-In-Tr)*VERB PAIR* ◉◖◗ The Intransitive Verb is hajimaru {{始まる}},

Hajiˈmemaˈshō - Haˈjimeru (始)

p. 80. The Transitive verb is Hajimeru-to begin {始}, p. 82.

(077-jg)*GENERAL MEANING (EXAMPLES)* ☼📖 *verb (transitive)* ❶ To begin, to start.

(838-su)**SUPER-TERM**

136.Hajiˈmemaˈshō

(015-w1)*WORD 1* ᵂᵂ ☞ hajime {{始め}}, p. 81

(077-jg)*GENERAL MEANING (EXAMPLES)* ☼📖 *verb (polite volitional form)* ❶ Let's get started, let's start, let's begin.

(211-1)始めましょう

(211-al)*ALTERNATIVES OR SEE ALSO*

✐✐ 初めましょう

#hajimemashō {{始めましょう}}##

(250-hi)はじめましょう (hir.)

(466-cha)*CHARACTERISTICS* ⓘ A Six-character, which consists of 1 Chinese Logograms and 5 Hiˈra-ga-ˈna Characters.

(800-tag)*TAGS* 💻 #hajimemasho, #hajimemashou, #hajimemashoo, hajime-masho, hajime masho

137.Haˈjimeru (始)

(000-it)*INCLUDING TERMS (EXAMPLES)*

👁✉ hajimaru {{始まる}}, p. 80; hajime {{始め}}, p. 81.

(077-jg)*GENERAL MEANING (EXAMPLES)* ☼📖 *verb (transitive)* ❶ To begin, to start.

(185-ch)*CHINESE (PINYIN)* 👁📖 *shǐ*

(211-1)始 (212-2)Hatsu-first {初}, p. 88

(211-ka+hi)始める

(211-ka+hiAlt)創める

(250-hi)はじめる (hir.)

(256-kat)ハジメル (kat.)

(610-In-Tr)*VERB PAIR* 👁◖ The Intransitive Verb is hajimaru {{始まる}}, p. 80. The Transitive verb is Hajimeru-to begin {始}, p. 82.

(810-vpTr)**VERB PAIR – TRANSITIVE PART**

#Hajimeru-to begin {始}##

(600-vt)**Form**	Shimo Ichidan Transitive (~eru)
Terminal	hàjímérú
Plain ~te Request	hàjímété
Polite ~te Request	hàjímété kudaˈsai
Plain Imperative	hàjíméró
Stem	hàjímé
Polite Imperative	haˈjime naˈsai
Formal	hàjímémá⁺s[ù]

See

List of Commands, p. 25

(275-tō)はじめる [hàjímérú]

(325-kr)*KANJI READINGS* 🖊🎨 Go-on:
し (shi). Kan-on: し (shi). Kun: は
じめる (hajimeru, 始める); はじめ
(hajime, 始め); はじまる (hajimaru,
始まる).

(800-tag)*TAGS* 💻 #begin, #start

(830-ik)**IMPORTANT KANJI**

138. Hak-ˈkyū (hachikyū)

(001-REF-rom)Hak-ˈkyū ☞ hachikyu
{{八級}}, p. 77

(002-REF-hi)はっきゅう ☞ はちきゅ
う

#hakkyū (hachikyū)##

(800-tag)*TAGS* 💻 #hakkyu, hak-kyu,
hak kyu

139. ˈHan (半)

(000-it)*INCLUDING TERMS (EXAMPLES)*
👁✉ hangetsu {{半月}}, p. 84;
hanmi {{半身}}, p. 85

(077-jg)*GENERAL MEANING (EXAM-
PLES)* ✿📖 noun ❶ Half
#Han-half {半}##

(185-ch)*CHINESE (PINYIN)* ☺📖 **bàn**

(211-1)半

(250-hi)はん (hir.)

(833-kan)**KANJI**

140. ˈHan (版)

(021-rb)*RESEARCH (FOR BOOKS)* ✍
noun, suffix ❶ Edition ❷ Printing
❸ Version

(211-1)版

#Han-edition {版}##

(250-hi)はん (hir.)

(833-kan)**KANJI**

141. ˈHan-getsu

(000-it)*INCLUDING TERMS (EXAMPLES)*
👁✉ hangetsudachi {{半月立ち}},
p. 84

(011-k1)*KANJI 1* ☛ Han-half {半}, p.
83

(012-k2)*KANJI 2* ☛ Tsuki-moon {月},
p. 253

(061-ka)*KATA* 形 **AKA** Sēshan (セー
シャン), Sehshan, Seshan ,Seishan
(セイシャン), Seisan, Sesan, Jusan,
Half-moon **Style** Shōrei (昭霊)
Group None **Enbusen** ˈJū-ji-ˈgata
(十字形) - 十 Shape **Number of
movements (approximately)** 41

(077-jg)*GENERAL MEANING (EXAM-
PLES)* ✿📖 *adverbial noun* ❶ Half-
moon

(185-ch)*CHINESE (PINYIN)* ☺📖 **bànyuè**

(211-1)半月

(250-hi)はんげつ (hir.)

#hangetsu {{半月}}##

(062-mk)*FUNAKOSHI MAIN BOOK - KATA*

MK 1922 original 7 (list beginning), 51 (list Enbusen), 236. **1925 Ishida** 20 (list beginning), 58 (list Enbusen), 241. **1925 Teramoto** 26 (list beginning), 52 (list Enbusen), 146. **1935 Suzuki-Johnston** 9 (list styles), 34 (list names), 40 (list Enbusen), 113. **1935 Ohshima** 8-9 (list styles), 36 (list names), 144.

(256-kat)ハンゲツ (kat.)

(280-po)pol:HANGECY

(466-cha)*CHARACTERISTICS* ⓘ A Two-character, which consists of 2 Chinese Logograms and 0 Hiˈra-ga-ˈna Characters.

(800-tag)*TAGS* 🖥 #hangetsu, han-getsu, han getsu

(838-su)**SUPER-TERM**

142. ˈHan-getsu ˈDachi

(015-w1)*WORD 1* ⟨W⟩ ☞ hangetsu {{半月}}, p. 84

(016-w2)*WORD 2* ⟨W⟩ ☞ tachi {{立ち}}, p. 228

(030-st)*STANCE* 立 **AKA** Half-moon Stance, Crescent Stance, Grounded Stance, Rooted Stance, Hourglass Stance. In our opinion, the right translation is simply Hangetsu Stance, because the stance is named after the Kata. According to higher opinions, the Kata is named after the stance[36]. **Category** Middle Height Front Stances

(089-no)*NOTES AND EXAMPLES* 📖✎ The knees[37] and the feet point medially. This stance is wider than ˈSanchin Daˈchi (三戦立ち).

(466-cha)*CHARACTERISTICS* ⓘ A Four-character, which consists of 4 Chinese Logograms and 1 Hiˈra-ga-ˈna Characters.

(211-1)半月立ち (212-2)半月立

#hangetsudachi {{半月立ち}}##

Masters 5 – Hangetsu-dachi by Bamgboye Sensei
List of Sensei Demonstrations next to Values, p. 10
List of large photos - p. 10
Bobby Bamgboye of Nigeria WSKF demonstrates Hangetsu-dachi. Photographer: Joel Ibanga.

(134-re)*RELATED TERMS* ◉∞ sanchin-dachi {{三戦立ち}}, p. 203

(250-hi)はんげつだち (hir.)

(280-po)pol:HANGECYDACI

(483-td)**T⤳d** ⌂ Due to the ˈRen-daku laws, the unvoiced consonant /T/ may get a Dak[u]-ˈten (゛) and become ~/d/ as a suffix. Example ↳ ˈTachi（た ち）turns into Ki-ˈba Daˈchi（きばだち）.

(800-tag)*TAGS* 💻 #hangetsudachi, hangetsu-dachi, hangetsu dachi

(838-su)**SUPER-TERM**

143. ˈHan-mi

(000-it)*INCLUDING TERMS (EXAMPLES)* ◉✉ hanmidachi {{半身立ち}}, p. 86

(011-k1)*KANJI 1* ☛ Han-half {半}, p. 83

(012-k2)*KANJI 2* ☛ Mi-body {身}, p. 169

(070-kt)*KARATE MEANING* ✋📖 *noun or adjective* ① Half-facing.

(078-mg)*FUNAKOSHI MAIN BOOK - GENERALLY* **⛩MG 1935 Ohshima** 30

(077-jg)*GENERAL MEANING (EXAMPLES)* ☼📖 *noun* ❶ Half of the

ˈHan-mi - ˈHan-mi Daˈchi body, half-body, half of one's body, one side of one's body.

(185-ch)*CHINESE (PINYIN)* ☯📖

bànshēn

#hanmi {{半身}}##

(079-ng)*FUNAKOSHI NYUMON TERAMOTO - GENERALLY* **⛩NG** 53

(139-an)*ANTONYMS* ◉↻ shōmen {{正面}}, p. 217

(211-1)半身

(250-hi)はんみ (hir.)

(275-tō)は ん み [hànmí]

(466-cha)*CHARACTERISTICS* ① A Two-character, which consists of 2 Chinese Logograms and 0 Hiˈra-ga-ˈna Characters.

(800-tag)*TAGS* 💻 #hanmi, han-mi, han mi

(838-su)**SUPER-TERM**

144. ˈHan-mi Daˈchi

(015-w1)*WORD 1* ᵂᵂ ☛ hanmi {{半身}}, p. 85

(016-w2)*WORD 2* ᵂᵂ ☛ tachi {{立ち}}, p. 228

(030-st)*STANCE* 立 **AKA** Half-facing Stance, Half-body Posture **Category** Various views.

ˈHan-shin (hanmi) - Haˈra (腹)

(136-se)*SEE ALSO* 👁➕ renojidachi {{レの字立ち}}, p. 195

(211-1)半身立ち (212-2)半身立

(250-hi)はんみだち (hir.)

(800-tag)*TAGS* 🖥 #hanmitachi #hanmidachi {{半身立ち}}##

Figure 1 – Shotokai's Hanmi-dachi[38]

(466-cha)*CHARACTERISTICS* ⓘ A Four-character, which consists of 3 Chinese Logograms and 1 Hiˈra-ga-ˈna Characters.

(483-td)**TↃd** 🜁 Due to the ˈRen-daku laws, the unvoiced consonant /T/ may get a Dak[u]-ˈten (゛) and become ~/d/ as a suffix. Example 🔧 ˈTachi (たち) turns into Ki-ˈba Daˈchi (きばだち).

145. ˈHan-shin (hanmi)

(001-REF-rom)ˈHan-shin ☞ hanmi {{半身}}, p. 85

(002-REF-hi)はんしん ☞ はんみ #hanshin (hanmi)##

(275-tō)は|んしん| [hàńshíń]

(800-tag)*TAGS* 🖥 #hanshin, han-shin, han shin

146. Haˈra (腹)

(077-jg)*GENERAL MEANING (EXAMPLES)* ☀📖 *noun* ❶ Abdomen, belly, stomach ❷ Courage ❸ Willpower ❹ Feelings, emotions ❺ Mind ❻ Real intentions, true motive ❼ Inside, inner part, interior.

(089-no)*NOTES AND EXAMPLES* 📖✎ Haˈra-kiˈri (腹切り) – ˈSep-ˈpuku (切腹) means suicide by disembowelment (abdomen cutting).

(134-re)*RELATED TERMS* 👁∞ tanden {{丹田}}, p. 232

(185-ch)*CHINESE (PINYIN)* 👁📖 *fù, fŭ*

(203-hi)⏳☉ (250-hi)はら (hir.) #Hara-abdomen {腹}##

(211-1)腹 (211-al)*ALTERNATIVES OR SEE ALSO* ✎✐ 肚, お腹, 御腹, 御中

(275-tō)は|ら| [hàrá゛]

(313-ka)*KANJI* ✐ The Phono-semantic Compound Logogram Haˈra-abdomen (腹). (313k-cn)**Components** 🝔 [semantic 肉 | phonetic 复]. (313k-ra)**Radical** ✚ 肉 月 月 meat. (313k-cs)**Composition** ✗ Left: 月, right: 复. (313k-re)**Readings (examples)** 🔧

Go-on: ふく (fuku). Kan-on: ふく (fuku). Kun: はら (haˈra).

(830-ik)**IMPORTANT KANJI**

147.Haˈrai

(000-it)*INCLUDING TERMS (EXAMPLES)*

👁✉ ashibarai {{足払い}}, p. 38; gedanbarai {{下段払い}}, p. 69

(011-k1)*KANJI 1* ☞ Harau-to sweep {払}, p. 88

(070-kt)*KARATE MEANING* ✋📖 *noun* ① Sweeping.

(077-jg)*GENERAL MEANING (EXAMPLES)* ☼📖 *noun* ❶ Sweeping, clearing out, clearing away, disposing of, getting rid of ❷ Payment.

(089-no)*NOTES AND EXAMPLES* 📖✎

Maˈe-ˈbarai [màébá⁺rài] (前払い), for instance, is a prepayment.

#harai {{払い}}##

(211-sh-2)払い (simp.)

(211-ky-1)拂い (trad.)

(250-hi)はらい (hir.)

(275-tō)は ら い [hàrá⁺ì]

(480-hb)**H⟲b** 🔔 Due to the ˈRendaku laws, the unvoiced consonant /H/ may get a Dak[u]-ˈten (゛) and become ~/b/ as a suffix. Example ↲

ˈHon (ほん) turns into ˈSan-bon (さんぼん).

(466-cha)*CHARACTERISTICS* ① A Two-character, which consists of 1 Chinese Logograms and 1 Hiˈra-ga-ˈna Characters.

148.Haˈrau (払)

(000-it)*INCLUDING TERMS (EXAMPLES)*

👁✉ harai {{払い}}, p. 87

(070-kt)*KARATE MEANING* ✋📖 *verb* ① To sweep (e.g., a leg), to knock aside.

(077-jg)*GENERAL MEANING (EXAMPLES)* ☼📖 *verb* ❶ To brush off, to wipe away, to dust off, to sweep away [39] ❷ To clear out, to clear away, to dispose of, to get rid of ❸ To pay.

(186-cs)*CHINESE SIMPLIFIED* (払) ☯📖 *fǎn* (187-ct)*CHINESE TRADITIONAL* (拂) ☯📖 *fú*

(705-gv)*GODAN VERB* 🏍⑤ **Terminal Form** {u* 💧※ but not i*-ru or e*-ru} Haˈrau [hàrá⁺ù] (払う), which means to clear away. **Polite Form** {i*-masu}   Haˈraimas[u] [hàráímá⁺sù] (払います).

(211-sh-2)払 (simp.) (211-ky-1)拂 (trad.)

(250-hi)はらう(hir.)

(275-tō)は ⎡ら⎤ う [hàráˈù]

(830-ik)**IMPORTANT KANJI**

#Harau-to sweep {払}##

(313-ka.1c)*COMMON* ✐ (313-ka.1e)**Radical**

【common】 ✛ 手 扌 ⺘.

(313-ka.2s)*SIMPLIFIED (SHINJITAI)* ✐ The Compound Ideogram Haˈrau-to sweep (払) (simp.). (313-ka.2g)**Building Blocks** 【*simp.*】 ✖ Left: 扌 (abbreviated form of 手), right: ム. (313-ka.2R)**Readings** 【*simp.*】 ✿ Kan-on: ひつ (hitsu); ふつ (ˈfutsu). Kun: はらう (haˈrau); はらい (haˈrai).

(313-ka.3t)*TRADITIONAL (KYUJITAI)* ✐ The Phono-semantic Compound Logogram Haˈrau-to sweep (拂) (trad.). (313-ka.3c)**Components** 【trad.】 ⛁ [semantic 扌 | phonetic 弗]. (313-ka.3g)**Building Blocks** 【trad.】 ✖ Left: 扌 (abbreviated form of 手), right: 弗. (313-ka.3r)**Readings** 【trad.】 ✿ Kan-on: ひつ (hitsu); ふつ (ˈfutsu). Kun: はらう (haˈrau).

■ 149.Haˈtsu (初)

(000-it)*INCLUDING TERMS (EXAMPLES)* ◉ ✉ shodan {{初段}}, p. 217; shoshin {{初心}}, p. 219

(077-jg)*GENERAL MEANING (EXAMPLES)* ☼ 📖 *adjective* ❶ First ❷ New

(089-no)*NOTES AND EXAMPLES* 📖 ✎ Haˈjimete (初めて) means for the first time. Haˈjimeˈmash[i]te (はじめまして) means nice to meet You.

(134-re)*RELATED TERMS* ◉ ∞ hajime {{始め}}, p. 81

(185-ch)*CHINESE (PINYIN)* ◉ 📖 *chū*

(211-1)初 (211-al)*ALTERNATIVES OR SEE ALSO* ✐✐ 初, 祄, 刜, 仞, 廲

#Hatsu-first {初}##

(250-hi)はつ (hir.)

(275-tō)は ⎡つ⎤ [hàtsúˈ]

(280-po)pol:HACY

(313-ka)*KANJI* ✐ The Compound Ideogram Haˈtsu-first (初). (313k-cn)**Components** ⛁ [ネ | 刀]. (313k-ra)**Radical** ✛ 刀 刂 ⺈ sword. (313k-cs)**Composition** ✖ Left: ネ, right: 刀. (313k-re)**Readings (examples)** ✿

Go-on: そ (so). Kan-on: しょ (sho). Kun: はじめ (hajime, 初め); はじめて (hajimete, 初めて); はつ (hatsu, 初). Nanori: し (shi); もと (moto).

(830-ik)**IMPORTANT KANJI**

150.Haˈyashi (林)

(000-it)*INCLUDING TERMS (EXAMPLES)*

👁✉ shōrin {{少林}}, p. 218

(077-jg)*GENERAL MEANING (EXAMPLES)* ✿📖 *noun* ❶ Grove, copse. ❷ Forest, woods.

(185-ch)*CHINESE (PINYIN)* 👁📖 *lín*

(211-1)林 (250-hi)はやし (hir.)

(275-tō)はやし [hàyáshí⁺]

(800-tag)*TAGS* 💻 #hayashi, #haiashi #Hayashi-grove {林}##

(313-ka)*KANJI* 🖌 The Same-compound Pictogram Haˈyashi-grove (林).

(313k-cn)**Components** 🗠 [木 | 木].

(313k-ra)**Radical** ✦ 木 . (313k-cs)**Composition** ✖ Left: 木, right: 木.

(313k-re)**Readings (examples)** ✊ Go-on and Kan-on: りん (ˈRin). Kun: はやし (Haˈyashi).

(830-ik)**IMPORTANT KANJI**

151.ˈHe[i] (Hira)

(001-REF-rom)ˈHe[i] 1 ☞ Hira-calm {平}, p. 98

(002-REF-hi)へい ☞ ひら

#hei (hira)##

(280-po)pol:HEE

(256-kat)ヘイ (kat.) (275-tō)へ─ [héⁱè]

(800-tag)*TAGS* 💻 #hey 1, #heh 1

152.ˈHe[i] (閉)

(000-it)*INCLUDING TERMS (EXAMPLES)*

👁✉ heisokudachi {{閉足立ち}}, p. 96

(077-jg)*GENERAL MEANING (EXAMPLES)* ✿📖 *adjective* ❶ Closed.

(185-ch)*CHINESE (PINYIN)* 👁📖 *bì*

(211-1)閉

#Hei-closed {閉}##

(250-hi)へい (hir.)

(256-kat)ヘイ (kat.)

(275-tō)へ─ [héⁱè]

(280-po)pol:HEE

(800-tag)*TAGS* 💻 #hey 2, #heh 2

(833-kan)**KANJI**

153.ˈHe[i]-an

(000-it)*INCLUDING TERMS (EXAMPLES)*

👁✉ heiangodan {{平安五段}}, p. 91; heiannidan {{平安二段}}, p.

92; heiansandan {{平安三段}}, p. 93; heianshodan {{平安初段}}, p. 91; heianyodan {{平安四段}}, p. 94

(011-k1)*KANJI 1* ☜ Hira-calm {平}, p. 98

(012-k2)*KANJI 2* ☜ An-calm {安}, p. 33

(060-kg)*KATA GROUP* 形形形 **AKA** Pinan (ピンアン), Pin'an, Binan, Pingan, Chiang Nan, Channan[40], Peace, Peaceful Mind, Peaceful and Safe **Style** Shōrin (少林) **Number of Kata** Five

(077-jg)*GENERAL MEANING (EXAMPLES)* ☼📖 *noun* ❶ Peace, tranquility

(089-no)*NOTES AND EXAMPLES* 📖✎ The Heian period (平安時代) ran from 794 to 1185.

(185-ch)*CHINESE (PINYIN)* ☯📖 *píng'ān*

(211-1)平安
#heian {{平安}}##

(062-mk)*FUNAKOSHI MAIN BOOK - KATA* 🛡**MK 1922 original** 6 (list beginning), 51 (list Enbusen), 63. **1925 Ishida** 20 (list beginning), 58-59 (list Enbusen), 69. **1925 Teramoto** 26 (list beginning), 52 (list Enbusen), 58. **1935 Suzuki-Johnston** 9 (list styles), 32 (list names), 40 (list Enbusen), 43. **1935 Ohshima** 8-9 (list styles), 35 (list names), 48.

(250-hi)へいあん (hir.)

(256-kat)ヘイアン (kat.)

(275-tō)へ―あん [hèéáń]

(280-po)pol: HEEAN

(466-cha)*CHARACTERISTICS* ⓘ A Two-character, which consists of 2 Chinese Logograms and 0 Hiˈra-ga-ˈna Characters.

(800-tag)*TAGS* 💻 #hei-an, hei an, #hean, #hehan

(838-su)**SUPER-TERM**

154.ˈHe[i]-an ˈSho-dan

(015-w1)*WORD 1* W̅ ☜ heian {{平安}}, p. 90

(016-w2)*WORD 2* W̅ ☜ shodan {{初段}}, p. 217

(061-ka)*KATA* 形 **AKA** Pinan (ピンアン) Shodan, Pin'an Shodan, Binan Shodan, Heian Ichidan, Pinan Ichidan, Heian Sono Ichi, Pinan Sono Ichi, Peace First, Peaceful

Mind One, Peaceful Way First Level **Style** Shōrin （少林） **Group** ˈHe[i]-an （平安） **Enbusen** ˈKō-ji-ˈgata (工字形) - 工 Shape **Number of movements (approximately)** 21

(089-no)*NOTES AND EXAMPLES* 📖✍

Some schools keep the historic name - Heian Nidan.

(211-1)平安初段

(250-hi)へいあんしょだん (hir.)

#heianshodan {{平安初段}}##

(062-mk)*FUNAKOSHI MAIN BOOK - KATA*

🔱**MK 1922 original** 6 (list beginning), 51 (list Enbusen), 209. **1925 Ishida** 20 (list beginning), 58 (list Enbusen), 210. **1925 Teramoto** 26 (list beginning), 52 (list Enbusen), 128. **1935 Suzuki-Johnston** 9 (list styles), 32 (list names), 40 (list Enbusen), 43. **1935 Ohshima** 8-9 (list styles), 35 (list names), 48.

(256-kat)ヘイアンショダン (kat.)

(280-po)pol:HEEANSHODAN

(466-cha)*CHARACTERISTICS* ⓘ A Four-character, which consists of 4 Chinese Logograms and 0 Hiˈra-ga-ˈna Characters.

ˈHe[i]-an-ˈgo-dan - ˈHe[i]-an-ˈgo-dan

(800-tag)*TAGS* 💻 #heian-shodan, heian shodan

(838-su)**SUPER-TERM**

155. ˈHe[i]-an-ˈgo-dan

(015-w1)*WORD 1* W/W ☛ heian {{平安}}, p. 90

(016-w2)*WORD 2* W/W ☛ godan {{五段}}, p. 71

(061-ka)*KATA* 形 **AKA** Pinan (ピンアン) Godan, Pin'an Godan, Binan Godan, Heian Sono Go, Pinan Sono Go, Peace Fifth, Peaceful Mind Five, Peaceful Way Fifth Level **Style** Shōrin (少林) **Group** ˈHe[i]-an (平安) **Enbusen** ˈTe[i]-ji-ˈgata （丁字形） - 丁 Shape **Number of movements (approximately)** Once 23 (1922, 1925), later 25 (1935, 1958)

(211-1)平安五段

(250-hi)へいあんごだん (hir.)

(280-po)pol:HEEANGODAN

#heiangodan {{平安五段}}##

(062-mk)*FUNAKOSHI MAIN BOOK - KATA*

🔱**MK 1922 original** 6 (list beginning), 51 (list Enbusen), 222. **1925 Ishida** 20 (list beginning), 58 (list Enbusen), 225. **1925 Teramoto** 26 (list beginning), 52 (list Enbusen),

137. **1935 Suzuki-Johnston** 9 (list styles), 32 (list names), 40 (list Enbusen), 67. **1935 Ohshima** 8-9 (list styles), 35 (list names), 79.

(466-cha)*CHARACTERISTICS* ⓘ A Four-character, which consists of 4 Chinese Logograms and 0 Hiˈra-ga-ˈna Characters.

(800-tag)*TAGS* 🖥 #heian-godan, heian godan, #hean godan, #heyan godan, #heian 5

(838-su)**SUPER-TERM**

156. ˈHe[i]-an-ˈni-dan

List of large photos - p. 10

(015-w1)*WORD 1* ᵂᵂ ☛ heian {{平安}}, p. 90

(016-w2)*WORD 2* ᵂᵂ ☛ nidan {{二段}}, p. 184

(061-ka)*KATA* 形 **AKA** Pinan (ピンアン) Nidan, Pin'an Nidan, Binan Nidan, Heian Sono Ni, Pinan Sono Ni, Peace Second, Peaceful Mind Two, Peaceful Way Second Level **Style** Shōrin (少林) **Group** ˈHe[i]-an (平安) **Enbusen** ˈKō-ji-ˈgata (工字形) - 工 Shape **Number of movements (approximately)** 26

(089-no)*NOTES AND EXAMPLES* 📖✍

Some schools keep the historic name - Heian Shodan.

(211-1)平安二段

(250-hi)へいあんにだん (hir.)

#heiannidan {{平安二段}}##

(062-mk)*FUNAKOSHI MAIN BOOK - KATA*

⛵**MK 1922 original** 6 (list beginning), 51 (list Enbusen), 63. **1925 Ishida** 20 (list beginning), 58 (list Enbusen), 69. **1925 Teramoto** 26 (list beginning), 52 (list Enbusen), 58. **1935 Suzuki-Johnston** 9 (list styles), 32 (list names), 40 (list Enbusen), 51. **1935 Ohshima** 8-9 (list styles), 35 (list names), 54.

(280-po)pol:HEEANNIDAN

(466-cha)*CHARACTERISTICS* ⓘ A Four-character, which consists of 4 Chinese Logograms and 0 Hiˈra-ga-ˈna Characters.

(800-tag)*TAGS* 🖥 #heian-nidan, heian nidan, heyan nidan, Heian 2

(838-su)**SUPER-TERM**

157. ˈHe[i]-an-ˈsan-dan

(015-w1)*WORD 1* ᵂᵂ ☛ heian {{平安}}, p. 90

(016-w2)*WORD 2* W̲W ☛ sandan {{三段}}, p. 204

(061-ka)*KATA* 形 **AKA** Pinan （ピンアン） Sandan, Pin'an Sandan, Binan Sandan, Heian Sono San, Pinan Sono San, Peace Third, Peaceful Mind Three, Peaceful Way Third Level **Style** Shōrin （少林） **Group** ˈHe[i]-an （平安） **Enbusen** ˈTe[i]-jiˈgata （丁字形） - 丁 Shape **Number of movements (approximately)** Once 24 (1922, 1925), later 23 (1935, 1958)

(211-1)平安三段

(250-hi)へいあんさんだん (hir.)

(256-kat)ヘイアンサンダン (kat.)

(280-po)pol:HEEANSANDAN #heiansandan {{平安三段}}##

(062-mk)*FUNAKOSHI MAIN BOOK - KATA*

🛡**MK 1922 original** 6 (list beginning), 51 (list Enbusen) (mistakenly called 二段 instead of 三段 in the T Shape column), 213. **1925 Ishida** 20 (list beginning), 58 (list Enbusen), 215. **1925 Teramoto** 26 (list beginning), 52 (list Enbusen), 131. **1935 Suzuki-Johnston** 9 (list styles), 32

ˈHe[i]-an-ˈyo-dan - ˈHe[i]-an-ˈyo-dan (list names), 40 (list Enbusen), 57. **1935 Ohshima** 8-9 (list styles), 35 (list names), 62.

(466-cha)*CHARACTERISTICS* ⓘ A Four-character, which consists of 4 Chinese Logograms and 0 Hiˈra-ga-ˈna Characters.

(800-tag)*TAGS* 🖥 #heian-sandan, heian sandan

(838-su)**SUPER-TERM**

158. ˈHe[i]-an-ˈyo-dan

(015-w1)*WORD 1* W̲W ☛ heian {{平安}}, p. 90

(016-w2)*WORD 2* W̲W ☛ yodan {{四段}}, p. 277

(061-ka)*KATA* 形 **AKA** Pinan （ピンアン） Yodan, Pin'an Yodan, Binan Yodan, Heian Yondan, Pinan Yondan, Pin'an Yondan, Binan Yondan, Heian Sono Yon, Pinan Sono Yon, Heian Sono Shi, Pinan Sono Shi, Peace Fourth, Peaceful Mind Four, Peaceful Way Fourth Level **Style** Shōrin （少林） **Group** ˈHe[i]-an （平安） **Enbusen** Do-ˈji-gaˈta （土字形） - 土 Shape **Number of movements (approximately)** 27

(211-1)平安四段 (250-hi)へいあんよだ

ん (hir.) (280-po)pol:HEEANYODAN

#heianyodan {{平安四段}}##

(062-mk)*FUNAKOSHI MAIN BOOK - KATA*

📖**MK** **1922 original** 6 (list begin-

ning), 51 (list Enbusen), 217. **1925**

Ishida 20 (list beginning), 59 (list

Enbusen), 220. **1925 Teramoto** 26

(list beginning), 52 (list Enbusen),

134. **1935 Suzuki-Johnston** 9 (list

styles), 32 (list names), 40 (list

Enbusen), 62. **1935 Ohshima** 8-9

(list styles), 35 (list names), 71.

(466-cha)*CHARACTERISTICS* ⓘ A Four-

character, which consists of 4 Chi-

nese Logograms and 0 Hiˈra-ga-ˈna

Characters.

(800-tag)*TAGS* 💻 #heian-yodan, heian

yodan, #hayan yodan, #heian jodan,

#heian 4

(838-su)**SUPER-TERM**

159.ˈHe[i]-kō

(000-it)*INCLUDING TERMS (EXAMPLES)*

👁✉ heikodachi {{平行立ち}}, p.

95

(012-k2)*KANJI 1* ☛ Hira-calm {{平}}, p.

98

(011-k1)*KANJI 2* ☛ Gyo-line {{行}}, p.

75

(077-jg)*GENERAL MEANING (EXAM-*

PLES) ☼📖 adjective ❶ Parallel

(185-ch)*CHINESE (PINYIN)* ☯📖

píngxíng

(211-1)平行 (212-2)並行

#heikō {{平行}}##

(250-hi)へいこう (hir.)

(280-po)pol:HEEKOO

(466-cha)*CHARACTERISTICS* ⓘ A Two-

character, which consists of 2 Chi-

nese Logograms and 0 Hiˈra-ga-ˈna

Characters.

(800-tag)*TAGS* 💻 #heiko, hei-ko, hei

ko, heikoh, heikoo, heikou

160.He[i]-ˈkō-daˈchi

💣☀ Not to be confused with hei-

sokudachi {{閉足立ち}}, p. 96

(030-st)*STANCE* 立 **AKA** Parallel

Stance **Category** High Stances

(089-no)*NOTES AND EXAMPLES* 📖✎

The feet are usually shoulder-width

apart. In Ōshima Dōjō, for instance,

He[i]-ˈkō-daˈchi is the regular Yō-i

Stance (p. 277).

(015-w1)*WORD 1* ᵂ/ᵂ ☛ heikō {{平行}},

p. 94

(016-w2)*WORD* 2 W⁄W ☛ tachi {{立ち}}, p. 228

(466-cha)*CHARACTERISTICS* ⓘ A Four-character, which consists of 3 Chinese Logograms and 1 Hiˈra-ga-ˈna Characters.

(211-1)平行立ち

(212-2)平行立

#heikodachi {{平行立ち}}##

Masters 6 - Heikodachi by Bamgboye Sensei
List of Sensei Demonstrations next to Values, p. 10
List of large photos - p. 10
Bobby Bamgboye of Nigeria WSKF demonstrates Heiki-dachi. Photographer: Joel Ibanga.

(250-hi)へいこうだち (hir.)

(280-po)pol:HEEKOODACI

(483-td)**Tɔd** 🔉 Due to the ˈRen-daku laws, the unvoiced consonant /T/ may get a Dak[u]-ˈten (゛) and become ~/d/ as a suffix. Example ↯ ˈTachi (たち) turns into Ki-ˈba Daˈchi (きばだち).

(800-tag)*TAGS* ⌨ #heiko-dachi, heiko dachi, #hekodachi

161.He[i]-soˈku-daˈchi

💣✳ Not to be confused with heiko-dachi {{平行立ち}}, p. 95

(011-k1)*KANJI 1* ☛ Hei-closed {閉}, p. 89

(012-k2)*KANJI 2* ☛ Ashi-foot {足}, p. 37

(016-w2)*WORD* 2 W⁄W ☛ tachi {{立ち}}, p. 228

(030-st)*STANCE* 立 **AKA** Closed-leg Stance, Closed Feet Stance, Close-leg Stance, Feet-together Stance **Category** High Stances

(089-no)*NOTES AND EXAMPLES* 📖✎

The big toes are touching or almost touching. The second stance of Heian Sandan; in other words, the second and the third movements of Heian Sandan are performed in He[i]-soˈku-daˈchi.

(211-1)閉足立ち(212-2)閉足立

(250-hi)へいそくだち (hir.)

(483-td)**Tɔd** 🔉 Due to the ˈRen-daku laws, the unvoiced consonant /T/ may get a Dak[u]-ˈten (゛) and become ~/d/ as a suffix. Example ↯

ˈHi (日) - ˈHi (日)

ˈTachi (たち) turns into Ki-ˈba Daˈchi (きばだち).

#heisokudachi {{閉足立ち}}##

Masters 7 - Heisokudachi by Bamgboye Sensei
List of Sensei Demonstrations next to Values, p. 10
Bobby Bamgboye of Nigeria WSKF demonstrates Heisoku-dachi (including Bassai-dai's). Photographer: Joel Ibanga.

(031-ms)*FUNAKOSHI MAIN BOOK - STANCES* 🐢MS **1922 original** 30 (list), 30. **1925 Ishida** 41 (list), 41. **1925 Teramoto** 40 (list), 40. **1935 Suzuki-Johnston** 22 (list), 22. **1935 Ohshima** 19 (list), 20.

(032-ns)*FUNAKOSHI NYUMON TERAMOTO - STANCES* 🐢NS 59

(280-po)pol:HEESOKUDACI

(466-cha)*CHARACTERISTICS* ⓘ A Four-character, which consists of 3 Chinese Logograms and 1 Hiˈra-ga-ˈna Characters.

(800-tag)*TAGS* 💻 #heisoku-dachi, heisoku dachi #hesokudachi

(838-su)**SUPER-TERM**

(000-it)*INCLUDING TERMS (EXAMPLES)*

👁✉ mikka {{三日}}, p. 171

(077-jg)*GENERAL MEANING (EXAMPLES)* ☼📖 *temporal noun* ❶ Day *noun* ❷ Sun

(185-ch)*CHINESE (PINYIN)* ☯📖 *rì*

(480-hb)**H⊃b** 🔔 Due to the ˈRendaku laws, the unvoiced consonant /H/ may get a Dak[u]-ˈten (ﾞ) and become ~/b/ as a suffix. Example ↲ ˈHon (ほん) turns into ˈSan-bon (さんぼん).

(211-1)日

(250-hi)ひ (hir.)

#Hi-day {日}##

(313-ka)*KANJI* ✒ The Pictogrammatic Radical (Radical 72) Hi-day (日).
(313k-cn)**Components** 🗂 No components - a Simple Logogram. (313k-ra)**Radical** ✦ 日 day. (313k-cs)**Composition** ✗ 口, 一. (313k-re)**Readings (examples)** 🗣 Go-on: にち [níˈchì] (ˈnichi) – as in ˈKonˈnichi wa (今日は), which means hello. Kan-on: じつ (jitsu). Kun: ひ (hi) – as in Gets[u]-ˈyō-bi

[gètsúyóⁱòbì] （月曜日）, which means Monday; か (ka).

(830-ik)**IMPORTANT KANJI**

163.ˈHi (臂)

(000-it)*INCLUDING TERMS (EXAMPLES)*

👁✉ enpi {{猿臂}}, p. 62

(077-jg)*GENERAL MEANING (EXAMPLES)* ✿📖 *noun* ❶ Elbow.

(133-sy)*SYNONYMS* 👁= Hiji-elbow {肘}, p. 97

(185-ch)*CHINESE (PINYIN)* 🌐📖 ***bì, bèi, bei***

(211-1)臂 (211-al)*ALTERNATIVES OR SEE ALSO* ✎✎ 肘, 肱. (250-hi)ひ (hir.)

#Hi-elbow {臂}##

(325-kr)*KANJI READINGS* ✎🗣 Go-on: ひ (hi). Kan-on: ひ (hi). Kun: ひじ (hiji, 臂).

(481-hp)**H⤵p** 🔔 Due to the ˈRendaku laws, the unvoiced consonant /H/ may get a Han-dak[u]-ten (゚) and become ~/p/ as a suffix. Example 🔔 ˈHon (ほん) turns into ˈIppon (いっぽん).

(833-kan)**KANJI**

164.Hiˈdari (左)

(077-jg)*GENERAL MEANING (EXAMPLES)* ✿📖 *adjective* ❶ Left.

(185-ch)*CHINESE (PINYIN)* 🌐📖 ***zuǒ***

(211-1)左 (211-al)*ALTERNATIVES OR SEE ALSO* ✎✎ 左

#Hidari-left {左}##

(250-hi)ひだり (hir.)

(275-tō)ひ だり [hìdárí]

(833-kan)**KANJI**

(838-su)**SUPER-TERM**

165.Hiˈji (肘)

(077-jg)*GENERAL MEANING (EXAMPLES)* ✿📖 *noun* ❶ Elbow.

(133-sy)*SYNONYMS* 👁= Hi-elbow {臂}, p. 97

(185-ch)*CHINESE (PINYIN)* 🌐📖 ***zhǒu***

(211-1)肘

(211-al)*ALTERNATIVES OR SEE ALSO* ✎✎ 肱, 臂

(250-hi)ひじ (hir.) (275-tō)ひ じ [hìjíⁱ]

(885-tag)*TAGS* 💻 #elbow 2

#Hiji-elbow {肘}##

(313-ka)*KANJI* ✎ The Phono-semantic Compound Pictogram[41] Hiji-elbow (肘). (313k-cn)**Components** 🔧 [月 | 寸

]. (313k-ra)**Radical** ✦ 肉月月 meat.

(313k-cs)**Composition** ⚔ Left: 月 , right: 寸 . (313k-re)**Readings (examples)** 🗣 Go-on: ちゅう (chū). Kan-on: ちゅう (chū). Kun: ひじ (hiji, 肘).

(830-ik)**IMPORTANT KANJI**

166.ˈHira (平)

(000-it)*INCLUDING TERMS (EXAMPLES)*
👁✉ heian {{平安}}, p. 90; heikō {{平行}}, p. 94; hiragana {{平仮名}}, p. 99 ; hiraken {{平拳}}, p. 99; Tenohira-palm {掌}, p. 244 (alternative spelling)

(077-jg)*GENERAL MEANING (EXAMPLES)* ☼📖 *adjective* ❶ Calm, gentle, peaceful ❷ Ordinary, usual, common, plain, mediocre ❸ Flat, even, level.

(133-sy)*SYNONYMS* 👁= An-calm {安}, p. 33

(185-ch)*CHINESE (PINYIN)* 🌐📖 *píng* as in *píng'ān* (平安)[42]

(211-1)平

(211-al)*ALTERNATIVES OR SEE ALSO* ✎✎ 平, 秤, 苹

#Hira-calm {平}##

(250-hi)ひら (hir.)

(256-kat)ヒラ (kat.)

(275-tō) ⬚ひ ら [híˎ ràˎ]

(313-ka)*KANJI* ✎ The Simple Logogram ˈHira-calm (平). (313k-cn)**Components** 🔧 No components - a Simple Logogram. (313k-ra)**Radical** ✦ 干 dry. (313k-cs)**Composition** ⚔ 干ヽ. (313k-re)**Readings (examples)** 🗣 Go-on: びょう (byō). Kan-on: へい (hei). Tō-on: ひん (hin). Kan'yō-on: ひょう (hyō). Kun: たいら (taira, 平ら); ひら (ˈhira, 平). Nanori: おさむ (osamu).

(830-ik)**IMPORTANT KANJI**

167.Hiˈra-ga-ˈna

(011-k1)*KANJI* 1 ☞ Hira-calm {平}, p. 98

(015-w1)*WORD* 1 ᵂᵂ ☞ kana {{仮名}}, p. 126

(020-re)*RESEARCH* 🔍 *noun* ❶ A Japanese cursive syllabic script, used along with ˈKan-ji and Kaˈta-ka-na. The Hiˈra-ga-ˈna 46 monographs (basic Characters) are あいうえお, かきくけこ, さしすせそ, たちつ

てと，なにぬねの，はひふへほ，ま
みむめも，やゆよ，らりるれろ，わ
を，ん．

(134-re)*RELATED TERMS* 👁∞ katakana

{{片仮名}}, p. 136

#hiragana {{平仮名}}##

(211-1)ひら仮名 (212-2)平仮名

(250-hi)ひらがな (hir.)

(466-cha)*CHARACTERISTICS* ⓘ A Four-
character, which consists of 2 Chinese Logograms and 2 Hiˈra-ga-ˈna
Characters.

(482-kg)**K⟳g** 🔔 Due to the ˈRen-
daku laws, the unvoiced consonant
/K/ may get a Dak[u]-ˈten (゛) and
become ~/g/ as a suffix. Example 🦶
Keˈri (けり) turns into Maˈe-geˈri (
まえげり).

(800-tag)*TAGS* 💻 #hira-ga-na, hira ga
na

168.Hiˈra-ken

💣※ This term has different meanings.

(011-k1)*KANJI 1* ☞ Hira-calm {平}, p.
98

(012-k2)*KANJI 2* ☞ Ken-fist {拳}, p.
140

(211-1)平拳 (250-hi)ひらけん (hir.)

(089-no)*NOTES AND EXAMPLES* 📖🖋

The striking area may be the Proximal InterPhalangeal Joints (PIP).
One of Hiraken's meanings is a kind
of a cat slap – it can be viewed as
the opposite of Ura-ken. Used for
striking the sole in Kappō (活法) -
resuscitation techniques, which are
practiced in some Shotokan schools.

(800-tag)*TAGS* 💻 #hira-ken, hira ken

#hiraken {{平拳}}##

Anatomy 2 - Hiraken

(040-ul)*UPPER LIMB STRIKE & ANATOMY*

手 **AKA** Ryotoken, Flat Fist, Half-
fist, Four-knuckle Fist, Fore-
knuckle Fist, Leopard Fist, Leopard
Blow, Leopard Punch **Category**
Strike

(041-mu)*FUNAKOSHI MAIN BOOK - UPPER*

LIMB **MUL** 1935 **Suzuki-
Johnston** 19. **1935 Ohshima** 18.

(466-cha)*CHARACTERISTICS* ⓘ A Two-
character, which consists of 2 Chinese Logograms and 0 Hiˈra-ga-ˈna
Characters.

169.Hiˈza (膝)

(000-it)*INCLUDING TERMS (EXAMPLES)*

👁✉ hizagashira {{膝頭}}, p. 100; hizazuchi {{膝鎚}}, p. 101

(077-jg)*GENERAL MEANING (EXAMPLES)* ☼📖 *noun* ❶ Knee

(185-ch)*CHINESE (PINYIN)* 👁📖 **xī**

(211-1)膝

(250-hi)ひざ (hir.)

(885-tag)*TAGS* 💻 #knee, #knee strike, #kneecap, #straight knee, #front knee, #curved knee, #side knee, #roundhouse knee, #clinch fighting #Hiza-knee {膝}##

(275-tō)ひ ざ [hìzá]

(313-ka)*KANJI* ✎ The Phono-semantic Compound Logogram Hiˈza-knee (膝). (313k-cn)**Components** [semantic 月 | phonetic 桼]. (313k-ra)**Radical** ⊹ 肉 月 月 meat. (313k-cs)**Composition** ✄ Left: 月, right: 桼. (313k-re)**Readings (examples)** ✊ Go-on: しち (shichi). Kan-on: しつ (shitsu). Kun: ひざ (hiza).

(830-ik)**IMPORTANT KANJI**

170.Hiˈza-ˈgashira

(011-k1)*KANJI 1* ☞ Hiza-knee {膝}, p. 100

(012-k2)*KANJI 2* ☞ Atama-head {頭}, p. 40

(077-jg)*GENERAL MEANING (EXAMPLES)* ☼📖 *noun* ❶ Patella, knee-cap, front of the knee.

(211-1)膝頭 (250-hi)ひざがしら (hir.)

(275-tō)ひ ざ が しら [hìzágáˈshìrà] #hizagashira {{膝頭}}##

(276-tō2)ひ ざ が しら [hìzágáshírá]

(466-cha)*CHARACTERISTICS* ⓘ A Two-character, which consists of 2 Chinese Logograms and 0 Hiˈra-ga-ˈna Characters.

(800-tag)*TAGS* 💻 #hiza-gashira, hiza gashira, hizakashira

171.Hiˈza-geˈri (hizazuchi)

(001-REF-rom)Hiˈza-geˈri ☞ hizazuchi {{膝鎚}}, p. 101 #hizageri (hizazuchi)##

(211-1)膝蹴り (250-hi)ひざげり (hir.)

(800-tag)*TAGS* 💻 #hiza-geri, hiza geri

172.Hiˈza-z[u]ˈchi

(011-k1)*KANJI 1* ☞ Hiza-knee {膝}, p. 100

(012-k2)*KANJI 2* ☞ Tsuchi-hammer {鎚}, p. 252

(045-ll)*LOWER LIMB STRIKE & ANATOMY*

足 **AKA** Hizageri, Knee Hammer, Knee Strike, Knee Kick, Hammer Knee, Kneeing **Category** Knee

(046-ml)*FUNAKOSHI MAIN BOOK - LOWER LIMB* 🔖**MLL** 1922 original 46 (list), 48 **1925 Ishida** 56 (list), 57 **1925 Teramoto** 49 (list), 51 **1935 Suzuki-Johnston** 27 (list), 28 **1935 Ohshima** 23 (list), 25

#hizazuchi {{膝鎚}}##

(211-1)膝鎚 (250-hi)ひざづち (hir.)

(466-cha)*CHARACTERISTICS* ⓘ A Two-character, which consists of 2 Chinese Logograms and 0 Hiˈra-ga-ˈna Characters.

(484-tsz)**TsⳢz** 🔔 Due to the ˈRendaku laws, the unvoiced consonant /Ts/ may get a Dak[u]-ˈten (゛) and become ~/z/ as a suffix. Example ↰ Ts[u]ˈki 2 (つき) turns into Oˈi-z[u]ˈki (おいづき).

(800-tag)*TAGS* 🖥 #hiza-zuchi, hiza zuchi, #hizatsuchi, #hiza-tsuchi, #hiza tsuchi

173. ˈHo (歩)

(000-it)*INCLUDING TERMS (EXAMPLES)*

👁✉ naihanchi {{内歩進}}, p. 177

(077-jg)*GENERAL MEANING (EXAMPLES)* ⚙📖 *noun* ❶ Step. #Ho-step {歩}##

(185-ch)*CHINESE (PINYIN)* 🔊📖 *bù*

(211-1)歩 (250-hi)ほ (hir.)

(833-kan)**KANJI**

174. ˈHon (本)

(000-it)*INCLUDING TERMS (EXAMPLES)*

👁✉ gohon {{五本}}, p. 71; ippon {{一本}}, p. 105; kihon {{基本}}, p. 146; sanbon {{三本}}, p. 202

(077-jg)*GENERAL MEANING (EXAMPLES)* ⚙📖 *noun* ❶ Source, origin, root, stem, base, basis, foundation *adjective* ❷ Original, true, real, genuine, main, head, principal, regular, proper, natural *noun* ❸ Book, volume *counter* ❹ Counter for long slender cylindrical objects (bananas, bottles, pens, trees, buses) and for other things *adjective prefix* ❺ This, present, current.

(089-no)*NOTES AND EXAMPLES* 📖✍ **1** ˈHon-tō (本当) means truth **2** This is the same Moˈto as in Admiral Yaˈma-moˈto (山本).

Hon-source {本}##

(136-se)*SEE ALSO* 👁➕ Moto-origin { 元}, p. 173

(185-ch)*CHINESE (PINYIN)* ☯📖 **běn**

(211-1)本

(250-hi)ほん (hir.)

(302-kn)*KANJI NOTES* 🖌✍ The lower part of the Logogram emphasizes the roots in the ground[43].

(313-ka)*KANJI* 🖌 The Pictogram 'Hon-source (本). (313k-cn)**Components** 🏴 No components - a Simple Logo-gram. (313k-ra)**Radical** ✛ 木 tree. (313k-cs)**Composition** 仌 木, 一. (313k-re)**Readings (examples)** 🗣 Go-on: ほん (hon). Kan-on: ほん (hon). Kun: もと (moto, 本).

(830-ik)**IMPORTANT KANJI**

175.Ho-ˈshin (goshin)

(001-REF-rom)Ho-ˈshin ☞ goshin {{護身}}, p. 72

#hoshin (goshin)##

(213-3)保身 (250-hi)ほしん (hir.)

(800-tag)*TAGS* 💻 #ho-shin, ho shin

176.ˈI (意)

(000-it)*INCLUDING TERMS (EXAMPLES)*

👁✉ yōi {{用意}}, p. 277

(077-jg)*GENERAL MEANING (EXAMPLES)* ☼📖 *noun* ❶ Meaning, intention, desire ❷ Feelings ❸ Thoughts, idea

(185-ch)*CHINESE (PINYIN)* ☯📖 **yì**[44]

(211-1)意 (250-hi)い (hir.)

I-meaning {意}##

(302-kn)*KANJI NOTES* 🖌✍ Its radical is 心 忄 小 heart

(325-kr)*KANJI READINGS* 🖌🗣 Go-on: い (i). Kan-on: い (i). Kun: おもい (omoi, 意い); こころ (kokoro, 意).

(833-kan)**KANJI**

177.I-ˈai

(012-k2)*KANJI 2* ☞ Au-to unite {合}, p. 41

(070-kt)*KARATE MEANING* 🖐📖 *noun* ① Responding to sudden attacks from Sei-za (正座); I (居) means sitting ② Responding to sudden attacks from a Natural-stance Position or another High Stance ③ Responding to sudden attacks generally.

(089-no)*NOTES AND EXAMPLES* 📖✍ I-ˈai-goshi-dachi (居合腰立ち) is a One-leg Kneeling Stance – as the first stance of enpi {{燕飛}}, p. 63.

I-ˈai-dō (居合道) and I-ˈai-jutsu (居合術) are arts of drawing a sword.

(211-1)居合 (212-2)居合い

(250-hi)いあい (hir.)

(275-tō)い あい [ìáí]

#iai {{居合}}##

(071-dl)🔥 AA *DOJO LANGUAGE* ⏳📖 *noun* ① Sitting together, Situational Kumite.

(078-mg)*FUNAKOSHI MAIN BOOK – GENERALLY* **MG** 1935 **Suzuki-Johnston** 185 **1935 Ohshima** 223, 235

(134-gr-re)*GROUP* 👁(͡°͜ʖ͡°) The following terms are related: iai {{居合}}, p. 103, mokusō {{黙想}}, p. 171, seiza {{正座}}, p. 207, zazen {{座禅}}, p. 283

(466-cha)*CHARACTERISTICS* ⓘ A Two-character, which consists of 2 Chinese Logograms and 0 Hiˈra-ga-ˈna Characters.

(800-tag)*TAGS* 💻 #iay, #yay, i-ai, i ai, #yai

178.Iˈchi (一)

(000-it)*INCLUDING TERMS (EXAMPLES)* 👁✉ ichijigata {{一字形}}, p. 104; ikkyū {{一級}}, p. 104; ippon {{一本}}, p. 105

(077-jg)*GENERAL MEANING (EXAMPLES)* ⚙📖 *noun* ❶ One

(185-ch)*CHINESE (PINYIN)* 🌐📖 *yī*

(211-1)一 (212-2)1 つ (211-ka+hi) 一つ

#Ichi-one {一}##

(211-al)*ALTERNATIVES OR SEE ALSO* ✏✏ 弌, 壱, 壹, 䐥, 齹, 嫳

(250-hi)いち (hir.)

(275-tō)い ち [ìchíˈ]

(800-tag)*TAGS* 💻 #chi, #1

(833-kan)**KANJI**

(838-su)**SUPER-TERM**

179.Iˈchi-ji-ˈgata

(011-k1)*KANJI 1* ☛ Ichi-one {一}, p. 103

(012-k2)*KANJI 2* ☛ Ji-character {字}, p. 109

(013-k3)*KANJI 3* ☛ Kata-shape {形}, p. 134

(070-kt)*KARATE MEANING* ✋📖 *noun* ① Straight Line Pattern, Single Line Shape, Character-one Pattern, 一 Pattern, 一 Character Figure, Capital letter I Form, —— Shape, | Shape.

(134-re)*RELATED TERMS* 👁∞ enbusen {{演武線}}, p. 61

(211-1)一字形 (211-al)*ALTERNATIVES OR SEE ALSO* 🖊🖊 一字型

(250-hi)いちじがた (hir.)

#ichijigata {{一字形}}##

(068-me)*FUNAKOSHI MAIN BOOK - ENBUSEN* 🐢**MEN** **1922 original 50-51 1925 Ishida 58 1925 Tera-moto 52 1935 Suzuki-Johnston 40-41 1935 Ohshima 41**

(466-cha)*CHARACTERISTICS* ① A Three-character, which consists of 3 Chinese Logograms and 0 Hiˈra-ga-ˈna Characters.

(482-kg)**K↻g** 🔔 Due to the ˈRen-daku laws, the unvoiced consonant /K/ may get a Dak[u]-ˈten (゛) and become ~/g/ as a suffix. Example 🦵 Keˈri (けり) turns into Maˈe-geˈri (まえげり).

(800-tag)*TAGS* 🖥 #ichiji-gata, ichiji gata

180.Ik-ˈkyū

(011-k1)*KANJI 1* ☞ Ichi-one {一}, p. 103

(012-k2)*KANJI 2* ☞ Kyū-rank {級}, p. 158

(070-kt)***KARATE MEANING*** ✋📖 *adjective* ① First ˈKyū.

(077-jg)*GENERAL MEANING (EXAMPLES)* ☼📖 *adjective* ❶ First de-gree, level one, first-class, 1st grade.

(185-ch)*CHINESE (PINYIN)* ☯📖 *yījí*

(466-cha)*CHARACTERISTICS* ① A Two-character, which consists of 2 Chinese Logograms and 0 Hiˈra-ga-ˈna Characters.

#ikkyū {{一級}}##

(095-3t)*THE THREE TEACHINGS* **3**👣

IKKYŪ (一休) (1394-1481) was a prominent Japanese Zen Buddhist monk. But the second Kanji in his surname (Yasumu-to rest {休}, p. 276) is different from the second Kanji in our Ik-ˈkyū (Kyū-rank {級}, p. 158).

(211-1)一級 (250-hi)いっきゅう (hir.)

(280-po)pol:IKKJUU

(800-tag)*TAGS* 🖥 #ikkyu, i-kkyu, i kkyu, #ikkiu, ikkyuu, ikkyuh, #ikiu, #ikyu

181.Iˈkusa(戦)

(000-it)*INCLUDING TERMS (EXAMPLES)*

👁✉ sanchindachi {{三戦立ち}}, p. 203

(077-jg)*GENERAL MEANING (EXAMPLES)* ☼📖 *noun* ❶ War, battle

(185-ch)*CHINESE (PINYIN)* 🌐📖 **zhàn**

(211-1)戦 (211-al)*ALTERNATIVES OR SEE ALSO* ✒✒ 戦, 战, 兵, 軍

#Ikusa-war {戦}##

(250-hi)いくさ (hir.)

(275-tō)い く さ [ìkúsá⁺]

(276-tō2)い く さ [ìkúsá]

(325-kr)*KANJI READINGS* ✒🗣 Go-on: せん (sen). Kan-on: せん (sen). Kun: いくさ (ikusa, 戦); たたかう (tatakau, 戦う).

(833-kan)**KANJI**

182.ˈIp-pon

(000-it)*INCLUDING TERMS (EXAMPLES)*

👁✉ ipponken {{一本拳}}, p. 106; ipponkumite {{一本組手}}, p. 106

(011-k1)*KANJI 1* ☛ Ichi-one {一}, p. 103

(012-k2)*KANJI 2* ☛ Hon-source {本}, p. 102

(077-jg)*GENERAL MEANING (EXAMPLES)* ☼📖 *counter* ❶ One slender cylindrical object (bananas, bottles, pens, trees, buses) ❷ Ippon, a point, full point ❸ Blow.

(134-re)*RELATED TERMS* 👁∞ wazaari {{技有り}}, p. 268

(185-ch)*CHINESE (PINYIN)* 🌐📖 **yīběn**

(211-1)一本

#ippon {{一本}}##

(211-al)*ALTERNATIVES OR SEE ALSO* ✒✒ 1本 (250-hi)いっぽん (hir.) (275-tō)い っぽん [í⁺ppòn]

(466-cha)*CHARACTERISTICS* ① A Two-character, which consists of 2 Chinese Logograms and 0 Hiˈra-ga-ˈna Characters.

(481-hp)**H➲p** 🔔 Due to the ˈRen-daku laws, the unvoiced consonant /H/ may get a Han-dak[u]-ten (゜) and become ~/p/ as a suffix. Example 🔱 ˈHon (ほん) turns into ˈIp-pon (いっぽん).

(800-tag)*TAGS* ⌨ ip-pon, ip pon, #ipon

(838-su)**SUPER-TERM**

183.Ip-ˈpon ˈKumi-te

(000-it)*INCLUDING TERMS (EXAMPLES)*

👁✉ jiyūipponkumite {{自由一本組手}}, p. 113

(015-w1)*WORD 1* W̲ ☛ ippon {{一本}}, p. 105

(016-w2)*WORD 2* W̲ ☛ kumite {{組手}}, p. 157

(070-kt)*KARATE MEANING* 🖐📖 *noun phrase* ① One-time Sparring, One Step Sparring.

(838-su)**SUPER-TERM**

#ipponkumite {{一本組手}}##

(134-re)*RELATED TERMS* 👁∞ tennokataura {{天の形裏}}, p. 242

(211-1)一本組手

(250-hi)いっぽんくみて (hir.)

(466-cha)*CHARACTERISTICS* ① A Four-character, which consists of 4 Chinese Logograms and 0 Hiˈra-ga-ˈna Characters.

(800-tag)*TAGS* 🖥 #ippon-kumite, ippon kumite, #iponkumite

184.Ip-ˈpon-ken

(000-it)*INCLUDING TERMS (EXAMPLES)*

👁✉ nakadaipponken {{中高一本拳}}, p. 179

(015-w1)*WORD 1* W̲ W̲ ☛ ippon {{一本}}, p. 105

(040-ul)*UPPER LIMB STRIKE & ANATOMY*

手 **AKA** One-knuckle Fist, One Knuckle Punch, One Knuckle Strike, One Finger Punch, One Finger Strike, One Point Fist, Singe Point Fist **Category** Strike, Closed-fist

(089-no)*NOTES AND EXAMPLES* 📖✑

The impact area is the second or third Proximal Interphalangeal Joint.

#ipponken {{一本拳}}##

(013-k3)*KANJI 3* ☛ Ken-fist {拳}, p. 140

(041-mu)*FUNAKOSHI MAIN BOOK - UPPER LIMB* **MUL** 1922 original 29, **1925 Ishida** 39-40 **1925 Teramoto** 39 **1935 Suzuki-Johnston** 19 **1935 Ohshima** 18

(211-1)一本拳

(250-hi)いっぽんけん (hir.)

(466-cha)*CHARACTERISTICS* ① A Three-character, which consists of 3 Chinese Logograms and 0 Hiˈra-ga-ˈna Characters.

(800-tag)*TAGS* 🖥 #ippon-ken, ippon ken, #iponken

185.I'ri (入)

Script 4 – Iri-entering Western Zhou Bronze Inscriptions 1

Script 5 – Iri-entering Western Zhou Bronze Inscriptions 2

List of large photos - p. 10

(000-it)*INCLUDING TERMS (EXAMPLES)*

👁✉ irimi {{入り身}}, p. 107

(077-jg)*GENERAL MEANING (EXAMPLES)* ✿📖 *noun* ❶ Entering.

(185-ch)*CHINESE (PINYIN)* 👁📖 *rù*

(302-kn)*KANJI NOTES* 🖊🖌 Contains two strokes. It depicts an arrowhead[45]; whenever performing I'ri-'mi, we should remember the penetrating arrowhead. According to another opinion, the Kanji depicts roots penetrating the ground[46]. Can You recognize the Logogram in the ancient Chinese script on page 28? #Iri-entering {{入}}##

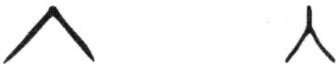

Script 6 – Iri-entering Shang Oracle Bone Script

Script 7 – Iri-entering Liushutong Transcribed ancient scripts

(211-1)入

(211-al)*ALTERNATIVES OR SEE ALSO*

🖊🖊 入, 入

(250-hi)いり (hir.)

(313-ka)*KANJI* 🖊 The Simple Ideogrammatic Radical (Radical 11) I'ri-entering （入）. (313k-cn)**Components** 🖳 No components - a Simple Logogram (313k-ra)**Radical** ⟊ 入ヘ enter (313k-cs)**Composition** 㡀 ヘ

(313k-re)**Readings (examples)** 🗣 Kun: いる (iru, 入る); いり (iri). Nanori: いり (iri); いる (iru).

(830-ik)**IMPORTANT KANJI**

186.I'ri-'mi

List of large photos - p. 10

(011-k1)*KANJI* 1 ☛ Iri-entering {入}, p. 107

(012-k2)*KANJI* 2 ☛ Mi-body {身}, p. 169

(070-kt)*KARATE MEANING* ✋📖 *noun* ① Entering into a technique, entering an attack, penetrating an attack, entering the opponent.

(134-re)*RELATED TERMS* 👁∞ Long Ma; tennomon {{天の門}}, p. 243; tokkōzuki {{特攻突き}}, p. 247

(211-1)入り身

(250-hi)いりみ (hir.)

#irimi {{入り身}}##

(191-ot)*OTHER MARTIAL ARTS TERMI-NOLOGY* ✿ ⚡ Maˈru-haˈshi (Maˈru-baˈshi) (丸橋), Bridge of Life, Log Bridge.

(466-cha)*CHARACTERISTICS* ⓘ A Three-character, which consists of 2 Chinese Logograms and 1 Hiˈra-ga-ˈna Characters.

(071-dl)💧 🅰🅰 *DOJO LANGUAGE* ⏳📖 ① Entering the body, into the body.

(800-tag)*TAGS* 💻 #iri-mi, iri mi, #marubashi, #maru bashi

(838-su)**SUPER-TERM**

187.Iˈ TO-SU ˈAn-kō

(013-k3)*KANJI* 3 ☞ An-calm {安}, p. 33

(029-pe)*PERSONS* 👪 Iˈ TO-SU ˈAn-kō (ˈShu-ri, 1831 - 1915) was a famous Okinawan Kaˈra-te-ka, considered by many the father of modern Kaˈra-te. A student of Maˈtsu-mura (p. 165). One of the two main teachers of Fuˈna-koˈshi (p. 67).

(216-ea)糸洲 安恒 (E.)

#itosuankō {{糸洲 安恒}}##

(185-ch)*CHINESE (PINYIN)* ☯📖 ***Mìzhōu ānhéng***

(217-we)安恒 糸洲 (W.)

(466-cha)*CHARACTERISTICS* ⓘ A Four-character, which consists of 2 Chinese Logograms and 2 Hiˈra-ga-ˈna Characters.

(800-tag)*TAGS* 💻 #ankoitosu, anko ito-su, #itosu, ito-su, ito su

188.Iˈwa 岩

(000-it)*INCLUDING TERMS (EXAMPLES)* 👁✉ gankaku {{岩鶴}}, p. 68

(077-jg)*GENERAL MEANING (EXAMPLES)* ✿📖 *noun* ❶ Rock.

(185-ch)*CHINESE (PINYIN)* ☯📖 ***yán***

(211-1)岩 (211-al)*ALTERNATIVES OR SEE ALSO* ✎✎ 巖, 磐

#Iwa-rock {岩}##

(250-hi)いわ (hir.)

(275-tō)い|わ| [ìwá˩]

(325-kr)*KANJI READINGS* ✎🗣 Go-on: げん (gen). Kan-on: がん (gan). Kun: いわ (iwa, 岩).

(833-kan)**KANJI**

189.ˈJi (字)

(000-it)*INCLUDING TERMS (EXAMPLES)* 👁✉ chōji {{丁字}}, p. 51; dojigata {{土字形}}, p. 58; hachiji {{八字}}, p. 78; ichijigata {{一字形}}, p. 104; jūjigata {{十字形}}, p. 115;

jūjiuke {{十字受け}}, p. 116; kanji {{漢字}}, p. 127; kōjigata {{工字形}}, p. 149; renojidachi {{レの字立ち}}, p. 195.

(211-1)字

#Ji-character {字}##

(077-jg)*GENERAL MEANING (EXAMPLES)* ✿📖 *noun* ❶ Character (e.g., ˈKan-ji) ❷ Letter.

(250-hi)じ (hir.)

(256-kat)ジ (kat.)

(185-ch)*CHINESE (PINYIN)* ☯📖 **zì** as in *hànzì*

(885-tag)*TAGS* 💻 #gi, #character, #letter, #kanji

(833-kan)**KANJI**

190. ˈJi (慈)

(000-it)*INCLUDING TERMS (EXAMPLES)*

👁✉ jion {{慈恩}}, p. 110

(077-jg)*GENERAL MEANING (EXAMPLES)* ✿📖 *noun* ❶ Mercy.

(185-ch)*CHINESE (PINYIN)* ☯📖 **cí**

(211-1)慈 (250-hi)じ (hir.)

(313-ka)*KANJI* 🖊 The Phono-semantic Compound Logogram ˈJi-mercy (慈).

#Ji-mercy {慈}##

(256-kat)ジ (kat.)

(313k-cn)**Components** ⚇ [phonetic 茲 | semantic 心] (313k-ra)**Radical** ✦ 心 忄 小 heart (313k-cs)**Composition** ✻ Top: 茲, bottom: 心 (313k-re)**Readings (examples)** 🗣 Go-on: じ (ji). Kan-on: し (shi).

(830-ik)**IMPORTANT KANJI**

191. ˈJi (自)

(000-it)*INCLUDING TERMS (EXAMPLES)*

👁✉ jiyū {{自由}}, p. 112; shizen {{自然}}, p. 214

(077-jg)*GENERAL MEANING (EXAMPLES)* ✿📖 *prefix* ❶ self-

(089-no)*NOTES AND EXAMPLES* 📖✍ Ji-ˈten-sha (自転車) means bicycle. #Ji-self {自}##

(185-ch)*CHINESE (PINYIN)* ☯📖 **zì, zí**

(211-1)自

(250-hi)じ (hir.)

(325-kr)*KANJI READINGS* 🖊🗣 Go-on: じ (ji). Kan-on: し (shi).

(833-kan)**KANJI**

192. Ji-ˈon

(000-it)*INCLUDING TERMS (EXAMPLES)*

👁✉ jiongamae {{慈恩構え}}, p. 111

(011-k1)*KANJI 1* ☛ Ji-mercy {慈}, p. 109

(012-k2)*KANJI 2* ☛ On-obligation {恩}, p. 190

(060-kg)*KATA GROUP* 形形形 **AKA** Mercy-compassion, Love and Goodness, Temple Sound, Temple Bells **Style** Shōrei (昭霊) **Number of Kata** Three

(089-no)*NOTES AND EXAMPLES* 📖✎ The Kata included in this group are Ji'in, Jion, and Jitte

(095-3t)*THE THREE TEACHINGS* **3** The Kata may be named after[47] a Japanese monk and Martial Arts teacher named Jion (1351–1409), after a Chinese Buddhist Temple called *ci'ēn* (慈恩寺), or after a Buddhist saint[48]. Since Jion is a name, the Kata should be translated plainly as Jion.

(800-tag)*TAGS* 💻 #ji-on, ji on

(185-ch)*CHINESE (PINYIN)* 🌐📖 *ci'ēn*

(211-1)慈恩

#jion {{慈恩}}##

(061-ka)*KATA* 形 **AKA** Mercy-compassion, Love and Goodness,

Temple sound, Temple bells **Style** Shōrei (昭霊) **Group** Jion (慈恩) **Enbusen** ˈKō-ji-ˈgata (工字形) - 工 Shape **Number of movements (approximately)** 47

(062-mk)*FUNAKOSHI MAIN BOOK - KATA*

📖**MK 1922 original** 7 (list beginning), 51 (list Enbusen), 266 **1925 Ishida** 20 (list beginning), 58 (list Enbusen), 279 **1925 Teramoto** 26 (list beginning), 52 (list Enbusen), 168 **1935 Suzuki-Johnston** 9 (list styles), 34 (list names), 40 (list Enbusen), 137 **1935 Ohshima** 8-9 (list styles), 36-37 (list names), 190

(077-jg)*GENERAL MEANING (EXAMPLES)* ✿📖 *noun* ❶ Deep compassion

(250-hi)じおん (hir.) (256-kat)ジオン (kat.)

(466-cha)*CHARACTERISTICS* ⓘ A Two-character, which consists of 2 Chinese Logograms and 0 Hiˈra-ga-ˈna Characters.

(838-su)**SUPER-TERM**

193.Ji-ˈon ˈGamae

💣 Not to be confused with Ji-ˈaino Kamaˈe (慈愛の構え)

(015-w1)*WORD 1* $\frac{W}{W}$ ☞ jion {{慈恩}}, p. 110

(016-w2)*WORD 2* $\frac{W}{W}$ ☞ kamae {{構え}}, p. 123

(070-kt)*KARATE MEANING* ✋📖 *noun phrase* ① The Jion Kata Group's (Ji'in, Jion, and Jitte) Standby Position.

(466-cha)*CHARACTERISTICS* ⓘ A Four-character, which consists of 3 Chinese Logograms and 1 Hiˈra-ga-ˈna Characters.

#jiongamae {{慈恩構え}}##

Masters 8 - Jiongamae by Bamgboye Sensei
List of Sensei Demonstrations next to Values, p. 10
Bobby Bamgboye of Nigeria WSKF demonstrates Jion-gamae. Photographer: Joel Ibanga.

(211-1)**慈恩構え**

(250-hi)**じおんがまえ** (hir.)

(800-tag)*TAGS* 💻 #jion-gamae, jion gamae, #jionkamae

194.Jit-ˈte

(011-k1)*KANJI 1* ☞ Jū-ten {十}, p. 114

(012-k2)*KANJI 2* ☞ Te-hand {手}, p. 234

(061-ka)*KATA* 形 **AKA** Jutte, Ten Hands **Style** Once Shōrei (昭霊) (1922), later Shōrin (少林) (1925), and then Shōrei (昭霊) again (1935, 1958) **Group** Jion (慈恩) **Enbusen** ˈJū-ji-ˈgata (十字形) - 十 Shape **Number of movements (approximately)** 24

(089-no)*NOTES AND EXAMPLES* 📖🖌 In our opinion, the Kata is called Ten Hands due to the ten hand-strikes up to the first Kiai; some of them come in pairs. Ten Hands and ten hands only - after the first Kiai the palm does not strike anymore. One must wonder, then, what does the open-palm sequence that follows the Ya-ma-zuki mean. And the obvious answer is dealing with a rod. In the rest of the strikes, we use the elbow area. Pay attention to the fact, that there are no Shutō-uke in this Kata.

#jitte {{十手}}##

(062-mk)*FUNAKOSHI MAIN BOOK - KATA*

📚**MK 1922 original** 7 (list beginning), 51 (list Enbusen) (mistakenly

Ji-ˈyū - Ji-ˈyū Ip-ˈpon ˈKumi-te

appears twice), 261 **1925 Ishida** 20 (list beginning), 58 (list Enbusen), 272 **1925 Teramoto** 26 (list beginning), 52 (list Enbusen), 164 **1935 Suzuki-Johnston** 9 (list styles), 33 (list names), 40 (list Enbusen), 120 **1935 Ohshima** 8-9 (list styles), 35-36 (list names), 157.

(077-jg)*GENERAL MEANING (EXAMPLES)* ☼📖 *noun* ❶ Short truncheon (実手)

(185-ch)*CHINESE (PINYIN)* ☯📖 ***shí shǒu***

(211-1)十手 (250-hi)じって (hir.) (256-kat)ジッテ (kat.) (275-tō)じ⬚って⬚ [jìtté]

(466-cha)*CHARACTERISTICS* ⓘ A Two-character, which consists of 2 Chinese Logograms and 0 Hiˈra-ga-ˈna Characters.

(800-tag)*TAGS* 💻 #jit-te, jit te, #jite

(838-su)**SUPER-TERM**

195.Ji-ˈyū

(000-it)*INCLUDING TERMS (EXAMPLES)*

👁✉ jiyūipponkumite {{自由一本組手}}, p. 113; jiyūkumite {{自由組手}}, p. 113

(011-k1)*KANJI 1* ☞ Ji-self {自}, p. 109

(077-jg)*GENERAL MEANING (EXAMPLES)* ☼📖 *noun* ❶ Freedom

(089-no)*NOTES AND EXAMPLES* 📖✎ Ji-ˈyū-gaˈta (自由形) means free style.

(185-ch)*CHINESE (PINYIN)* ☯📖 ***zìyóu***

(211-1)自由

#jiyū {{自由}}##

(211-al)*ALTERNATIVES OR SEE ALSO*

🖌🖌 自繇

(250-hi)じゆう (hir.)

(275-tō)じ⬚ゆ⬚う [jìyúˈù]

(280-po)pol:DZIJUU

(466-cha)*CHARACTERISTICS* ⓘ A Two-character, which consists of 2 Chinese Logograms and 0 Hiˈra-ga-ˈna Characters.

(800-tag)*TAGS* 💻 #jiyu, ji-yu, ji yu, #ju, #jiu, jiyuu, jiyuh

196.Ji-ˈyū Ip-ˈpon ˈKumi-te

(015-w1)*WORD 1* ᴟᴟ ☞ jiyū {{自由}}, p. 112

(016-w2)*WORD 2* ᴟᴟ ☞ ipponkumite {{一本組手}}, p. 106

(070-kt)*KARATE MEANING* ✋📖 AKA Jiyū-ippon Gumite *noun phrase* ① Semi-free One Attack Sparring ②

Free One-time Sparring, Freestyle One-step Sparring.

(211-1) 自由一本組手

(466-cha) *CHARACTERISTICS* ⓘ A Six-character, which consists of 6 Chinese Logograms and 0 Hiˈra-ga-ˈna Characters.

#jiyūipponkumite {{自由一本組手}}##

(250-hi) じゆういっぽんくみて (hir.)

(481-hp) **H⊃p** ⌂ Due to the ˈRen-daku laws, the unvoiced consonant /H/ may get a Han-dak[u]-ten (゜) and become ~/p/ as a suffix. Example ↳ ˈHon (ほん) turns into ˈIp-pon (いっぽん).

(800-tag) *TAGS* 💻 #jiyuipponkumite, jiyu-ippon-kumite, jiyu ippon kumite, #juipponkumite, #juiponkumite, #jiyuippongumite

(838-su)SUPER-TERM

197.Ji-ˈyū-ˈkumi-te

(015-w1) *WORD 1* 🆆 ☞ jiyū {{自由}}, p. 112

(016-w2) *WORD 2* 🆆 ☞ kumite {{組手}}, p. 157

(070-kt) *KARATE MEANING* 🖐 📖 AKA Jiyū Gumite *noun* ① Free Sparring, Freestyle Sparring

(133-sy) *SYNONYMS* 👁= randori {{乱取り}}, p. 195

(211-1) 自由組手

#jiyūkumite {{自由組手}}##

(250-hi) じゆうくみて (hir.)

(280-po) pol:DZIJUUKUMITE

(466-cha) *CHARACTERISTICS* ⓘ A Four-character, which consists of 4 Chinese Logograms and 0 Hiˈra-ga-ˈna Characters.

(800-tag) *TAGS* 💻 #jiyukumite, jiyu-kumite, jiyu kumite, #jukumite, #ji-yugumite, #ju kumite, #kukumite

(838-su)SUPER-TERM

198.ˈJō (Ue)

(001-REF-rom) ˈJō ☞ Ue-top {上}, p. 262

(002-REF-hi) じょう ☞ うえ

#Jō (Ue)##

(275-tō) じょ ― [jóˈò]

(800-tag) *TAGS* 💻 #jo, joo, jou, joh

199.ˈJō-dan

(011-k1) *KANJI 1* ☞ Ue-top {上}, p. 262

(012-k2) *KANJI 2* ☞ Dan-level {段}, p.

56

(070-kt)*KARATE MEANING* ✋📖 *noun*

① Upper body, Upper Level, Upper Section, High Section ② Philtrum.

(185-ch)*CHINESE (PINYIN)* ☯📖 ***shàng-duàn***

(211-1)上段

#jōdan {{上段}}##

(250-hi)じょうだん (hir.)

(466-cha)*CHARACTERISTICS* ⓘ A Two-character, which consists of 2 Chinese Logograms and 0 Hiˈra-ga-ˈna Characters.

(800-tag)*TAGS* 🖥 #jodan, jo-dan, jo dan, joodan, johdan, joudan

(838-su)**SUPER-TERM**

200. ˈJō-wan

(011-k1)*KANJI 1* ☞ Ue-top {上}, p. 262

(012-k2)*KANJI 2* ☞ Ude-arm {腕}, p. 260

(077-jg)*GENERAL MEANING (EXAMPLES)* ✿📖 *noun* ❶ Upper arm, brachium, the proximal portion of the upper limb. Extends from the shoulder to the elbow.

(185-ch)*CHINESE (PINYIN)* ☯📖 ***shàngwàn***

#jōwan {{上腕}}##

(211-1)上腕

(250-hi)じょうわん (hir.)

(275-tō)じょ 一わん [jòówáń]

(466-cha)*CHARACTERISTICS* ⓘ A Two-character, which consists of 2 Chinese Logograms and 0 Hiˈra-ga-ˈna Characters.

(800-tag)*TAGS* 🖥 #jowan, jo-wan, jo wan

201. ˈJu (jiyū)

(001-REF-rom)ˈJu ☞ jiyū {{自由}}, p. 112

#ju (jiyū)##

202. ˈJū (十)

(000-it)*INCLUDING TERMS (EXAMPLES)* 👁✉ jitte {{十手}}, p. 111; jūdan {{十段}}, p. 115; jūjigata {{十字形}}, p. 115; jūjiuke {{十字受け}}, p. 116

(077-jg)*GENERAL MEANING (EXAMPLES)* ✿📖 *noun* ❶ Ten

(185-ch)*CHINESE (PINYIN)* ☯📖 ***shí***

(211-1)十

#Jū-ten {十}##

(211-al)*ALTERNATIVES OR SEE ALSO* ✎✎ 拾

(250-hi)じゅう (hir.)

(275-tō)じゅ う [júˑù]

(280-po)pol:DZIUU

(800-tag)*TAGS* 🖥 #ju 1, juu, juh, #10

(833-kan)**KANJI**

(838-su)**SUPER-TERM**

203. ˈJū-dan

(011-k1)*KANJI 1* ☞ Jū-ten {十}, p. 114

(012-k2)*KANJI 2* ☞ Dan-level {段}, p. 56

(070-kt)*KARATE MEANING* ✋📖 *noun*

① Tenth Level ② Tenth dan, tenth degree black belt ③ Ten.

(077-jg)*GENERAL MEANING (EXAMPLES)* ✿📖 *noun* ❶ Tenth grade, level ten, tenth rank, tenth degree. #jūdan {{十段}}##

(211-1)十段

(250-hi)じゅうだん (hir.)

(466-cha)*CHARACTERISTICS* ① A Two-character, which consists of 2 Chinese Logograms and 0 Hiˈra-ga-ˈna Characters.

(800-tag)*TAGS* 🖥 #judan, ju-dan, ju dan

204. ˈJū-ji-ˈgata

(011-k1)*KANJI 1* ☞ Jū-ten {十}, p. 114

(012-k2)*KANJI 2* ☞ Ji-character {字}, p. 109

(013-k3)*KANJI 3* ☞ Kata-shape {形}, p. 134

(070-kt)*KARATE MEANING* ✋📖 *noun*

① Cross Pattern, Cross Shape, Cruciform, Character-ten Pattern, 十 Pattern, 十 Character Figure, Plus Shape, + Shape.

(134-re)*RELATED TERMS* 👁∞ enbusen {{演武線}}, p. 61

(211-1)十字形 (211-al)*ALTERNATIVES OR SEE ALSO* ✐✐ 十字型

(800-tag)*TAGS* 🖥 #jujigata, juji-gata, juji gata
#jūjigata {{十字形}}##

(068-me)*FUNAKOSHI MAIN BOOK - ENBUSEN* 📕**MEN** 1922 **original** 50-51 **1925 Ishida** 58 **1925 Teramoto** 52 **1935 Suzuki-Johnston** 40 **1935 Ohshima** 41

(250-hi)じゅうじがた (hir.)

(466-cha)*CHARACTERISTICS* ① A Three-character, which consists of 3 Chinese Logograms and 0 Hiˈra-ga-ˈna Characters.

(482-kg)**Kↄg** 🔔 Due to the ˈRendaku laws, the unvoiced consonant /K/ may get a Dak[u]-ˈten (˚) and

ˈJū-ji-uˈke - Juˈtsu (術)

become ~/g/ as a suffix. Example ✎ Keˈri (けり) turns into Maˈe-geˈri (まえげり).

205. ˈJū-ji-uˈke

(011-k1) *KANJI 1* ☛ Jū-ten {十}, p. 114

(012-k2) *KANJI 2* ☛ Ji-character {字}, p. 109

(015-w1) *WORD 1* ᵂᵂ ☛ uke {{受け}}, p. 262

(070-kt) *KARATE MEANING* ✋📖 AKA Kosa Uke *noun* ① Cross-arm Block, Cross Block, X Block

(466-cha) *CHARACTERISTICS* ⓘ A Four-character, which consists of 3 Chinese Logograms and 1 Hiˈra-ga-ˈna Characters.

(211-1)十字受け

(250-hi) じゅうじうけ (hir.)

#jūjiuke {{十字受け}}##

Masters 9 - Jūjiuke by Bamgboye Sensei
List of Sensei Demonstrations next to Values, p. 10
List of large photos - p. 10

Bobby Bamgboye of Nigeria WSKF demonstrates Jūji-uke. Photographer: Joel Ibanga.

(256-kat)ジュウジウケ (kat.)

(800-tag) *TAGS* 💻 #jujiuke, juji-uke, juji uke

206. Juˈtsu (術)

(000-it) *INCLUDING TERMS (EXAMPLES)* 👁✉ bujutsu {{武術}}, p. 47

(077-jg) *GENERAL MEANING (EXAMPLES)* ☼📖 *noun* ❶ Art, technique, skill ❷ Trick, magic ❸ Means, resources.

(089-no) *NOTES AND EXAMPLES* 📖✎ Bi-ˈjuts[u]-kan (美術館) means museum.

(136-se) *SEE ALSO* 👁✚ Waza-technique {技}, p. 267

(185-ch) *CHINESE (PINYIN)* 👁📖 *shù* - as in *wǔshù* (武術)

(211-1)術 (250-hi) じゅつ (hir.)

(256-kat)ジュツ (kat.)

#Jutsu-art {術}##

(275-tō) じゅ[つ] [jùtsú˧]

(276-tō2) [じゅ]つ [jú˧tsù]

(280-po) pol:DZIUCY

(313-ka)*KANJI* ✎ The Phono-semantic Compound Logogram Juˈtsu-art (術). (313k-cn)**Components** ⬚ [semantic 行 | phonetic 朮]. (313k-ra)**Radical** ⚘ 行 go. (313k-cs)**Composition** ⚔ Outside: 行, center: 朮. (313k-re)**Readings (examples)** ✊ Go-on: じゅつ (jutsu).

(800-tag)*TAGS* 💻 #jitsu, #yutsu

(830-ik)**IMPORTANT KANJI**

207.Jūt-ˈte (jitte)

(001-REF-rom)Jūt-ˈte ☞ jitte {{十手}}, p. 111

#jūtte (jitte)##

(800-tag)*TAGS* 💻 #jutte, jut-te, jut te, #jute

208.K[u]ˈtsu (Kagamu)

(001-REF-rom)K[u]ˈtsu ☞ Kagamu-to stoop {屈}, p. 120

#Kutsu (Kagamu)##

(256-kat)クツ (kat.)

(280-po)pol:KCY

209.Kaˈchi

(000-it)*INCLUDING TERMS (EXAMPLES)*

👁✉ akanokachi {{赤の勝ち}}, p. 32

(011-k1)*KANJI* ɪ ☛ Katsu-to win {勝}, p. 138

(077-jg)*GENERAL MEANING (EXAMPLES)* ☼📖 *noun* ❶ Victory, win

(211-1)勝ち

#kachi {{勝ち}}##

(250-hi)かち (hir.)

(275-tō)か ち [kàchíˑ]

(466-cha)*CHARACTERISTICS* ⓘ A Two-character, which consists of 1 Chinese Logograms and 1 Hiˈra-ga-ˈna Characters.

210.ˈKaeru (返)

(000-it)*INCLUDING TERMS (EXAMPLES)*

👁✉ kaesu {{返す}}, p. 119; kaeshi {{返し}}, p. 118; kaette {{返って}}, p. 119

(077-jg)*GENERAL MEANING (EXAMPLES)* ☼📖 *verb (intransitive)* ❶ To return[49], to come back, to go back. ❷ To reverse, to turn over (to move in the opposite direction or to interchange front and back).

(185-ch)*CHINESE (PINYIN)* ☯📖 *fǎn*

(211-1)返

(211-ka+hi)返る

(211-ka+hiAlt)反る

(250-hi)かえる (hir.)

(256-kat)カエル (kat.)

ˈKaeshi - ˈkaesu

(275-tō) か え る [káˈèrù]

(280-po)pol:KAERY

(800-tag)TAGS 🖥 #return

#Kaeru-to return {返}##

(600-vt)Form	Godan Intransitive ~ru (v. su)
Terminal	káˈèrù
Plain ~te Request	káˈèttè
Polite ~te Request	káˈèttè kudaˈsai
Plain Imperative	káˈèrè
Stem	ˈkaeri
Polite Imperative	kaˈeri naˈsai
Formal	kàérímáˈs[ù]

See

List of Commands, p. 25

(325-kr)KANJI READINGS 🖋👤 Go-on: ほん (hon). Kan-on: はん (han). Kun: かえす (kaesu, 返す); かえる (kaeru, 返る).

(610-In-Tr)VERB PAIR 👁◑ The Intransitive Verb is Kaeru-to return {返}, p. 118. The Transitive verb is kaesu {{返す}}, p. 119.

(811-vpIn)**VERB PAIR – INTRANSITIVE PART**

(830-ik)**IMPORTANT KANJI**

211. ˈKaeshi

(000-it)INCLUDING TERMS (EXAMPLES)

👁✉ tsubamegaeshi {{燕返し}}, p. 256

(011-k1)KANJI 1 ☞ Kaeru-to return {返}, p. 118

(019-ste)STEM FORM OF ❗ ☞ kaesu {{返す}}, p. 119

(077-jg)GENERAL MEANING (EXAMPLES) ☼📖 noun ❶ Return, reversal.

#kaeshi {{返し}}##

(211-1)返し

(211-al)ALTERNATIVES OR SEE ALSO

🖋🖊 反し

(250-hi)かえし (hir.)

(466-cha)CHARACTERISTICS ⓘ A Two-character, which consists of 1 Chinese Logograms and 1 Hiˈra-ga-ˈna Characters.

212. ˈkaesu

(011-k1)KANJI 1 ☞ Kaeru-to return {返}, p. 118

(077-jg)GENERAL MEANING (EXAMPLES) ☼📖 verb (transitive) ❶ To return something, to put back, to restore.

(135-ge)GERUND 👁⏩ kaeshi {{返し}}, p. 118

(211-1)返す (212-2)反す

(250-hi)かえす (hir.)

(256-kat)**カエス** (kat.)

(275-tō)か̲えす [ká⁺èsù]

(280-po)pol:KAESY

(610-In-Tr)*VERB PAIR* 👁◑ The Intransitive Verb is Kaeru-to return {返}, p. 118. The Transitive verb is kaesu {{返す}}, p. 119.

#kaesu {{返す}}##

(600-vt)**Form**	**Godan Transitive ~su**
Terminal	ká⁺èsù
Plain ~te Request	ká⁺èsh[ì]tè
Polite ~te Request	ká⁺èsh[ì]tè kudaˈsai
Plain Imperative	ká⁺èsè
Stem	ˈkaeshi
Polite Imperative	kaˈeshi naˈsai
Formal	kàéshímá⁺s[ù]

See

List of Commands, p. 25

(466-cha)*CHARACTERISTICS* ⓘ A Two-character, which consists of 1 Chinese Logograms and 1 Hiˈra-ga-ˈna Characters.

(810-vpTr)**VERB PAIR – TRANSITIVE PART**

213. ˈKaette

♦※ Not to be confused with kaiten {{回転}}

(018-te)*TE FORM OF* ❗ ☞ Kaeru-to return {返}, p. 118

(070-kt)*KARATE MEANING* ✋📖 AKA Kaete (返て) *verb (imperative mood)* ① Turn around! turn! Pivot! Assume Opposite Direction!

See

List of Commands, p. 25

(133-sy)*SYNONYMS* 👁= mawatte {{回って}}, p. 168

(466-cha)*CHARACTERISTICS* ⓘ A Three-character, which consists of 1 Chinese Logograms and 2 Hiˈra-ga-ˈna Characters.

(211-1)**返って**

(250-hi)**かえって** (hir.)

#kaette {{返って}}##

Masters 10 - Kaette by Le Bas Sensei
List of Sensei Demonstrations next to Values, p. 10
Sophie Le Bas of France Shōtōkan demonstrates Kaette. Photographer: Patrick Schoeffer.

(610-In-Tr)*VERB PAIR* 👁◑ The Intransitive Verb is Kaeru-to return {返},

p. 118. The Transitive verb is kaesu {{返す}}, p. 119.

(800-tag)*TAGS* ⌨ #kaete (かえて)

(838-su)**SUPER-TERM**

214.Kaˈgamu (屈)

(000-it)*INCLUDING TERMS (EXAMPLES)*

👁 ✉ kōkutsu {{後屈}}, p. 150; zenkutsu {{前屈}}, p. 284

(077-jg)*GENERAL MEANING (EXAMPLES)* ⚙ 📖 *verb* ❶ To stoop, to lean over, to bend down ❷ To crouch.

(185-ch)*CHINESE (PINYIN)* 🌓📖 *qū*

(203-hi)⏳⊙ (250-hi)かがむ (hir.)

(211-1)屈

(211-al)*ALTERNATIVES OR SEE ALSO*

✐ 屧, 屈, 㲍, 屈, 㞎

(211-ka+hi)屈む

(275-tō)か がむ [kàgámú]

(280-po)pol:KAGAMY

(830-ik)**IMPORTANT KANJI**

#Kagamu-to stoop {屈}##

(313-ka)*KANJI* ✐ The Compound Ideogram Kaˈgamu-to stoop (屈). (313-cn)**Components** ⛲ [尸 | 出] (313-ra)**Radical** ✛ 尸 corpse (313-cs)**Composition** ✗ Top-left: 尸, bot-tom-right: 出 (313k-re)**Readings (examples)** ✊ Go-on: くち (kuchi); ごち (gochi). Kan-on: くつ (kutsu). Kun: かがむ (kagamu, 屈む).

(705-gv)*GODAN VERB* 🏍⑤ **Terminal Form** {u* ✺ but not i*-ru or e*-ru} Kaˈgamu (屈む), which means to bend down. **Polite Form** {i*-masu} Kaˈgamimas[u] (屈みます).

215.Kaˈgi·zuˈki

(015-w1)*WORD 1* ☝ tsuki {{突き}}, p. 253

(040-ul)*UPPER LIMB STRIKE & ANATOMY*

手 **AKA** Kaku-zuki (角突), Mawashi-zuki, Hook Thrust, Hook Punch, Hook Strike, Square Punch, ˈZen-wan ˈMizu-ˈnagare Kaˈmae (前腕水流れ構え), **Category** Strike, Closed-fist.

(089-no)*NOTES AND EXAMPLES* 📖✍ Considered a close-range technique; hence common in Tekki Kata Group.

(466-cha)*CHARACTERISTICS* ① A Three-character, which consists of 2 Chinese Logograms and 1 Hiˈra-gaˈna Characters.

(211-1)鈎突き (212-2)鈎突

(250-hi)かぎづき (hir.)

#kagizuki {{鉤突き}}##

Masters 11 - Kagizuki by Le Bas Sensei
List of Sensei Demonstrations next to Values, p. 10

Sophie Le Bas of France Shōtōkan demonstrates Kagi-zuki (Miˈzu-naˈgare ˈKamae). Photographer: Patrick Schoeffer.

(280-po)pol:KAGIDZYKI

(484-tsz)**Ts↺z** 🔔 Due to the ˈRendaku laws, the unvoiced consonant /Ts/ may get a Dak[u]-ˈten (゛) and become ~/z/ as a suffix. Example ↯ Ts[u]ˈki 2 (つき) turns into Oˈi-z[u]ˈki (おいづき).

(800-tag)*TAGS* 💻 #kagi-zuki, kagi zuki, #kakuzuki

216. ˈKai (Mawaru)

(001-REF-rom)ˈKai ☞ Mawaru-to turn {回}, p. 165

#Kai (Mawaru)##

(250-hi)かい (hir.)

217. ˈKaite

ˈKai (Mawaru) - ˈKai-ten

(001-REF-rom)ˈKaite ☞ kaette {{返って}}, p. 119

(009-REF-kan)回て ☞ 返って

#kaite##

(002-REF-hi)かいて ☞ かえって

(800-tag)*TAGS* 💻 #kaitte

218. ˈKai-ten

💣※ Not to be confused with kaette {{返って}}

💣※ Not to be confused with ˈKai-ten (回天) - *huítiān*

(011-k1)*KANJI 1* ☛ Mawaru-to turn {回}, p. 165

(012-k2)*KANJI 2* ☛ Korogaru-to rotate {転}, p. 153

(077-jg)*GENERAL MEANING (EXAMPLES)* ☼📖 *noun* ❶ Rotation [50], turning.

(211-1)回転

#kaiten {{回転}}##

(089-no)*NOTES AND EXAMPLES* 📖✎ Ji-ten-sha (自転車) means bicycle.

(211-al)*ALTERNATIVES OR SEE ALSO* ✐✐ 廻転 (250-hi)かいてん (hir.)

(275-tō)かいてん [kàitéń]

(466-cha)*CHARACTERISTICS* ⓘ A Two-character, which consists of 2 Chi-

nese Logograms and 0 Hiˈra-ga-ˈna Characters.

(800-tag)*TAGS* 🖥 #kai-ten, kai ten

219.Kaˈkato (踵)

(000-it)*INCLUDING TERMS (EXAMPLES)*

👁✉ kakatogeri {{踵蹴り, p. 123; kakatootoshigeri {{踵落とし蹴り}}, p. 122

(077-jg)*GENERAL MEANING (EXAMPLES)* ⚙📖 *noun* ❶ Heel

(185-ch)*CHINESE (PINYIN)* 👁📖 ***zhǒng***

(203-hi)⏳☉ (250-hi)かかと (hir.)

(302-kn)*KANJI NOTES* ✒✎ Contains 16 strokes. This Logogram is outside the list of Jō-yō ˈKan-ji, belonging to the Hyō-gai ˈKan-ji.
#Kakato-heel {踵}##

(211-1)踵

(313-ka)*KANJI* ✎ The Phono-semantic Compound Logogram Kaˈkato-heel (踵). (313k-cn)**Components** 🗂 [semantic 足 | phonetic 重] (313k-ra)**Radical** ✚ 足 ⻊ foot (313k-cs)**Composition** ✗ Left: ⻊ , right: 重 (313k-re)**Readings (examples)** 🎤 Go-on: しゅ (shu). Kan-on: しょう

(shō). Kun: かかと (kakato, 踵); くびす (kubisu, 踵).

(885-tag)*TAGS* 🖥 #heel

(830-ik)**IMPORTANT KANJI**

220.Kaˈkato ˈOtosh[i] Geˈri

(011-k1)*KANJI 1* ☛ Kakato-heel {踵}, p. 122

(012-k2)*KANJI 2* ☛ Otosu-to drop {落}, p. 193

(013-k3)*KANJI 3* ☛ keri {{蹴り}}, p. 140

(070-kt)*KARATE MEANING* 🖐📖 AKA Otoshi Kakato Geri, Kakato Geri *noun phrase* ① Heel-drop kick , Axe Kick, Heel Axe Kick, Dropping Heel Kick, Falling Heel Kick, Ax Kick.

(211-1)踵落とし蹴り (212-2)かかと落とし蹴り (213-3)踵落し蹴り
#kakatootoshigeri {{踵落とし蹴り}}##

(089-no)*NOTES AND EXAMPLES* 📖✎ The target – usually the head or the shoulder – is hit from above.

(136-se)*SEE ALSO* 👁➕ Kakato-geri (250-hi)かかとおとしげり (hir.)

(466-cha)*CHARACTERISTICS* ⓘ A Six-character, which consists of 3 Chinese Logograms and 3 Hiˈra-ga-ˈna Characters.

(800-tag)*TAGS* 🖥 #kakato-otoshi-geri, kakato otoshi geri, #kakatootoshikeri

221. Kaˈkato-geˈri

(011-k1)*KANJI 1* ☞ Kakato-heel {踵}, p. 122

(012-k2)*KANJI 2* ☞ keri {{蹴り}}, p. 140

(070-kt)*KARATE MEANING* 🖐📖 *noun*
① Heel Kick ② Heel Kick to the back ③ Heel Kick to the jaw.

(136-se)*SEE ALSO* 👁✚ Kakato-otoshi-geri

#kakatogeri {{踵蹴り}}##

(211-1)踵蹴り (250-hi)かかとげり (hir.)

(466-cha)*CHARACTERISTICS* ⓘ A Three-character, which consists of 2 Chinese Logograms and 1 Hiˈra-ga-ˈna Characters.

(800-tag)*TAGS* 🖥 kakato-geri, kakato geri, #kakatokeri

222. Kaˈmae

💣✳ Not to be confused with kamaete {{構えて}}, p. 125

👁✉ bassaigamae {{抜塞構え}}, p. 43; jiongamae {{慈恩構え}}, p. 111; kankūgamae {{観空構え}}, p. 128

(011-k1)*KANJI 1* ☞ Kamaeru-to prepare {構}, p. 124

(019-ste)*STEM FORM OF* ❗ ☞ Kamaeru-to prepare {構}, p. 124

(070-kt)*KARATE MEANING* 🖐📖 *noun*
① Standby, readiness, preparedness, state of being prepared in body (身構え) and in mind (心構え)[51].

(466-cha)*CHARACTERISTICS* ⓘ A Two-character, which consists of 1 Chinese Logograms and 1 Hiˈra-ga-ˈna Characters.

(211-1)構え

(250-hi)かまえ (hir.)

(838-su)**SUPER-TERM**

#kamae {{構え}}##

Masters 12 - Kamae by Le Bas Sensei

Sophie Le Bas of France Shōtōkan demonstrates Kamae. Photographer: Patrick Schoeffer.

(077-jg)*GENERAL MEANING (EXAMPLES)* ✿📖 *noun* ❶ Posture (of the entire body), pose ❷ Stance ❸ Structure, construction ❹ Readiness, preparedness ❺ Determination.

(134-gr-re)*GROUP* 👁(ᵔᵔ) The following terms are related: hajime {{始め}}, p. 81; kamae {{構え}}, p. 123; kamaete {{構えて}}, p. 125; naore {{直れ}}, p. 180; yame {{止め}}, p. 271; yasume {{休め}}, p. 274; yōi {{用意}}, p. 277

223.Kaˈmaeru (構)

(000-it)*INCLUDING TERMS (EXAMPLES)* 👁✉ kamae {{構え}}, p. 123; kamaete {{構えて}}, p. 125

(077-jg)*GENERAL MEANING (EXAMPLES)* ✿📖 *verb (transitive)* ❶ To prepare.

(135-ge)*GERUND* 👁▶▶ kamae {{構え}}, p. 123

(185-ch)*CHINESE (PINYIN)* ☻📖 *gòu*

(211-1)構

(211-ka+hi)構える

(212-2)搆

(213-3)构

(214-4)遘

(250-hi)かまえる (hir.)

(256-kat)カマエル (kat.)

(275-tō)か まえ る [kàmáéˑrù]

(885-tag)*TAGS* 💻 #prepare

(830-ik)IMPORTANT KANJI

#Kamaeru-to prepare {構}##

(600-vt)Form	Shimo Ichidan Transitive (~eru)
Terminal	kàmáéˑrù
Plain ~te Request	kàmáˑètè
Polite ~te Request	kàmáˑètè kudaˈsai
Plain Imperative	kàmáéˑrò
Stem	kaˈmae
Polite Imperative	kaˈmae naˈsai
Formal	kàmáémáˑs[ù]

See

List of Commands, p. 25

(313-ka)*KANJI* ✎ The Phono-semantic Compound Logogram Kaˈmaeru-to prepare (構). (313k-cn)**Components** ⧉ [semantic 木 | phonetic 冓] (313k-ra)**Radical** ✛ 木 tree (313k-cs)**Composition** ✗ Left: 木, right: 冓 (313k-re)**Readings (examples)** 🖌 Go-on: く (ku). Kan-on: こう (kō).

Kun: かまえる (kamaeru, 構える);
かまえ (kamae, 構え); かまう
(kamau, 構う).

224. Kaˈmaete

💣※ Not to be confused with kamae
{{構え}}, p. 123

(018-te)*TE FORM OF* **!** ☞ Kamaeru-to
prepare {構}, p. 124

(070-kt)*KARATE MEANING* ✋📖 *verb
(imperative mood)* ① Stand ready!,
get ready!, be prepared!, assume
position!, assume stance!, in position!, take a certain posture!, take a
stand!

See

List of Commands, p. 25

(211-1)構えて (250-hi)かまえて (hir.)

(275-tō)か[ま]えて [kàmá⁺ètè]

#kamaete {{構えて}}##

(466-cha)*CHARACTERISTICS* ⓘ A
Three-character, which consists of 1
Chinese Logograms and 2 Hiˈra-ga-
ˈna Characters.

(134-gr-re)*GROUP* 👁👥 The following
terms are related: hajime {{始め}},
p. 81; kamae {{構え}}, p. 123;
kamaete {{構えて}}, p. 125; naore

{{直れ}}, p. 180; yame {{止め}},
p. 271; yasume {{休め}}, p. 274;
yōi {{用意}}, p. 277

(800-tag)*TAGS* 🖥 #kamaite, #kamaette

(838-su)**SUPER-TERM**

225. ˈKan (観)

(000-it)*INCLUDING TERMS (EXAMPLES)*
👁✉ kankū {{観空}}, p. 127

(077-jg)*GENERAL MEANING (EXAM-
PLES)* ☯📖 *noun, noun suffix* ❶
Observation, contemplation, observation meditation, Vipassanā[52], in-
sight ❷ Look, appearance ❸ Out-
look on-, view of- ❹ Sight, specta-
cle

(089-no)*NOTES AND EXAMPLES* 📖✍
ˈMiru [mí⁺rù] (見る, 視る, 観る)
means to see.

(185-ch)*CHINESE (PINYIN)* ☯📖 *guān*
Middle Chinese: *kuan*

(203-hi)⏳☉ (250-hi)かん (hir.)

(211-al)*ALTERNATIVES OR SEE ALSO*
✒✒ 觀, 观, 覌

#Kan-observation {観}##

(211-1)観

(256-kat)カン (kat.)

(302-kn)*KANJI NOTES* 🖊 ✍ Contains 18 strokes.

(313-ka)*KANJI* 🖊 The Phono-semantic Compound Logogram ˈKan-observation (観). (313k-cn)**Components** ⛨ [phonetic 雚 | semantic 見] (313k-ra)**Radical** ✛ 見 see (313k-cs)**Composition** ⚔ Left: 雚, right: 見 (313k-re)**Readings (examples)** 🕯 Go-on: かん (kan) – historically くわん (kwan). Kan-on: かん (kan) – historically くわん (kwan). Kun: みる (miru, 観る); しめす (shimesu).

(830-ik)**IMPORTANT KANJI**

226. ˈKan (館)

(000-it)*INCLUDING TERMS (EXAMPLES)* 👁 ✉ budōkan {{武道館}}, p. 47; shōtōkan {{松濤館}}, p. 221

(077-jg)*GENERAL MEANING (EXAMPLES)* ⚙📖 *noun* ❶ Hall, large building, building, house

(185-ch)*CHINESE (PINYIN)* 👂📖 *guǎn*

(211-1)館

#Kan-hall {館}##

(089-no)*NOTES AND EXAMPLES* 📖✍

To-ˈsho-kan（図書館）means li-brary, and Bi-ˈjuts[u]-kan (美術館) means museum.

(250-hi)かん (hir.)

(275-tō)か ん [káˈǹ]

(833-kan)**KANJI**

(838-su)**SUPER-TERM**

227. Ka-ˈna

(000-it)*INCLUDING TERMS (EXAMPLES)* 👁 ✉ hiragana {{平仮名}}, p. 99; katakana {{片仮名}}, p. 136

(020-re)*RESEARCH* ✍ *noun* ❶ Japanese syllabic script (Hiragana - cursive, Katakana - angular)

(203-hi)⏳ ☉

(250-hi)かな (hir.)

(211-1)仮名

#kana {{仮名}}##

(211-al)*ALTERNATIVES OR SEE ALSO* 🖊🖊 假名, 仮字

(275-tō)か な [kàná]

(466-cha)*CHARACTERISTICS* ⓘ A Two-character, which consists of 0 Chinese Logograms and 2 Hiˈra-ga-ˈna Characters.

(800-tag)*TAGS* 💻 #ka-na, ka na, #gana

228. ˈKan-ji

(012-k2)*KANJI 2* ☛ Ji-character {字}, p. 109

(020-re)*RESEARCH* ✑ *noun* ❶ Chinese Logogram used in the Japanese writing system, Chinese Character, Han Character, Hanzi, Kanji.

(185-ch)*CHINESE (PINYIN)* 🌐📖 *hànzì*

(211-al)*ALTERNATIVES OR SEE ALSO*

✑✑ 汉字

#kanji {{漢字}}##

(211-1)漢字

(250-hi)かんじ (hir.)

(275-tō)かんじ [kànjí]

(466-cha)*CHARACTERISTICS* ⓘ A Two-character, which consists of 2 Chinese Logograms and 0 Hiˈra-ga-ˈna Characters.

(800-tag)*TAGS* 💻 #kan-ji, kan ji

229. ˈKan-kū

(000-it)*INCLUDING TERMS (EXAMPLES)*

👁✉ kankūgamae {{観空構え}}, p. 128; kankūdai {{観空大}}, p. 129

(011-k1)*KANJI 1* ☛ Kan-observation {観}, p. 125

(012-k2)*KANJI 2* ☛ Sora-sky {空}, p. 224

(060-kg)*KATA GROUP* 形形形 **AKA** Kwankū, Kūshankū (公相君), Kūsankū (公相君), Kōshōkun (公相君), Kōsōkun (公相君), Kong Sang Koon (공상군), Gazing Heavenward, Sky-gazing, To Look at the Sky, Viewing the Sky, Contemplating the Sky, Night Fighting Kata. **Style** Shōrin (少林). **Number of Kata** Two.

(095-3t)*THE THREE TEACHINGS* **3**🎎 The Chinese Logogram 公 in the alternative spellings of the Kata, is the Kō in ˈKō-an (公案). Kōan, in a nutshell, is a Zen story.

#kankū {{観空}}##

(062-mk)*FUNAKOSHI MAIN BOOK - KATA*

📘**MK 1922 original** 6 (list beginning), 51 (list Enbusen), 135 **1925 Ishida** 20 (list beginning), 59 (list Enbusen), 137 **1925 Teramoto** 26 (list beginning), 52 (list Enbusen), 92 **1935 Suzuki-Johnston** 9 (list styles), 33 (list names), 40 (list Enbusen), 80 **1935 Ohshima** 8-9 (list styles), 36 (list names), 103.

(211-1)観空 (250-hi)かんくう (hir.)

(280-po)pol:KANKYY

(466-cha)*CHARACTERISTICS* ⓘ A Two-character, which consists of 2 Chinese Logograms and 0 Hiˈra-ga-ˈna Characters.

(089-no)*NOTES AND EXAMPLES* 📖✎ In Ōshima Dōjō - for instance - the name refers specifically to ˈKan-kū-ˈdai (観空大), since the small Kata is not practiced.

(800-tag)*TAGS* 💻 #kanku, kan-kū, kan kū

(838-su)**SUPER-TERM**

230. ˈKan-kū ˈGamae

(015-w1)*WORD 1* ᵂᵂ ☞ kankū {{観空}}, p. 127

(016-w2)*WORD 2* ᵂᵂ ☞ kamae {{構え}}, p. 123

(070-kt)*KARATE MEANING* ✋📖 AKA Heaven Hands *noun phrase* ⓘ ˈKan-kū-ˈdai's (観空大) standby position, ˈKan-kū-ˈdai's ˈYō-I posture.

(482-kg)**K⟳g** 🔔 Due to the ˈRen-daku laws, the unvoiced consonant /K/ may get a Dak[u]-ˈten (゚) and become ~/g/ as a suffix. Example ✍

Keˈri (けり) turns into Maˈe-geˈri (まえげり).

(466-cha)*CHARACTERISTICS* ⓘ A Four-character, which consists of 3 Chinese Logograms and 1 Hiˈra-ga-ˈna Characters.

(800-tag)*TAGS* 💻 #kankugamae, kankū-gamae, kankū gamae, #kankukamae #kankūgamae {{観空構え}}##

Masters 13 – Kankū-gamae by Pavlović Sensei
List of Sensei Demonstrations next to Values, p. 10
Maria Anette Pavlović of Sweden Kase-ha demonstrates Kankū-gamae. Photographer: Denis Sopovic.

(090-te)*TELL YOUR STUDENTS* 📖☺ There is a Taekwondo Ḳata named Gwang-Gae (광개) that begins in a similar way, only there the hands are already up.

(089-no)*NOTES AND EXAMPLES* 📖✎ The hand gesture resembles the palms' position in the O-ˈgasawara-ryū's[53] (小笠原流) bowing[54] while kneeling (座礼).

(211-1)観空構え

(250-hi)かんくうがまえ (hir.)

231. ˈKan-kū-ˈdai

(015-w1)*WORD 1* W ☛ kankū {{観空}}, p. 127

(061-ka)*KATA* 形 **AKA** Kanku Major, Kanku Shodan, Kwankū dai, Kūshankū dai (公相君大), Kūsankū dai (公相君大), Kōshōkun dai (公相君大), Kōsōkun dai (公相君大), Kong Sang Koon (공상군) (Korean), Gazing Heavenward big, Sky-gazing big, To Look at the Sky big, Viewing the Sky big, Contemplating the Sky big **Style** Shōrin (少林) **Group** ˈKan-kū (観空) **Enbusen** Do-ˈji-gaˈta (土字形) - 土 Shape **Number of movements (approximately)** Once 60 (1922, 1925), later 65 (1935, 1958)

(089-no)*NOTES AND EXAMPLES* 📖✍ In Ōshima Dōjō - for instance - the Kata is called simply ˈKan-kū, since the small Kata is not practiced #kankūdai {{観空大}}##

ˈKan-kū-ˈdai - ˈKan-setsu-geˈri

(013-k3)*KANJI 3* ☛ Dai-big {大}, p. 56

(062-mk)*FUNAKOSHI MAIN BOOK - KATA*

📖**MK 1922 original** 6 (list beginning), 51 (list Enbusen), 135 **1925 Ishida** 20 (list beginning), 59 (list Enbusen), 137 **1925 Teramoto** 26 (list beginning), 52 (list Enbusen), 92 **1935 Suzuki-Johnston** 9 (list styles), 33 (list names), 40 (list Enbusen), 80 **1935 Ohshima** 8-9 (list styles), 36 (list names), 103

(211-1)観空大

(250-hi)かんくうだい (hir.)

(256-kat)カンクウダイ (kat.)

(466-cha)*CHARACTERISTICS* ① A Three-character, which consists of 3 Chinese Logograms and 0 Hiˈra-gaˈna Characters.

(800-tag)*TAGS* 💻 #kankudai, kankū-dai, kankū dai

(838-su)**SUPER-TERM**

232. ˈKan-setsu-geˈri

(016-w2)*WORD 2* W ☛ keri {{蹴り}}, p. 140

(070-kt)*KARATE MEANING* ✋📖 *noun* ① Knee Joint Kick, Joint Kick, Dislocation Kick, low side kick to the knee, Stomping Joint Kick.

(134-re)*RELATED TERMS* 👁∞ fumikomi {{踏み込み}}, p. 66, fumikiri {{踏み切り}}, p. 65

#kansetsugeri {{関節蹴り}}##

(211-1)関節蹴り

(250-hi)かんせつげり (hir.)

(466-cha)*CHARACTERISTICS* ⓘ A Four-character, which consists of 3 Chinese Logograms and 1 Hiˈra-ga-ˈna Characters.

(800-tag)*TAGS* 🖳 #kansetsu-geri, kansetsu geri, #kanzetsugeri, #kansetzugeri, #kansetsukeri, #kansezugeri

233. Kaˈra (Sora)

(001-REF-rom)Kaˈra ☞ Sora-sky {空}, p. 224

#Kara (Sora)##

(250-hi)から (hir.) (275-tō)か ら [kàráˈ]

234. ˈKara (唐)

(000-it)*INCLUDING TERMS (EXAMPLES)* 👁✉ karate {{空手}}, p. 131 (alternative spelling)

(077-jg)*GENERAL MEANING (EXAMPLES)* ☼📖 *noun* ❶ The Táng Dynasty ❷ China.

(185-ch)*CHINESE (PINYIN)* ☯📖 ***tang***

(211-1)唐

#Kara-china {唐}##

(211-al)*ALTERNATIVES OR SEE ALSO* ✎✎ 漢, 韓, 鬺, 獛, 獤

(250-hi)から (hir.) (275-tō)か ら [káˈrà]

(325-kr)*KANJI READINGS* ✎🗣 Go-on: どう (dō). Kan-on: とう (tō) – as in Tō-de (唐手). Kun: から (ˈkara, 唐).

(833-kan)**KANJI**

235. Kaˈrada (Tai)

(001-REF-rom)Kaˈrada ☞ Tai-body {体}, p. 228

(250-hi)からだ (hir.)

#Karada (Tai)##

(275-tō)か らだ [kàrádá]

236. Kaˈra-te

💣※ This term has alternative spellings, using different Kanji.

(000-it)*INCLUDING TERMS (EXAMPLES)* 👁✉ karategi {{空手着}}, p. 131; karatedō {{空手道}}, p. 132; karateka {{空手家}}, p. 132

(011-k1-s1)*KANJI 1 SPELLING 1* ☞ Sora-sky {空}, p. 224

(011-k1-s2)*KANJI 1 SPELLING 2* ☞ Kara-china {唐}, p. 130

(012-k2)*KANJI* 2 ☛ Te-hand {手}, p. 234

(077-jg)*GENERAL MEANING (EXAMPLES)* ✿📖 *noun* ❶ Karate, a martial art developed in the ˈRyū-kyū Kingdom *adjective* ❷ Empty handed.

(090-te)*TELL YOUR STUDENTS* 📖☺ The Heart Sūtra states, that form is emptiness and emptiness is form.

(838-su)**SUPER-TERM**
#karate {{空手}}##

(078-mg)*FUNAKOSHI MAIN BOOK* - *空手*
v. *唐手* 🖤**MG** 1935 **Suzuki-Johnston** 2-3 1935 **Ohshima** 3-4

(185-ch)*CHINESE (PINYIN)* ☯📖
kōngshǒu

(189-ok)*OKINAWAN* ● Tō-dī (トーディー)

(211-1)空手 (212-2)空手

(213-3)唐手 (alternative spelling)

(250-hi)からて (hir.)

(256-kat)カラテ (kat.)

(275-tō)からて [kàráté]

(466-cha)*CHARACTERISTICS* ⓘ A Two-character, which consists of 2 Chi-

nese Logograms and 0 Hiˈra-ga-ˈna Characters.

(800-tag)*TAGS* 💻 #kara-te, kara te

237.Kaˈra-te ˈGi

(015-w1)*WORD* 1 ꟿ ☛ karate {{空手}}, p. 131

(013-k3)*KANJI* 3 ☛ Tsuku-to wear {着}, p. 254

(077-jg)*GENERAL MEANING (EXAMPLES)* ✿📖 *noun* ❶ Karate uniform

(089-no)*NOTES AND EXAMPLES* 📖✎
AKA Karate I (空手衣), Keikogi (稽古着), Dōjōgi, Ki ("Gi"), Dōgi (道着). The top part is called Uwagi (上着). The trousers are called Sh[i]ˈta-baˈki (下穿き) or Zubon (ズボン).

#karategi {{空手着}}##

(211-1)空手着 (250-hi)からてぎ (hir.)

(466-cha)*CHARACTERISTICS* ⓘ A Three-character, which consists of 3 Chinese Logograms and 0 Hiˈra-ga-ˈna Characters.

(482-kg)**K⌐g** 🔔 Due to the ˈRendaku laws, the unvoiced consonant /K/ may get a Dak[u]-ˈten (゛) and become ~/g/ as a suffix. Example ↳

Keˑri (けり) turns into Maˑe-geˑri (まえげり).

(800-tag)*TAGS* 🖳 #karategi, karate-gi, karate gi, #karateki, #karatei

238.Kaˑra-te-dō

(015-w1)*WORD 1* ☝ karate {{空手}}, p. 131

(013-k3)*KANJI 3* ☛ Dō-way{道}, p. 57

(077-jg)*GENERAL MEANING (EXAMPLES)* ✿📖 *noun* ❶ The way of Karate, the way of the empty hand ❷ Karate

(185-ch)*CHINESE (PINYIN)* ☯📖

kōngshǒudào

(800-tag)*TAGS* 🖳 #karatedo, karate-do, karate do

#karatedō {{空手道}}##

(211-1)空手道

(211-al)*ALTERNATIVES OR SEE ALSO*

✐✐ 空手道

(250-hi)からてどう (hir.)

(466-cha)*CHARACTERISTICS* ⓘ A

Three-character, which consists of 3 Chinese Logograms and 0 Hiˑra-gaˑna Characters.

(838-su)**SUPER-TERM**

239.Kaˑra-te-ka

(015-w1)*WORD 1* 🆆🆆 ☝ karate {{空手}}, p. 131

(077-jg)*GENERAL MEANING (EXAMPLES)* ✿📖 *noun* ❶ Karate practitioner ❷ Karate expert

(211-1)空手家

(250-hi)からてか (hir.)

#karateka {{空手家}}##

(466-cha)*CHARACTERISTICS* ⓘ A

Three-character, which consists of 3 Chinese Logograms and 0 Hiˑra-gaˑna Characters.

(800-tag)*TAGS* 🖳 #karateka, karate-ka, karate ka

240.Kaˑru (刈)

(133-sy)*SYNONYMS* 👁= Kiru-to cut { 切}, p. 148

(077-jg)*GENERAL MEANING (EXAMPLES)* ✿📖 *verb* ❶ To cut ❷ To harvest, to reap, to mow.

(185-ch)*CHINESE (PINYIN)* 👁📖 ***yì***

(211-1)刈

(211-al)*ALTERNATIVES OR SEE ALSO*

✐✐ 苅る, 苅, 乂, 艾, 刈

#Karu-to cut {刈}##

(211-ka+hi)刈る

(250-hi)かる (hir.)

(275-tō)か る [kàrú]

(280-po)pol:KARY

(325-kr)*KANJI READINGS* ✎🗣 Go-on: げ (ge). Kan-on: がい (gai). On: かい (kai). Kun: かる (karu, 刈る).

(833-kan)**KANJI**

241. Ka'shira (Atama)

(001-REF-rom)Ka'shira ☞ Atama-head { 頭}, p. 40

#Kashira (Atama)##

(250-hi)かしら (hir.)

(275-tō)か しら [kàshírá˖]

242. Ka'ta (型)

💣 Do not confuse: Kata-shape {形 }, p. 134 with Kata-type {型}, p. 133!

(070-kt)*KARATE MEANING* 🖐📖 *noun*

① See Kata-shape {形}, p. 134

(077-jg)*GENERAL MEANING (EXAMPLES)* ⚙📖 *noun* ❶ Pattern, template, form ❷ Type, style ❸ Movement form in Martial Arts and in sports.

(095-3t)*THE THREE TEACHINGS* **3** 💰 This is not the famous Chinese concept of pattern (or law). The neo-Confucian pattern, which can be

Ka'shira (Atama) - Ka'ta (型) found in other doctrines as well, is pronounced *Lǐ* (理).

(185-ch)*CHINESE (PINYIN)* ☯📖 **xíng**

(211-l)型 (211-al)*ALTERNATIVES OR SEE ALSO* ✎✎ 荊, 形

(250-hi)かた (hir.) (256-kat)カタ (kat.)

#Kata-type {型}##

(275-tō)か た [kàtá˖]

(313-ka)*KANJI* ✎ The Phono-semantic Compound Logogram Ka'ta-type (型). (313k-cn)**Components** ⛭ [phonetic 刑 | semantic 土] (313k-ra)**Radical** ✦ 土 earth (313k-cs)**Composition** ✂ Top: 刑, bottom: 土 (313k-re)**Readings (examples)** 🗣 Go-on: ぎょう (gyō). Kan-on: けい (kei). Kun: かた (ka'ta, 型); がた (ga'ta, がた).

(302-kn)*KANJI NOTES* ✎✍ As for the two spellings of Ka'ta and *xíng* - 形 and 型: In both Japanese and Chinese, usually, 形 is used for shape and 型 is used for type.

(885-tag)*TAGS* 💻 #pattern, #type

(830-ik)**IMPORTANT KANJI**

(838-su)**SUPER-TERM**

243. Kaˈta (形)

💣✴ Do not confuse: Kata-shape {形}, p. 134 with Kata-type {型}, p. 133!

(000-it) *INCLUDING TERMS (EXAMPLES)*

👁✉ dojigata {{土字形}}, p. 58; ichijigata {{一字形}}, p. 104; jūjigata {{十字形}}, p. 115; kōjigata {{工字形}}, p. 149; teijigata {{丁字形}}, p. 236; Tennokata {{天の形}}, p. 241.

(070-kt) *KARATE MEANING* ✋📖 *noun*
① Form, routine, sequence, practice form, choreographed training form including defenses and attacks.

(077-jg) *GENERAL MEANING (EXAMPLES)* ☼📖 *noun* ❶ Shape, figure, form

(133-sy) *SYNONYMS* 👁= Kata-type {型}, p. 133

(302-kn) *KANJI NOTES* ✎✍ As for the two spellings of Kaˈta and *xíng* - 形 and 型: In both Japanese and Chinese, usually, 形 is used for shape and 型 is used for type.

#Kata-shape {形}##

(089-no) *NOTES AND EXAMPLES* 📖✍

We say to our students, that the Kata is wiser than its performer.

(185-ch) *CHINESE (PINYIN)* ☯📖 ***xíng***

(211-1) 形

(211-al) *ALTERNATIVES OR SEE ALSO*
✎✎ 形, 型, 容, 躰, 貌

(250-hi) かた (hir.)

(256-kat) カタ (kat.)

(275-tō) か た [kàtáˈ]

(313-ka) *KANJI* ✎ The Compound Ideogram Kaˈta-shape (形). (313k-cn) **Components** ⊞ [开 | 彡] (313k-ra) **Radical** ✦ 彡 hair (313k-cs) **Composition** ✗ Left: 开, right: 彡 (313k-re) **Readings (examples)** 🗣
Go-on: ぎょう (gyō). Kan-on: けい (kei) – as in Do-ˈji-ke[i] (土字形). Kun: かた (kaˈta); かたち [kàtáchí] (katachi); かたぎ (katagi). Nanori: ち (chi).

(830-ik) **IMPORTANT KANJI**

244. Kaˈta (方)

(000-it) *INCLUDING TERMS (EXAMPLES)*

👁✉ anata {{貴方}}, p. 33

(077-jg)*GENERAL MEANING (EXAMPLES)* ☼📖 *noun* ❶ Direction, way ❷ Person (polite)

(185-ch)*CHINESE (PINYIN)* ☯📖 ***fang***

(211-1)方

(250-hi)かた (hir.) (256-kat)カタ (kat.)

(275-tō)か|た| [kàtá˺]

(830-ik)**IMPORTANT KANJI**

#Kata-direction {方}##

(313-ka)*KANJI* 🖋 The Compound Ideogrammatic Radical (Radical 70) Ka'ta-direction (方). (313k-cn)**Components** 🖧 [一 丨 刀]. (313k-ra)**Radical** ✦ 方 direction. (313k-cs)**Composition** ⚒ 丶, 万. (313k-re)**Readings (examples)** 🗣 Go-on and Kan-on: ほう (hō) – as in Ze'n-pō [zèńpóó] (前方). Kun: かた (ka'ta). Nanori: まさ (masa).

245. 'Kata (片)

(000-it)*INCLUDING TERMS (EXAMPLES)*

👁✉ katakana {{片仮名}}, p. 136; katawa {{片輪}}, p. 137

(077-jg)*GENERAL MEANING (EXAMPLES)* ☼📖 *adjective, prefix* ❶ One of a pair ❷ Incomplete, not whole, imperfect

(185-ch)*CHINESE (PINYIN)* ☯📖 ***piàn, piān***

(211-1)片

#Kata-incomplete {片}##

(250-hi)かた (hir.) (256-kat)カタ (kat.)

(302-kn)*KANJI NOTES* 🖋✍ A Radical (Radical 91). Contains 4 strokes.

(325-kr)*KANJI READINGS* 🖋🗣 Go-on: へん (hen). Kan-on: へん (hen). Kun: かた (kata, 片); ひら (hira, 片).

(833-kan)**KANJI**

246. 'Kata (肩)

(077-jg)*GENERAL MEANING (EXAMPLES)* ☼📖 *noun* ❶ Shoulder.

(185-ch)*CHINESE (PINYIN)* ☯📖 ***jiān***

(203-hi)⌛☉ (250-hi)かた (hir.)

(211-1)肩

(211-al)*ALTERNATIVES OR SEE ALSO*

🖋🖋 肩, 肩

#Kata-shoulder {肩}##

(256-kat)カタ (kat.)

(275-tō)|か|た [ká˺tà]

(325-kr)*KANJI READINGS* 🖋🗣 Go-on: けん (ken). Kan-on: けん (ken). Kun: かた (kata, 肩).

(833-kan)**KANJI**

247. Kaˈta-ka-ˈna

(011-k1)*KANJI 1* ☛ Kata-incomplete { 片}, p. 135

(016-w2)*WORD 2* W ☛ kana {{仮名}}, p. 126

(020-re)*RESEARCH* 🔍 *noun* ❶ A Japanese angular syllabic script, used along with ˈKan-ji and Hiragana. The Kaˈta-ka-na 48 monographs (basic Characters) are アイウエオ, カキクケコ, サシスセソ, タチツテト, ナニヌネノ, ハヒフヘホ, マミムメモ, ヤユヨ, ラリルレロ, ワヰヱヲ, ン.

(206-kata)⧗❍

(256-kat)カタカナ (kat.) #katakana {{片仮名}}##

(134-re)*RELATED TERMS* 👁∞ hiragana {{平仮名}}, p. 99

(250-hi)かたかな (hir.)

(211-1)片仮名

(211-al)*ALTERNATIVES OR SEE ALSO* ✍✍ 片假名

(275-tō)か た か な [kàtákáˉnà]

(276-tō2)か た かな [kàtáˉkànà]

(466-cha)*CHARACTERISTICS* ⓘ A Four-character, which consists of 0 Chinese Logograms and 4 Katakana Characters.

(800-tag)*TAGS* 🖥 #kata-kana, kata kana

248. Kaˈtana (刀)

(000-it)*INCLUDING TERMS (EXAMPLES)* 👁✉ haitō {{背刀}}, p. 80; seiryūtō {{青龍刀}}, p. 206; shutō {{手刀}}, p. 210; sokutō {{足刀}}, p. 223.

(077-jg)*GENERAL MEANING (EXAMPLES)* ✿📖 *noun* ❶ Sword ❷ Knife.

(185-ch)*CHINESE (PINYIN)* 🌐📖 *dāo*

(211-1)刀

(211-var) 刂 (right)

(250-hi)かたな (hir.)

(275-tō)か た な [kàtáná˧]

(276-tō2)か た な [kàtá˧nà]

#Katana-sword {刀}##

(302-kn)*KANJI NOTES* ✍✍ Contains 2 strokes.

(313-ka)*KANJI* ✍ The Pictogrammatic Radical (Radical 18) Kaˈtana-sword (刀). (313k-cn)**Components** 🔀 No components - a Simple Logogram.

(313k-ra)**Radical** ✦ 刀 刂 ⌒ sword.

(313k-cs)**Composition** ⚔ Top-right: 刁, bottom-left: 丿. (313k-re)**Readings (examples)** 🐾 Go-on: と (to); とう (tō). Kan-on: とう (tō). Kun: かたな (katana, 刀).

(830-ik)**IMPORTANT KANJI**

249.Kaˈta-wa

(000-it)*INCLUDING TERMS (EXAMPLES)* 👁✉ katawaguruma {{片輪車}}, p. 137

(011-k1)*KANJI 1* ☞ Kata-incomplete { 片}, p. 135

(012-k2)*KANJI 2* ☞ Wa-ring {輪}, p. 267

(077-jg)*GENERAL MEANING (EXAMPLES)* ⚙📖 *adjective* ❶ Crippled. #katawa {{片輪}}##

(211-1)片輪

(211-al)*ALTERNATIVES OR SEE ALSO*

✒✒ 片端

(250-hi)かたわ (hir.)

(466-cha)*CHARACTERISTICS* ⓘ A Two-character, which consists of 2 Chinese Logograms and 0 Hiˈra-ga-ˈna Characters.

250.Kaˈta-wa-guruma

💣✳ Not to be confused with Kaˈta-guruˈma (肩車) - Shoulder Wheel. Kata-shoulder {肩}, p. 135, does not appear in this term.

(015-w1)*WORD 1* ᵂᵂ ☞ katawa {{片輪}}, p. 137

(055-tt)*THROWING TECHNIQUE* 投技

Old Name Bikko-daoshi (跛倒), Bikko-taoshi (跛倒) **AKA** Kata-sha-rin, Kata-rin-sha, Crippled wheel, Half wheel

(077-jg)*GENERAL MEANING (EXAMPLES)* ⚙📖 *noun* ❶ Crippled wheel.

(089-no)*NOTES AND EXAMPLES* 📖✎

Kaˈta-wa-guruma is a fascinating part of the japanese folklore and includes a rolling burning wheel. A close term in Japanese mythology is Wa Nyū-dō (輪入道).

(211-1)片輪車

(250-hi)かたわぐるま (hir.)

#katawaguruma {{片輪車}}##

(056-mt)*FUNAKOSHI MAIN BOOK - THROWING TECHNIQUES* 🛡MTT

1922 original 57 (Bikko-daoshi) **1925 Ishida** Does not appear **1925 Teramoto** Does not appear **1935**

Suzuki-Johnston 196 (Kata-sha-rin) **1935 Ohshima** 229 (Kata-wa-guruma)

(466-cha)*CHARACTERISTICS* ① A Three-character, which consists of 3 Chinese Logograms and 0 Hiˈra-ga-ˈna Characters.

(482-kg)**K⊃g** 🔔 Due to the ˈRen-daku laws, the unvoiced consonant /K/ may get a Dak[u]-ˈten (゛) and become ~/g/ as a suffix. Example 🌶 Keˈri (けり) turns into Maˈe-geˈri (まえげり).

(800-tag)*TAGS* 💻 #katawa-guruma, katawa guruma, #katawakuruma

251. ˈKatsu (勝)

(000-it)*INCLUDING TERMS (EXAMPLES)* 👁✉ kachi {{勝ち}}, p. 117; shōbu {{勝負}}, p. 216

(077-jg)*GENERAL MEANING (EXAMPLES)* ✿📖 *verb* ❶ To win.

(185-ch)*CHINESE (PINYIN)* ☻📖 ***shèng, shēng***

(705-gv)*GODAN VERB* 🏍⑤ **Terminal Form** {u* 💧 but not i*-ru or e*-ru} ˈKatsu (勝る), which means to win.

Polite Form {i*-masu} ˈKachimas[u] (勝ります).

#Katsu-to win {勝}##

(211-1)勝つ (250-hi)かつ (hir.)

(275-tō) かつ [káˈtsù]

(280-po)pol:KACY

(313-ka)*KANJI* 🖌 The Phono-semantic Compound Logogram ˈKatsu-to win (勝). (313k-cn)**Components** 🖧 [phonetic 朕 | semantic 力]. (313k-ra)**Radical** ✛ 力 power. (313k-cs)**Composition** ✂ Left: 月, right: 券. (313k-re)**Readings (examples)** 🗣 Go-on and Kan-on: しょう (shō). Kun: かつ (katsu).

(830-ik)**IMPORTANT KANJI**

252. Ke-ˈage

(000-it)*INCLUDING TERMS (EXAMPLES)* 👁✉ yokogerikeage {{横蹴り蹴上げ}}, p. 279

(011-k1)*KANJI 1* ☛ Keru-to kick {蹴}, p. 142

(015-w1)*WORD 1* ʷ/ʷ ☛ age {{上げ}}, p. 30

(070-kt)*KARATE MEANING* ✋📖 *noun* ① Snap (kick), flick (kick).

(077-jg)GENERAL MEANING (EXAMPLES) ✿📖 *noun* ❶ Riser ❷ Rise.

(185-ch)CHINESE (PINYIN) ☯📖 **cù**

shàng

#keage {{蹴上げ}}##

(134-re)RELATED TERMS 👁∞ keageru {{蹴上げる}}, p. 139

(211-1)蹴上げ

(212-2)蹴上

(250-hi)けあげ (hir.)

(466-cha)CHARACTERISTICS ⓘ A Tree-character, which consists of 2 Chinese Logograms and 1 Hiˈra-ga-ˈna Characters.

(800-tag)TAGS 💻 #ke-age, ke age

(838-su)**SUPER-TERM**

253.Ke-ˈageru

(011-k1)KANJI 1 ☞ Keru-to kick {蹴}, p. 142

(015-w1)WORD 1 ^W_W ☞ ageru {{上げる}}, p. 31

(077-jg)GENERAL MEANING (EXAMPLES) ✿📖 *verb (transitive)* ❶ To kick up.

(466-cha)CHARACTERISTICS ⓘ A Four-character, which consists of 2 Chi-

nese Logograms and 2 Hiˈra-ga-ˈna Characters.

#keageru {{蹴上げる}}##

(134-re)RELATED TERMS 👁∞ keage {{蹴上げ}}, p. 139

(211-1)蹴上げる   (250-hi)けあげる (hir.)

(711-sh)SHIMO ICHIDAN VERB 🏍①↻

Terminal Form {e*-ru} Ke-ˈageru (蹴上げる), which means to kick up.   **Polite Form** {-masu} Keˈagemas[u] (蹴上げます).

254.Ke-ˈkomi

(000-it)INCLUDING TERMS (EXAMPLES) 👁✉ yokogerikekomi {{横蹴り蹴込み}}, p. 280

(011-k1)KANJI 1 ☞ Keru-to kick {蹴}, p. 142

(015-w1)WORD 1 ^W_W ☞ komi {{込み}}, p. 153

(070-kt)KARATE MEANING 🖐📖 *noun, adjective, preposition* ① Thrust (kick), penetrating (kick), into (kick), push (kick).

(077-jg)GENERAL MEANING (EXAMPLES) ✿📖 *noun* ❶ Riser ❷ Footboard

#kekomi {{蹴込み}}##

(089-no)*NOTES AND EXAMPLES* 📖✍ 込

is a Japanese-coined character.

(185-ch)*CHINESE (PINYIN)* 🌐📖 *cùyū*

(211-1)蹴込み

(250-hi)けこみ (hir.)

(466-cha)*CHARACTERISTICS* ⓘ A

Three-character, which consists of 2

Chinese Logograms and 1 Hiˈra-ga-

ˈna Characters.

(800-tag)*TAGS* 🖥 #ke-komi, ke komi

(838-su)**SUPER-TERM**

255. ˈKen (拳)

(000-it)*INCLUDING TERMS (EXAMPLES)*

👁✉ hiraken {{平拳}}, 99; ip-

ponken {{一本拳}}, p. 106; seiken

{{正拳}}, p. 206; uraken {{裏拳}},

p. 265

(077-jg)*GENERAL MEANING (EXAM-*

PLES) ☼📖 *noun* ❶ Fist

(185-ch)*CHINESE (PINYIN)* 🌐📖 *quán*

as in *tàijíquán* (太極拳) – Tai Chi

(211-1)拳 (211-al)*ALTERNATIVES OR SEE*

ALSO 🖊🖊 捲

(250-hi)けん (hir.) (256-kat)ケン (kat.)

#Ken-fist {拳}##

(313-ka)*KANJI* 🖊 The Phono-semantic

Compound Logogram ˈKen-fist (拳

). (313k-cn)**Components** 🔣 [phonetic

𠬞 | semantic 手] (313k-ra)**Radical** ✋

手 扌 龵 hand (313k-cs)**Composition** 🔨

Top: 𠬞 , bottom: 手 (313k-

re)**Readings (examples)** 🔊 Go-on:

げん (gen). Kan-on: けん (ken).

Kun: こぶし (kobushi, 拳).

(830-ik)**IMPORTANT KANJI**

(838-su)**SUPER-TERM**

256. Keˈri

(000-it)*INCLUDING TERMS (EXAMPLES)*

👁✉; kakatootoshigeri {{踵落とし

蹴り}}, p. 122; kakatogeri {{踵蹴

り}, p. 123; kansetsugeri {{関節蹴

り}}, p. 130; keriwaza {{蹴り技}},

p. 141; maeashigeri {{前足蹴り}},

p. 161; maegeri {{前蹴り}}, p. 162;

mawashigeri {{回し蹴り}}, p. 167;

mikazukigeri {{三日月蹴り}}, p.

170; nidangeri {{二段蹴り}}, p.

184; tobigeri {{飛び蹴り}}, p. 246;

ushirogeri {{後ろ蹴り}}, p. 265;

yokogeri {{横蹴り}}, p. 279

#keri {{蹴り}}##

(011-k1)*KANJI 1* ☛ Keru-to kick {蹴}, p. 142

(077-jg)*GENERAL MEANING (EXAMPLES)* ☼📖 *noun* ❶ Kick.

(211-1)蹴り (256-kat)ケリ(kat.)

(250-hi)けり (hir.) (275-tō)け|り [kèríˈ]

(466-cha)*CHARACTERISTICS* ⓘ A Two-character, which consists of 1 Chinese Logograms and 1 Hiˈra-ga-ˈna Characters.

(800-tag)*TAGS* 🖥 #geri

(838-su)**SUPER-TERM**

257. Keˈri-waˈza

(015-w1)*WORD 1* ^W_W ☛ keri {{蹴り}}, p. 140

(012-k2)*KANJI 2* ☛ Waza-technique {技}, p. 267

(077-jg)*GENERAL MEANING (EXAMPLES)* ☼📖 *noun* ❶ Kicking technique.

(133-sy)*SYNONYMS* 👁= ashigeri {{足蹴り}}, p. 38; ashiwaza {{足技}}, p. 39

#keriwaza {{蹴り技}}##

(185-ch)*CHINESE (PINYIN)* 🌐📖 *cù jì*

(211-1)蹴り技

(250-hi)けりわざ (hir.)

(466-cha)*CHARACTERISTICS* ⓘ A Three-character, which consists of 2 Chinese Logograms and 1 Hiˈra-ga-ˈna Characters.

(800-tag)*TAGS* 🖥 #keri-waza, keri waza

258. ˈKeru (蹴)

(000-it)*INCLUDING TERMS (EXAMPLES)* 👁✉ keage {{蹴上げ}}, p. 139; keageru {{蹴上げる}}, p. 139; kekomi {{蹴込み}}, p. 140; keri {{蹴り}}, p. 140

(077-jg)*GENERAL MEANING (EXAMPLES)* ☼📖 *verb* ❶ To kick ❷ To refuse, to reject.

(185-ch)*CHINESE (PINYIN)* 🌐📖 *cù*

(482-kg)**K⊃g** ♫ Due to the ˈRendaku laws, the unvoiced consonant /K/ may get a Dak[u]-ˈten (゙) and become ~/g/ as a suffix. Example ↳ Keˈri (けり) turns into Maˈe-geˈri (まえげり).

(705-gv)*GODAN VERB* 🏍⑤ **Terminal Form** {u* ✺ but not i*-ru or e*-ru} ˈKeru [kéˈrù] (蹴る), which means to kick. **Polite Form** {i*-masu}

ˈKi (気) - ˈKi (気)

Keˈrimas[u] [kèrímá⁺sù] (蹴ります).

#Keru-to kick {蹴}##

(211-1)蹴

(250-hi)ける (hir.)

(275-tō)け|る [ké⁺rù]

(313-ka)*KANJI* ✐ The Phono-semantic Compound Ideogram [55] ˈKeru-to kick (蹴). (313k-cn)**Components** 🖧 [semantic 足 | semantic and phonetic 就]. (313k-ra)**Radical** ✦ 足⻊ foot.

(313k-cs)**Composition** ✂ Left: ⻊ (abbreviated form of 足), right: 就. (313k-re)**Readings (examples)** 🗣 Go-on: すく (suku). Kan-on: しゅく (shuku). Kan'yō-on: しゅう (shū). Kun: ける (keru, 蹴る).

(302-kn)*KANJI NOTES* ✐ ✍ Contains 19 Strokes.

(731-vn)*VERB NOTES* 🏍 ✍ Originally a Shiˈmo-ˈichi-dan Verb[56].

(830-ik)**IMPORTANT KANJ**

259. ˈKi (気)

(000-it)*INCLUDING TERMS (EXAMPLES)* 👁 ✉ kiai {{気合}}, p. 144; genki {{元気}}, p. 69; ogenkidesuka {{お元気ですか}}, p. 187.

(077-jg)*GENERAL MEANING (EXAMPLES)* ✿ 📖 *noun, suffix* ❶ Vital energy ❷ Breath, gas, atmosphere, air ❸ Spirit, mind, heart, feeling, mood ❹ Condition, state ❺ Nature, quality, temperament ❻ Sign, indication, trace, seeming, feeling, appearance.

(089-no)*NOTES AND EXAMPLES* 📖 ✍ ˈKū-ki [kú⁺ùkì] (空気) means air. ˈTen-ki (天気) means weather.

(185-ch)*CHINESE (PINYIN)* ☯ 📖 *qì*

(211-sh-2)气 (simp.)

(211-ky-1)氣 (trad.)

(250-hi)き (hir.) (256-kat)キ (kat.)

(302-kn)*KANJI NOTES* ✐ ✍ It arguably depicts the smell of fermenting rice[57]. Unseen, but very present.

(830-ik)**IMPORTANT KANJI**

#Ki-energy {気}##

(313-ka.1c)*COMMON* ✐ (313-ka.1e)**Radical 【common】** ✦ 气 steam. (313-ka.1r)**Readings 【common】** 🗣 Go-on: け (ke). Kan-on: き (ki). Kun: いき (iki, 気).

(313-ka.2s)*SIMPLIFIED (SHINJITAI)* 🖋 The Phono-semantic Compound Ideogram 'Ki-energy (気) (simp.). (313-ka.2C)**Components** 【simp.】 🖧 [phonetic 气 | semantic 米]. (313-ka.2g)**Composition** 【simp.】 🛠 Top-right: 气, bottom-left: 乂.

(313-ka.3t)*TRADITIONAL (KYUJITAI)* 🖋 The Phono-semantic Compound Ideogram 'Ki-energy (氣) (trad.). (313-ka.3c)**Components** 【trad.】 🖧 [phonetic 气 | semantic 米]. (313-ka.3g)**Composition** 【trad.】 🛠 Top-right: 气, bottom-left: 米.

(800-tag)*TAGS* 💻 #chi, #qi

260. 'Ki (騎)

(000-it)*INCLUDING TERMS (EXAMPLES)* 👁✉ kiba {{騎馬}}, p. 144; tekki {{鉄騎}}, p. 237

(077-jg)*GENERAL MEANING (EXAMPLES)* ☼📖 *noun, verb* ❶ Horseback riding ❷ To ride a horse ❸ To sit astride[58] ❹ Cavalry ❺ Horseman.

(185-ch)*CHINESE (PINYIN)* ☯📖 ***qí***[59]

(211-1)騎 (211-al)*ALTERNATIVES OR SEE ALSO* 🖋🖋 骑

(302-kn)*KANJI NOTES* 🖋✍ Contains 18 strokes.

#Ki-riding {騎}##

(250-hi)き (hir.)

(256-kat)キ (kat.)

(313-ka)*KANJI* 🖋 The Phono-semantic Compound Logogram 'Ki-riding (騎). (313k-cn)**Components** 🖧 [semantic 馬 | phonetic 奇] (313k-ra)**Radical** ✦ 馬 horse (313k-cs)**Composition** 🛠 Left: 馬, right: 奇 (313k-re)**Readings (examples)** 🗣 Go-on: ぎ (gi). Kan-on: き (ki). Kun: のる (noru, 騎る).

(830-ik)**IMPORTANT KANJI**

261.Ki-'ai

(011-k1)*KANJI 1* ☛ Ki-energy {気}, p. 142

(012-k2)*KANJI 2* ☛ Au-to unite {合}, p. 41

(070-kt)*KARATE MEANING* ✋📖 *noun* ① Union of Energy, Spirit Unification ② Spirit Yell, shouting to focus energy ④ Vocal expulsion of air.

(077-jg)*GENERAL MEANING (EXAMPLES)* ☼📖 *noun* ❶ Scream, yell ❷

ˈKi-ba - Ki-ˈba Daˈchi

Fighting spirit, combat motivation, combat effort.

(185-ch)*CHINESE (PINYIN)* ☯📖 *qìhé*

(211-al)*ALTERNATIVES OR SEE ALSO*

✐✐ 氣合, 气合

#kiai {{気合}}##

(089-no)*NOTES AND EXAMPLES* 📖✍

ˈAi-ki-dō [àíkí⁺dòò] (合気道) contains the Logograms of Ki-ˈai (気合), only inversely.

(211-1)気合

(212-2)気合い

(250-hi)きあい (hir.)

(466-cha)*CHARACTERISTICS* ⓘ A Two-character, which consists of 2 Chinese Logograms and 0 Hiˈra-ga-ˈna Characters.

(800-tag)*TAGS* 🖥 #kyai, ki-ai, ki ai

(838-su)**SUPER-TERM**

262. ˈKi-ba

(000-it)*INCLUDING TERMS (EXAMPLES)*

👁✉ kibadachi {{騎馬立ち}}, p. 145

(011-k1)*KANJI 1* ☚ Ki-riding {騎}, p. 143

(012-k2)*KANJI 2* ☚ Uma-horse {馬}, p. 264

(077-jg)*GENERAL MEANING (EXAMPLES)* ☼📖 *noun* ❶ Horse-riding ❷ Horseback rider

(185-ch)*CHINESE (PINYIN)* ☯📖 *qímǎ*

#kiba {{騎馬}}##

(211-1)騎馬

(211-al)*ALTERNATIVES OR SEE ALSO*

✐✐ 骑马

(250-hi)きば (hir.)

(466-cha)*CHARACTERISTICS* ⓘ A Two-character, which consists of 2 Chinese Logograms and 0 Hiˈra-ga-ˈna Characters.

(800-tag)*TAGS* 🖥 #ki-ba, ki ba

263. Ki-ˈba Daˈchi

(015-w1)*WORD 1* ʷ/ʷ ☚ kiba {{騎馬}}, p. 144

(016-w2)*WORD 2* ʷ/ʷ ☚ tachi {{立ち}}, p. 228

(030-st)*STANCE* 立 **AKA** Nai-han-chi-dachi (内歩進立ち, ナイハンチ立ち), Horse Stance, Horse Mounting Stance, Horse Riding Stance, Horse Rider Stance, Straddle Stance, Straddle Leg Stance, Rider Stance, Cavalry Horse Stance **Category** Low Frontal Stances

(089-no)*NOTES AND EXAMPLES* 📖🖋

Kibadachi is also the old name of the Tekki Kata.

(134-re)*RELATED TERMS* 👁∞ tekki {{鉄騎}}, p. 237

(136-se)*SEE ALSO* 👁➕ shikodachi {{四股立ち}}, p. 209

(466-cha)*CHARACTERISTICS* ⓘ A Four-character, which consists of 3 Chinese Logograms and 1 Hiˈra-ga-ˈna Characters.

(185-ch)*CHINESE (PINYIN)* 👁📖 *qímǎ lì*

(190-kf)*KUNG FU TERMINOLOGY* 👁🕇

Mǎ bù (馬步)

(211-1)騎馬立ち

(212-2)騎馬立

#kibadachi {{騎馬立ち}}##

Masters 14 - Kibadachi by Bamgboye Sensei
List of Sensei Demonstrations next to Values, p. 10
Bobby Bamgboye of Nigeria WSKF demonstrates Kiba-dachi. Photographer: Joel Ibanga.

(031-ms)*FUNAKOSHI MAIN BOOK - STANCES* 📚MS **1922 original** 30 (list) (San-chin-dachi), 34 (San-chin-dachi) **1925 Ishida** 41 (list), 46 **1925 Teramoto** 40 (list), 42 **1935 Suzuki-Johnston** 22 (list), 23 **1935 Ohshima** 19 (list), 20.

(032-ns)*FUNAKOSHI NYUMON TERAMO-TO - STANCES* 📚NS 59 (list), 60-61.

(250-hi)きばだち (hir.)

(256-kat)キバダチ (kat.)

(483-td)**TꞒd** 🔊 Due to the ˈRen-daku laws, the unvoiced consonant /T/ may get a Dak[u]-ˈten (゛) and become ~/d/ as a suffix. Example 🕇 ˈTachi（たち）turns into Ki-ˈba Daˈchi（きばだち）.

(800-tag)*TAGS* 💻 #kiba-dachi, kiba dachi, #kibatachi

(838-su)**SUPER-TERM**

264.Ki-ˈhon

(011-k1)*KANJI 1* ☛ Moto-origin {元}, p. 173 (alternative spelling)

(012-k2)*KANJI 2* ☛ Hon-source {本}, p. 102

(070-kt)*KARATE MEANING* ✋📖 *noun*

① Basic training, basic techniques.

(077-jg)*GENERAL MEANING (EXAMPLES)* ☼📖 *noun* ❶ Foundation, basis ❷ Standard

(185-ch)*CHINESE (PINYIN)* 😊📖 ***jīběn***

#kihon {{基本}}##

(211-1)基本

(250-hi)きほん (hir.)

(275-tō)き|ほん| [kìhón]

(466-cha)*CHARACTERISTICS* ⓘ A Two-character, which consists of 2 Chinese Logograms and 0 Hi˙ra-ga-˙na Characters.

(800-tag)*TAGS* 🖥 #ki-hon, ki hon

(838-su)**SUPER-TERM**

265.Ki˙me

💣✳ This term has alternative spellings, using different Kanji.

(011-k1-s1)*KANJI 1 SPELLING 1* ☞ Ki-meru-to decide {決}, p. 147

(011-k1-s2)*KANJI 1 SPELLING 2* ☞ Ki-wameru-to act excessively {極}, p. 148

(070-kt)*KARATE MEANING* ✋📖 *noun* ① Focus, maximization ② Determination, decisiveness, intention ③ Sensible power, energy ④ Efficiency ⑤ Contraction, tension at the right moment.

(077-jg)*GENERAL MEANING (EXAMPLES)* ☼📖 *noun* ❶ Agreement, rule (something that has been decided)

#kime {{決め}}##

(089-no)*NOTES AND EXAMPLES* 📖✎ Has nothing to do with the Logogram ˙Ki-energy (気).

(211-1)決め

(211-al)*ALTERNATIVES OR SEE ALSO* 🖌🖌 極め

(250-hi)きめ (hir.)

(256-kat)キメ (kat.)

(466-cha)*CHARACTERISTICS* ⓘ A Two-character, which consists of 1 Chinese Logograms and 1 Hi˙ra-ga-˙na Characters.

(838-su)**SUPER-TERM**

266.Ki˙meru (決)

(000-it)*INCLUDING TERMS (EXAMPLES)* 👁✉ kime {{決め}}, p. 146

(077-jg)*GENERAL MEANING (EXAMPLES)* ☼📖 *verb (transitive)* ❶ To decide, to choose, to determine. ❷ To persist in doing, to go through with. ❸ To carry out something successfully. ❹ To burst. ❺ To kill.

(133-sy)*SYNONYMS* 👁 = Kiwameru-to act excessively {極}, p. 148

(185-ch)*CHINESE (PINYIN)* 🔊📖 *jué*

(211-1)決 (212-2)渓

(211-ka+hi)決める

(211-ka+hiAlt)極める

(250-hi)きめる (hir.) (256-kat)キメる (kat.)

(275-tō)き[め]る [kìmérú]

(276-tō2)き[め]る [kìmérú⁺]

#Kimeru-to decide {決}##

(280-po)pol:KIMERY

(313-ka)*KANJI* 🖋 The Phono-semantic Compound Logogram Kiˈmeru-to decide (決). (313k-cn)**Components** 🔡 [semantic 氵 | phonetic 夬] (313k-ra)**Radical** ✦ 水 氵 氺 water. (313k-cs)**Composition** ✗ Left: 氵, right: 夬. (313k-re)**Readings (examples)** 🗣 Go-on: けち (kechi). Kan-on: けつ (ketsu). Kun: きまる (kimaru, 決まる); きめる (kimeru, 決める).

(711-sh)*SHIMO ICHIDAN VERB* 🏍①↻

Terminal Form {e*-ru} Kiˈmeru [kìmérú] (決める), which means to decide. **Polite Form** {-masu}

Ki'memas[u] [kìmémá⁺sù] (決めます).

267. ˈKiri

(000-it)*INCLUDING TERMS (EXAMPLES)*

👁✉ fumikiri {{踏み切り}}, p. 65

(011-k1)*KANJI 1* ☛ Kiru-to cut {切}, p. 148

(077-jg)*GENERAL MEANING (EXAMPLES)* ⚙📖 *noun* ❶ Counter for cuts ❷ End, stop ❸ Limits.

(211-1)切り

(212-2)限り

(213-3)限

#kiri {{切り}}##

(089-no)*NOTES AND EXAMPLES* 📖✍ Haˈra-kiˈri (腹切り) – ˈSep-ˈpuku (切腹) means suicide by disembowelment (abdomen cutting)

(250-hi)きり (hir.)

(466-cha)*CHARACTERISTICS* ① A Two-character, which consists of 1 Chinese Logograms and 1 Hiˈra-ga-ˈna Characters.

268. ˈKiru (切)

(000-it)*INCLUDING TERMS (EXAMPLES)*

👁✉ kiri {{切り}}, p. 147

(077-jg)*GENERAL MEANING (EXAMPLES)* ☼📖 *verb* ❶ To cut.

(133-sy)*SYNONYMS* 👁= Karu-to cut { 刈}, p. 132

(185-ch)*CHINESE (PINYIN)* 🌐📖 *qiē*

(211-1)切

(705-gv)*GODAN VERB* 🏍⑤ **Terminal Form** {u* ✎* but not i*-ru or e*-ru} ˈKiru [kíˈrù] (切る), which means to cut. **Polite Form** {i*-masu} Kiˈrimas[u] [kìrímáˈsù] (切ります).

(731-vn)*VERB NOTES* 🏍✍ Exceptional ˈGo-dan Verb (i*-ru or e*-ru). #Kiru-to cut {切}##

(250-hi)きる (hir.) (275-tō)き|る [kíˈrù]

(313-ka)*KANJI* ✎ The Phono-semantic Compound Logogram ˈKiru-to cut (切). (313k-cn)**Components** 🔠 [phonetic 七 | semantic 刀]. (313k-ra)**Radical** ✛ Radical: 刀 刂 ⼑ sword. (313k-cs)**Composition** ✖ Left: 七, right: 刀. (313k-re)**Readings (examples)** 🎺 Go-on: せち (sechi); さい (sai). Kan-on: せつ (setsu); せい (sei). Kun: きる (kiru, 切る); きれ

る (kireru, 切れる). Nanori: きつ (kitsu); きり (kiri); ぎり (giri).

269.Kiˈwameru (極)

(000-it)*INCLUDING TERMS (EXAMPLES)* 👁✉ kime {{決め}}, p. 146 (alternative spelling); taikyoku {{太極}}, p. 230.

(077-jg)*GENERAL MEANING (EXAMPLES)* ☼📖 *verb (transitive)* ❶ To act excessively, to carry to extremes, to go to the end of something. ❷ To reach the limits of something, to reach the peak of something, to exhaust completely, to have nothing left, to carry to the end, to complete. ❸ To be extremely something. & The meanings of Kimeru-to decide {決}, p. 147

(133-sy)*SYNONYMS* 👁= Kimeru-to decide {決}, p. 147

(185-ch)*CHINESE (PINYIN)* 🌐📖 *jí*

(211-1)極

(212-2)极

#Kiwameru-to act excessively {極}##

(211-ka+hi)極める

(211-ka+hiAlt)窮める

(250-hi)きわめる (hir.)

(313-ka)*KANJI* 🖊 The Phono-semantic Compound Logogram Kiˈwameru- to act excessively (極). (313k-cn)**Components** 🖧 [semantic 木 | phonetic 亟] (313k-ra)**Radical** ✦ 木 tree (313k-cs)**Composition** ⚔ Left: 木, right: 亟 . (313k-re)**Readings (examples)** 👊 Go-on: ごく (goku). Kan-on: きょく (kyoku). Kun: きわめる (kiwameru, 極める); きわまる (kiwamaru, 極まる); きめる (ki-meru, 極める); きまる (kimaru, 極まる).

(830-ik)IMPORTANT KANJI

270.Kiˈzami Zuˈki (maete)

(001-REF-rom) Kiˈzami Zuˈki ☞ maete {{前手}}, p. 162

(002-REF-hi)きざみ突き ☞ まえて #kizamizuki (maete)##

(800-tag)*TAGS* 💻 #kizaminozuki (きざみの突き), #kizamitsuki

271.ˈKō-ji-ˈgata

(012-k2)*KANJI* 2 ☛ Ji-character {字}, p. 109

(013-k3)*KANJI 3* ☛ Kata-shape {形}, p. 134

Kiˈzami Zuˈki (maete) - ˈKō-ji-ˈgata

(070-kt)*KARATE MEANING* 🖐📖 *noun*

① I Pattern, I Shape, H Pattern, H Shape, Character-ko Pattern, 工 Pattern, 工 Character Figure, 90° rotated H Shape

(134-re)*RELATED TERMS* 👁∞ enbusen {{演武線}}, p. 61

(211-1)工字形 (211-al)*ALTERNATIVES OR SEE ALSO* 🖌🖊 工字型

(250-hi)こうじがた (hir.)

(800-tag)*TAGS* 💻 #kojigata, koji-gata, koji gata
#kōjigata {{工字形}}##

(068-me)*FUNAKOSHI MAIN BOOK - ENBUSEN* 🥋**MEN** 1922 original 51 **1925 Ishida** 58 **1925 Teramoto** 52 **1935 Suzuki-Johnston** 40 **1935 Ohshima** 41

(466-cha)*CHARACTERISTICS* ① A Three-character, which consists of 3 Chinese Logograms and 0 Hiˈra-gaˈna Characters.

(482-kg)**K⤳g** 🔔 Due to the ˈRendaku laws, the unvoiced consonant /K/ may get a Dak[u]-ˈten (゛) and become ~/g/ as a suffix. Example ✔

ˈKō-k[u]tsu - ˈKō-k[u]tsu-ˈdachi

Keˈri (けり) turns into Maˈe-geˈri (まえげり).

272. ˈKō-k[u]tsu

(000-it)*INCLUDING TERMS (EXAMPLES)*

👁✉ kōkutsudachi {{後屈立ち}}, p. 150

(011-k1)*KANJI 1* ☛ Ato-behind {後}, p. 41

(012-k2)*KANJI 2* ☛ Kagamu-to stoop { 屈}, p. 120

(070-kt)*KARATE MEANING* ✋📖 *noun* ① ˈKō-k[u]tsu-ˈdachi (後屈立ち)

(077-jg)*GENERAL MEANING (EXAMPLES)* ☼📖 *noun, verb* ❶ Retroflexion, back bend, bending backwards.

(185-ch)*CHINESE (PINYIN)* 👁📖 *hòu qū*

(211-1)後屈

#kōkutsu {{後屈}}##

(139-an)*ANTONYMS* 👁↺ zenkutsu {{ 前屈}}, p. 284

(250-hi)こうくつ (hir.)

(256-kat)コウクツ (kat.)

(280-po)pol:KOOKCY

(466-cha)*CHARACTERISTICS* ⓘ A Two-character, which consists of 2 Chinese Logograms and 0 Hiˈra-ga-ˈna Characters.

(800-tag)*TAGS* 🖥 #kokutsu, kō-kutsu, kō kutsu, kookutsu, kohkutsu, kou-kutsu, koktsu, kokuzu

(838-su)**SUPER-TERM**

273. ˈKō-k[u]tsu-ˈdachi

(015-w1)*WORD 1* W/W ☛ kōkutsu {{ 後屈}}, p. 150

(016-w2)*WORD 2* W/W ☛ tachi {{立ち}}, p. 228

(030-st)*STANCE* 立 **AKA** ˈKō-k[u]tsu, ˈKōkutsu ˈShi-se[i] (後屈姿勢) ˈKō-kutsu Shitsu (後屈膝), Kokutsu Stance, Back Stance, Back Long Stance, Rear-bending, Back-leg-bent Stance, Rear Knee Bent Stance, Rear Knee Flexion Stance, Rear Bending **Category** Low Sidewise Stances.

(139-an)*ANTONYMS* 👁↺ zenkutsu-dachi {{前屈立ち}}, p. 285

(185-ch)*CHINESE (PINYIN)* 👁📖 *hòu qū lì*

(211-1)後屈立ち (212-2)後屈立

(466-cha)*CHARACTERISTICS* ⓘ A Four-character, which consists of 3 Chinese Logograms and 1 Hiˈra-ga-ˈna Characters.

#kōkutsudachi {{後屈立ち}}##

(031-ms)*FUNAKOSHI MAIN BOOK - STANCES* 🎴**MS** 1922 original 30 (list), 33 (後屈姿勢) **1925 Ishida** 41 (list), 44 **1925 Teramoto** 40 (list), 41 **1935 Suzuki-Johnston** 22 (list), 23 **1935 Ohshima** 19 (list), 20.

(032-ns)*FUNAKOSHI NYUMON TERAMO-TO - STANCES* 🎴**NS** 59 (list), 60

(250-hi) こうくつだち (hir.)

(483-td)**T⤳d** 🔔 Due to the ‛Ren-daku laws, the unvoiced consonant /T/ may get a Dak[u]-‛ten (゛) and become ~/d/ as a suffix. Example ⸬ ‛Tachi (たち) turns into Ki-‛ba Da‛chi (きばだち).

(800-tag)*TAGS* 🖥 #kokutsudachi, kō-kutsu dachi, kō kutsu dachi, kookutsudachi, kohkutsudachi, koukutsudachi, koktsudachi

(838-su)**SUPER-TERM**

274.Ko‛koro (心)

(000-it)*INCLUDING TERMS (EXAMPLES)*

👁✉ shoshin {{初心}}, p. 219

(077-jg)*GENERAL MEANING (EXAMPLES)* ✿📖 *noun* ❶ Heart ❷ Mind, spirit

(185-ch)*CHINESE (PINYIN)* 🌐📖 *xīn*

(211-1)心

(211-al)*ALTERNATIVES OR SEE ALSO* ✎✎忄, 灬

(250-hi) こころ (hir.) (256-kat) ココロ (kat.)

(275-tō) こ[ころ] [kòkóró゛]

(276-tō2) こ[ころ] [kòkó゛rò]

(800-tag)*TAGS* 🖥 #shin #Kokoro-heart {心}##

(302-kn)*KANJI NOTES* ✎🖌 Contains 4 strokes.

(313-ka)*KANJI* ✎ The Pictogrammatic[60] Radical (Radical 61) Ko‛koro-heart (心). (313k-cn)**Components** ⛭ No components - a Simple Logogram (313k-ra)**Radical** ✛ 心忄小 heart (313k-cs)**Composition** 乂ノㄴヽヽ (313k-re)**Readings (examples)** 🗣 Go-on: しん (shin). Kan-on: しん (shin). Kun: こころ (kokoro, 心).

(830-ik)**IMPORTANT KANJI**

275.‛Ko-ma

(000-it)*INCLUDING TERMS (EXAMPLES)*

👁✉ komanage {{独楽投げ}}, p. 152

(077-jg)*GENERAL MEANING (EXAMPLES)* ☼📖 *noun* ❶ Spinning top

(185-ch)*CHINESE (PINYIN)* 🌐📖 *dúlè*

(203-hi)⏳☉

(250-hi)こま (hir.)

#koma {{独楽}}##

(211-1)独楽 (275-tō)｜こ￤ま [kóˈmà]

(466-cha)*CHARACTERISTICS* ① A Two-character, which consists of 0 Chinese Logograms and 2 Hiˈra-ga-ˈna Characters.

(800-tag)*TAGS* 💻 #ko-ma, ko ma

276.Ko-ˈma Naˈge

(015-w1)*WORD 1* ᵂ ☛ koma {{独楽}}, p. 152

(016-w2)*WORD 2* ᵂ ☛ nage {{投げ}}, p. 174

(055-tt)*THROWING TECHNIQUE* 投技

Old Name Neji-daoshi (捻倒, 捻ぢ倒, 捻じ倒), Neji-taoshi, Neiji-daoshi, Chin-tō (捻倒) **AKA** Spinning-top Throw, Twisting Down, Twisting Takedown.

(089-no)*NOTES AND EXAMPLES* 📖✍

The following illustration is taken from *KLARE ONDERRICHTINGE DER VOORTREFFELIJKE WORSTEL-KONST*

by Nicolaes Petter, Plate 36 (Plate 2 of Sixth Part on Chest Grips). It is considered by many very similar to Ko-ma Nage.

(211-1)独楽投げ

#komanage {{独楽投げ}}##

Figure 2 - Romeyn de Hooghe, Amsterdam, 1674

(056-mt)*FUNAKOSHI MAIN BOOK - THROWING TECHNIQUES* 📚MTT

1922 original 53 (Neji-daoshi) **1925 Ishida** 60 (Chin-tō) **1925 Teramoto** 53 (list), 54 (Neji-daoshi) **1935 Suzuki-Johnston** 194 (Ko-ma Nage) **1935 Ohshima** 227 (list), 228 (Ko-ma Nage).

(212-2)独楽投 (250-hi)こまなげ (hir.)

(466-cha)*CHARACTERISTICS* ① A Four-character, which consists of 3 Chinese Logograms and 1 Hiˈra-ga-ˈna Characters.

(800-tag)*TAGS* 💻 #koma-nage, koma nage

277.ˈKomi

(000-it)*INCLUDING TERMS (EXAMPLES)*

👁✉ fumikomi {{踏み込み}}, p. 66; kekomi {{蹴込み}}, p. 140

(077-jg)*GENERAL MEANING (EXAMPLES)* ☼📖 *adverb or noun* ❶ Including.

(089-no)*NOTES AND EXAMPLES* 📖✍ 込 is a Japanese-coined character.

(211-1)込み

#komi {{込み}}##

(250-hi)こみ (hir.)

(256-kat)コミ (kat.)

(275-tō)こ み [kòmíˈ]

(466-cha)*CHARACTERISTICS* ⓘ A Two-character, which consists of 1 Chinese Logograms and 1 Hiˈra-ga-ˈna Characters.

278.Koˈrogaru (転)

(000-it)*INCLUDING TERMS (EXAMPLES)*

👁✉ kaiten {{回転}}, p. 121

(077-jg)*GENERAL MEANING (EXAMPLES)* ☼📖 *noun* ❶ To rotate, to roll[61]

(089-no)*NOTES AND EXAMPLES* 📖✍ Jiˈten-sha (自転車) means bicycle. ˈTen-ten [tèńtéń] (転々, 転転) means rolling about, as well as moving from place to place.

(134-re)*RELATED TERMS* 👁∞ (134-re)*RELATED TERMS* 👁∞ Mawaru-to turn {回}, p. 165

(185-ch)*CHINESE (PINYIN)* ☯📖 *zhuǎn*

#Korogaru-to rotate {転}##

(211-1)転 (211-ka+hi)転がる

(211-al)*ALTERNATIVES OR SEE ALSO* ✒✒ 轉, 转 (250-hi)ころがる (hir.)

(275-tō)こ ろがる [kòrógárú]

(280-po)pol:KOROGARY

(325-kr)*KANJI READINGS* ✒🗣 Go-on: てん (ten). Kan-on: てん (ten). Kun: ころぶ (korobu, 転ぶ); ころがる (korogaru, 轉がる); ころげる (korogeru, 轉げる).

(800-tag)*TAGS* 💻 #korobu, #korogeru

(833-kan)**KANJI**

279.ˈKō-sa

(000-it)*INCLUDING TERMS (EXAMPLES)*

👁✉ kosadachi {{交差立ち}}, p. 154

(077-jg)*GENERAL MEANING (EXAMPLES)* ☼📖 *noun* ❶ Crossing, intersection

(185-ch)*CHINESE (PINYIN)* ☯📖

jiāochāi

(211-1)交差 (211-al)*ALTERNATIVES OR SEE ALSO* ✎✎ 交差, 交叉

#kosa {{交差}}##

(250-hi)こうさ (hir.)

(275-tō)こ－さ [kóˈòsà]

(276-tō2)こ－さ [kòósá]

(466-cha)*CHARACTERISTICS* ⓘ A Two-character, which consists of 2 Chinese Logograms and 2 Hiˈra-ga-ˈna Characters.

280. ˈKō-sa-dachi

(015-w1)*WORD 1* ᵂ ☛ kosa {{交差}}, p. 154

(016-w2)*WORD 2* ᵂ ☛ tachi {{立ち}}, p. 228

(030-st)*STANCE* 立 **AKA** Crossed Stance, Crossing Stance **Category** Middle height front stances

(211-1)交差立ち

(212-2)交差立

(250-hi)こうさだち (hir.)

#kosadachi {{交差立ち}}##

(466-cha)*CHARACTERISTICS* ⓘ A Four-character, which consists of 3 Chinese Logograms and 1 Hiˈra-ga-ˈna Characters.

(483-td)**Tↄd** ⌂ Due to the ˈRen-daku laws, the unvoiced consonant /T/ may get a Dak[u]-ˈten (゛) and become ~/d/ as a suffix. Example ↳ ˈTachi (たち) turns into Ki-ˈba Daˈchi (きばだち).

281. Koˈshi (腰)

(077-jg)*GENERAL MEANING (EXAMPLES)* ☼📖 *noun* ❶ Hips, pelvis ❷ Waist, lower back, lumbar region ❸ Back.

(089-no)*NOTES AND EXAMPLES* 📖✎ I-ˈai-goshi-dachi (居合腰立ち) is a One-leg Kneeling Stance – as the first stance of enpi {{燕飛}}, p. 63.

(185-ch)*CHINESE (PINYIN)* ☯📖 *yāo*

(211-1)腰

(211-al)*ALTERNATIVES OR SEE ALSO* ✎✎ 腰

(250-hi)こし (hir.)

#Koshi-hips {腰}##

(256-kat)コシ (kat.)

(313-ka)*KANJI* ✎ The Phono-semantic Compound Logogram Koˈshi-hips (腰). (313k-cn)**Components** ⛁ [semantic 月 | phonetic 要] (313k-ra)**Radical**

✦ 肉月月 meat (313k-cs)**Composition**

✗ Left: 月 , right: 要 (313k-re)**Readings (examples)** ✎ Go-on: よう (yō). Kan-on: よう (yō). Kun: こし (koshi, 腰).

(885-tag)*TAGS* 💻 #hip

(830-ik)**IMPORTANT KANJI**

282.Koshi 2

(011-k1)*KANJI 1* ☞ Tora-tiger {虎}, p. 249

(012-k2)*KANJI 2* ☞ Ato-toe {趾}, p. 40

(045-ll)*LOWER LIMB STRIKE & ANATOMY*

足 **AKA** Ball of the Foot, Tiger's paw, Tiger Tow, see Synonyms **Category** Foot Anatomy

(089-no)*NOTES AND EXAMPLES* 📖✍

Metatarso-Phalangeal Joints. Some would say that especially the first and the second MTP Joints. Others would say that especially when the toes are dorsiflexed.

(047-nl)*FUNAKOSHI NYUMON TERAMOTO – LOWER LIMB* 📚**NLL** 48 (list), 57 #koshi {{虎趾}}##

(133-sy)*SYNONYMS* ☞= The following can mean ball of the foot: chūsoku (nakaashi), p. 55; Jō-soku-tei (上足底); koshi {{虎趾}}, p. 155; nakaashi (中足), p. 178; maeashi {{前足}}, p. 161; Zen-soku (前足).

(185-ch)*CHINESE (PINYIN)* 👁📖 **hǔ zhǐ**

(211-1)虎趾

(250-hi)こし (hir.)

(256-kat)コシ (kat.)

(466-cha)*CHARACTERISTICS* ⓘ A Two-character, which consists of 2 Chinese Logograms and 0 Hiˈra-ga-ˈna Characters.

283.Kō-ˈshō-kun (kankū)

(001-REF-rom) Kō-ˈshō-kun ☞ kankū {{観空}}, p. 127

#kōshōkun (kankū)##

(800-tag)*TAGS* 💻 #koshokun

284.Kō-ˈsō-kun (kankū)

(001-REF-rom)Kō-ˈsō-kun ☞ kankū {{観空}}, p. 127

#kōsōkun (kankū)##

(800-tag)*TAGS* 💻 #kosokun

285.Kuˈbi (首)

(000-it)*INCLUDING TERMS (EXAMPLES)* 👁✉ kubiwa {{首輪}}, p. 156; shuri {{首里}}, p. 222

(077-jg)*GENERAL MEANING (EXAMPLES)* ⚙📖 *noun* ❶ Neck ❷ Head

(185-ch)*CHINESE (PINYIN)* ☯📖 ***shǒu***

(211-1)首

#Kubi-neck {首}##

(211-al)*ALTERNATIVES OR SEE ALSO* 🖌🖌 頸, 頚, 㑨, 百

(256-kat)クビ (kat.) (250-hi)くび (hir.)

(275-tō)く[び] [kùbí]

(302-kn)*KANJI NOTES* 🖌✍ A Radical (Radical 185)

(833-kan)**KANJI**

286.Ku'bi-wa

(011-k1)*KANJI 1* ☛ Kubi-neck {首}, p. 156

(012-k2)*KANJI 2* ☛ Wa-ring {輪}, p. 267

(055-tt)*THROWING TECHNIQUE* 投 技 **Old Name** Ku'bi-wa (頸環) **AKA** Encircle the Neck, To Encircle the Neck, Neck Ring, Neck Circle, Around the Neck

(077-jg)*GENERAL MEANING (EXAMPLES)* ☼📖 *noun* ❶ Collar ❷ Necklace

(089-no)*NOTES AND EXAMPLES* 📖✍ Yu'bi-'wa [yùbíwá] (指輪), for instance, is a finger ring, and U'de-wa [ùdéwá] (腕輪) means bracelet.

(134-re)*RELATED TERMS* 👁∞ udewa {{腕輪}}, p. 261

(185-ch)*CHINESE (PINYIN)* ☯📖 ***shǒulún***

#kubiwa {{首輪}}##

(056-mt)*FUNAKOSHI MAIN BOOK - THROWING TECHNIQUES* **MTT** **1922 original** 58 (頸環) **1925 Ishida** 64 **1925 Teramoto** 53 (list), 56 **1935 Suzuki-Johnston** 195 **1935 Ohshima** 227 (list), 228-229

(203-hi)⌛⊙ (250-hi)くびわ (hir.)

(211-1)首輪

(211-al)*ALTERNATIVES OR SEE ALSO* 🖌🖌 首轮, 頚輪, 頸環, 頸輪

(466-cha)*CHARACTERISTICS* ⓘ A Two-character, which consists of 2 Chinese Logograms and 0 Hi'ra-ga-'na Characters.

(800-tag)*TAGS* 💻 #kubiwa, #kubi-wa, #kubi wa

287.Ku'mi (組)

(000-it)*INCLUDING TERMS (EXAMPLES)* 👁✉ kumite {{組手}}, p. 157

(077-jg)*GENERAL MEANING (EXAMPLES)* ☼📖 *noun* ❶ Set, pack ❷

Class, group[62], team, crew, association.

(313-ka)*KANJI* 🖊 The Phono-semantic Compound Logogram Kuˈmi-set (組). (313k-cn)**Components** 🖧 [semantic 糸 | phonetic 且]. (313k-ra)**Radical** ✛ 糸 糸 silk. (313k-cs)**Composition** ✗ Left: 糸 , right: 且. (313k-re)**Readings (examples)** 🗣 Go-on: す (su). Kan-on: そ (so). On: しょ (sho). Kun: く み (kumi, 組み); くみひも (kumi-himo); くむ (kumu, 組む).

#Kumi-set {組}##

(185-ch)*CHINESE (PINYIN)* ☯📖 *zǔ*

(211-1)組

(211-ka+hi)組み

(250-hi)くみ (hir.)

(275-tō)く み [kùmí˙]

(705-gv)*GODAN VERB* 🏍⑤ **Terminal Form** {u* 🔥 but not i*-ru or e*-ru} ˈKumu [kú˙mù] (組 む), which means to assemble. **Polite Form** {i*-masu} Kuˈmimas[u] [kùmímá˙sù] (組みます).

(730-vt)*VERB TRANSLATION* 🏍📖 To assemble, to put together, to construct ❷ To unite, to join ❸ To wrestle, to grapple.

(830-ik)**IMPORTANT KANJI**

288.Kuˈmi-ˈte

(000-it)*INCLUDING TERMS (EXAMPLES)*

👁✉ gohonkumite {{五本組手}}, p. 71; ipponkumite {{一本組手}}, p. 106; jiyūkumite {{自由組手}}, p. 113; sanbonkkumite {{三本組手}}, p. 202

(011-k1)*KANJI 1* ☞ Kumi-set {組}, p. 157

(012-k2)*KANJI 2* ☞ Te-hand {手}, p. 234

(070-kt)*KARATE MEANING* ✋📖 *noun* ① Sparring, facing an opponent, training against an adversary, combat training with a partner.

#kumite {{組手}}##

(071-dl)🔥 **AA** *DOJO LANGUAGE* ⏳📖 *phrase* ① Grappling hands

(211-1)組手

(212-2)組み手

(250-hi)くみて (hir.)

(280-po)pol:KYMITE

ˈKū-san-ˈkū (kankū) - ˈKyū (級)

(466-cha)*CHARACTERISTICS* ① A Two-character, which consists of 2 Chinese Logograms and 0 Hiˈra-ga-ˈna Characters.

(800-tag)*TAGS* 🖥 #kumi-te, kumi te

(838-su)**SUPER-TERM**

289. ˈKū-san-ˈkū (kankū)

(001-REF-rom)Kū-san-kū ☞ kankū {{観空}}, p. 127

#kūsankū (kankū)##

(256-kat)**クーサンクー** (kat.)

(800-tag)*TAGS* 🖥 #kusanku

290. ˈKū-shan-ˈkū (kankū)

(001-REF-rom)Kū-shan-kū ☞ kankū {{観空}}, p. 127

#kūshankū (kankū)##

(256-kat)**クーシャンクー** (kat.)

(800-tag)*TAGS* 🖥 #kushanku

291. Kwan (his.) (Kan)

(001-REF-rom)Kwan ☞ Kan-observation {観}, p. 125

#Kwan (Kan)##

(250-hi)**くわん** (hir. his.)

292. Kwan-kū (kankū)

(001-REF-rom)Kwan-kū ☞ kankū {{観空}}, p. 127

#kwankū (kankū)##

(800-tag)*TAGS* 🖥 #kwanku

293. ˈKyū (九)

(077-jg)*GENERAL MEANING (EXAMPLES)* ☼📖 *noun* ❶ Nine.

(185-ch)*CHINESE (PINYIN)* ☯📖 *jiǔ*

(211-1)**九**

(250-hi)**きゅう** (hir.)

(275-tō) きゅう [kyúˑù]

#Kyū-nine {九}##

(280-po)pol:KJUU

(325-kr)*KANJI READINGS* 🖌🗣 Go-on: く (ku). Kan-on: きゅう (kyū).

(800-tag)*TAGS* 🖥 #kyuu, kyuh

(833-kan)**KANJI**

(838-su)**SUPER-TERM**

294. ˈKyū (級)

(000-it)*INCLUDING TERMS (EXAMPLES)* 👁✉ gokyū {{五級}}, p. 72; hachikyu {{八級}}, p. 77; ikkyū {{一級}}, p. 104

(070-kt)*KARATE MEANING* ✋📖 *noun* ① Junior rank, rank below Dan.

(185-ch)*CHINESE (PINYIN)* ☯📖 *jí*

#Kyū-rank {級}##

(077-jg)*GENERAL MEANING (EXAMPLES)* ☼📖 *noun* ❶ Rank, class, grade, level

(211-1)**級** (250-hi)**きゅう** (hir.)

(280-po)pol:KJUU

(990-tag)*TAGS* 🖥 #kyuu, kyuh

(833-kan)**KANJI**

295. ˈMa (間)

☀ Not to be confused with Ma-ai (間合い).

(000-it)*INCLUDING TERMS (EXAMPLES)*

👁✉ maai {{間合}}, p. 160

(071-dl)☀**AA** *DOJO LANGUAGE* ⧗📖

noun ① Ma-ai (間合い).

(077-jg)*GENERAL MEANING (EXAMPLES)* ☼📖 *noun* ❶ Space (between), gap, distance [63]. ❷ Time (between), pause, break.

(089-no)*NOTES AND EXAMPLES* 📖✎

Ma meaning negative space or time, is an important concept in Japanese art[64]. Intervals are considered rich in energy[65].

(185-ch)*CHINESE (PINYIN)* 👁📖 *jiān*

(211-1)間 (211-al)*ALTERNATIVES OR SEE ALSO* ✎✎ 间, 閒

(250-hi)ま (hir.)

#Ma-space {間}##

Script 8 – Ma-space Western Zhou Bronze Inscriptions

QR Code 2 – Ma-space Logogram (Aski8rpK_PI&t=88s)

List of QR Codes (Video), p. 11

(256-kat)マ (kat.)

(313-ka)*KANJI* ✎ The Compound Ideogram ˈMa-space (間). (313k-cn)**Components** ⬚ [門 gate (door) | 日 sun (once moon – moonlight peeking through a door - 閒)] (313k-ra)**Radical** ✦ 門 gate (313k-cs)**Composition** ✗ Top, left and right: 門 , bottom: 日 (313k-re)**Readings (examples)** ✊ Go-on: けん (ken). Kan-on: かん (kan) – as in Ji-ˈkan (時間) which means time. Kun: あいだ (aida, 間), ま (ma, 間).

(830-ik)**IMPORTANT KANJI**

(838-su)**SUPER-TERM**

296. Ma-aˈi

(011-k1)*KANJI 1* ☞ Ma-space {間}, p. 159

(012-k2)*KANJI 2* ☞ Au-to unite {合}, p. 41

(070-kt)*KARATE MEANING* ✋📖 ① Personal space, personal distance ② Proper distance from the opponent, distancing, right meeting distance ③ Actual distance between opponents ④ Set of values such as distance and timing.

ˈMae (前) - Maˈe ˈAshi-geˈri

(211-1)間合 (212-2)間合い

#maai {{間合}}##

(077-jg)*GENERAL MEANING (EXAM-PLES)* ☼📖 *noun* ❶ Distance ❷ Break, pause ❸ Suitable time, appropriate opportunity.

(185-ch)*CHINESE (PINYIN)* � 📖 ***jiān hé***

(250-hi)まあい (hir.)

(466-cha)*CHARACTERISTICS* ⓘ A Two-character, which consists of 2 Chinese Logograms and 0 Hiˈra-ga-ˈna Characters.

297. ˈMae (前)

(000-it)*INCLUDING TERMS (EXAMPLES)* 👁✉ maeashi {{前足}}, p. 161; maegeri {{前蹴り}}, p. 162; maete {{前手}}, p. 162; zenkutsu {{前屈}}, p. 284

(077-jg)*GENERAL MEANING (EXAM-PLES)* ☼📖 *preposition, adjective, adverb* ❶ Front, fore part, head ❷ In front of ❸ Before (chronologically), previously, ago

(089-no)*NOTES AND EXAMPLES* 📖✎ Maˈe-ˈbarai [màébáˈràì] (前払い), for instance, is a prepayment.

(134-re)*RELATED TERMS* 👁∞ Saki-previous {先}, p. 201; Omote-front {表}, p. 190

#Mae-front {前}##

(139-an)*ANTONYMS* 👁↺ Ato-behind {後}, p. 41

(185-ch)*CHINESE (PINYIN)* ☺📖 ***qián***

(211-1)前

(211-al)*ALTERNATIVES OR SEE ALSO* ✒✒ 前, 歬, 剬, 歬, 𣥺

(250-hi)まえ (hir.)

(275-tō)ま え [máˈè]

(325-kr)*KANJI READINGS* ✒🗣 Go-on: ぜん[zéˈǹ] (zen) – as in ˈZen-wan (前腕) which means forearm. Kun: まえ (mae, 前).

(833-kan)**KANJI**

298. Maˈe ˈAshi-geˈri

●⃰ This term has different meanings.

(015-w1)*WORD 1* ʷ/ʷ ☛ maeashi {{前足}}, p. 161

(016-w2)*WORD 2* ʷ/ʷ ☛ keri {{蹴り}}, p. 140

(070-kt)*KARATE MEANING* ✋📖 *noun phrase* ① Front-leg kick (generally, any kind) ② Mae-ashi Mae-geri, Front Leg Front Kick, Front kick with the front leg.

#maeashigeri {{前足蹴り}}##

(211-1)前足蹴り

(212-2) 前足蹴

(250-hi)**まえあしげり** (hir.)

(466-cha)*CHARACTERISTICS* ⓘ A four-character, which consists of 3 Chinese Logograms and 1 Hiʹra-ga-ʹna Characters.

(800-tag)*TAGS* 🖥 #maeashigeri, mae-ashigeri, mae ashi geri

299.Maʹe-aʹshi

💣※ This term has different meanings.

💣※ Not to be confused with maeashigeri {{前足蹴り}}, p. 161.

(000-it)*INCLUDING TERMS (EXAMPLES)*

👁✉ maeashigeri {{前足蹴り}}, p. 161

(011-k1)*KANJI 1* ☞ Mae-front {前}, p. 160

(012-k2)*KANJI 2* ☞ Ashi-foot {足}, p. 37

(070-kt)*KARATE MEANING* ✋📖 AKA Zen-soku *noun* ① Front foot ②

Front leg ③ With the front leg, using the front leg ④ Ball of the foot.

(133-sy)*SYNONYMS* 👁= The following can mean ball of the foot: chūsoku (nakaashi), p. 55; Jō-soku-tei (上足底); koshi {{虎趾}}, p. 155; nakaashi (中足), p. 178; maeashi {{前足}}, p. 161; Zen-soku (前足).

#maeashi {{前足}}##

(077-jg)*GENERAL MEANING (EXAMPLES)* ☼📖 *noun* ❶ Forefoot, anterior aspect of the foot (including the metatarsal area).

(134-re)*RELATED TERMS* 👁∞ nakaashi (中足), p. 178

(185-ch)*CHINESE (PINYIN)* 👁📖 *qiánzú*

(211-1)前足

(211-al)*ALTERNATIVES OR SEE ALSO*

✎✎ 前脚, 前肢

(250-hi)**まえあし** (hir.)

(256-kat)**マエアシ** (kat.)

(275-tō)ま え あし [màéáshí]

(276-tō2)ま え あし [màéʹàshì]

(466-cha)*CHARACTERISTICS* ⓘ A Two-character, which consists of 2 Chi-

nese Logograms and 0 Hiˈra-ga-ˈna Characters.

300.Maˈe-geˈri

(011-k1)*KANJI 1* ☛ Mae-front {前}, p. 160

(015-w1)*WORD 1* ^W_W ☛ keri {{蹴り}}, p. 140

(045-ll)*LOWER LIMB STRIKE & ANATOMY*

足 **AKA** Front Kick, Forward Kick **Category** Kick

(046-ml)*FUNAKOSHI MAIN BOOK - LOWER LIMB* ☵**MLL** 1935 Ohshima 23 (list), 23

(077-jg)*GENERAL MEANING (EXAMPLES)* ☼📖 *noun* ❶ Front kick.

(185-ch)*CHINESE (PINYIN)* ☯📖 *qián cù*

(211-1)前蹴り

(466-cha)*CHARACTERISTICS* ⓘ A Three-character, which consists of 2 Chinese Logograms and 1 Hiˈra-ga-ˈna Characters.

#maegeri {{前蹴り}}##

(212-2)前蹴

(250-hi)まえげり (hir.)

(482-kg)**K↻g** ⌂ Due to the ˈRendaku laws, the unvoiced consonant /K/ may get a Dak[u]-ˈten (゛) and

become ~/g/ as a suffix. Example ↳ Keˈri (けり) turns into Maˈe-geˈri (まえげり).

(493-g)**G** ⌂👂🎵 Sometimes, /g/ may be pronounced differently than [g]. /g/ in the middle of a word, especially when pronounced by the older generation, may sound [ŋ]. Example ↳ Maˈe-geˈri will be pronounced [Maˈe-neˈri].

(800-tag)*TAGS* ▭ #mae-geri, mae geri, maigeri, mai-geri, mae keri, mae-keri

(838-su)**SUPER-TERM**

301.ˈMae-te

☀ This term is not related to kamaete {{構えて}}.

(011-k1)*KANJI 1* ☛ Mae-front {前}, p. 160

(012-k2)*KANJI 2* ☛ Te-hand {手}, p. 234

(070-kt)*KARATE MEANING* ✋📖 **AKA** Kizami-zuki *noun* ① Jab, Jabbing Punch, Front Arm Punch.

(133-sy)*SYNONYMS* 👁= kizamizuki , p. 149

#maete {{前手}}##

(185-ch)*CHINESE (PINYIN)* ☯📖 **qián**

shǒu

(211-1)前手 (250-hi)まえて（まえで）(hir.)

(466-cha)*CHARACTERISTICS* ⓘ A Two-character, which consists of 2 Chinese Logograms and 0 Hiˈra-ga-ˈna Characters.

(800-tag)*TAGS* 💻 #mae-te, mae te, maede, mae-de, mae de

(838-su)**SUPER-TERM**

302.Maˈki-waˈra

(077-jg)*GENERAL MEANING (EXAMPLES)* ☼📖 *noun* ❶ Straw post, padded post, punching post. Used for hitting.

(089-no)*NOTES AND EXAMPLES* 📖✎ As for the first Kanji – ˈMaki (巻): Toˈra-no-Maˈki (虎の巻), created by Hōan KOSUGI (Misai KOSUGI), is Shōtōkan's symbol[66].
#makiwara {{巻藁}}##

(185-ch)*CHINESE (PINYIN)* ☯📖

juàngǎo

(211-1)巻藁 (212-2)巻き藁
(250-hi)まきわら (hir.)

(466-cha)*CHARACTERISTICS* ⓘ A Two-character, which consists of 2 Chinese Logograms and 0 Hiˈra-ga-ˈna Characters.

303.ˈManji (卍)

(000-it)*INCLUDING TERMS (EXAMPLES)* 👁✉ manjiuke {{卍受け}}, p. 164

(077-jg)*GENERAL MEANING (EXAMPLES)* ☼📖 *noun* ❶ Swastika (especially counterclockwise).

(089-no)*NOTES AND EXAMPLES* 📖✎ Comes from 卍字 – Man-ji, which means Man Character.

(185-ch)*CHINESE (PINYIN)* ☯📖 **wàn**

(211-1)卍

(211-al)*ALTERNATIVES OR SEE ALSO* ✐✐卍字, 乐, 万字

#Manji-swastika {卍}##

(250-hi)まんじ(hir.)

(275-tō)まんじ [màńjí]

(276-tō2)まんじ [máˈǹjì]

(302-kn)*KANJI NOTES* ✐✎ This Logogram is outside the list of Jō-yō ˈKan-ji, belonging to the Hyō-gai ˈKan-ji. Contains 6 strokes.

(325-kr)*KANJI READINGS* ✐🗣 Go-on: もん (mon). Kan-on: ばん (ban).

Kan'yō-on: まん (man). Kun: まん じ (manji, 卍).

(833-kan)**KANJI**

304. ˈManji Uˈke

(011-k1)*KANJI* *1* ☞ Manji-swastika {卍}, p. 163

(012-k2)*KANJI* *2* ☞ uke {{受け}}, p. 262

(070-kt)*KARATE MEANING* 🖐📖 AKA Manji Kamae (卍 構 え), Manji Gamae *noun phrase* ① Swastika Block, Bent Cross Block, Snow-flake Block.

(089-no)*NOTES AND EXAMPLES* 📖✎ The last movement of Heian Godan.

(466-cha)*CHARACTERISTICS* ⓘ A Three-character, which consists of 2 Chinese Logograms and 1 Hiˈra-ga-ˈna Characters.

#manjiuke {{卍受け}}##

Masters 15 - Manjiuke by Bamgboye Sensei
List of Sensei Demonstrations next to Values, p. 10

Bobby Bamgboye of Nigeria WSKF demonstrates Manji-uke. Photographer: Joel Ibanga.

(185-ch)*CHINESE (PINYIN)* ☯📖 **wàn shòu**

(211-1)卍受け (212-2)卍受

(250-hi)まんじうけ (hir.)

(800-tag)*TAGS* 🖥 #manji-uke, manji uke

305. ˈMatsu (松)

(000-it)*INCLUDING TERMS (EXAMPLES)* 👁✉ matsumurasōkon {{松村 宗棍}}, p. 165; shōtō {{松濤}}, p. 220

(077-jg)*GENERAL MEANING (EXAMPLES)* ☼📖 *noun* ❶ Pine tree.

(185-ch)*CHINESE (PINYIN)* ☯📖 **sōng**[67]

(211-1)松

(250-hi)まつ (hir.)

#Matsu-pine {松}##

(256-kat)マツ (kat.)

(275-tō) ま つ [máˈtsù]

(280-po)pol:MACY

(325-kr)*KANJI READINGS* ✐🗣 Go-on: じゅ (ju). Kan-on: しょう (shō). Kun: まつ (matsu, 松).

(833-kan)**KANJI**

306. MAˈTSU-MURA ˈSō-kon

(011-k1)*KANJI 1* ☞ Matsu-pine {松}, p. 164

(029-pe)*PERSONS* 👪 MAˈTSU-MURA ˈSō-kon (ˈShu-ri , ~1809 - ~1899) was a famous Okinawan Kaˈra-te-ka. Among his students, we can find several legendary teachers, including Iˈto-su (p. 108), A-ˈsato (p. 36) and Fuˈna-koˈshi (p. 67).

(185-ch)*CHINESE (PINYIN)* ☯📖

Sōngcūn Zōng gùn

#matsumurasōkon {{ 松村 宗棍 }}##

(216-ea)松村 宗棍 (E.)

(217-we)宗棍 松村 (W.)

(466-cha)*CHARACTERISTICS* ⓘ A Four-character, which consists of 2 Chinese Logograms and 2 Hiˈra-ga-ˈna Characters.

(800-tag)*TAGS* 💻 #matsumurasokon, #sokon matsumura, #sokonmatsumura

307.Maˈwaru (回)

(000-it)*INCLUDING TERMS (EXAMPLES)*

👁✉ kaiten {{ 回転 }}, p. 121; mawashi {{回し}}, p. 166; mawasu {{回す}}, p. 167; mawatte {{回って}}, p. 168.

(077-jg)*GENERAL MEANING (EXAMPLES)* ✿📖 *verb (intransitive)* ❶ To turn, to revolve.

(134-re)*RELATED TERMS* 👁∞

Korogaru-to rotate {転}, p. 153

(185-ch)*CHINESE (PINYIN)* 👁📖 ***huí***

(610-In-Tr)*VERB PAIR* 👁◖ The Intransitive Verb is Mawaru-to turn {回}, p. 165. The Transitive verb is mawasu {{回す}}, p. 167.

(211-1)回

(211-ka+hi)回る

(211-ka+hiAlt)廻る

(212-2)囘

(250-hi)まわる (hir.)

(256-kat)マワル (kat.)

(275-tō)ま[わ]る [màwárú]

(800-tag)*TAGS* 💻 #turn

#Mawaru-to turn {回}##

(600-vt)**Form**	**Godan Intransitive ~ru (v. su)**
Terminal	màwárú
Plain ~te Request	màwátté
Polite ~te Request	màwátté kudaˈsai
Plain Imperative	màwáré
Stem	màwárí
Polite Imperative	maˈwari naˈsai
Formal	màwárímá⁺s[ù]

See

List of Commands, p. 25

(280-po)pol:MAŁARY

(313-ka)*KANJI* ✐ The Same-compound Pictogram Maˈwaru-to turn (回).

(313k-cn)**Components** 🖧 [口 | 口].

(313k-ra)**Radical** ✛ 口 enclosure. (313k-cs)**Composition** ✗ Outside: 口, center: 口. (313k-re)**Readings (examples)** ✊ Go-on: え (e). Kan-on: かい (kai). Tō-on: うい (ui). Kun: まわす (mawasu, 回す); まわる (maˈwaru, 回る).

(811-vpIn)**VERB PAIR – INTRANSITIVE PART**

(830-ik)**IMPORTANT KANJI**

308.Maˈwashi

(000-it)*INCLUDING TERMS (EXAMPLES)* 👁✉ mawashigeri {{回し蹴り}}, p. 167

(011-k1)*KANJI 1* ☛ Mawaru-to turn {回}, p. 165

(019-ste)*STEM FORM OF* ❗ ☛ mawasu {{回す}}, p. 167

(070-kt)*KARATE MEANING* ✋📖 *adjective* ① Circular.

#mawashi {{回し}}##

(077-jg)*GENERAL MEANING (EXAMPLES)* ☼📖 *noun* ❶ Loincloth, Sumo belt[68] ❷ Mantle, cape.

(211-1)回し (212-2)廻し

(250-hi)まわし (hir.)

(466-cha)*CHARACTERISTICS* ① A Two-character, which consists of 1 Chinese Logograms and 1 Hiˈra-ga-ˈna Characters.

309.Maˈwashi-geˈri

(000-it)*INCLUDING TERMS (EXAMPLES)* 👁✉ gyakumawashigeri {{逆回し蹴り}}, p. 74

(015-w1)*WORD 1* ᵂᵂ ☛ mawashi {{回し}}, p. 166

(016-w2)*WORD 2* ᵂᵂ ☛ keri {{蹴り}}, p. 140

(045-ll)*LOWER LIMB STRIKE & ANATOMY* 足 **AKA** Roundhouse Kick, Round Kick, Turning Kick, Spin Kick **Category** Kick

(046-ml)*FUNAKOSHI MAIN BOOK - LOWER LIMB* 📖**MLL** 1935 Ohshima 23 (list), 24

(185-ch)*CHINESE (PINYIN)* 👁📖 *huí cù*

(211-1)回し蹴り (212-2)回し蹴

(800-tag)*TAGS* ⌨ #mawashi-geri, mawashi geri, #mawashikeri #mawashigeri {{回し蹴り}}##

(250-hi)まわしげり (hir.)

(482-kg)**KↃg** 🔔 Due to the ˈRendaku laws, the unvoiced consonant /K/ may get a Dak[u]-ˈten (゛) and become ~/g/ as a suffix. Example 🖐 Keˈri (けり) turns into Maˈe-geˈri (まえげり).

(493-g)**G** 👂🔊 Sometimes, /g/ may be pronounced differently than [g]. /g/ in the middle of a word, especially when pronounced by the older generation, may sound [ŋ]. Example 🖐 Maˈe-geˈri may be pronounced [Maˈe-neˈri].

(466-cha)*CHARACTERISTICS* ⓘ A Four-character, which consists of 2 Chinese Logograms and 2 Hiˈra-ga-ˈna Characters.

(838-su)**SUPER-TERM**

310.maˈwasu

(011-k1)*KANJI 1* ☚ Mawaru-to turn {回}, p. 165

(077-jg)*GENERAL MEANING (EXAMPLES)* ✿📖 *verb (transitive)* ❶ To turn, to rotate.

(135-ge)*GERUND* 👁 ▶▶ mawashi {{回し}}, p. 166

(610-In-Tr)*VERB PAIR* 👁◖ The Intransitive Verb is Mawaru-to turn {回}, p. 165. The Transitive verb is mawasu {{回す}}, p. 167.

(211-1)回す

(212-2)廻す

(250-hi)まわす (hir.) (256-kat)マワス (kat.)

(810-vpTr)**VERB PAIR – TRANSITIVE PART**

#mawasu {{回す}}##

(600-vt)**Form**	Godan Transitive ~su
Terminal	màwású
Plain ~te Request	màwásh[í]té
Polite ~te Request	màwásh[í]té kudaˈsai
Plain Imperative	màwásé
Stem	maˈwashi
Polite Imperative	maˈwashi naˈsai
Formal	màwáshímá⁺s[ù]

See List of **Commands**, p. 25

(275-tō)ま わす [màwású]

(466-cha)*CHARACTERISTICS* ⓘ A Two-character, which consists of 1 Chi-

nese Logograms and 1 Hiˈra-ga-ˈna Characters.

311.Maˈwatte

(018-te)*TE FORM OF* ❗ ☞ Mawaru-to turn {回}, p. 165

(070-kt)*KARATE MEANING* ✋📖 AKA Maware *verb (imperative mood)* ① Turn around! turn![69] pivot! assume opposite direction!

See

List of Commands, p. 25

(133-sy)*SYNONYMS* 👁= kaette {{返って}}, p. 119

(211-1)回って (250-hi)まわって (hir.)

(275-tō)ま わって [màwátté]

(466-cha)*CHARACTERISTICS* ⓘ A Three-character, which consists of 1 Chinese Logograms and 2 Hiˈra-ga-ˈna Characters.

#mawatte {{回って}}##

Masters 16 - Mawatte by Le Bas Sensei
List of Sensei Demonstrations next to Values, p. 10

Sophie Le Bas of France Shōtōkan demonstrates Mawatte. Photographer: Patrick Schoeffer.

(610-In-Tr)*VERB PAIR* 👁◖◗ The Intransitive Verb is Mawaru-to turn {回}, p. 165. The Transitive verb is mawasu {{回す}}, p. 167.

(800-tag)*TAGS* 💻 #mawate

(838-su)**SUPER-TERM**

312.ˈMen (面)

(000-it)*INCLUDING TERMS (EXAMPLES)* 👁✉ shōmen {{正面}}, p. 217; sokumen {{側面}}, 224

(077-jg)*GENERAL MEANING (EXAMPLES)* ✿📖 *noun suffix* ❶ Side, aspect *noun* ❷ Surface ❸ Face

(185-ch)*CHINESE (PINYIN)* 👁📖 *miàn* #Men-side {面}##

(211-1)面 (211-al)*ALTERNATIVES OR SEE ALSO* ✒✒ 麵, 麺, 頰

(250-hi)めん (hir.) (256-kat)メン (kat.)

(302-kn)*KANJI NOTES* ✒✎ A Radical (Radical 176)

(833-kan)**KANJI**

313.ˈMi (身)

(000-it)*INCLUDING TERMS (EXAMPLES)* 👁✉ goshin {{護身}}, p. 72; hanmi {{半身}}, p. 85; irimi {{入り身}}, p. 107

(077-jg)*GENERAL MEANING (EXAMPLES)* ✿📖 *noun* ❶ Body ❷ Oneself, identity, somebody, person ❸ One's place, one's position, one's station, one's social standing ❹ Main part ❺ Blade ❻ Flesh, meat.

(089-no)*NOTES AND EXAMPLES* 📖✍ Shus-ˈshin (出身) is a birthplace or generally a person's origin.

(133-sy)*SYNONYMS* 👁= Tai-body {体}, p. 228

#Mi-body {身}##

(185-ch)*CHINESE (PINYIN)* ☯📖 *shēn*

(211-1)身

(250-hi)み (hir.)

(302-kn)*KANJI NOTES* ✍✍ It depicts a pregnant woman.

(313-ka)*KANJI* ✍ The Pictogrammatic Radical (Radical 158) ˈMi-body (身). (313k-cn)**Components** 🝆 No components - a Simple Logogram. (313k-ra)**Radical** ✛ 身 body. (313k-cs)**Composition** 夂 身 . (313k-re)**Readings (examples)** 🗣 Go-on:

しん (shin). Kan-on: しん (shin). Kun: み (mi, 身).

(830-ik)**IMPORTANT KANJI**

314.Miˈgi (右)

(077-jg)*GENERAL MEANING (EXAMPLES)* ✿📖 *adjective* ❶ Right (direction), right hand side, the opposite of left.

(185-ch)*CHINESE (PINYIN)* ☯📖 *yòu*

(211-1)右

(250-hi)みぎ (hir.)

#Migi-right {右}##

(211-al)*ALTERNATIVES OR SEE ALSO*

✍✍ 又, 広

(302-kn)*KANJI NOTES* ✍✍ Contains 5 strokes.

(833-kan)**KANJI**

315.Mi-ˈka-z[u]ˈki

(000-it)*INCLUDING TERMS (EXAMPLES)* 👁✉ mikazukigeri {{三日月蹴り}}, p. 170

(015-w1)*WORD* ↗ 🆆 ☞ mikka {{三日}}, p. 171

(013-k3)*KANJI* 3 ☞ Tsuki-moon {月}, p. 253

(077-jg)*GENERAL MEANING (EXAMPLES)* ✿📖 *noun* ❶ New moon, crescent moon

(185-ch)*CHINESE   (PINYIN)* ☯ 📖

sānrìyuè

(211-1)三日月 (211-al)*ALTERNATIVES OR*

SEE ALSO ✎✎ 朒

#mikazuki {{三日月}}##

(250-hi)みかづき (hir.)

(275-tō)み|かづき| [mìkázúkí]

(466-cha)*CHARACTERISTICS* ⓘ   A

Three-character, which consists of 3

Chinese Logograms and 0 Hiˈra-ga-

ˈna Characters.

(484-tsz)**Ts↷z** 🔔 Due to the ˈRen-

daku laws, the unvoiced consonant

/Ts/ may get a Dak[u]-ˈten (゛) and

become ~/z/ as a suffix. Example ↳

Ts[u]ˈki 2（つき）turns into Oˈi-

z[u]ˈki（おいづき）.

(800-tag)*TAGS* 🖥 #mikkazuki

316.Mi-ˈka-z[u]ˈki Geˈri

(015-w1)*WORD 1* ᵂᵂ ☞ mikazuki {{三日

月}}, p. 170

(016-w2)*WORD 2* ᵂᵂ ☞ keri {{蹴り}},

p. 140

(045-ll)*LOWER LIMB STRIKE & ANATOMY*

足 **AKA** Crescent Kick, Crescent-

moon Kick, New Moon Kick **Cate-**

gory Kick

(046-ml)*FUNAKOSHI MAIN BOOK - LOW-*

ER LIMB 🐟**MLL** 1922 original 45

(list), 46 **1925 Ishida** 56 (list), 56

1925 Teramoto 49 (list), 50 **1935**

Suzuki-Johnston 27 (list), 28 **1935**

Ohshima 23 (list), 25

(466-cha)*CHARACTERISTICS* ⓘ A Five-

character, which consists of 4 Chi-

nese Logograms and 1 Hiˈra-ga-ˈna

Characters.

#mikazukigeri {{三日月蹴り}}##

(211-1)三日月蹴り

(212-2)三日月蹴

(250-hi)みかづきげり (hir.)

(482-kg)**K↷g** 🔔 Due to the ˈRen-

daku laws, the unvoiced consonant

/K/ may get a Dak[u]-ˈten (゛) and

become ~/g/ as a suffix. Example ↳

Keˈri（けり）turns into Maˈe-geˈri（

まえげり）.

(484-tsz)**Ts↷z** 🔔 Due to the ˈRen-

daku laws, the unvoiced consonant

/Ts/ may get a Dak[u]-ˈten (゛) and

become ~/z/ as a suffix. Example ↳

Ts[u]ˈki 2（つき）turns into Oˈi-

z[u]ˈki（おいづき）.

(800-tag)*TAGS* 🖥 #mikazukikeri (みか

づきけり) - Mi-ˈka-z[u]ˈki Keˈri

(838-su)**SUPER-TERM**

317.Mik-ˈka

(000-it)*INCLUDING TERMS (EXAMPLES)*

👁✉ mikazuki {{三日月}}, p. 170

(011-k1)*KANJI 1* ☛ San-three {三}, p. 201

(012-k2)*KANJI 2* ☛ Hi-day {日}, p. 96

(077-jg)*GENERAL MEANING (EXAMPLES)* ☼📖 noun ❶ The third day of the month ❷ Three days.

(211-1)三日 (212-2) 3 日

#mikka {{三日}}##

(250-hi)みっか (hir.)

(275-tō)みっか [mìkká]

(466-cha)*CHARACTERISTICS* ⓘ A Two-character, which consists of 2 Chinese Logograms and 0 Hiˈra-ga-ˈna Characters.

(800-tag)*TAGS* 🖥 #mik-ka, mik ka, #mika, mi-ka, mi ka

318.Mok[u]-ˈsō

(011-k1)*KANJI 1* ☛ Moku-silence {黙}, p. 172

(012-k2)*KANJI 2* ☛ Sō-thought {想}, p. 222

(070-kt)*KARATE MEANING* ✋📖 verb (imperative mode) ① Begin meditation! a call to meditate ② Close Your eyes!

See

List of Commands, p. 25

(077-jg)*GENERAL MEANING (EXAMPLES)* ☼📖 noun ❶ Meditation, silent contemplation

(185-ch)*CHINESE (PINYIN)* 👁📖

mòxiǎng

#mokusō {{黙想}}##

(134-gr-re)*GROUP* 👁(😣) The following terms are related: iai {{居合}}, p. 103, mokusō {{黙想}}, p. 171, seiza {{正座}}, p. 207, zazen {{座禅}}, p. 283

(211-1)黙想 (250-hi)もくそう (hir.)

(280-po)pol:MOKSOO

(466-cha)*CHARACTERISTICS* ⓘ A Two-character, which consists of 2 Chinese Logograms and 0 Hiˈra-ga-ˈna Characters.

(800-tag)*TAGS* 🖥 #mokuso, #mokso

(838-su)**SUPER-TERM**

319.ˈMoku (黙)

(000-it)*INCLUDING TERMS (EXAMPLES)*

👁✉ mokusō {{黙想}}, p. 171

(077-jg)*GENERAL MEANING (EXAMPLES)* ☼📖 *noun* ❶ Silence

(185-ch)*CHINESE (PINYIN)* ☯📖 ***mò***

#Moku-silence {黙}##

(211-1)黙 (212-2)默

(250-hi)もく (hir.)

(280-po)pol:MOKY

(833-kan)**KANJI**

320. ˈMon (門)

(000-it)*INCLUDING TERMS (EXAMPLES)*

👁✉ tennomon {{天の門}}, p. 243

(077-jg)*GENERAL MEANING (EXAMPLES)* ☼📖 *noun* ❶ Gate

(185-ch)*CHINESE (PINYIN)* ☯📖 ***mén*** as in *tiān'ānmén* (天安門)

(302-kn)*KANJI NOTES* 🖌🖎 Can You recognize the Logogram in the ancient Chinese script on page 28? #Mon-gate {門}##

門 **Script 9 - Mon-gate Western Zhou Bronze Inscriptions**

(211-1)門

(212-2)门

(250-hi)もん (hir.)

(302-kn)*KANJI NOTES* 🖌🖎 A Radical (Radical 169)

(833-kan)**KANJI**

321. ˈMoro (諸)

(000-it)*INCLUDING TERMS (EXAMPLES)*

👁✉ morote {{諸手}}, p. 172

(077-jg)*GENERAL MEANING (EXAMPLES)* ☼📖 *prefix* ❶ Many ❷ Together ❸ Both.

(185-ch)*CHINESE (PINYIN)* ☯📖 ***zhū***

#Moro-many {諸}##

(211-1)諸 (211-al)*ALTERNATIVES OR SEE ALSO* 🖊🖎 諸, 諸, 両, 双 (250-hi)もろ (hir.)

(302-kn)*KANJI NOTES* 🖊🖎 Contains 15 strokes.

(833-kan)**KANJI**

322. Moˈro-te

(011-k1)*KANJI 1* ☛ Moro-many {諸}, p. 172

(012-k2)*KANJI 2* ☛ Te-hand {手}, p. 234

(070-kt)*KARATE MEANING* ✋📖 *adjective* ① Double handed, two hand, two-armed, double arm, double forearm, two-fisted ② Augmented.

(077-jg)*GENERAL MEANING (EXAMPLES)* ☼📖 *adjective* ❶ Including both hands #morote {{諸手}}##

(185-ch)*CHINESE   (PINYIN)* ☯📖

zhūshǒu

(211-1) **諸手**

(211-al)*ALTERNATIVES OR SEE ALSO*

✐✎ **両手, 双手**

(250-hi) **もろて** (hir.)

(466-cha)*CHARACTERISTICS* ⓘ A Two-character, which consists of 2 Chinese Logograms and 0 Hiˈra-ga-ˈna Characters.

323. Moˈto (元)

(000-it)*INCLUDING TERMS (EXAMPLES)*

👁✉ ashimoto {{足元}}, p. 38; genki {{元気}}, p. 69; kihon {{基本}}, p. 146 (alternative spelling); ogenkidesuka {{お元気ですか}}, p. 187

(077-jg)*GENERAL MEANING (EXAMPLES)* ☼📖 *noun* ❶ Origin, source, root, base, basis, foundation, beginning[70], starting point ❷ Cause.

(136-se)*SEE ALSO* 👁✚ Hon-source {本}, p. 102

(185-ch)*CHINESE (PINYIN)* ☯📖 **yuan**

(095-3t)*THE THREE TEACHINGS* 𝟛ⓢ In Traditional Chinese Medicine, there

Moˈto (元) - Muˈsubi-daˈchi is a term called *yuán* point, which is relevant for Kaˈra-te as well[71].

(302-kn)*KANJI NOTES* ✐✎ 二 is the historic[72] version of the Simple Ideogram Uˈe-top (上).

#Moto-origin {元}##

(211-1) **元**

(212-2) **本**

(213-3) **原**

(214-4) **基**

(215-5) **素**

(250-hi) **もと** (hir.)

(275-tō) も|と| [mòtóˑ]

(276-tō2) も|と| [mòtó]

(313-ka)*KANJI* ✐ The Pictogram Moˈto-origin (元). (313k-cn)**Components** ⛓ [二 | ル]. (313k-ra)**Radical** ⚘ ル legs. (313k-cs)**Composition** ⚒ Top: 二, bottom: ル. (313k-re)**Readings (examples)** 👄 Go-on: ごん (gon). Kan-on: げん (gen). Tō-on: がん (gan). Kun: もと (moto). Nanori: はじめ (hajime).

(830-ik)**IMPORTANT KANJ**

324. Muˈsubi-daˈchi

(016-w2)*WORD 2* W̲ ☛ tachi {{立ち}}, p. 228

(030-st)*STANCE* 立 **AKA** Informal Attention Stance, Joining Stance, Closed Heel Stance, Heels Together Stance, Knot Stance, V Stance, V-shape Stance, Ready Stance, Formal Attention Stance **Category** High Stances

(089-no)*NOTES AND EXAMPLES* 📖✍

The heels touch one another, and the toes are at 45 degrees.

(032-ns)*FUNAKOSHI NYUMON TERAMOTO - STANCES* ❧**NS** 59 (list), 59.

(466-cha)*CHARACTERISTICS* ⓘ A Four-character, which consists of 2 Chinese Logograms and 2 Hiˈra-ga-ˈna Characters.

(185-ch)*CHINESE (PINYIN)* ☯📖 *jié lì*

(211-1)結び立ち

#musubidachi {{結び立ち}}##

Masters 17 - Musubidachi by Bamgboye Sensei
List of Sensei Demonstrations next to Values, p. 10

Bobby Bamgboye of Nigeria WSKF demonstrates Musubi-dachi. Photographer: Joel Ibanga.

(212-2)結び立

(213-3)V字立

(250-hi)むすびだち (hir.)

(483-td)**T⊃d** 🔔 Due to the ˈRen-daku laws, the unvoiced consonant /T/ may get a Dak[u]-ˈten (゛) and become ~/d/ as a suffix. Example 🖋 ˈTachi (たち) turns into Ki-ˈba Daˈchi (きばだち).

(800-tag)*TAGS* 📖 #musubitachi

325. ˈNage

(000-it)*INCLUDING TERMS (EXAMPLES)* 👁✉ komanage {{独楽投げ}}, p. 152; nagewaza {{投げ技}}, p. 175

(011-k1)*KANJI 1* ☛ Nageru-to throw {投}, p. 175

(077-jg)*GENERAL MEANING (EXAMPLES)* ☯📖 *noun* ❶ Throw ❷ Fall #nage {{投げ}}##

(211-1)投げ

(250-hi)なげ (hir.)

(466-cha)*CHARACTERISTICS* ⓘ A Two-character, which consists of 1 Chinese Logograms and 1 Hiˈra-ga-ˈna Characters.

326.Naˈgeru (投)

(000-it)*INCLUDING TERMS (EXAMPLES)*

👁✉ nage {{投げ}}, p. 174

(077-jg)*GENERAL MEANING (EXAMPLES)* ✿📖 *verb (transitive)* ❶ To throw.

(185-ch)*CHINESE (PINYIN)* ☯📖 *tóu*

(211-1)投

(211-ka+hi)投げる

(711-sh)*SHIMO ICHIDAN VERB* 🏍①↻

Terminal Form {e*-ru} Naˈgeru [nàgé⁺rù] (投げる), which means to throw. **Polite Form** {-masu} Naˈgemas[u] [nàgémá⁺sù] (投げます).

#Nageru-to throw {投}##

(250-hi)なげる (hir.)

(275-tō)な げ る [nàgé⁺rù]

(313-ka)*KANJI* ✐ The Phono-semantic Compound Logogram Naˈgeru-to throw (投). (313k-cn)**Components** 🔣 [semantic 扌 | phonetic 殳] (313k-ra)**Radical** ✛ 手 扌 𰀀 hand (313k-cs)**Composition** 🗡 Left: 扌, right: 殳 (313k-re)**Readings (examples)** 🗣

Go-on: ず (zu). Kan-on: とう (tō). Kun: なげる (nageru, 投げる).

(830-ik)**IMPORTANT KANJI**

327.Naˈge-waˈza

(015-w1)*WORD 1* Ⓦ Ⓦ ☛ nage {{投げ}}, p. 174

(013-k3)*KANJI 3* ☛ Waza-technique {技}, p. 267

(056-mt)*FUNAKOSHI MAIN BOOK - THROWING TECHNIQUES* 📘MTT

1922 original 51-61 **1925 Ishida** 59-65 **1925 Teramoto** 53 (list), 54-56 **1935 Suzuki-Johnston** 192-201 **1935 Ohshima** 227 (list), 228-232.

(185-ch)*CHINESE (PINYIN)* ☯📖 *tóu jì*

#nagewaza {{投げ技}}##

(077-jg)*GENERAL MEANING (EXAMPLES)* ✿📖 *noun* ❶ Throwing technique.

(211-1)投げ技

(211-al)*ALTERNATIVES OR SEE ALSO* ✎✎ 投技, 投げ業

(250-hi)なげわざ (hir.)

(466-cha)*CHARACTERISTICS* ① A Three-character, which consists of 2 Chinese Logograms and 1 Hiˈra-gaˈna Characters.

328.ˈNa-ha

(000-it)*INCLUDING TERMS (EXAMPLES)*

👁✉ nahate {{那覇手}}, p. 176

(028-pl)*PLACES* 🌐 Historically, the village of Naha played an important part in the development of the Okinawan martial arts. Today, the capital city of Okinawa Prefecture.

(134-re)*RELATED TERMS* 👁∞ shuri {{首里}}, p. 222

(185-ch)*CHINESE (PINYIN)* ☯📖 *nàbà*

#naha {{那覇}}##

(189-ok)*OKINAWAN* ● ˈNā-fa

(211-1) 那 覇　(211-al)*ALTERNATIVES OR SEE ALSO* 🖊🖊 那覇

(250-hi) なは (hir.)

(275-tō) な|は [ná⁺hà]

(466-cha)*CHARACTERISTICS* ⓘ A Two-character, which consists of 2 Chinese Logograms and 0 Hiˈra-ga-ˈna Characters.

329. ˈNa-ha-te

(015-w1)*WORD 1* ᵂ/ᵂ ☞ naha {{那覇}}, p. 176

(013-k3)*KANJI 3* ☞ Te-hand {手}, p. 234

(025-sch)*SCHOOLS* ⛩ *name* Karate styles that are attributed to Naha.

They belong to the ˈShō-re[i]-ryū (昭霊流) - the heavy and short Karate styles, which resemble the southern schools of Chinese martial arts[73].

(133-sy)*SYNONYMS* 👁= shōreiryū {{昭霊流}}, p. 218

#nahate {{那覇手}}##

(139-an)*ANTONYMS* 👁↺ shurite {{首里手}}, p. 222; tomarite {{泊手}}, p. 248; shōrinryū {{少林流}}, p. 219

(189-ok)*OKINAWAN* ● ˈNā-fa-dī (ナーファディー)

(211-1)那覇手

(250-hi)なはて (hir.)

(466-cha)*CHARACTERISTICS* ⓘ A Three-character, which consists of 3 Chinese Logograms and 0 Hiˈra-ga-ˈna Characters

330. Nai-ˈhan-chi

(011-k1)*KANJI 1* ☞ Uchi-inside {内}, p. 258

(012-k2)*KANJI 2* ☞ Ho-step {歩}, p. 101

(013-k3)*KANJI 3* ☞ Shin-to advance {進}, p. 213

(070-kt)*KARATE MEANING* ✋📖 *name*

① The Tekki Kata (page 237)

(133-sy)*SYNONYMS* 👁= tekki {{鉄騎}}, p. 237

(185-ch)*CHINESE (PINYIN)* 👁📖 ***nèi bù jìn, nèi pàn zhàn, nèi fàn zhì***

(189-ok)*OKINAWAN* ● Naifanchi (ナイファンチ), Naifanchin (ナイファンチン), Naifuanchin, Naifanchen (ナイファンチェン)

(211-1)**内歩進**

(211-al)*ALTERNATIVES OR SEE ALSO*

✍✍ 内畔戦, 内範置

(250-hi)ないはんち (hir.)

(256-kat)ナイハンチ (kat.)

#naihanchi {{内歩進}}##

(089-no)*NOTES AND EXAMPLES* 📖✍

Naihanchi Kata translates to or called Internal Divided Conflict, Internally Divided Conflict, Internal Struggle, Internal Opposing Energy, Inside & Outside Battle, Advanced Inward Stepping and Sideways Fighting[74]. Chi could mean a battle. The Characters 進 (Shin) and 戦 (Sen) appear as suffixes, in at least one version of each name - ˈSan-chin and Nai-ˈhan-chi. ˈSan-chin (*sānzhàn*) means three (三) battles, and is written 三戦, 三戦, 三進 or 参戦. Nowadays, Nai-ˈhan-chi is written 内歩進, 内畔戦 or 内範置, but the original ideographic spelling is obscure[75].

(466-cha)*CHARACTERISTICS* ① A Three-character, which consists of 3 Chinese Logograms and 0 Hiˈra-gaˈna Characters.

(800-tag)*TAGS* 💻 #naifanchi, #naihanchin

331. ˈNaka (中)

(000-it)*INCLUDING TERMS (EXAMPLES)* 👁✉ chūdan {{中段}}, p. 54; chūsokukotsu {{中足骨}}, p. 55; nakaashi (中足), p. 178; nakadaka {{中高}}, 179

(077-jg)*GENERAL MEANING (EXAMPLES)* ☼📖 *noun et al.* ❶ Middle, center, central, mean ❷ Inside, in, within, among ❸ China, Chinese, Sino-

(185-ch)*CHINESE (PINYIN)* 👁📖 ***zhōng, zhòng***

(211-1)中 (211-al)*ALTERNATIVES OR SEE ALSO* ✍✍ 内, 裡

(250-hi)なか (hir.)

#Naka-middle {中}##

(136-se)*SEE ALSO* 👁➕ Uchi-inside { 内}, p. 258

(275-tō) な か [náˈkà]

(313-ka)*KANJI* ✏ The Simple Picogram ˈDaka-middle (中). (313k-cn)**Components** 🔠 No components - a Simple Logogram. (313k-ra)**Radical** ✚ | line. (313k-cs)**Composition** ✕ Merging of 口 and | . (313k-re)**Readings (examples)** 🗣 Go-on: ちゅう (chū); じゅう (jū). Kan-on: ちゅう (chū); じゅう (jū). Kun: なか (ˈnaka, 中); うち (uˈchi, 中).

(830-ik)**IMPORTANT KANJI**

332.Naˈka-aˈshi

(011-k1)*KANJI 1* ☛ Naka-middle {中}, p. 178

(012-k2)*KANJI 2* ☛ Ashi-foot {足}, p. 37

(077-jg)*GENERAL MEANING (EXAMPLES)* ⚙📖 *noun* ❶ Mid-foot, the metatarsal area, the area of the long bones of the foot, the area of the arch of the foot ❷ Ball of the foot

(134-re)*RELATED TERMS* 👁∞ maeashi {{前足}}, p. 161

(211-1)中足

(250-hi)なかあし (hir.)

#nakaashi (中足)##

(133-sy)*SYNONYMS* 👁= The following can mean ball of the foot: chūsoku (nakaashi), p. 55; Jō-soku-tei (上足底); koshi {{虎趾}}, p. 155; nakaashi (中足), p. 178; maeashi {{前足}}, p. 161; Zen-soku (前足).

(466-cha)*CHARACTERISTICS* ⓘ A Two-character, which consists of 2 Chinese Logograms and 0 Hiˈra-ga-ˈna Characters.

(800-tag)*TAGS* 💻 #nakaashi, naka-ashi, naka ashi

333.Naˈka-daˈka

(000-it)*INCLUDING TERMS (EXAMPLES)* 👁✉ nakadakaipponken {{中高一本拳}}, p. 179

(011-k1)*KANJI 1* ☛ Naka-middle {中}, p. 178

(012-k2)*KANJI 2* ☛ Taka-quantity {高}, p. 231

(077-jg)*GENERAL MEANING (EXAMPLES)* ✿📖 *noun* ❶ Medium and high-level. *no-adjective (~ の)* ❷ Convex, arched, curved outward. ❸ Type of Japanese pitch accent.

(211-1)中高

(250-hi)なかだか (hir.)

#nakadaka {{中高}}##

(089-no)*NOTES AND EXAMPLES* 📖✎

Naˈka-daˈka-gaˈta (中高型) is one of the Japanese pitch accent patterns, along with with Aˈtama-ˈdaka-ˈgata (頭高型), O-daka-gata (尾高型) and Hei-ban-gata (平板型).

(136-se)*SEE ALSO* 👁➕ chūkō (nakadaka), p. 54

(466-cha)*CHARACTERISTICS* ⓘ A Two-character, which consists of 2 Chinese Logograms and 0 Hiˈra-ga-ˈna Characters.

(800-tag)*TAGS* 💻 #nakadaka, nakadaka, naka daka

334. Naˈka-daˈka-ip-ˈpon-ken

(015-w1)*WORD 1* ᵂ/ᵂ ☞ nakadaka {{中高}}, p. 179

(016-w2)*WORD 2* ᵂ/ᵂ ☞ ipponken {{一本拳}}, p. 106

(040-ul)*UPPER LIMB STRIKE & ANATOMY*

手 **AKA** Chūkōipponken, Middle Finger Knuckle Fist, Middle Finger One Knuckle Fist, Middle Finger Single-point Fist, Middle Knuckle Fist, Middle High One-knuckle Fist, Single-point Index Finger Fist, Middle Finger Strike, Middle Finger Punch **Category** Strike

(089-no)*NOTES AND EXAMPLES* 📖✎

The index finger (人差し指) may be used instead of the middle finger.

(466-cha)*CHARACTERISTICS* ⓘ A Five-character, which consists of 5 Chinese Logograms and 0 Hiˈra-ga-ˈna Characters.

(211-1)中高一本拳

(250-hi)なかだかいっぽんけん (hir.)

#nakadakaipponken {{中高一本拳}}##

Anatomy 3 - Nakadaka Ipponken

(041-mu)*FUNAKOSHI MAIN BOOK - UPPER LIMB* 🖤**MⓄL** 1922 original 29 1925 **Ishida** 39 (Chuko Ipponken) 1925 **Teramoto** 39 (Chuko Ipponken) **1935** Suzuki-Johnston 19 **1935 Ohshima** 18

(042-nu)*FUNAKOSHI NYUMON TERAMOTO – UPPER LIMB* 🦭**NUL** 48 (list)

(185-ch)*CHINESE (PINYIN)* ☯📖

Zhōnggāo yī běn quán

(483-td)**T⊃d** 🔔 Due to the ˈRen-daku laws, the unvoiced consonant /T/ may get a Dak[u]-ˈten (゛) and become ~/d/ as a suffix. Example 🖌 ˈTachi (た ち) turns into Ki-ˈba Daˈchi (きばだち).

(800-tag)*TAGS* 🖥 #nakatakaipponken (なかたかいっぽんけん), #nakadakaiponken, #naka daka ippon ken

335. ˈNana (Shichi)

(001-REF-rom)ˈNana ☞ Shichi-seven {七}, p. 209

#Nana (Shichi)##

(002-REF-hi)なな ☞ しち

336.Naˈore

(018-imp)*IMPERATIVE FORM OF* ❗ ☞

Naoru-to be fixed {直}, p. 181

(070-kt)*KARATE MEANING* ✋📖 AKA Naotte *verb (imperative mood)* ① Rest! relax! ② Recover to Natural Stance! return to Natural Position! See

List of Commands, p. 25

(077-jg)*GENERAL MEANING (EXAMPLES)* ⚙📖 *verb (imperative mood)*

❶ Get fixed!

(134-gr-re)*GROUP* 👁(👥) The following terms are related: hajime {{始め}}, p. 81; kamae {{構え}}, p. 123; kamaete {{構えて}}, p. 125; naore {{直れ}}, p. 180; yame {{止め}}, p. 271; yasume {{休め}}, p. 274; yōi {{用意}}, p. 277

#naore {{直れ}}##

QR Code 3 – Yame, Yasume & Naore Lily (wJ7a_kGZ2GQ)
List of QR Codes (Video), p. 11

(133-sy)*SYNONYMS* 👁= yasume {{休め}}, p. 274

(211-1)直れ

(250-hi)なおれ (hir.)

(275-tō)な お れ [nàóˈrè]

(610-In-Tr)*VERB PAIR* 👁◀▶ The Intransitive Verb is Naoru-to be fixed {直}, p. 181. The Transitive verb is naosu {{直す}}, p. 182.

(466-cha)*CHARACTERISTICS* ⓘ A Two-character, which consists of 1 Chi-

nese Logograms and 1 Hiˑra-ga-ˈna Characters.

(838-su)**SUPER-TERM**

337.Naˑoru (直)

(000-it)*INCLUDING TERMS (EXAMPLES)*

👁✉ chokuzuki {{直突き}}, p. 52; naore {{直れ}}, p. 180; naosu {{直す}}, p. 182.

(077-jg)*GENERAL MEANING (EXAMPLES)* ☼📖 ❶ *verb (intransitive)* To be fixed, to be repaired. ❷ *adjective* Straight.

(185-ch)*CHINESE (PINYIN)* 👁📖 *zhí*

(325-kr)*KANJI READINGS* ✒🗣 Go-on: じき (jiki). Kan-on: ちょく (choku). Kun: なおす (naosu, 直す); なおる (naoru, 直る).

(211-1)直 (211-ka+hi)直る

(212-2)直

(211-ka+hiAlt)治る

(250-hi)なおる (hir.)

#Naoru-to be fixed {直}##

(600-vt)**Form**	**Godan Intransitive ~ru (v. su)**
Terminal	nàó⁺rù
Plain ~te Request	nàó⁺ttè
Polite ~te Request	nàó⁺ttè kudaˑsai
Plain Imperative	nàó⁺rè
Stem	naˑori
Polite Imperative	naˑori naˑsai
Formal	nàórímá⁺s[ù]

See

List of Commands, p. 25

(256-kat)ナオル (kat.)

(275-tō)な お る [nàó⁺rù]

(610-In-Tr)*VERB PAIR* 👁◑ The Intransitive Verb is Naoru-to be fixed {直}, p. 181. The Transitive verb is naosu {{直す}}, p. 182.

(811-vpIn)**VERB PAIR – INTRANSITIVE PART**

(830-ik)**IMPORTANT KANJI**

338.naˑosu

(011-k1)*KANJI 1* ☛ Naoru-to be fixed {直}, p. 181

(077-jg)*GENERAL MEANING (EXAMPLES)* ☼📖 *verb (transitive)* ❶ To fix, to correct, to repair.

(466-cha)*CHARACTERISTICS* ⓘ A Two-character, which consists of 1 Chinese Logograms and 1 Hiˑra-ga-ˈna Characters.

(211-1)直す (212-2)治す

(250-hi)なおす (hir.)

(256-kat)ナオス (kat.)

(275-tō)な お す [nàó⁺sù]

(810-vpTr)**VERB PAIR – TRANSITIVE PART**

#naosu {{直す}}##

(600-vt)**Form**   **Godan Transitive ~su**

Terminal	nàóˈsù
Plain ~te Request	nàóˈsh[ì]tè
Polite ~te Request	nàóˈsh[ì]tè kudaˈsai
Plain Imperative	nàóˈsè
Stem	naˈoshi
Polite Imperative	naˈoshi naˈsai
Formal	nàóshímáˈs[ù]

See

List of **Commands**, p. 25

(610-In-Tr) *VERB PAIR* 👁◑ The Intransitive Verb is Naoru-to be fixed {直}, p. 181. The Transitive verb is naosu {{直す}}, p. 182.

339. ˈNeko (猫)

(000-it)*INCLUDING TERMS (EXAMPLES)*

👁✉ nekoashi {{猫足}}, p. 182

(077-jg)*GENERAL MEANING (EXAMPLES)* ✿📖 *noun* ❶ Cat

(185-ch)*CHINESE (PINYIN)* 👁📖 ***māo, máo, miáo***

(189-ok)*OKINAWAN* ● Mayā (まやー)

(203-hi)⏳☉ (206-kata)⏳○

(250-hi)ねこ (hir.) (256-kat)ネコ(kat.)

(211-al)*ALTERNATIVES OR SEE ALSO*

✎✎ 猫

#Neko-cat {猫}##

(275-tō)ね こ [néˈkò]

(313-ka)*KANJI* ✎ The Phono-semantic Compound Logogram ˈNeko-cat (猫). (313k-cn)**Components** 🔲 [semantic 犬 | phonetic 苗] (313k-ra)**Radical** ✛ 犬 (313k-cs)**Composition** ✗ Left: 犭, right: 苗 (313k-re)**Readings (examples)** ✊ Go-on: みょう (myō). Kan-on: びょう (byō). Kun: ねこ (neko, 猫).

(830-ik)**IMPORTANT KANJI**

340. Neˈko-aˈshi

(000-it)*INCLUDING TERMS (EXAMPLES)*

👁✉ nekoashidachi {{猫足立ち}}, p. 183

(011-k1)*KANJI 1* ☞ Neko-cat {猫}, p. 182

(012-k2)*KANJI 2* ☞ Ashi-foot {足}, p. 37

(077-jg)*GENERAL MEANING (EXAMPLES)* ✿📖 *noun* ❶ Stealthy footsteps ❷ Carved table leg

(185-ch)*CHINESE (PINYIN)* 👁📖 ***Māozú***

#nekoashi {{猫足}}##

(211-1)猫足

(211-al)*ALTERNATIVES OR SEE ALSO*

✎✎ 猫脚

(250-hi)ねこあし (hir.)

(466-cha)*CHARACTERISTICS* ⓘ A Two-character, which consists of 2 Chinese Logograms and 0 Hiʼra-ga-ʼna Characters.

341.Neˈko-aˈshi Daˈchi

(015-w1)*WORD 1* 🖢 ☛ nekoashi {{猫足}}, p. 182

(016-w2)*WORD 2* 🖢 ☛ tachi {{立ち}}, p. 228

(030-st)*STANCE* 立 **AKA** Nekoashi, Cat Stance, Cat Legs, Cat Leg Stance, Cat's Paw Stance, Cat Foot Stance **Category** Low frontal stances

(031-ms)*FUNAKOSHI MAIN BOOK - STANCES* 🐟**MS** 1922 original 30 (list), 48 **1925 Ishida** 41 (list), 45 **1925 Teramoto** 40 (list), 42 **1935 Suzuki-Johnston** 22 (list), 23 **1935 Ohshima** 19 (list), 20

#nekoashidachi {{猫足立ち}}##

(211-1)猫足立ち

(212-2)猫足立

(250-hi)ねこあしだち (hir.)

Neˈko-aˈshi Daˈchi - ˈNi (二)

(466-cha)*CHARACTERISTICS* ⓘ A Four-character, which consists of 3 Chinese Logograms and 1 Hiʼra-ga-ʼna Characters.

(483-td)**T⤳d** 🕮 Due to the ˈRen-daku laws, the unvoiced consonant /T/ may get a Dak[u]-ˈten (゛) and become ~/d/ as a suffix. Example 🏴 ˈTachi (たち) turns into Ki-ˈba Daˈchi (きばだち).

(838-su)**SUPER-TERM**

342.ˈNi (二)

(000-it)*INCLUDING TERMS (EXAMPLES)* 👁✉ nidan {{二段}}, p. 184

(077-jg)*GENERAL MEANING (EXAMPLES)* ☼🕮 *noun* ❶ Two.

(089-no)*NOTES AND EXAMPLES* 🕮✍ The Kaʼta-ka-ʼna (p. 136) Character that reads /ni/ is 二, resembling the ˈKan-ji. The Hiʼra-ga-ʼna (p. 99) Character Ni also contains two parallel lines - に.

#Ni-two {二}##

(185-ch)*CHINESE (PINYIN)* ☻🕮 *èr*

(211-1)二

(211-al)*ALTERNATIVES OR SEE ALSO*

✎✎ 二, 弍, 弐, 貳, 貮, 贰

(250-hi)に (hir.)

(800-tag)*TAGS* 🖥 #2

(833-kan)**KANJI**

(838-su)**SUPER-TERM**

343.ˈNi-dan

(000-it)*INCLUDING TERMS (EXAMPLES)*

◉⊠ heiannidan {{平安二段}}, p. 92; nidangeri {{二段蹴り}}, p. 184; tekkinidan {{鉄騎二段}}, p. 238.

(011-k1)*KANJI 1* ☞ Ni-two {二}, p. 183

(012-k2)*KANJI 2* ☞ Dan-level {段}, p. 56

(070-kt)*KARATE MEANING* 🖐📖 *noun* ① Second Level ② Second dan, second degree black belt ③ Two.

(800-tag)*TAGS* 🖥 #ni-dan, ni dan #nidan {{二段}}##

(077-jg)*GENERAL MEANING (EXAMPLES)* ⚙📖 *noun* ❶ Second grade, level two, second rank, second-degree

(211-1)二段

(250-hi)にだん (hir.)

(466-cha)*CHARACTERISTICS* ① A Two-character, which consists of 2 Chinese Logograms and 0 Hiˈra-ga-ˈna Characters.

(838-su)**SUPER-TERM**

344.Ni-ˈdan-geˈri

💣※ Not to be confused with tobigeri {{飛び蹴り}}, p. 246!

(015-w1)*WORD 1* ₩ ☞ nidan {{二段}}, p. 184

(016-w2)*WORD 2* ₩ ☞ keri {{蹴り}}, p. 140

(045-ll)*LOWER LIMB STRIKE & ANATOMY*

足 **AKA** Double Kick, Double Front Kick, Two Level Kick, Two Step Kick **Category** Kick

(046-ml)*FUNAKOSHI MAIN BOOK – LOWER LIMB* 📕**MLL** 1935 Ohshima 23 (list), 25

(211-1)二段蹴り

#nidangeri {{二段蹴り}}##

(134-re)*RELATED TERMS* ◉∞ tobigeri {{飛び蹴り}}, p. 246

(212-2)二段蹴

(250-hi)にだんげり (hir.)

(466-cha)*CHARACTERISTICS* ① A Four-character, which consists of 3 Chinese Logograms and 1 Hiˈra-ga-ˈna Characters.

(482-kg)**K⊃g** 🔔 Due to the ˈRen-daku laws, the unvoiced consonant

/K/ may get a Dak[u]-ˈten (ﾟ) and become ~/g/ as a suffix. Example ↰ Keˈri (けり) turns into Maˈe-geˈri (まえげり).

345.Nuk[i]-ˈte

💣＊ Do not confuse: Tsuranuku-to pierce {貫}, p. 257 as in nukite {{ 貫手}}, p. 185 with Nuku-to extract {抜}, p. 186 as in bassai {{抜塞}}, p. 43 and as in Iai-do's Nuˈki-ts[u]ˈke (抜き付け)!

(011-k1)*KANJI 1* ☛ Tsuranuku-to pierce {貫}, p. 257

(012-k2)*KANJI 2* ☛ Te-hand {手}, p. 234

(040-ul)*UPPER LIMB STRIKE & ANATOMY* 手 **AKA** Spear Hand, Spear Hand Strike, Spear Hand Attack, X-finger Thrust (X-hon-tsuki), Piercing Hand **Category** Strike

(185-ch)*CHINESE (PINYIN)* ☻📖 *Guàn shǒu*

(211-1)貫手 (212-2)貫き手 #nukite {{貫手}}##

(041-mu)*FUNAKOSHI MAIN BOOK – UPPER LIMB* 🐢**MUL** 1922 original 27-28, 41 (list), 42 **1925 Ishida** 37-38, 53

(list), 54 **1925 Teramoto** 39, 46 (list), 47 **1935 Suzuki-Johnston** 20-21, 24 (list), 24 **1935 Ohshima** 18-19, 21 (list), 21

(042-nu)*FUNAKOSHI NYUMON TERAMO-TO – UPPER LIMB* 🐢**NUL** 48 (list), 55-56

(077-jg)*GENERAL MEANING (EXAMPLES)* ☼📖 *noun* ❶ Spear Hand

(250-hi)ぬきて (hir.)

(466-cha)*CHARACTERISTICS* ① A Two-character, which consists of 2 Chinese Logograms and 0 Hiˈra-gaˈna Characters.

346.Nuˈku (抜)

💣＊ Do not confuse: Tsuranuku-to pierce {貫}, p. 257 as in nukite {{ 貫手}}, p. 185 with Nuku-to extract {抜}, p. 186 as in bassai {{抜塞}}, p. 43 and as in Iai-do's Nuˈki-ts[u]ˈke (抜き付け)!

(000-it)*INCLUDING TERMS (EXAMPLES)* ☻✉ bassai {{抜塞}}, p. 43

(077-jg)*GENERAL MEANING (EXAMPLES)* ☼📖 *verb* ❶ To extract, to take out, to pull out ❷ To pierce, to break through, to go through ❸ To carry through, to do to the end

(134-re)*RELATED TERMS* ◉∞ Tsura-nuku-to pierce {貫}, p. 257

(211-sh-1)抜 (simp.) (211-sh-2)拔 (simp.)

(211-ky-1)拔 (trad.) (250-hi)ぬく (hir.)

(275-tō)ぬ⟨く⟩ [nùkú]

#Nuku-to extract {抜}##

(313-ka)*KANJI* ✍ The Phono-semantic Compound Logogram Nuˈku-to extract（抜）. (313k-cn)**Components** ⛁ [semantic 扌 | phonetic 友]. (313k-ra)**Radical** ✚ 手 扌 龵 hand. (313k-cs)**Composition** ✄ Left: 扌, right: 友. (313k-re)**Readings (examples)** ♣ Go-on: ばち (bachi). Kan-on: はつ (hatsu). Kan'yō-on: ばつ (batsu). Kun: ぬく (nuˈku, 抜く); ぬける (nukeru, 抜ける); ぬかる (nukaru, 抜かる).

(705-gv)*GODAN VERB* 🏍⑤ **Terminal Form** {u* ✴ but not i*-ru or e*-ru} Nuˈku [nùkú] (抜く), which means to extract. **Polite Form** {i*-masu} Nukimas[u] (抜きます).

(830-ik)**IMPORTANT KANJI**

347.ˈObi (帯)

(070-kt)*KARATE MEANING* ✋📖 *noun* ① Belt.

(077-jg)*GENERAL MEANING (EXAMPLES)* ✿📖 *noun* ❶ Kimono sash, Obi.

(090-te)*TELL YOUR STUDENTS* 📖☺ Usually, we want a knot that does not require a very long belt, does not create tails that disturb the hands, and is very secure even if the belt is stiff. To ensure stability, tuck both ends behind two layers. Take Your time to adjust the knot for tightness. As for the wrapping, in some cases the Single Line Style (Full Overlap Style, Hollywood Style) – without the cross on the back - makes it easier to tie the knot properly. The Low Single Loop (Two Feeds) Knot (see QR codes above) will not come undone easily. The Heigh-Above Tucks Knot (see QR codes above) is another very secure knot. The Granny Knot is both modest and trustworthy, if rotated in the end.

(185-ch)*CHINESE (PINYIN)* ☯📖 **Dài**

(211-1)帯 (211-al)*ALTERNATIVES OR SEE ALSO* ✍✍ 帯

(250-hi)おび (hir.)

#Obi-belt {帯}##

QR Code 4 – Square, Heigh-Below Tucks, **Heigh-Above Tucks** Knots (4ynrdB7UTqQ)

QR Code 5 – **Low Single Loop (Two Feeds)** Knot (BuLRrRArnsw)

QR Code 6 – Low Single Loop (One Feed) & Heigh-Below Tucks Knots (s8C7TxxGcaw)

QR Code 7 –Low Tucks Knot (hFbgxI-zZo8)

List of QR Codes (Video), p. 11

(089-no)*NOTES AND EXAMPLES* 📖✍

The knot that is commonly used is Koˈma-ˈmusubi - こま結び (駒結び), also known as a Square Knot (本結び); many Karateka are familiar with the name Fortune Cookie Knot. The Granny Knot (縦結び) works fine as well, if properly adjusted. Anyways, the Overhand Knot (止め結び) forms the bases of most of the complicated knots that we use. We recommend trying lesser-known knots. Change the knot

from time to time – it is good for Your brain.

(275-tō)おび [óˈbì]

(885-tag)*TAGS* 🖥 #belt, #sash

(833-kan)**KANJI**

348.Oˈgen-kides[u]ˈka?

(011-k1)*KANJI 1* ☞ Moto-origin {元}, p. 173

(012-k2)*KANJI 2* ☞ Ki-energy {気}, p. 142

(077-jg)*GENERAL MEANING (EXAMPLES)* ☼📖 *phrase* ❶ How are You? how are You doing? Are You well?

(211-1)お元気ですか

(800-tag)*TAGS* 🖥 #ogenki-desuka, ogenki desuka, #ogenkideska #ogenkidesuka {{お元気ですか}}#

(250-hi)おげんきですか (hir.)

(409-o)*HIRAGANA* ☉ The prefix ˈO (お〜) (御) is an honorific prefix.

(409-ka)*HIRAGANA* ☉ The particle ˈKa (か) is a question denominator.

(466-cha)*CHARACTERISTICS* ① A Six-character, which consists of 2 Chinese Logograms and 4 Hiˈra-ga-ˈna Characters.

349.Oˈi-z[u]ˈki

List of large photos - p. 10

(011-k1)*KANJI 1* ☞ Ou-to chase {追}, p. 193

(015-w1)*WORD 1* ʷ/ʷ ☞ tsuki {{突き}}, p. 253

(040-ul)*UPPER LIMB STRIKE & ANATOMY* 手 **AKA** Jun-z[u]ki (順 突), Chase Thrust, Chasing Thrust, Step Through Punch, Lunge Punch, Front Punch, Equal-sided Punch, Ipsilateral Thrust. **Category** Strike, closed fist.

(041-mu)*FUNAKOSHI MAIN BOOK - UPPER LIMB* 🖤**MUL** 1935 Ohshima 29 (list), 31

(089-no)*NOTES AND EXAMPLES* 📖✎

Oizuki is the ultimate ipsilateral movement. For further research about human ipsilateral gait (German: Passgang beim Menschen), both in general and in Japanese martial arts, we recommend searching for ˈNanba-ˈaruki (ナンバ歩き) – Nanba walking. We also recommend looking for ˈNanba-ˈhashiri (ナンバ走り) – Nanba running.

(138-co)*COORDINATE TERMS* 👁≈ gyakuzuki {{逆突き}}, p. 73

(185-ch)*CHINESE (PINYIN)* 🌐📖 *Zhuītū*

(211-1)追い突き

(212-2)追い突 (213-3)追突

#oizuki {{追い突き}}##

Figure 3 - Chasing Tiger
Circa 400 A.D. mosaic, featuring a tiger (p. 249) pursuing an ibex. Uncovered during a 2023 excavation in the remains of an ancient synagogue located in Huqoq, Israel.
Special thanks: Prof. Jodi Magness & Jim Haberman, University of North Carolina at Chapel Hill

(090-te)*TELL YOUR STUDENTS* 📖☻

What does a chase thrust mean practically, other than the obvious answers? For instance, imagine that the opponent is with his back to You, like any prey running from a predator. Accordingly, You have nothing to be afraid of when You leap.

(250-hi)おいづき (hir.)

(280-po)pol:OIDZYKI

(466-cha)*CHARACTERISTICS* ⓘ A Four-character, which consists of 2 Chinese Logograms and 2 Hiˈra-ga-ˈna Characters.

(484-tsz)**Ts↻z** 🔔 Due to the ˈRen-daku laws, the unvoiced consonant /Ts/ may get a Dak[u]-ˈten (゛) and become ~/z/ as a suffix. Example ✎ Ts[u]ˈki 2（つき）turns into Oˈi-z[u]ˈki（おいづき）.

(800-tag)*TAGS* 💻 #oitsuki, oizki, outski

(838-su)**SUPER-TERM**

350.Ōkī

(011-k1)*KANJI 1* ☞ Dai-big {大}, p. 56

(077-jg)*GENERAL MEANING (EXAMPLES)* ✿📖 *adjective* ❶ Big, great

(211-1)**大きい** (212-2)**おっきい**

(250-hi)**おおきい** (hir.)

(275-tō)お おき い [òókíˈì]

#ōkī {{**大きい**}}##

(466-cha)*CHARACTERISTICS* ⓘ A Three-character, which consists of 1 Chinese Logograms and 2 Hiˈra-ga-ˈna Characters.

(800-tag)*TAGS* 💻 #oki, ooki, ohkii, okii, ookii, ōkii

351.Oˈki-nawa

(028-pl)*PLACES* 🌐 *name* ❶ The largest island of the Ryūkyū Islands, the main island in the Okinawa Islands ❷ The Ryūkyū Islands, most of Japan's southwestern archipelago.

(185-ch)*CHINESE (PINYIN)* ☯📖

Chōngshéng

(134-re)*RELATED TERMS* 👁∞ ryūkyū {{琉球}}, p. 198

#okinawa {{沖縄}}##

(189-ok)*OKINAWAN* 🌑 Uchinā（うちなー）

(211-1)**沖縄**

(250-hi)**おきなわ** (hir.)

(275-tō)お き な わ [òkínáwá]

(466-cha)*CHARACTERISTICS* ⓘ A Two-character, which consists of 2 Chinese Logograms and 0 Hiˈra-ga-ˈna Characters.

352.Oˈmote (表)

(000-it)*INCLUDING TERMS (EXAMPLES)* 👁✉ tennokataomote {{天の形表}}, p. 242

(077-jg)*GENERAL MEANING (EXAMPLES)* ✿📖 *adjective* ❶ Front ❷ Surface

(134-re)*RELATED TERMS* 👁∞ Mae-front {前}, p. 160

(185-ch)*CHINESE (PINYIN)* ☯📖 ***biǎo***

#Omote-front {表}##

(139-an)*ANTONYMS* 👁↺ Ura-back {裏}, p. 264

(211-1)表

(212-2)衣

(250-hi)おもて (hir.)

(275-tō)おもて [òmóté꜄]

(833-kan)**KANJI**

353.'On (恩)

(000-it)*INCLUDING TERMS (EXAMPLES)* 👁✉ jion {{慈恩}}, p. 110

(077-jg)*GENERAL MEANING (EXAMPLES)* ☼📖 *noun* ❶ Obligation ❷ Debt of gratitude ❸ Favor ❹ Grace, kindness, goodness

(185-ch)*CHINESE (PINYIN)* ☯📖 ***ēn***

(250-hi)おん (hir.) (203-hi)⌛⊙

(211-1)恩 (211-al)*ALTERNATIVES OR SEE ALSO* 🖌🖌 恩 (256-kat)オン (kat.)

#On-obligation {恩}##

(313-ka)*KANJI* 🖌 The Phono-semantic Compound Logogram 'On-obligation (恩). (313k-cn)**Components** 品 [phonetic 因 | semantic 心] (313k-ra)**Radical** ✦ 心 忄 㣺 heart (313k-cs)**Composition** ⚒ Top: 因, bottom: 心

(313k-re)**Readings (examples)** 🗣 Go-on: おん (on). Kan-on: おん (on).

(830-ik)**IMPORTANT KANJI**

354.O-ne'gai-shi'mas[u]

(077-jg)*GENERAL MEANING (EXAMPLES)* ☼📖 *interjection (polite)* ❶ Please, kindly, if You would be so kind, if it pleases You.

(211-1)お願いします

(212-2)御願いします (250-hi)おねがいします (hir.)

(275-tō)おねがいします

[ònégáí shímá꜄sṳ̀]

#onegaishimasu {{お願いします}}##

(466-cha)*CHARACTERISTICS* ⓘ A Six-character, which consists of 1 Chinese Logograms and 5 Hi'ra-ga-'na Characters.

(409-o)*HIRAGANA* ⊙ The prefix 'O (お～) (御) is an honorific prefix.

(800-tag)*TAGS* 💻 #onegai-shimasu, onegai shimasu, o negai shimasu

(838-su)**SUPER-TERM**

355. ʹOs[u] (Ossu)

(001-REF-rom)ʹOs[u] ☞ ossu {{押忍}},

p. 192

#osu (ossu)##

(002-REF-hi)おす ☞ おっす

356. Osaʹe

(000-it)*INCLUDING TERMS (EXAMPLES)*

👁✉ osaeuke {{押え受け}}, p.

191

(011-k1)*KANJI 1* ☛ Osu-to push {押},

p. 192

(077-jg)*GENERAL MEANING (EXAMPLES)* ☼📖 *noun* ❶ Pressure ❷

Weight ❸ Control, keeping control.

(211-1)押え

#osae {{押え}}##

(211-al)*ALTERNATIVES OR SEE ALSO*

✎✎抑え, 押さえ

(250-hi)おさえ (hir.)

(466-cha)*CHARACTERISTICS* ⓘ A Two-

character, which consists of 1 Chi-

nese Logograms and 1 Hiʹra-ga-ʹna

Characters.

357. Oʹsae Uʹke

(015-w1)*WORD 1* ᵂ𝘞 ☛ osae {{押え}},

p. 191

(016-w2)*WORD 2* ᵂ𝘞 ☛ uke {{受け}}, p.

262

(089-no)*NOTES AND EXAMPLES* 📖✎

One example is movement 12 of

Heian Nidan (1973, p. 57 illustra-

tion 15). Another example is

movement 3 of Jitte (1973, p. 158

illustration 8).

(466-cha)*CHARACTERISTICS* ⓘ A Four-

character, which consists of 2 Chi-

nese Logograms and 2 Hiʹra-ga-ʹna

Characters.

(185-ch)*CHINESE (PINYIN)* ☯📖 *Yā*

shòu

(211-1)押え受け (212-2)押え受

#osaeuke {{押え受け}}##

Masters 18 - Osaeuke by Bamgboye Sensei
List of Sensei Demonstrations next to Values, p. 10
List of large photos - p. 10
Bobby Bamgboye of Nigeria WSKF
demonstrates Osae-uke. Photographer:
Joel Ibanga.

(070-kt)*KARATE MEANING* ✋📖 *noun*

phrase ① Pressing Block, Pushing

ˈOs-s[u] – Oˈtosu (落)

Block, Pressure Block, Press Block ② Palm Block.

(250-hi)おさえうけ (hir.)

358. ˈOs-s[u]

(011-k1)*KANJI 1* ☞ Osu-to push {押}, p. 192

(071-dl)💣✳ᴀᴀ *DOJO LANGUAGE* ⏳📖 *interjection* ① Yes sir! no sir! right sir! got it sir! very much sir! salutation, respectful greeting, sign of respect and enthusiasm, sign of acknowledgement.

(089-no)*NOTES AND EXAMPLES* 📖✎

According to some schools, even in Shōtōkan, this term is much too familiar for a Dōjō. Hai (はい) is used instead.

(185-ch)*CHINESE (PINYIN)* ☯📖 **Yārěn**

#ossu {{押忍}}##

(203-hi)⏳☉

(250-hi)おっす (hir.)

(250-hi-Alt)おす (hir.)

(211-1)押忍

(211-al)*ALTERNATIVES OR SEE ALSO*

✐✐ 押っ忍

(275-tō)お̲す̲ [óˑssù]

(466-cha)*CHARACTERISTICS* ⓘ A

Three-character, which consists of 0 Chinese Logograms and 3 Hiˑraˑgaˑˈna Characters.

(800-tag)*TAGS* 💻 #oss, #os

359. Oˈsu (押)

(077-jg)*GENERAL MEANING (EXAMPLES)* ⚙📖 *verb (transitive)* ❶ To push, to press ❷ To press down.

(000-it)*INCLUDING TERMS (EXAMPLES)*

👁✉ osae {{押え}}, p. 191; ossu {{押忍}}, p. 192

(139-an)*ANTONYMS* 👁↺ Hiku-to pull {引}, p. 76

#Osu-to push {押}##

(185-ch)*CHINESE (PINYIN)* ☯📖 **yā**

(211-1)押

(211-ka+hi)押す

(250-hi)おす (hir.)

(275-tō)お̲す̲ [òsú]

(280-po)pol:OSY

(833-kan)**KANJI**

360. Oˈtosu (落)

(000-it)*INCLUDING TERMS (EXAMPLES)*

👁✉ kakatootoshigeri {{踵落とし蹴り}}, p. 122; taniotoshi {{谷落}}, p. 233

(077-jg)*GENERAL MEANING (EXAMPLES)* ✿📖 *verb (transitive)* ❶ To drop.

(185-ch)*CHINESE (PINYIN)* ☯📖 *luò, lào, luō*

(211-1)落

(211-al)*ALTERNATIVES OR SEE ALSO*

✐✐ 落す

#Otosu-to drop {落}##

(211-ka+hi)落とす

(250-hi) おとす (hir.) (256-kat) オトす (kat.)

(275-tō)お と す [òtóˑsù]

(325-kr)*KANJI READINGS* ✐🗣 Go-on: らく (raku). Kan-on: らく (raku). Kun: おちる (ochiru, 落ちる); おとす (otosu, 落とす). Nanori: おち (ochi)

(800-tag)*TAGS* 🖥 #ochi

(833-kan)**KANJI**

361.Oʹu (追)

(000-it)*INCLUDING TERMS (EXAMPLES)* 👁✉ oizuki {{追い突き}}, p. 188.

(077-jg)*GENERAL MEANING (EXAMPLES)* ✿📖 *verb (transitive)* ❶ To chase, to pursue, to run after

(185-ch)*CHINESE (PINYIN)* ☯📖 *zhuī*

(203-hi)⧗⊙ (250-hi)おう (hir.)

(211-1)追

(211-ka+hi)追う, 逐う

(705-gv)*GODAN VERB* 🏍⑤ **Terminal Form** {u* ✹ but not i*-ru or e*-ru} Oʹu [òú] (追う), which means to chase. **Polite Form** {i*-masu} Oʹimas[u] [òímáˑsù] (追います). #Ou-to chase {追}##

(211-al)*ALTERNATIVES OR SEE ALSO*

✐✐ 追, 追

(313-ka)*KANJI* ✐ The Phono-semantic Compound Logogram Oʹu-to chase (追). (313k-cn)**Components** 🖧 [semantic 辶 | phonetic 𠂤] (313k-ra)**Radical** ✚ 辶 辵辶 walk (313k-cs)**Composition** ✗ Bottom-left: 辶, top-right: 𠂤 (313k-re)**Readings (examples)** 🗣 Go-on: つい (tsui). Kan-on: つい (tsui). On: たい (tai). Kun: おう (ou, 追う).

(830-ik)**IMPORTANT KANJI**

362.ʹŌ-yō

(070-kt)*KARATE MEANING* ✋📖 *noun* ① The result of Kata practical analysis, the extracted technique.

(077-jg)*GENERAL MEANING (EXAMPLES)* ☼📖 *noun* ❶ Application, practical use.

(089-no)*NOTES AND EXAMPLES* 📖✍

Shares a common Kanji with yōi {{用意}}, p. 277.

(134-re)*RELATED TERMS* 👁∞ bunkai {{分解}}, p. 48

#ōyō {{応用}}##

(211-1)応用

(250-hi)おうよう (hir.)

(275-tō)お―よ― [òóyóó]

(466-cha)*CHARACTERISTICS* ⓘ A Two-character, which consists of 2 Chinese Logograms and 0 Hiˈra-ga-ˈna Characters.

(800-tag)*TAGS* 💻 #oyo, o-yo, o yo, ouyou, ooyoo, oio

363. Pas-ˈsai (bassai)

(001-REF-rom)Pas-ˈsai ☞ bassai {{拔塞}}, p. 43

#passai (bassai)##

(002-REF-hi)ぱっさい ☞ ばっさい

364. ˈPēji (頁)

(000-it)*INCLUDING TERMS (EXAMPLES)* 👁✉ pejisansho {{頁参照}}, p. 194

(021-rb)*RESEARCH (FOR BOOKS)* ✍ *noun* ❶ Page ❷ Leaf.

#Peji-page {{頁}}##

(206-kata)🔧⭕ (256-kat)ページ (kat.)

(211-1)頁 (275-tō)ペ―ジ [péˈèjì]

(833-kan)**KANJI**

365. ˈPēji ˈSan-shō

(011-k1)*KANJI 1* ☞ Peji-page {{頁}}, p. 194

(012-k2)*KANJI 2* ☞ San-three {{三}}, p. 201

(021-rb)*RESEARCH (FOR BOOKS)* ✍ *phrase* ❶ See page!

(089-no)*NOTES AND EXAMPLES* 📖✍ 12

頁参照 means see page 12.

(211-1)頁参照

#pejisansho {{頁参照}}##

(466-cha)*CHARACTERISTICS* ⓘ A Theree-character, which consists of 3 Chinese Logograms and 0 Hiˈra-ga-ˈna Characters.

(800-tag)*TAGS* 💻 #pejisansho, peji-san-so, peji sansho, peji san sho

366. ˈPin-an (Pin'an) (heian)

(001-REF-rom)ˈPin-an ☞ heian {{平安}}, p. 90

#pinan (heian)##

(002-REF-hi)ぴんあん ☞ へいあん

(256-kat) ピンアン (kat.)

367. ˈPon (Hon)

(001-REF-rom) ˈPon ☞ Hon-source {本},
p. 102

#Pon (Hon)##

(002-REF-hi) ぽん ☞ ほん

368. ˈRan-doˈri

(015-w1) *WORD 1* ᵂ/ᵂ ☛ tori {{取り}}, p.
250

(077-jg) *GENERAL MEANING (EXAMPLES)* ☼📖 *noun* ❶ Freestyle practice, Jiyūkumite ❷ Slow Jiyūkumite, one-on-one slow motion free sparring, soft sparring

(133-sy) *SYNONYMS* 👁= jiyūkumite
{{自由組手}}, p. 113

(185-ch) *CHINESE (PINYIN)* ☯📖 *Luàn
qǔ*

(211-1) 乱取り (212-2) 乱取

(250-hi) らんどり(hir.)

#randori {{乱取り}}##

(211-al) *ALTERNATIVES OR SEE ALSO*
✐✐

乱捕, 乱捕り

(466-cha) *CHARACTERISTICS* ⓘ A
Three-character, which consists of 2
Chinese Logograms and 1 Hiˈra-ga-
ˈna Characters.

(483-td) 𝐓⟳𝐝 ⌂ Due to the ˈRen-daku laws, the unvoiced consonant /T/ may get a Dak[u]-ˈten (゛) and become ~/d/ as a suffix. Example ↯ ˈTachi (た ち) turns into Ki-ˈba Daˈchi (きばだち).

369. Re ˈno Ji Daˈchi

(012-k2) *KANJI 2* ☛ Ji-character {字},
p. 109

(015-w1) *WORD 1* ᵂ/ᵂ ☛ tachi {{立ち}},
p. 228

(030-st) *STANCE* 立 **AKA** Character レ Stance, L-Stance, L-shaped Stance **Category** Sidewise High Stances

(089-no) *NOTES AND EXAMPLES* 📖✎ Most of the weight is on the posterior foot.

(136-se) *SEE ALSO* 👁+ hanmidachi
{{半身立ち}}, p. 86

(211-1) レの字立ち

(212-2) レの字立

#renojidachi {{レの字立ち}}##

(250-hi) れのじだち (hir.)

(409-no) *HIRAGANA* ☉ The particle ˈNo (の) is a genitive case marker, which indicates possession: of, -'s

(466-cha)*CHARACTERISTICS* ⓘ A Five-character, which consists of 3 Chinese Logograms and 2 Hiˈra-ga-ˈna Characters.

(483-td)**T⤸d** 🔔 Due to the ˈRen-daku laws, the unvoiced consonant /T/ may get a Dak[u]-ˈten (゙) and become ~/d/ as a suffix. Example 🔥 ˈTachi（たち）turns into Ki-ˈba Daˈchi（きばだち）.

370. ˈRe[i] (礼)

(070-kt)*KARATE MEANING* ✋📖 *verb (imperative mood)* ① Bow!

See

List of Commands, p. 25

(077-jg)*GENERAL MEANING (EXAMPLES)* ✿📖 *noun* ❶ Thanks, gratitude ❷ Bow, expression of appreciation ❸ Manners.

(185-ch)*CHINESE (PINYIN)* 😊📖 *Lǐ*

(203-hi)⏳☉ (250-hi)れい (hir.)

#Rei-thanks {礼}##

(211-1)礼

(211-al)*ALTERNATIVES OR SEE ALSO*

✒🖌 禮, 礼

(275-tō)れー [ré⁺è]

(275-tō)れー [ré゙è]

(280-po)pol:REE

(800-tag)*TAGS* 🖥 #re, #ree

(833-kan)**KANJI**

371. ˈRe[i] (霊)

(000-it)*INCLUDING TERMS (EXAMPLES)*

👁✉ shōreiryū {{昭霊流}}, p. 218

(077-jg)*GENERAL MEANING (EXAMPLES)* ✿📖 *noun* ❶ Sole, spirit.

(185-ch)*CHINESE (PINYIN)* 😊📖 *líng*

(211-1)霊 (211-al)*ALTERNATIVES OR SEE ALSO* ✒🖌 靈, 灵, 魂, 魄

#Rei-sole {霊}##

(250-hi)れい (hir.) (275-tō)れー [ré⁺è]

(280-po)pol:REE

(302-kn)*KANJI NOTES* ✒🖌 Contains 15 strokes.

(800-tag)*TAGS* 🖥 #re, #ree

(833-kan)**KANJI**

372. ˈRen (連)

(000-it)*INCLUDING TERMS (EXAMPLES)*

👁✉ renzoku {{連続}}, p. 197

(077-jg)*GENERAL MEANING (EXAMPLES)* ✿📖 *noun suffix* ❶ Set, group ❷ Counter for things strung in a line.

(185-ch)*CHINESE (PINYIN)* 😊📖 *lián*

#Ren-set {連}##

(211-1)連 (211-al)*ALTERNATIVES OR SEE ALSO* ✒🖌 连, 嗹

(250-hi)れん (hir.)

(833-kan)**KANJI**

373. ˈRen-zoku

(011-k1)*KANJI 1* ☞ Ren-set {連}, p. 196

(077-jg)*GENERAL MEANING (EXAMPLES)* ✿📖 *adjective* ❶ Consecutive, serial, continuing.

(185-ch)*CHINESE (PINYIN)* 😊📖 *Liánxù*

(211-1) 連 続 (211-al)*ALTERNATIVES OR SEE ALSO* 🖌✒ 連續

#renzoku {{連続}}##

(250-hi)れんぞく (hir.)

(275-tō)れんぞく [rènzókú]

(466-cha)*CHARACTERISTICS* ⓘ A Two-character, which consists of 2 Chinese Logograms and 0 Hiˈra-ga-ˈna Characters.

374. ˈRin (Hayashi)

(001-REF-rom)ˈRin ☞ Hayashi-grove {林}, p. 89

#Rin (Hayashi)##

(002-REF-hi)りん ☞ はやし

375. Roˈku (六)

(077-jg)*GENERAL MEANING (EXAMPLES)* ✿📖 *noun* ❶ Six

(185-ch)*CHINESE (PINYIN)* 😊📖 *liù, lù*

(211-1)六

(250-hi)ろく (hir.)

#Roku-six {六}##

(275-tō)ろく [ròkú]

(280-po)pol:ROKY (800-tag)*TAGS* 💻 #6

(833-kan)**KANJI**

(838-su)**SUPER-TERM**

376. Rˈyū (流)

(000-it)*INCLUDING TERMS (EXAMPLES)* 👁✉ shōreiryū {{昭霊流}}, p. 218; shōrinryū {{少林流}}, p. 219

(077-jg)*GENERAL MEANING (EXAMPLES)* ✿📖 *noun* ❶ Art style ❷ School of thought.

(133-sy)*SYNONYMS* 👁= Ha-school {派}, p. 76

#Ryū-style {流}##

(185-ch)*CHINESE (PINYIN)* 😊📖 *liú*

(211-1)流

(250-hi)りゅう (hir.)

(275-tō)りゅう [ryúù]

(280-po)pol:RJU

(800-tag)*TAGS* 💻 #ryu, #riu, #riyu

(833-kan)**KANJI**

377. Ryˈū-kyˈū

(028-pl)*PLACES* 🌏 *name* A chain of Japanese islands that stretch southwest from ˈKyūshū (きゅうしゅう) to Taiwan.

(134-re)*RELATED TERMS* 👁∞ okinawa {{沖縄}}, p. 189

(185-ch)*CHINESE (PINYIN)* 🌐📖 ***Liúqiú***

(211-1)琉球

(250-hi)りゅうきゅう (hir.)

#ryūkyū {{琉球}}##

(275-tō)りゅ う き ゅ う [ryùúkyúˈù]

(280-po)pol:RJUUKJUU

(466-cha)*CHARACTERISTICS* ⓘ A Two-character, which consists of 2 Chinese Logograms and 0 Hiˈra-ga-ˈna Characters.

(800-tag)*TAGS* 🖥 #ryukyu, #riukiu, #rukiu

378. ˈSabaki

(000-it)*INCLUDING TERMS (EXAMPLES)* 👁✉ ashisabaki {{足捌き}}, p. 37; taisabaki {{体捌き}}, p. 229

(011-k1)*KANJI 1* ☛ Sabaku-to handle {捌}, p. 198

(077-jg)*GENERAL MEANING (EXAMPLES)* ✿📖 *noun* ❶ Handling, control, use *noun suffix* ❷ ~work (as in footwork).

#sabaki {{捌き}}##

(203-hi)⏳☉

(250-hi)さばき (hir.)

(211-1)捌き

(256-kat)サバキ (kat.)

(466-cha)*CHARACTERISTICS* ⓘ A Two-character, which consists of 1 Chinese Logograms and 1 Hiˈra-ga-ˈna Characters.

379.Saˈbaku (捌)

(000-it)*INCLUDING TERMS (EXAMPLES)* 👁✉ sabaki {{捌き}}, p. 198

(077-jg)*GENERAL MEANING (EXAMPLES)* ✿📖 *verb* ❶ To handle, to deal with, to manage.

(185-ch)*CHINESE (PINYIN)* 🌐📖 ***bā***

(302-kn)*KANJI NOTES* 🖌✍ This Logogram is outside the list of Jō-yō ˈKan-ji, belonging to the Hyō-gai ˈKan-ji.

(705-gv)*GODAN VERB* 🏍⑤ **Terminal Form** {u* 💥 but not i*-ru or e*-ru} Sabaku (さばく), which means to handle. **Polite Form** {i*-masu} Sabakimas[u] (さばきます).

(211-1)捌

(250-hi)さばく (hir.)

#Sabaku-to handle {捌}##

(280-po)pol:SABAKY

(313-ka)*KANJI* ✐ The Phono-semantic Compound Logogram Saˈbaku-to handle (捌). (313k-cn)**Components** ⛭ [semantic 扌 | phonetic 別]. (313k-ra)**Radical** ✛ 手 扌 ⺘ hand. (313k-cs)**Composition** ⚔ Left: 扌 (abbreviated form of 手), right: 別.

(313k-re)**Readings (examples)** 🗣 On (unclassified): はつ (hatsu); はち (hachi). Kun: さばく (sabaku, 捌く); さばける (sabakeru, 捌ける); はける (hakeru, 捌ける); はかす (hakasu, 捌かす).

(830-ik)**IMPORTANT KANJI**

380. ˈSai (塞)

(000-it)*INCLUDING TERMS (EXAMPLES)* 👁✉ bassai {{抜塞}}, p. 43

(077-jg)*GENERAL MEANING (EXAMPLES)* ⚙📖 *noun* ❶ Fortress, fort[76] *verb* ❷ To block, to obstruct ❸ To shut, to close.

(185-ch)*CHINESE (PINYIN)* 🌏📖 *sāi, sè, sēi*

(705-gv)*GODAN VERB* 🏍⑤ **Terminal Form** {u* 🌢 but not i*-ru or e*-ru}

Fusagu (塞ぐ), which means to block. **Polite Form** {i*-masu} fusagimas[u] (塞ぎます).

#Sai-fortress {塞}##

(211-1)塞

(250-hi)さい (hir.)

(313-ka)*KANJI* ✐ The Compound Ideogram ˈSai-fortress (塞). (313k-cn)**Components** ⛭ [宀 | 工 | 廾]. (313k-ra)**Radical** ✛ 土 earth. (313k-cs)**Composition** ⚔ Top: 寒, bottom: 土. (313k-re)**Readings (examples)** 🗣 Go-on: そく (soku); さい (ˈsai). Kan-on: そく (soku); さい (ˈsai).

(830-ik)**IMPORTANT KANJI**

381. ˈSai-go

(012-k2)*KANJI 2* ☜ Ato-behind {後}, p. 41

(077-jg)*GENERAL MEANING (EXAMPLES)* ⚙📖 *adjective* ❶ Last.

(185-ch)*CHINESE (PINYIN)* 🌏📖 *zuìhòu*

(211-1)最後

#saigo {{最後}}##

(250-hi)さいご (hir.)

(466-cha)*CHARACTERISTICS* ① A Two-character, which consists of 2 Chi-

nese Logograms and 0 Hiˈra-ga-ˈna Characters.

382. ˈSak[u]-sha

(021-rb)*RESEARCH (FOR BOOKS)* 🔍

noun ❶ Author, writer, creator

(211-1)作者

(250-hi)さくしゃ (hir.)

(800-tag)*TAGS* 💻 #saku-sha, saku sha #sakusha##

(275-tō) さ く しゃ [sá⁺kɐ̀shà]

(466-cha)*CHARACTERISTICS* ⓘ A Two-character, which consists of 2 Chinese Logograms and 0 Hiˈra-ga-ˈna Characters

383. Saˈka Ts[u]ˈchi

(011-k1)*KANJI 1* ☛ Gyaku-reverse {逆}, p. 73

(012-k2)*KANJI 2* ☛ Tsuchi-hammer {槌}, p. 252

(055-tt)*THROWING TECHNIQUE* 投技

Old Name Taˈni ˈOtoshi (谷落)
AKA Saka Zuchi, Gyaku Tsuchi, Gyaku Zuchi, Upside-down Hammer, Reverse Hammer Throw, To Hammer Upside Down, Push off a Cliff, Valley Drop

(185-ch)*CHINESE (PINYIN)* ☯📖 *Nì chuí*

(211-1)逆槌

(250-hi)さかつち (hir.)

#sakatsuchi {{逆槌}}##

(056-mt)*FUNAKOSHI MAIN BOOK - THROWING TECHNIQUES* 📖MTT

1922 original 52 (list), 55 (Taˈni ˈOtoshi) **1925 Ishida** 62 (Taˈni ˈOtoshi) **1925 Teramoto** 53 (list), 55 (Taˈni ˈOtoshi) **1935 Suzuki-Johnston** 201 (Gyaku Zuchi) **1935 Ohshima** 227 (list), 232 (Sakatsuchi)

(466-cha)*CHARACTERISTICS* ⓘ A Two-character, which consists of 2 Chinese Logograms and 0 Hiˈra-ga-ˈna Characters.

(800-tag)*TAGS* 💻 #sakazuchi (さかづち), #gyakutsuchi, gyakuzuchi

384. Saˈki (先)

(000-it)*INCLUDING TERMS (EXAMPLES)* 👁✉ senpai {{先輩}}, p. 208; sensei {{先生}}, p. 208.

(077-jg)*GENERAL MEANING (EXAMPLES)* ☯📖 *adjective* ❶ Previous, earlier, prior ❷ First

(134-re)*RELATED TERMS* 👁∞ Mae-front {前}, p. 160

(185-ch)*CHINESE (PINYIN)* ☯📖 *xiān*

#Saki-previous {先}##

(211-1)先

(211-ka+hi)先き

(250-hi)さき (hir.)

(275-tō)さ[き] [sàkí]

(325-kr)*KANJI READINGS* ✑🕨 Go-on:
せん (sen). Kan-on: せん (sen).
Kun: さき (saki, 先).

(833-kan)**KANJI**

385. ˈSam-bon (sanbon)

(001-REF-rom) ˈSam-bon ☞ sanbon
{{三本}}, p. 202

(800-tag)*TAGS* 🖥 #sam-bon, sam bon,
#sa(m)bon

#sambon (sanbon)##

(089-no)*NOTES AND EXAMPLES* 📖✑ ん

(*n*) is the only Kana that does not
end in a vowel sound.

386. Saˈmurai (侍)

(077-jg)*GENERAL MEANING (EXAM-
PLES)* ⚙📖 *noun* ❶ Warrior, samurai

(211-1)侍 (250-hi)さむらい (hir.)

(275-tō)さむらい [sàmúráí]

(833-kan)**KANJI**

#Samurai-warrior {侍}##

(133-gr-sy)*GROUP* 👁(😊😊) The following
terms are synonyms: Samurai-

ˈSam-bon (sanbon) - ˈSan (三)

warrior {侍}, p. 201; Bu-warrior {
武}, p. 45; Shi-warrior {士}, p. 211;
bushi {{武士}}, p. 48

387. ˈSan (三)

(000-it)*INCLUDING TERMS (EXAMPLES)*

👁✉ mikka {{三日}}, p. 171; sanbon {{三本}}, p. 202; sanchindachi
{{三戦立ち}}, p. 203; sandan {{三
段}}, p. 204.

(077-jg)*GENERAL MEANING (EXAM-
PLES)* ⚙📖 *noun* ❶ Three

(185-ch)*CHINESE (PINYIN)* 🌙📖 *sān*

(211-1)三

(212-2)参 (legal)

(250-hi)さん (hir.)

(256-kat)サン (kat.)

#San-three {三}##

(275-tō)さ[ん] [sàń]

(313-ka)*KANJI* ✑ The Simple Ideogram
ˈSan-three (三). (313k-cn)**Components**
🖧 No components - a Simple Logogram. (313k-cs)**Composition** ✗ Top:
一 , bottom: 二 . (313k-re)**Readings
(examples)** 🕨 Go-on and Kan-on:
さん (ˈSan). Kun: み (ˈMi).

(800-tag)*TAGS* 🖥 #3

(830-ik)**IMPORTANT KANJI**

(838-su)**SUPER-TERM**

388. ˈSan-bon

(000-it)*INCLUDING TERMS (EXAMPLES)*

👁✉ sanbonkkumite {{三本組手}}, p. 202

(011-k1)*KANJI 1* ☛ San-three {三}, p. 201

(012-k2)*KANJI 2* ☛ Hon-source {本}, p. 102

(077-jg)*GENERAL MEANING (EXAMPLES)* ☼📖 *counter* ❶ Three long slender cylindrical objects (bananas, bottles, pens, trees, buses)

(089-no)*NOTES AND EXAMPLES* 📖✎

Sa/n/-hon > Sa/n/-bon > Sa[m]-bon

(185-ch)*CHINESE (PINYIN)* ☻📖 *sānběn*

(211-1)三本

(466-cha)*CHARACTERISTICS* ⓘ A Two-character, which consists of 2 Chinese Logograms and 0 Hiˈra-ga-ˈna Characters.

#sanbon {{三本}}##

(212-2)3 本

(250-hi)さんぼん (hir.)

(256-kat)サンボン (kat.)

(480-hb)**H⟳b** 🔔 Due to the ˈRen-daku laws, the unvoiced consonant /H/ may get a Dak[u]-ˈten (゙) and become ~/b/ as a suffix. Example 🖑 ˈHon (ほん) turns into ˈSan-bon (さんぼん).

(492-nbmb)**/n/b 👂 [m]b** 🔔 The moraic nasal ん is realized as [m] when preceding /b/. Example 🖑 ˈSan-bon (さんぼん) is pronounced [ˈSam-bon]. In such cases, we recommend Karate researchers to look for both spellings (Sanbon and Sambon, for instance) in every search, due to different Romanization systems.

389. ˈSan-bon ˈKumi-te

(015-w1)*WORD 1* 🅆 ☛ sanbon {{三本}}, p. 202

(016-w2)*WORD 2* 🅆 ☛ kumite {{組手}}, p. 157

(070-kt)*KARATE MEANING* 🖑📖 *noun phrase* ① Three-time Sparring, Three-step Sparring.

(211-1)三本組手

(212-2)3 本組手

(250-hi)さんぼんくみて (hir.)

#sanbonkkumite {{三本組手}}##

(466-cha)*CHARACTERISTICS* ⓘ A Four-character, which consists of 4 Chinese Logograms and 0 Hi·ra-ga-·na Characters.

(800-tag)*TAGS* 🖥 #san-bon kumite, san bon kumite, #sambon kumite, sambon kumite, #sanbongumite, sanbon gummite, #sambongumite, sambon gumite

(838-su)**SUPER-TERM**

390. ·San-chin Da·chi

(011-k1)*KANJI 1* ☞ San-three {三}, p. 201

(012-k2)*KANJI 2* ☞ Ikusa-war {戦}, p. 105

(015-w1)*WORD 1* ^W_W ☞ tachi {{立ち}}, p. 228

(030-st)*STANCE* 立 **AKA** Uchi-hachiji Dachi (内八字立), Three Battles Stance, Crescent Stance, Grounded Stance, Rooted Stance, Rooting Stance, Hourglass Stance. ·San-chin is a name of a Shōrei-style Kata. In our opinion, the right translation is simply Sanchin Stance, since the stance is named after the Kata. **Category** Middle height front stances

(089-no)*NOTES AND EXAMPLES* 📖✎

The knees[77] and the feet point medially. This stance is narrower than ·Han-getsu ·Dachi.

(031-ms)*FUNAKOSHI MAIN BOOK - STANCES* 🐢**MS** 1922 original 30 (list), 34 **1925 Ishida** 41 (list) **1925 Teramoto** 40 (list).

#sanchindachi {{三戦立ち}}##

(134-re)*RELATED TERMS* ◉∞ hangetsu-dachi {{半月立ち}}, p. 84

(185-ch)*CHINESE (PINYIN)* ◉📖 **Sān zhàn Lì**

(211-1)三戦立ち

(211-al)*ALTERNATIVES OR SEE ALSO* ✎✎三戦立, 三戦立ち, 三進立ち, 参戦立ち, サンチン立ち

(250-hi)さんちんだち (hir.)

(466-cha)*CHARACTERISTICS* ⓘ A Four-character, which consists of 3 Chinese Logograms and 1 Hi·ra-ga-·na Characters.

(483-td)**T⊃d** 🏠 Due to the ·Ren-daku laws, the unvoiced consonant /T/ may get a Dak[u]-·ten (゛) and become ~/d/ as a suffix. Example ↯ ·Tachi (たち) turns into Ki-·ba Da·chi (きばだち).

(800-tag)*TAGS* 🖥 #sanshindachi, sanshin dachi, #sansendachi, sansen dachi, #sanchintachi, sanchin tachi

391. ˈSan-dan

(000-it)*INCLUDING TERMS (EXAMPLES)*

👁✉ heiansandan {{平安三段}}, p. 93; tekkisandan {{鉄騎三段}}, p. 239.

(011-k1)*KANJI 1* ☛ San-three {三}, p. 201

(012-k2)*KANJI 2* ☛ Dan-level {段}, p. 56

(070-kt)*KARATE MEANING* ✋📖 *noun* ① Third Level ② Third dan, third degree black belt ③ Three.

#sandan {{三段}}##

(077-jg)*GENERAL MEANING (EXAMPLES)* ⚙📖 *noun* ❶ Third grade, level three, third rank, third-degree.

(211-1)三段 (250-hi)さんだん (hir.)

(466-cha)*CHARACTERISTICS* ⓘ A Two-character, which consists of 2 Chinese Logograms and 0 Hiˈra-ga-ˈna Characters.

(800-tag)*TAGS* 💻 san-dan, san dan

(838-su)**SUPER-TERM**

392. ˈSaru (猿)

(000-it)*INCLUDING TERMS (EXAMPLES)*

👁✉ enpi {{猿臂}}, p. 62

(077-jg)*GENERAL MEANING (EXAMPLES)* ⚙📖 *noun* ❶ Monkey

(185-ch)*CHINESE (PINYIN)* 🔊📖 *yuán*

(211-1)猿

(250-hi)さる (hir.) (275-tō) さ る [sáˈrù]

#Saru-monkey {猿}##

(280-po)pol:SARY

(325-kr)*KANJI READINGS* ✏🗣 Go-on: おん (on). Kan-on: えん (en). Kun: さる (saru, 猿); まし (mashi, 猿); ましら (mashira, 猿ら). Nanori: さ (sa); さわ (sawa).

(833-kan)**KANJI**

393. ˈSe (背)

(000-it)*INCLUDING TERMS (EXAMPLES)*

👁✉ haitō {{背刀}}, p. 80; hai-wanuke {{背腕受け}}, p. 79

(077-jg)*GENERAL MEANING (EXAMPLES)* ⚙📖 *noun* ❶ Back, spine (exclusively for ˈSe reading) ❷ Rear side, reverse (exclusively for ˈSe reading) ❸ Ridge (of a mountain) (exclusively for ˈSe reading) ❹ Height, stature.

(325-kr)*KANJI READINGS* ✏🗣 Go-on: へ (he); べ (be); はい (hai). Kan-on: はい (hai). Kun: せ (se, 背) – as in Se-ˈnaka (背中); せい (sei, 背).

#Se-back {背}##

(089-no)*NOTES AND EXAMPLES* 📖✎ It seems that the *ridge* meaning is only relevant for the ˈSe reading[78]. So, apparently ˈHai-tō (背刀) cannot be translated as Ridge Hand. On the other hand, the *back*, the *rear side,* and the *reverse* meanings may also be exclusive for the ˈSe reading.

(185-ch)*CHINESE (PINYIN)* ☯📖 ***bèi***

(211-1)背

(250-hi)せ (hir.)

(885-tag)*TAGS* 🖥 #back

(833-kan)**KANJI**

394. ˈSe Uˈde Uˈke (haiwanuke)

(001-REF-rom) ˈSe Uˈde Uˈke ☞ hai-wanuke {{背腕受け}}, p. 79 #seudeuke (haiwanuke)##

(800-tag)*TAGS* 🖥 #se-ude-uke

395. ˈSe[i] Rˈyū

(000-it)*INCLUDING TERMS (EXAMPLES)* 👁✉ seiryūtō {{青龍刀}}, p. 206

(011-k1)*KANJI 1* ☞ Ao-blue {青}, p. 34

(077-jg)*GENERAL MEANING (EXAMPLES)* ☼📖 *noun phrase* ❶ The Azure Dragon, The Blue Dragon, The Green Dragon, The Blue-green Dragon, The Bluegreen Dragon of the East.

(095-3t)*THE THREE TEACHINGS* 3⃝👤 One of The Four Symbols (*Sì Xiàng*), along with The White Tiger of the West (p. 249).

(185-ch)*CHINESE (PINYIN)* ☯📖 ***qīnglóng***

#seiryū {{青龍}}##

(211-1)青龍

(212-2)青竜

(211-al)*ALTERNATIVES OR SEE ALSO*

✏✏ 蒼龍, 苍龙

(250-hi)せいりゅう (hir.)

(275-tō)せ—りょ— [sèéryóó]

(280-po)pol:SEERJUU

(466-cha)*CHARACTERISTICS* ⓘ A Two-character, which consists of 2 Chinese Logograms and 0 Hiˈra-ga-ˈna Characters.

(800-tag)*TAGS* 🖥 #seiryu, #seiriu

396. ˈSe[i]-ken

(011-k1)*KANJI 1* ☞ Shō-correct {正}, p. 216

(012-k2)*KANJI 2* ☞ Ken-fist {拳}, p. 140

(040-ul)*UPPER LIMB STRIKE & ANATOMY* 手 **AKA** Regular Fist, Proper Fist, Fore-fist, Front of the Fist, Straight

Fist, Fist **Category** Strike, Closed-fist.

(089-no)*NOTES AND EXAMPLES* 📖✎

The impact area is the distal side of MCP (metacarpophalangeal joints) II and III, with or without PIP (proximal interphalangeal joints) II and III

#seiken {{正拳}}##

(041-mu)*FUNAKOSHI MAIN BOOK - UPPER LIMB* 🐟**MUL** 1935 Ohshima 17

(185-ch)*CHINESE (PINYIN)* ☯📖 ***Zhèng quán***

(211-1)正拳

(250-hi)せいけん (hir.)

(280-po)pol:SEEKEN

(466-cha)*CHARACTERISTICS* ① A Two-character, which consists of 2 Chinese Logograms and 0 Hiˈra-ga-ˈna Characters.

397. ˈSe[i]-ryū-ˈtō

(015-w1)*WORD 1* ^W_W ☛ seiryū {{青龍}}, p. 205

(013-k3)*KANJI 3* ☛ Katana-sword {刀}, p. 136

(070-kt)*KARATE MEANING* ✋📖 AKA Ox-jaw Hand, Ox-jaw Strike, Seiryuto Uke *noun* ① Vertical

sword-hand strike, performed with an abduction of the wrist (radial deviation) along with a small extension.

(089-no)*NOTES AND EXAMPLES* 📖✎

Often described as the base of the Sh[u]-ˈtō (手 刀). Resembles *Gōngfū*'s Willow Leaf Palm.

#seiryūtō {{青龍刀}}##

Anatomy 4 - Seiryuto

(185-ch)*CHINESE (PINYIN)* ☯📖

Qīnglóng dāo

(211-1)青龍刀

(212-2)青竜刀

(250-hi)せいりゅうとう (hir.)

(280-po)pol:SEERJIUUTOO

(466-cha)*CHARACTERISTICS* ① A Three-character, which consists of 3 Chinese Logograms and 0 Hiˈra-ga-ˈna Characters.

(800-tag)*TAGS* 🖥 #seiryuto, #seiriuto

398. ˈSe[i]-za

(011-k1)*KANJI 1* ☛ Shō-correct {正}, p. 216

(012-k2)*KANJI 2* ☛ Za-seat {座}, p. 283

(077-jg)*GENERAL MEANING (EXAMPLES)* ☼📖 *noun* ❶ Traditional Japanese kneeled position, with the dorsal aspect of the feet facing down.

(134-gr-re)*GROUP* 👁(🔅) The following terms are related: iai {{居合}}, p. 103, mokusō {{黙想}}, p. 171, seiza {{正座}}, p. 207, zazen {{座禅}}, p. 283

(185-ch)*CHINESE (PINYIN)* ☯📖

zhèngzuò

(211-1)正座

#seiza {{正座}}##

Masters 19 - Seiza by Papkin Sensei

List of Sensei Demonstrations next to Values, p. 10

Gal Papkin Sensei of Israel Shotokan demonstrates Seiza. Photographer: Shlomi Ofir.

(212-2)正坐

(250-hi)せいざ (hir.)

(280-po)pol:SEEDZA

(466-cha)*CHARACTERISTICS* ① A Two-character, which consists of 2 Chinese Logograms and 0 Hiˈra-ga-ˈna Characters.

399. ˈSem-pai (senpai)

(001-REF-rom)ˈSem-pai ☞ senpai {{先輩}}, p. 208

#sempai (senpai)##

(885-tag)*TAGS* 🖥 #sem pai

400. ˈSen (Ikusa)

(001-REF-rom)ˈSen ☞ Ikusa-war {戦}, p. 105

#Sen (Ikusa)##

(002-REF-hi)せん ☞ いくさ

401. ˈSen (線)

(000-it)*INCLUDING TERMS (EXAMPLES)* 👁✉ enbusen {{演武線}}, p. 61

(077-jg)*GENERAL MEANING (EXAMPLES)* ☼📖 *noun* ❶ Line.

(211-1)線

#Sen-line {線}##

(250-hi)せん (hir.)

(133-sy)*SYNONYMS* 👁= Gyo-line {行}, p. 75

(833-kan)**KANJI**

402. ˈSen-pai

(011-k1)*KANJI I* ☞ Saki-previous {先}, p. 201

(070-kt)*KARATE MEANING* ✋📖 *noun* ① Senior student ② Assistant instructor (Shodan or Nidan for instance) ③ Senior.

(077-jg)*GENERAL MEANING (EXAMPLES)* ☼📖 *noun* ❶ Senior ❷ Superior, someone with a higher level of skill or experience *suffix* ❸ Honorific, honorary title

(089-no)*NOTES AND EXAMPLES* 📖✍

Sen-hai > Sen-pai > Se[m]-pai. Kōhai, (後輩), which means junior, is the antonym of Senpai.

(136-se)*SEE ALSO* 👁➕ sensei {{先生}}, p. 208

(185-ch)*CHINESE (PINYIN)* 🌐📖 *xiānbèi*

(211-1)先輩

(212-2)先輩

(250-hi)せんぱい (hir.)

#senpai {{先輩}}##

(275-tō)せ|ん|ぱい [sèńpái]

(280-po)pol:SEMPAJ

(466-cha)*CHARACTERISTICS* ⓘ A Two-character, which consists of 2 Chinese Logograms and 0 Hiˈra-ga-ˈna Characters.

(481-hp)**H⊃p** 🔔 Due to the ˈRen-daku laws, the unvoiced consonant /H/ may get a Han-dak[u]-ten (゜) and become ~/p/ as a suffix. Example 🔑 ˈHon (ほん) turns into ˈIp-pon (いっぽん).

(491-npmp)**/n/p** 👂 **[m]p** 🔔 The moraic nasal ん is realized as [m] when preceding /p/. Example 🔑 ˈEn-pi (えんぴ) is pronounced [ˈEm-pi]. In such cases, we recommend Karate researchers to look for both spellings (Enpi and Empi, for instance) in every search, due to different Romanization systems.

403. ˈSen-ˈse[i]

(011-k1)*KANJI* ェ ☞ Saki-previous {先}, p. 201

(077-jg)*GENERAL MEANING (EXAMPLES)* ☼📖 *noun* ❶ Teacher, master *suffix* ❷ Honorific, honorary title

(089-no)*NOTES AND EXAMPLES* 📖✍

The rules of Japanese honorifics apply to this term when used as an honorific (and not on its own): First, the term comes after the name (usually the surname): Funakosh-sensei, and not Sensei Funakoshi or Gichin Sensei. Second, one should not use this term when referring to oneself.
#sensei {{先生}}##

(136-se)*SEE ALSO* 👁+ senpai {{先輩}}, p. 208

(185-ch)*CHINESE (PINYIN)* ☻📖

xiānshēng

(189-ok)*OKINAWAN* ● Shinshī (しんしー)

(211-1)先生 (250-hi)せんせい (hir.)

(275-tō)せ|ん|せ|ー| [sèńséˈè]

(280-po)pol:SENSEE

(466-cha)*CHARACTERISTICS* ⓘ A Two-character, which consists of 2 Chinese Logograms and 0 Hiˈra-ga-ˈna Characters.

(838-su)**SUPER-TERM**

404.Sh[i]ˈchi (七)

(077-jg)*GENERAL MEANING (EXAMPLES)* ✿📖 *noun* ❶ Seven

(185-ch)*CHINESE (PINYIN)* ☻📖 ***qī***

(211-1)七 (250-hi)しち (hir.)

(275-tō)し|ち| [shꜛchíˈ]

(800-tag)*TAGS* 💻 #shchi, #7 #Shichi-seven {七}##

(325-kr)*KANJI READINGS* ✒🗣 Go-on: しち (shichi). Kan-on: しつ (shitsu). Kun: なな [náˈnà] (nana,

七); ななつ (nanatsu, 七つ); なの (nano, 七).

(838-su)**SUPER-TERM**

(833-kan)**KANJI**

405.ˈSh[i]-ˈko Daˈchi

(011-k1)*KANJI 1* ☞ Yon-four {四}, p. 280

(013-k3)*KANJI 3* ☞ tachi {{立ち}}, p. 228

(070-kt)*KARATE MEANING* ✋📖 AKA Jigotai-dachi *noun phrase* ① Square Stance, Wide Open-leg Horse Stance

(089-no)*NOTES AND EXAMPLES* 📖✎ Shiko (四股) is a Sumo term.

(136-se)*SEE ALSO* 👁+ kibadachi {{騎馬立ち}}, p. 145

(466-cha)*CHARACTERISTICS* ⓘ A Four-character, which consists of 3 Chinese Logograms and 1 Hiˈra-ga-ˈna Characters.

(185-ch)*CHINESE (PINYIN)* ☻📖 ***Sìgǔ lì***

(250-hi)しこだち (hir.) #shikodachi {{四股立ち}}##

Sh[u]-ˈtō - Sh[u]-ˈtō-uchi

Masters 20 - Shikodachi by Bamgboye Sensei
List of Sensei Demonstrations next to Values, p. 10
Bobby Bamgboye of Nigeria WSKF demonstrates Shiko-dachi. Photographer: Joel Ibanga.

(211-1)四股立ち (212-2)四股立

(280-po)pol:SZKODACI

(483-td)**Tↄd** 🔔 Due to the ˈRen-daku laws, the unvoiced consonant /T/ may get a Dak[u]-ˈten (゙) and become ~/d/ as a suffix. Example 🖐 ˈTachi (た ち) turns into Ki-ˈba Daˈchi (き ば だ ち).

406.Sh[u]-ˈtō

(000-it)*INCLUDING TERMS (EXAMPLES)*

👁✉ shutōuchi {{手刀打ち}}, p. 211, shutōuke {{手刀受け}}, p. 211.

(011-k1)*KANJI 1* ☛ Te-hand {手}, p. 234

(012-k2)*KANJI 2* ☛ Katana-sword {刀}, p. 136

(070-kt)*KARATE MEANING* 🖐📖 AKA Te-ˈgatana (て が た な), Knife-hand,

Handsword *noun* ① Ulnar border of the open palm.

(138-co)*COORDINATE TERMS* 👁≈ tettsui {{鉄槌}}, p. 245

#shutō {{手刀}}##

(185-ch)*CHINESE (PINYIN)* ☯📖

Shǒudāo

(139-an)*ANTONYMS* 👁↺ haitō {{背刀}}, p. 80

(211-1)手刀

(250-hi)しゅとう (hir.)

(256-kat)シュトウ (kat.)

(466-cha)*CHARACTERISTICS* ① A Two-character, which consists of 2 Chinese Logograms and 0 Hiˈra-ga-ˈna Characters.

(800-tag)*TAGS* 💻 #shuto, #shto #te-gatana (て が た な), #tekatana

407.Sh[u]-ˈtō-uchi

(015-w1)*WORD 1* W ☛ shutō {{手刀}}, p. 210

(016-w2)*WORD 2* W ☛ uchi {{打ち}}, p. 258

(070-kt)*KARATE MEANING* 🖐📖 AKA Teˈ gatana-uchi (て が た な う ち) *noun* ① Knifehand strike, handsword strike, Karate chop.

(185-ch) *CHINESE* *(PINYIN)* ☯📖

Shǒudāo dǎ

#shutōuchi {{手刀打ち}}##

(211-1) 手刀打ち

(212-2) 手刀打 (250-hi) しゅとううち

(hir.)

(466-cha) *CHARACTERISTICS* ⓘ A Four-character, which consists of 3 Chinese Logograms and 1 Hiˈra-ga-ˈna Characters.

(800-tag) *TAGS* 💻 #shutouchi, #shtouchi, #shotouchi

(838-su) **SUPER-TERM**

408. Sh[u]-ˈtō-uˈke

(015-w1) *WORD 1* ᵂ⁄ᵂ ☛ shutō {{手刀}}, p. 210

(016-w2) *WORD 2* ᵂ⁄ᵂ ☛ uke {{受け}}, p. 262

(070-kt) *KARATE MEANING* ✋📖 AKA Syuto-uke, Tegatana-uke *noun* ① Knifehand block, handsword block

(185-ch) *CHINESE* *(PINYIN)* ☯📖

Shǒudāo shòu

#shutōuke {{手刀受け}}##

(211-1) 手刀受け (212-2) 手刀受

(250-hi) しゅとううけ (hir.)

(466-cha) *CHARACTERISTICS* ⓘ A Four-character, which consists of 3 Chi-

nese Logograms and 1 Hiˈra-ga-ˈna Characters.

(800-tag) *TAGS* 💻 #shutouke, #shotouke, #shtouke, #syutouke

(838-su) **SUPER-TERM**

409. ˈShi (Yon)

(001-REF-rom) ˈShi ☞ Yon-four {四}, p. 280

#Shi (Yon)##

(002-REF-hi) し ☞ よん

410. ˈShi (士)

(000-it) *INCLUDING TERMS (EXAMPLES)*

👁✉ bushi {{武士}}, p. 48

(077-jg) *GENERAL MEANING (EXAMPLES)* ☼📖 *noun* ❶ Warrior, samurai ❷ Gentleman.

(211-1) 士 (250-hi) し (hir.)

(275-tō) | し | [shíˈ]

#Shi-warrior {士}##

(133-gr-sy) *GROUP* 👁😺 The following terms are synonyms: Samurai-warrior {侍}, p. 201; Bu-warrior {武}, p. 45; Shi-warrior {士}, p. 211; bushi {{武士}}, p. 48

(885-tag) *TAGS* 💻 #shy

(833-kan) **KANJI**

411. ˈShi-han

(070-kt)*KARATE MEANING* 🖐📖 *noun*

① Master instructor, head instructor ② Senior instructor, teacher of teachers.

(077-jg)*GENERAL MEANING (EXAMPLES)* ✿📖 *noun* ❶ Instructor *adjective, adjectival noun* ❷ Model.

(089-no)*NOTES AND EXAMPLES* 📖✎

Kyō-han (教範) means a manual or a teaching method.

(136-se)*SEE ALSO* 👁➕ sensei {{先生}}, p. 208

#shihan {{師範}}##

(185-ch)*CHINESE (PINYIN)* 👁📖 *Shīfàn*

Shīfù (師傅) means master.

(211-1)師範 (212-2)师范

(250-hi) しはん (hir.)

(275-tō)し はん [shíˈhàn]

(466-cha)*CHARACTERISTICS* ⓘ A Two-character, which consists of 2 Chinese Logograms and 0 Hiˈra-ga-ˈna Characters.

(800-tag)*TAGS* 💻 #shi-han

412. ˈShi-ji-ˈgata (dojigata)

(001-REF-rom)ˈShi-ji-ˈgata ☞ dojigata {{土字形}}, p. 58

#shijigata (dojigata)##

(800-tag)*TAGS* 💻 #shiji-gata, shiji gata

413. Shiˈmo (下)

(000-it)*INCLUDING TERMS (EXAMPLES)*

👁✉ ashimoto {{足元}}, p. 38 (alternative spelling); gedan {{下段}}, p. 69.

(077-jg)*GENERAL MEANING (EXAMPLES)* ✿📖 *noun* ❶ Bottom, lower portion, lower part *preposition* ❷ Down, under, below.

(095-3t)*THE THREE TEACHINGS* 3️⃣:

Here is a passage from one of the Four Books (Chinese classics)[79]:

'Man's nature is like water whirling round in a corner. Open a passage for it to the east, and it will flow to the east; open a passage for it to the west, and it will flow to the west. Man's nature is indifferent to good and evil, just as the water is indifferent to the east and west.'

Mencius replied, 'Water indeed will flow indifferently to the east or west, but will it flow indifferently up or down?

The water goes east, only because the east side is lower at that point. Our advice is: when moving in any horizontal direction, try to feel as if the gravity is the force that moves You. If You move to the left, it is because the left side is lower and pulls You.

(185-ch)*CHINESE (PINYIN)* ☯📖 **xià**

#Shimo-bottom {下}##

(139-an)*ANTONYMS* 👁↻ Ue-top {上}, p. 262

(211-1) 下

(250-hi) しも (hir.)

(275-tō) し|も| [shìmó⁺]

(313-ka)*KANJI* ✐ The Simple Ideogram Shiˈmo-bottom (下). (313k-cn)**Components** ⛏ No components - a Simple Logogram. (313k-ra)**Radical** ✦ 一 one. (313k-cs)**Composition** ✄ 一卜.

(313k-re)**Readings (examples)** 🗣 Go-on: げ (ge). Kan-on: か (ka) – as in ˈSei-ka-ˈtan-den (臍下丹田). Kun: した [shⅰtá] (sh[i]ˈta, 下) – as in Shita-muki (下向き); しも (Shiˈmo 下); もと [mòtó⁺] (moˈto, 下); さがる (sagaru, 下がる); さげる (sageru, 下げる); くだる (kudaru, 下る); くだす (kudasu, 下す); くださる (kudasaru, 下さる); おりる (oriru, 下りる); おろす (orosu, 下ろす).

(830-ik)**IMPORTANT KANJI**

414. ˈShin (進)

(000-it)*INCLUDING TERMS (EXAMPLES)*

👁✉ naihanchi {{内歩進}}, p. 177

(077-jg)*GENERAL MEANING (EXAMPLES)* ⚙📖 *verb* ❶ To advance.

(185-ch)*CHINESE (PINYIN)* ☯📖 **jìn**

(211-1)進 (211-al)*ALTERNATIVES OR SEE ALSO* ✐✐ 進 (250-hi) しん (hir.)

#Shin-to advance {進}##

(256-kat)シン (kat.)

(325-kr)*KANJI READINGS* ✐🗣 Go-on: しん (shin). Kan-on: しん (shin). On: じん (jin). Kun: すすむ (susumu, 進む); すすめる (susumeru, 進める).

(800-tag)*TAGS* 💻 #chin, #jin

(833-kan)**KANJI**

415. ˈShin-pan

(077-jg)*GENERAL MEANING (EXAMPLES)* ⚙📖 *noun* ❶ Referee.

(185-ch)*CHINESE (PINYIN)* ☯📖 **shěnpàn**

(275-tō) しんぱん [shíⁿpàn]

(276-tō2) |しんぱん| [shìⁿpáⁿ]

(800-tag)*TAGS* 💻 #shimpan, #shinban (しんばん)

(466-cha)*CHARACTERISTICS* ⓘ A Two-character, which consists of 2 Chinese Logograms and 0 Hiˈra-ga-ˈna Characters.

#shinpan {{審判}}##

(211-1)審判 (212-2)审判

(250-hi)しんぱん (hir.)

(491-npmp)**/n/p** 🎜 **[m]p** 🔔 The moraic nasal ん is realized as [m] when preceding /p/. Example 🗲 ˈEn-pi (えんぴ) is pronounced [ˈEm-pi]. In such cases, we recommend Karate researchers to look for both spellings (Enpi and Empi, for instance) in every search, due to different Romanization systems.

416. ˈShiro (白)

(000-it)*INCLUDING TERMS (EXAMPLES)*

👁 ✉ shiroi {{白い}}, p. 214

(077-jg)*GENERAL MEANING (EXAMPLES)* ☼📖 *noun* ❶ White (noun)

(185-ch)*CHINESE (PINYIN)* ☻📖 ***bái, bó***

#Shiro-white {白}##

(211-1)白 (250-hi)しろ (hir.)

(302-kn)*KANJI NOTES* 🖊🖌 A Radical (Radical 106). Contains 5 strokes.

(833-kan)**KANJI**

417. Shiˈroi

(077-jg)*GENERAL MEANING (EXAMPLES)* ☼📖 *adjective* ❶ White (adjective).

(011-k1)*KANJI 1* ☞ Shiro-white {白}, p. 214

(211-1)白い

(250-hi)しろい (hir.)

#shiroi {{白い}}##

(275-tō)し ろ い [shìró⁺ì]

(466-cha)*CHARACTERISTICS* ⓘ A Two-character, which consists of 1 Chinese Logograms and 1 Hiˈra-ga-ˈna Characters.

418. Shi-ˈzen

(000-it)*INCLUDING TERMS (EXAMPLES)*

👁 ✉ shizentai {{自然体}}, p. 215

(011-k1)*KANJI 1* ☞ Ji-self {自}, p. 109

(077-jg)*GENERAL MEANING (EXAMPLES)* ☼📖 *noun* ❶ Nature *adjective* ❷ Natural ❸ Spontaneous.

(185-ch)*CHINESE (PINYIN)* ☻📖 ***zìrán***

(189-ok)*OKINAWAN* ❶ Shijin (しじん)

#shizen {{自然}}##

(211-1)自然

(250-hi)しぜん (hir.)

(275-tō)し ぜ ん [shìzéń]

(466-cha)*CHARACTERISTICS* ⓘ A Two-character, which consists of 2 Chinese Logograms and 0 Hiˈra-ga-ˈna Characters.

419.Shi-ˈzen-tai

(015-w1)*WORD 1* Ⓦ ☞ shizen {{自然}}, p. 214

(013-k3)*KANJI 3* ☞ Tai-body {体}, p. 228 (077-jg)*GENERAL MEANING (EXAMPLES)* ✿📖 *noun* ❶ Natural posture ❷ Natural stance ❸ Open attitude, relaxed manner.

#shizentai {{自然体}}##

(185-ch)*CHINESE (PINYIN)* ☯📖 **Zìrántǐ**

(211-1) 自然体 (250-hi) しぜんたい (hir.)

(466-cha)*CHARACTERISTICS* ⓘ A Three-character, which consists of 3 Chinese Logograms and 0 Hiˈra-ga-ˈna Characters.

420.ˈShō (小)

💣☀ Do not confuse: Shō-small {小}, p. 215 with Shō-small {少}, p. 215.

(077-jg)*GENERAL MEANING (EXAMPLES)* ✿📖 *adjective* ❶ Small, little.

(089-no)*NOTES AND EXAMPLES* 📖✎

This is the Character we find in Ka-

ta names –Baˈssai-shō (拔塞小), ˈKankū-shō (観空小), ˈGojūshiho-shō (五十四步小)

(139-an)*ANTONYMS* 👁↻ Dai-big {大}, p. 56

#Shō-small {小}##

(185-ch)*CHINESE (PINYIN)* ☯📖 **xiǎo**

(211-1)小

(250-hi) しょう (hir.)

(256-kat) ショウ (kat.)

(275-tō) しょー [shó⁺ò]

(302-kn)*KANJI NOTES* ✎✏ A Radical (Radical 42). Contains 3 strokes.

(800-tag)*TAGS* 🖥 #sho 1, #small

(833-kan)**KANJI**

421.ˈShō (少)

💣☀ Do not confuse: Shō-small {小}, p. 215 with Shō-small {少}, p. 215.

(000-it)*INCLUDING TERMS (EXAMPLES)* 👁✉ shōrin {{少林}}, p. 218

(077-jg)*GENERAL MEANING (EXAMPLES)* ✿📖 *adjective, prefix et al.* ❶ Small, little ❷ few

(089-no)*NOTES AND EXAMPLES* 📖✎

S[u]ˈkoshi (少し) means a bit.

#Shō-small {少}##

(185-ch)*CHINESE (PINYIN)* ☯📖 **shǎo** In *Shàolín*'s case, *Shǎo* is only a name, and does not mean small

(211-1)少 (250-hi)しょう (hir.) (256-kat)ショウ (kat.)

(302-kn)*KANJI NOTES* ✒🖌 Contains 4 strokes.

(800-tag)*TAGS* 💻 #sho 2, #small

(833-kan)**KANJI**

422. ˈShō (正)

(000-it)*INCLUDING TERMS (EXAMPLES)* 👁✉ seiken {{正拳}}, p. 206; seiza {{正座}}, p. 207; shōmen {{正面}}, p. 217; taisho {{大正}}, p. 230.

(077-jg)*GENERAL MEANING (EXAMPLES)* ☼📖 *adjective* ❶ Correct, proper, right ❷ Regular

(185-ch)*CHINESE (PINYIN)* ☯📖 **zhèng**

(211-1)正 (211-al)*ALTERNATIVES OR SEE ALSO* ✒✒ 正しい , ただしい, せい

#Shō-correct {正}##

(250-hi)しょう (hir.)

(302-kn)*KANJI NOTES* ✒🖌 Contains 5 strokes.

(325-kr)*KANJI READINGS* ✒🗣 Go-on: しょう (shō). Kan-on: せい (sei).

Kun: ただしい (tadashii, 正しい); ただす (tadasu, 正す); まさ (masa, 正); まさに (masani, 正に). Nanori: おお (ō).

(800-tag)*TAGS* 💻 #sho

(833-kan)**KANJI**

423. ˈShō-bu

(011-k1)*KANJI 1* ☞ Katsu-to win {勝}, p. 138

(077-jg)*GENERAL MEANING (EXAMPLES)* ☼📖 *noun* ❶ Match, contest.

(185-ch)*CHINESE (PINYIN)* ☯📖

Shèngfù

(211-1)勝負 (250-hi)しょうぶ (hir.)

(275-tō) しょ －ぶ [shóˑòbù]

#shōbu {{勝負}}##

(280-po)pol:SZOOBY

(466-cha)*CHARACTERISTICS* ① A Two-character, which consists of 2 Chinese Logograms and 0 Hiˈra-ga-ˈna Characters.

(800-tag)*TAGS* 💻 #shobu

424.Sho-ˈdan

(000-it)*INCLUDING TERMS (EXAMPLES)* 👁✉ heianshodan {{平安初段}}, p. 91; tekkishodan {{鉄騎初段}}, p. 239.

(011-k1)*KANJI 1* ☛ Hatsu-first {初}, p. 88

(012-k2)*KANJI 2* ☛ Dan-level {段}, p. 56

(070-kt)*KARATE MEANING* ✋📖 AKA Ichi-dan *noun* ① First Level, beginning degree ② First dan, lowest black belt rank, first degree black belt ③ One.

#shodan {{初段}}##

(077-jg)*GENERAL MEANING (EXAMPLES)* ☼📖 *noun* ❶ First grade, lowest grade, level one, first rank, first-degree

(211-1)初段

(250-hi)しょだん (hir.)

(466-cha)*CHARACTERISTICS* ⓘ A Two-character, which consists of 2 Chinese Logograms and 0 Hiˈra-ga-ˈna Characters.

(800-tag)*TAGS* 💻 #sho-dan, sho dan

(838-su)**SUPER-TERM**

425. ˈShō-men

(011-k1)*KANJI 1* ☛ Shō-correct {正}, p. 216

(012-k2)*KANJI 2* ☛ Men-side {面}, p. 168

(071-dl)💣🔥 AA *DOJO LANGUAGE* 🗿📖 *noun* ① Full facing posture, front-facing posture, opposite of Hanmi.

(077-jg)*GENERAL MEANING (EXAMPLES)* ☼📖 *adjective* ❶ Front ❷ Main

(139-an)*ANTONYMS* 👁↻ hanmi {{半身}}, p. 85

#shōmen {{正面}}##

(185-ch)*CHINESE (PINYIN)* ☯📖

zhèngmiàn

(211-1)正面 (250-hi)しょうめん (hir.)

(275-tō)しょ 一め ん [shòómé⁺ǹ]

(466-cha)*CHARACTERISTICS* ⓘ A Two-character, which consists of 2 Chinese Logograms and 0 Hiˈra-ga-ˈna Characters.

(800-tag)*TAGS* 💻 #shomen

426. ˈShō-re[i]-ryū

(011-k1)*KANJI 1* ☛ Aki-bright {昭}, p. 32

(012-k2)*KANJI 2* ☛ Rei-sole {霊}, p. 196

(013-k3)*KANJI 3* ☛ Ryū-style {流}, p. 197

(070-kt)*KARATE MEANING* ✋📖 AKA Shokei Style *noun phrase* ① Heavy and short Karate styles. They resemble the southern schools of Chinese martial arts[80]. ② Heavy and short Kata style (within the same school).

(090-te)*TELL YOUR STUDENTS* 📖☺ The ˈShō in the beginning of the words ˈShō-re[i]-ryū (昭霊流) and ˈShō-rin-ryū (少林流) is not the same ˈShō! However, Funakoshi in his 1922 book, spells ˈShō-rin-ryū "昭林流". In the 1925 edition, the mistake is corrected.

#shōreiryū {{昭霊流}}##

(133-sy)*SYNONYMS* 👁= nahate {{那覇手}}, p. 176

(139-an)*ANTONYMS* 👁↻ shōrinryū {{少林流}}, p. 219; shurite {{首里手}}, p. 222; tomarite {{泊手}}, p. 248

(185-ch)*CHINESE (PINYIN)* 👁📖 *Zhāo líng*

(211-1)昭霊流

(250-hi)しょうれいりゅう (hir.)

(256-kat)ショウレイリュウ (kat.)

(466-cha)*CHARACTERISTICS* ⓘ A Three-character, which consists of 3

Chinese Logograms and 0 Hiˈra-ga-ˈna Characters.

(800-tag)*TAGS* 💻 #shoreiryu, shoreiryu, shorei ryu, shōre[i]-ryū, shōrei ryū

427. ˈShō-rin

(000-it)*INCLUDING TERMS (EXAMPLES)* 👁✉ shōrinryū {{少林流}}, p. 219

(011-k1)*KANJI 1* ☛ Shō-small {少}, p. 215

(012-k2)*KANJI 2* ☛ Hayashi-grove {林}, p. 89

(025-sch)*SCHOOLS* 🏯 *name* Shaolin Kung Fu (*Shǎolín gōngfū*), Shaolin Wushu (*Shǎolín wǔshù*), Shaolin Quan (*Shàolínquán*).

(028-pl)*PLACES* 🌏 *name* Shaolin Monastery, Shaolin Temple (*Shàolínsì*).

#shōrin {{少林}}##

(185-ch)*CHINESE (PINYIN)* 👁📖 *Shàolín Shào* (少) is short for *Shàoshìshān* (少室山).

(211-1)少林

(250-hi)しょうりん (hir.)

(466-cha)*CHARACTERISTICS* ⓘ A Two-character, which consists of 2 Chinese Logograms and 0 Hiˈra-ga-ˈna Characters.

(800-tag)*TAGS* 💻 #shorin, #shaolin

428.˙**Shō-rin-ryū**

(015-w1)*WORD 1* ʷ̲ʷ̲ ☛ shōrin {{少林}}, p. 218

(013-k3)*KANJI 3* ☛ Ryū-style {流}, p. 197

(070-kt)*KARATE MEANING* ✋📖 AKA Shaolin Style *noun* ① Light and long Karate styles. They resemble the northern schools of Chinese martial arts[81] ② Light and long Kata style (within the same school).

(133-sy)*SYNONYMS* 👁= shurite {{首里手}}, p. 222; tomarite {{泊手}}, p. 248

(139-an)*ANTONYMS* 👁↺ shōreiryū {{昭霊流}}, p. 218

(185-ch)*CHINESE (PINYIN)* 🐸📖 *Shàolín liú*

(211-1)少林流

(250-hi)しょうりんりゅう (hir.)

(256-kat)ショウリンリュウ (kat.)

#shōrinryū {{少林流}}##

(090-te)*TELL YOUR STUDENTS* 📖☺ The ˙Shō in the beginning of the words ˙Shō-re[i]-ryū (昭霊流) and ˙Shō-rin-ryū (少林流) is not the same

˙Shō! However, Funakoshi in his 1922 book, spells ˙Shō-rin-ryū "昭林流". In the 1925 edition, the mistake is corrected.

(190-kf)*KUNG FU TERMINOLOGY* 🐸🏃 *Běi shàolín* (北少林), *Běi pài* (北派), *Zhǎngquán, chángquán* (長拳).

(280-po)pol:SZOORINRJU

(466-cha)*CHARACTERISTICS* ① A Three-character, which consists of 3 Chinese Logograms and 0 Hi˙ra-ga-˙na Characters.

(800-tag)*TAGS* 💻 #shorinryu, #shorin-riu, #long

429.Sho-˙shin

(011-k1)*KANJI 1* ☛ Hatsu-first {初}, p. 88

(012-k2)*KANJI 2* ☛ Kokoro-heart {心}, p. 151

(077-jg)*GENERAL MEANING (EXAMPLES)* ⚙📖 *noun* ❶ Beginner's mind, beginner's attitude (in a good way) ❷ Original intention.

(095-3t)*THE THREE TEACHINGS* 3ˢ̃ A Zen concept.

#shoshin {{初心}}##

(185-ch)*CHINESE (PINYIN)* 🐸📖 *chūxīn*

(211-1)初心

(250-hi) しょしん (hir.)

(275-tō) しょ し ん [shòshín]

(466-cha) *CHARACTERISTICS* ⓘ A Two-character, which consists of 2 Chinese Logograms and 0 Hiˈra-ga-ˈna Characters.

430. ˈShō-te[i] (teishō)

(001-REF-rom) ˈShō-te[i] （掌底） ☞ teishō {{底掌}}, p. 236

#shōtei (teishō)##

(002-REF-hi) しょうてい ☞ ていしょう

(800-tag) *TAGS* 🖵 #shotei

431. ˈShō-tō

(000-it) *INCLUDING TERMS (EXAMPLES)* 👁✉ shōtōkan {{松濤館}}, p. 221

(011-k1) *KANJI 1* ☛ Matsu-pine {松}, p. 164

(029-pe) *PERSONS* 👪 *name* Gichin FUNAKOSHI'S (p. 67) pen name.

(077-jg) *GENERAL MEANING (EXAMPLES)* ⚙📖 *noun* ❶ Soughing of the wind in the pines, sound of the wind rustling in pine needles.

#shōtō {{松濤}}##

(185-ch) *CHINESE (PINYIN)* ☯📖

sōngtāo, sōngtáo

(211-1) 松濤 (212-2) 松涛

(250-hi) しょうとう (hir.)

(466-cha) *CHARACTERISTICS* ⓘ A Two-character, which consists of 2 Chinese Logograms and 0 Hiˈra-ga-ˈna Characters.

(800-tag) *TAGS* 🖵 #shoto

432. ˈShō-tō-kan

(015-w1) *WORD 1* ᵂ ☛ shōtō {{松濤}}, p. 220

(013-k3) *KANJI 3* ☛ Kan-hall {館}, p. 126

(025-sch) *SCHOOLS* 🎿 *name* Shōtōkan-ryū （松濤館流）, Karate style. Shōtōkan was the name of FUNAKOSHI's first official Dōjō (1936)[82].

(185-ch) *CHINESE (PINYIN)* ☯📖

Sōngtāo guǎn

(211-1) 松濤館

(212-2) 松涛館

(250-hi) しょうとうかん (hir.)

(466-cha) *CHARACTERISTICS* ⓘ A Three-character, which consists of 3 Chinese Logograms and 0 Hiˈra-ga-ˈna Characters.

(800-tag) *TAGS* 🖵 #shotokan, shoto kan, sho to kan

(838-su) **SUPER-TERM**

#shōtōkan {{松濤館}}##

(089-no)*NOTES AND EXAMPLES* 📖✎

Here are some names of Shotokan organizations: Japan Karate Association (JKA), Shotokai (Shōtōkai), Shotokan Karate-Do International Federation (SKIF), Japan Shotokan Karate Association (JSKA), International Shotokan Karate Federation (ISKF), Asai Shotokan Association International (ASAI), Shotokan Karate of America (SKA) and worldwide Ōshima Dōjō (Ohshima's Dojo, SOD), International Traditional Karate Federation (ITKF), World Traditional Karate Organization (WTKO), Kenkojuku Karate Association (KKA), Funakoshi Shotokan Karate Association (FSKA), Japan Karate Shotorenmei (JKS), Karate-nomichi World Federation (KWF) and World JKA Karate Association (WJKA).

433. ˈShō-wa

(011-k1)*KANJI 1* ☞ Aki-bright {昭}, p. 32

(021-rb)*RESEARCH (FOR BOOKS)* ✍

name ❶ The Shōwa (Hiˈro-hito) era - the Shōwa period, ran from December 25, 1926 to January 7, 1989. 1926 is considered Shōwa 1 - 昭和 1 年. Therefore 1935, for instance, is Shōwa 10 - 昭和 10 年. One may always subtract 1925 from the Gregorian calendar year.

(211-1)昭和 (250-hi)しょーわ (hir.)

(800-tag)*TAGS* 💻 #showa

#shōwa {{昭和}}##

(089-no)*NOTES AND EXAMPLES* 📖✎💣

Not to be confused with the other Shōwa or Jōwa eras.

(134-gr-re)*GROUP* 👁(☺) The following terms are related: shōwa {{昭和}}, p. 221; taisho {{大正}}, p. 230; toshi {年}, p. 251.

(466-cha)*CHARACTERISTICS* ⓘ A Two-character, which consists of 2 Chinese Logograms and 0 Hiˈra-gaˈna Characters.

434. ˈShu-ri

(000-it)*INCLUDING TERMS (EXAMPLES)* 👁✉ shurite {{首里手}}, p. 222

(011-k1)*KANJI 1* ☞ Kubi-neck {首}, p. 156

(028-pl)*PLACES* 🌏 *name* Historically, the royal capital of the Ryūkyū Kingdom. One of its most famous sites is the Shuri Castle. Shuri played an important part in the development of the Okinawan martial arts. Gi-ˈchin FUˈNA-KOSHI came from Shuri. Today, Shuri is a district of Naha.

(185-ch)*CHINESE (PINYIN)* ☯📖 ***Shŏulĭ***

#shuri {{首里}}##

(134-re)*RELATED TERMS* ☯∞ naha {{那覇}}, p. 176

(189-ok)*OKINAWAN* ☯ Sui (スイ), Shui or Shiyori (しより)

(211-1)首里 (250-hi)しゅり (hir.)

(275-tō) しゅ り [shú⁺rì]

(280-po)po‖:SZYRI

(466-cha)*CHARACTERISTICS* ⓘ A Two-character, which consists of 2 Chinese Logograms and 0 Hiˈra-ga-ˈna Characters.

435. Shu-ˈri-te

(015-w1)*WORD 1* ☞ shuri {{首里}}, p. 222

(013-k3)*KANJI 3* ☞ Te-hand {手}, p. 234

(025-sch)*SCHOOLS* 🏯 *name* Karate styles that are attributed to Shuri. They belong to the ˈShō-rin-ryū (少

林流) - the light and long styles, which resemble the northern schools of Chinese martial arts[83].

(133-sy)*SYNONYMS* 👁= shōrinryū {{少林流}}, p. 219; tomarite {{泊手}}, p. 248.

#shurite {{首里手}}##

(139-an)*ANTONYMS* 👁↻ nahate {{那覇手}}, p. 176; shōreiryū {{昭霊流}}, p. 218

(185-ch)*CHINESE (PINYIN)* ☯📖 ***Shŏu lĭ shŏu***

(189-ok)*OKINAWAN* ☯ Su-i-dī (スイディー).

(211-1)首里手 (250-hi)しゅりて (hir.)

(466-cha)*CHARACTERISTICS* ⓘ A Three-character, which consists of 3 Chinese Logograms and 0 Hiˈra-ga-ˈna Characters.

436. ˈSō (想)

(000-it)*INCLUDING TERMS (EXAMPLES)* 👁✉ mokusō {{黙想}}, p. 171

(077-jg)*GENERAL MEANING (EXAMPLES)* ☼📖 *noun* ❶ Thought, idea

(185-ch)*CHINESE (PINYIN)* ☯📖 ***xiǎng***

#Sō-thought {想}##

(203-hi)⌛☉ (250-hi)そう (hir.)

(211-1)想

(800-tag)*TAGS* 🖥 #so, soh, sou, soo

(833-kan)**KANJI**

437.ˈSok[u]-ˈshi (ashiyubi)

(001-REF-rom)ˈSok[u]-ˈshi ☞ ashiyubi {{足指}}, p. 39

#sokushi (ashiyubi)##

(800-tag)*TAGS* 🖥 #sokushi, soku-shi, soku shi, #sokshi

438.Sok[u]-ˈtō

(011-k1)*KANJI 1* ☛ Ashi-foot {足}, p. 37

(012-k2)*KANJI 2* ☛ Katana-sword {刀}, p. 136

(077-jg)*GENERAL MEANING (EXAMPLES)* ☼📖 *noun* ❶ Sword of the foot, foot sword, blade of the foot, lateral aspect of the foot.

(185-ch)*CHINESE (PINYIN)* ☯📖 ***Zú dāo***

#sokutō {{足刀}}##

(211-1)足刀

(250-hi)そくとう (hir.)

(466-cha)*CHARACTERISTICS* ① A Two-character, which consists of 2 Chinese Logograms and 0 Hiˈra-ga-ˈna Characters.

(800-tag)*TAGS* 🖥 #sokuto, #sokto

439.Soˈko (底)

(000-it)*INCLUDING TERMS (EXAMPLES)*

👁 ✉ teishō {{底掌}}, p. 236

(077-jg)*GENERAL MEANING (EXAMPLES)* ☼📖 *noun* ❶ Bottom ❷ Sole, bottom of the foot.

(185-ch)*CHINESE (PINYIN)* ❶📖 *dǐ*

(203-hi)⌛☉ (250-hi)そこ (hir.) (211-1)底

#Soko-bottom {底}##

(275-tō)そ[こ] [sòkó]

(325-kr)*KANJI READINGS* ✐🦻 Go-on: たい (tai). Kan-on: てい [té⁺è] (te[i]). Kun: そこ (soko, 底).

(800-tag)*TAGS* 🖥 #tei, #tee

(833-kan)**KANJI**

440.Soˈko-teˈnohira (teishō)

(001-REF-rom)Soˈko-teˈnohira ☞ teishō {{底掌}}, p. 236

(002-REF-hi)そこてのひら ☞ ていしょう

#sokotenohira (teishō)##

(211-1)底手の平

(212-2)底手のひら

441.Soˈku (Ashi)

(001-REF-rom)Soˈku ☞ Ashi-foot {足}, p. 37

#Soku (Ashi)##

(002-REF-hi) そく ☞ あし (280-po)pol:SOKY

442. ˈSoku-ˈmen

(012-k2)*KANJI* 2 ☛ Men-side {面}, p. 168

(077-jg)*GENERAL MEANING (EXAMPLES)* ✿📖 *noun* ❶ Side

(185-ch)*CHINESE (PINYIN)* ☻📖 ***cèmiàn***

(211-1)側面 (212-2)側面

#sokumen {{側面}}##

(250-hi)そくめん (hir.)

(466-cha)*CHARACTERISTICS* ⓘ A Two-character, which consists of 2 Chinese Logograms and 0 Hiˈra-ga-ˈna Characters.

443. ˈSora (空)

(000-it)*INCLUDING TERMS (EXAMPLES)* 👁✉ karate {{空手}}, p. 131; kankū {{観空}}, p. 127

(077-jg)*GENERAL MEANING (EXAMPLES)* ✿📖 *noun* ❶ Sky, heaven ❷ Air, empty air ❸ Emptiness.

(089-no)*NOTES AND EXAMPLES* 📖✍ ˈKū-ki (空気) means air.

(133-sy)*SYNONYMS* 👁= Ten-heaven {天}, p. 240

(185-ch)*CHINESE (PINYIN)* ☻📖 ***kōng***

(211-1)空 (211-al)*ALTERNATIVES OR SEE ALSO* 🖌🖌 空, 㒼, 空, 靈, 虚

#Sora-sky {空}##

(250-hi)そら (hir.)

(275-tō)そ ら [sóˈrà]

(313-ka)*KANJI* ✍ The Phono-semantic Compound Logogram ˈSora-sky (空). (313k-cn)**Components** 🔧 [semantic 穴 | phonetic 工] (313k-ra)**Radical** ✦ 穴 cave (313k-cs)**Composition** ✗ Top: 穴 , bottom: 工 (313k-re)**Readings (examples)** 👊 Go-on: く (ku); くう (kū). Kan-on: こう (kō). Kun: から (kaˈra [kàráˈ], 空); そら (ˈsora [sóˈrà], 空).

(830-ik)**IMPORTANT KANJI**

444. ˈSoto (外)

(000-it)*INCLUDING TERMS (EXAMPLES)* 👁✉ sotouke {{外受け}}, p. 225; sotoudeuke {{外腕受け}}, p. 226

(077-jg)*GENERAL MEANING (EXAMPLES)* ✿📖 *adjective, noun* ❶ Outside

(139-an)*ANTONYMS* 👁↺ Uchi-inside {内}, p. 258

(185-ch)*CHINESE (PINYIN)* ☻📖 ***wài***

(211-1)外 (211-al)*ALTERNATIVES OR SEE ALSO* ✐✐ 夘

#Soto-outside {外}##

(250-hi)そと (hir.)

(275-tō) そと [sóˈtò]

(302-kn)*KANJI NOTES* ✐✎ Contains 5 strokes.

(325-kr)*KANJI READINGS* ✐🔊 Go-on: げ (ge). Kan-on: がい (gai). Tō-on: うい (ui). Kun: そと (soto, 外); ほか (hoka, 外); はずす (hazusu, 外す).

(833-kan)**KANJI**

445.Soˈto Uˈke

(011-k1)*KANJI 1* ☞ Soto-outside {外}, p. 225

(015-w1)*WORD 1* ^W_W ☞ uke {{受け}}, p. 262

(070-kt)*KARATE MEANING* 🖐📖 AKA Soto-ude-uke *noun phrase* ① Outside block, outer block, external block ② From outside block, outside to inside block, inward block ③ Soˈto-uˈde Uˈke, outside arm block, outside forearm block, outer arm block, external arm block.

(133-sy)*SYNONYMS* 👁= sotoudeuke {{外腕受け}}, p. 226

(139-an)*ANTONYMS* 👁↺ uchiuke {{内受け}}, p. 259

(185-ch)*CHINESE (PINYIN)* 👁📖 ***Wài shòu***

(211-1)外受け (212-2)外受

#sotouke {{外受け}}##

(089-no)*NOTES AND EXAMPLES* 📖✎ Any of the adjectives "inner" or "outer", can be interpreted as centrifugal (outward) or centripetal (inward). Different schools give opposite meanings to Soto-uke and to Uchi-uke. Outer can mean coming from outside or going to outside. In this dictionary, the name goes after the origin of the movement - Uchi means centrifugal (beginning inside), and Soto means centripetal (beginning outside).

(250-hi)そとうけ (hir.)

(466-cha)*CHARACTERISTICS* ① A Three-character, which consists of 2 Chinese Logograms and 1 Hiˈra-gaˈna Characters.

(838-su)**SUPER-TERM**

446.Soˈto-uˈde Uˈke

(011-k1)*KANJI 1* ☞ Soto-outside {外}, p. 225

(015-w1)*WORD 1* ᵂ/ᵂ ☞ udeuke {{腕受け}}, p. 261

(070-kt)*KARATE MEANING* ✋📖 AKA Gai-wan Uke *noun phrase* ① Outside arm block, outside forearm block, outer arm block, external arm block ② From outside arm block, outside to inside arm block, inward arm block.

(133-sy)*SYNONYMS* 👁= sotouke {{外受け}}, p. 225

(134-re)*RELATED TERMS* 👁∞ tettsui {{鉄槌}}, p. 245

(139-an)*ANTONYMS* 👁↻ uchiudeuke {{内腕受け}}, p. 259

(185-ch)*CHINESE (PINYIN)* 👁📖 **Wài wàn shòu**

(211-1)外腕受け #sotoudeuke {{外腕受け}}##

(089-no)*NOTES AND EXAMPLES* 📖✍ Any of the adjectives "inner" or "outer", can be interpreted as centrifugal (outward) or centripetal (inward). Different schools give opposite meanings to Soto-ude-uke and to Uchi-ude-uke. Outer can mean coming from outside or going to outside. In this dictionary, the name goes after the origin of the movement - Uchi means centrifugal (beginning inside), and Soto means centripetal (beginning outside).

(212-2)外腕受

(250-hi)そとうでうけ (hir.)

(466-cha)*CHARACTERISTICS* ⓘ A Four-character, which consists of 3 Chinese Logograms and 1 Hiˈra-ga-ˈna Characters.

(800-tag)*TAGS* 🖥 #gaiwanuke, #gai-wan-uke, #gai-wan uke

447.Su-ˈbaraˈshī

(077-jg)*GENERAL MEANING (EXAMPLES)* ☼📖 *adjective* ❶ Great, terrific, wonderful, splendid, magnificent

(203-hi)⌛⊙

(250-hi)すばらしい (hir.)

(211-1)素晴らしい

(212-2)素晴しい

#subarashi##

(089-no)*NOTES AND EXAMPLES* 📖✍ As for the first Kan-ji (素), see Moto-origin { 元 }, p. 173 (alternative spelling).

(275-tō)す|ばらし|ˈ|い [sùbáráshíˈì]

(800-tag)*TAGS* 💻 #subarashi, su-barashi, su barashi

448. Su˙ru (為)

(077-jg)*GENERAL MEANING (EXAMPLES)* ✿📖 *verb* ❶ To do.

(185-ch)*CHINESE (PINYIN)* ☻📖 **wéi** as in *wúwéi* (無為)[84]

(203-hi)⧗☉ (250-hi)する (hir.)

(211-sh-2)为 (simp.) (211-ky-1)爲 (trad.)

#Suru-to do{為}##

(kan+hirSHI)為る

(kan+hirKYU)爲る

(275-tō)す|る| [sùrú]

(280-po)pol:SYRY

(833-kan)**KANJI**

449. ˈTa (田)

(000-it)*INCLUDING TERMS (EXAMPLES)*

👁✉ tanden {{丹田}}, p. 232

(077-jg)*GENERAL MEANING (EXAMPLES)* ✿📖 *noun* ❶ Rice field, paddy (the particularity to rice is unique to Japanese).

(185-ch)*CHINESE (PINYIN)* ☻📖 **tián** – field. 💣⁕ Not to be confused with *tiān* (p. 240), which means sky!

#Ta-paddy {田}##

(211-1)田

(250-hi)た (hir.)

(302-kn)*KANJI NOTES* ✏🖌 A Radical (Radical 102). Contains 5 strokes.

(325-kr)*KANJI READINGS* ✏🌿 Go-on: でん (den). Kan-on: てん (ten). Kun: た (ta, 田). Nanori: いなか (inaka).

(833-kan)**KANJI**

450. ˈTachi

(000-it)*INCLUDING TERMS (EXAMPLES)*

👁✉ fudōdachi {{不動立ち}}, p. 64;

hachijidachi {{八字立ち}}, p. 78;

hanmidachi {{半身立ち}}, p. 86;

heikodachi {{平行立ち}}, p. 95;

heisokudachi {{閉足立ち}}, p. 96;

kibadachi {{騎馬立ち}}, p. 145;

kōkutsudachi {{後屈立ち}}, p. 150;

kosadachi {{交差立ち}}, p. 154;

musubidachi {{結び立ち}}, p. 174;

nekoashidachi {{猫足立ち}}, p. 183;

renojidachi {{レの字立ち}}, p. 195; sanchindachi {{三戦立ち}}, p. 203;

shikodachi {{四股立ち}}, p. 209;

teijidachi {{丁字立ち}}, p. 235;

#tachi {{立ち}}##

yamadachi {{山立ち}}, p. 269;

zenkutsudachi {{前屈立ち}}, p. 285.

(011-k1)*KANJI 1* ☞ Tatsu-to stand {立}, p. 234

(070-kt)*KARATE MEANING* ✋📖 *noun* ① Stance, position of the lower limbs.

(077-jg)*GENERAL MEANING (EXAMPLES)* ✿📖 *noun* ❶ Departure ❷ Start.

(211-1)立ち

(250-hi)たち (hir.) (256-kat)タチ (kat.)

(466-cha)*CHARACTERISTICS* ① A Two-character, which consists of 1 Chinese Logograms and 1 Hiʹra-ga-ʹna Characters.

(800-tag)*TAGS* 🖥 #dachi

(838-su)**SUPER-TERM**

451. ˈTai (Futo)

(001-REF-rom)ˈTai-futo ☞ Futo-great {太}, p. 63

#Tai (Futo)##

(002-REF-hi)たい ☞ ふと

452. ˈTai (体)

(000-it)*INCLUDING TERMS (EXAMPLES)*

👁✉ shizentai {{自然体}}, p. 215;

taisabaki {{体捌き}}, p. 229.

(077-jg)*GENERAL MEANING (EXAMPLES)* ✿📖 *noun* ❶ Body ❷ Posture ❸ Shape, form.

(133-sy)*SYNONYMS* 👁= Mi-body {身}, p. 169

(185-ch)*CHINESE (PINYIN)* ☯📖 *bèn*

(211-1)体

(211-al)*ALTERNATIVES OR SEE ALSO* ✐✐ 体, 体, 體

#Tai-body {体}##

(250-hi)たい (hir.)

(256-kat)タイ (kat.) (275-tō)たい [táʼì]

(313-ka)*KANJI* ✐ The Compound Ideogram ˈTai-body (体). (313k-cn)**Components** 🔳 [亻 | 本] (313k-ra)**Radical** ✚ 人亻 human (骨) (313k-cs)**Composition** 🔀 亻 本 (313k-re)**Readings (examples)** 🎋 Go-on:

たい (tai). Kan-on: てい (tei). Kun: からだ (karada, 体)

(830-ik)**IMPORTANT KANJI**

453. ˈTai ˈSabaki

(011-k1)*KANJI 1* ☞ Tai-body {体}, p. 228

(015-w1)*WORD 1* ᵂ ☞ sabaki {{捌き}}, p. 198

(070-kt)*KARATE MEANING* ✋📖 *noun phrase* ① Body movements, whole body movement, bodywork, body shifting, body turning, dodging.

(185-ch)*CHINESE (PINYIN)* 🌐📖 ***Tǐ bā***

(250-hi)たいさばき (hir.)

#taisabaki {{体捌き}}##

(077-jg)*GENERAL MEANING (EXAMPLES)* ✿📖 *noun phrase* ❶ Defensive body movement (martial arts).

(211-1)体捌き

(212-2)体さばき

(466-cha)*CHARACTERISTICS* ⓘ A Three-character, which consists of 2 Chinese Logograms and 1 Hiˈra-gaˈna Characters.

454. ˈTai-kyoku

(011-k1)*KANJI 1* ☞ Futo-great {太}, p. 63

(012-k2)*KANJI 2* ☞ Kiwameru-to act excessively {極}, p. 148

(060-kg)*KATA GROUP* 形形形 **AKA** ˈTai-kyoku no Kaˈta (太極の形, 太極の型), Ki-ˈhon-gaˈta (基本形, 基本型), Kihon-kata, Ki-ˈhon no Gaˈta (基本の形, 基本の型), Kihon no Kata, First Cause, Beginning of the Universe Kata **Style** Shōrin (少林) **Number of Kata** Originally three

(062-mk)*FUNAKOSHI MAIN BOOK - KATA* 📖**MK** **1935 Ohshima** 9 (list styles), 35 (list names), 42-48

(077-jg)*GENERAL MEANING (EXAMPLES)* ✿📖 *noun* ❶ Chinese philosophical idea of the supreme ultimate[85] ❷ T'ai chi, Chinese martial art.

(090-te)*TELL YOUR STUDENTS* 📖☺ The Ten no Kata (p. 241) and the three Taikyoku Kata were developed by Gigo[86] FUNAKOSHI and his father Gichin[87] FUNAKOSHI.

(185-ch)*CHINESE (PINYIN)* 🌐📖 ***tàijí*** (Tai chi) as in *Tàijíquán* (Tai chi ch'üan) (太極拳).

#taikyoku {{太極}}##

(095-3t)*THE THREE TEACHINGS* **3**🝔:

Tàijí is a deep and old term in Chinese cosmology[88]. It could mean the source, the beginning, the great supreme, the supreme ultimate, the great pole, the supreme polarity[89], the highest top etcetera. Personally, we think that *tàijí* is the One, not exactly the *Dào* on one side and not the Two on the other side. The One is what *Dào* gave birth to, and what created the Two [90]. According to some Chinese classics, *tàijí* generates the *yáng* and the *yīn*, and those generate the Five Elements[91].

(134-re)*RELATED TERMS* 👁∞ Tennokata {{天の形}}, p. 241

(211-1)太極 (212-2)太极

(250-hi)たいきょく (hir.)

(275-tō)た いきょく [tàíkyókú]

(280-po)pol:TAJKKJOKY

(466-cha)*CHARACTERISTICS* ⓘ A Two-character, which consists of 2 Chinese Logograms and 0 Hiˈra-ga-ˈna Characters.

(800-tag)*TAGS* 💻 #taikioku, #taykyoku, #taikoku, #taykoku

(011-k1)*KANJI 1* ☛ Dai-big {大}, p. 56

(012-k2)*KANJI 2* ☛ Shō-correct {正}, p. 216

(021-rb)*RESEARCH (FOR BOOKS)* 📚 *name* ❶ The Taishō period - the Taishō era, ran from 30 July 1912 to 25 December 1926.

(211-1)大正 (250-hi)たいしょー (hir.)

(275-tō)た いしょ ー [tàíshóó]

(466-cha)*CHARACTERISTICS* ⓘ A Two-character, which consists of 2 Chinese Logograms and 0 Hiˈra-ga-ˈna Characters.

(800-tag)*TAGS* 💻 #tai-sho, tai sho #taisho {{大正}}##

(089-no)*NOTES AND EXAMPLES* 📖🖎

Although the Taishō period did not begin on January 1, 大正 11 年, for instance, is 1922. 💣※ It is a common mistake to assume that 大正 14 年, for instance, could mean 1925 or 1926. 大正 14 年 could only mean 1925. One may always subtract 1911 from the Gregorian calendar year.

(134-gr-re)*GROUP* 👁(ⓧⓧ The following terms are related: shōwa {{昭和}},

p. 221; taisho {{大正}}, p. 230; toshi {年}, p. 251.

456. ˈTaka (高)

(000-it)*INCLUDING TERMS (EXAMPLES)*

👁✉ nakadaka {{中高}}, p. 179

(077-jg)*GENERAL MEANING (EXAMPLES)* ☯📖 *noun* ❶ Quantity, amount *prefix* ❷ High~

#Taka-quantity {高}##

(089-no)*NOTES AND EXAMPLES* 📖✍

Taˈkai [tàká⁺ì] (高い) means tall or expensive.

(211-1)高 (250-hi)たか (hir.)

(833-kan)**KANJI**

457. ˈTama (玉)

(000-it)*INCLUDING TERMS (EXAMPLES)*

👁✉ yaridama {{槍玉}}, p. 273

(077-jg)*GENERAL MEANING (EXAMPLES)* ☯📖 *noun* ❶ Ball

(211-1)玉

(250-hi)たま (hir.)

#Tama-ball {玉}##

(089-no)*NOTES AND EXAMPLES* 📖✍

Taˈma-ts[u]ki (玉突き), for instance, means billiards, pool.

(800-tag)*TAGS* 🖥 #dama

(833-kan)**KANJI**

458. ˈTan (丹)

(000-it)*INCLUDING TERMS (EXAMPLES)*

👁✉ tanden {{丹田}}, p. 232

(077-jg)*GENERAL MEANING (EXAMPLES)* ☯📖 *noun* ❶ Elixir (life-prolonging substance), elixir made with cinnabar ❷ Cinnabar, mercury sulfide, chemical compound composed of mercury and sulfur ❸ Red earth containing cinnabar ❹ Red.

(095-3t)*THE THREE TEACHINGS* ☯ Connected to the Dàoist alchemical elixirs of life.

(185-ch)*CHINESE (PINYIN)* ☯📖 ***dān***

(250-hi)たん (hir.)

(256-kat)タン (kat.)

#Tan-elixir {丹}##

(211-1)丹 (211-al)*ALTERNATIVES OR SEE ALSO* ✒✍ 𠄌, 同

(302-kn)*KANJI NOTES* ✒✍ Contains 4 strokes.

(313-ka)*KANJI* ✒ The Compound Ideogram ˈTan-elixir (丹). (313k-cn)**Components** 🕸 [丶 | 井] (313k-ra)**Radical** ✚ 丶 dot (313k-cs)**Composition** 夊 冂 亠 (313k-re)**Readings (examples)** 🖌 Go-on: たん (tan). Kan-on: たん (tan).

Kun: あか (aka, 丹); あかい (akai, 丹い); に (ni, 丹).

(830-ik)IMPORTANT KANJI

459. ˈTan-den

(011-k1)*KANJI 1* ☞ Tan-elixir {丹}, p. 231

(012-k2)*KANJI 2* ☞ Ta-paddy {田}, p. 227

(077-jg)*GENERAL MEANING (EXAMPLES)* ✿📖 AKA Elixir Field, Cinnabar Field, Sea of *qì* (気) *noun* ❶ Three ˈKi 1 (気) focus flow centers, any of the three energy fields ❷ Three focus points, any of the three energy points ❸ Energy field that arguably extends from the level of acupuncture point CV-7 (one ˈSun below the navel) down to the level of acupoint CV-4[92]. This area is inferior to the level of the kidneys and superior to the level of the urinary bladder. CV-4 (REN-4) is an acupuncture point, located three ˈSun (寸) (four fingers) below the center of the navel and two ˈSun above the pubic symphysis. ❹ Energy point deep inside the body. The main opinions vary between the levels of CV-7[93], CV-6[94], CV-5[95] and CV-4[96].

(466-cha)*CHARACTERISTICS* ⓘ A Two-character, which consists of 2 Chinese Logograms and 0 Hiˈra-ga-ˈna Characters.

(134-re)*RELATED TERMS* 👁∞ Hara-abdomen {腹}, p. 86

#tanden {{丹田}}##

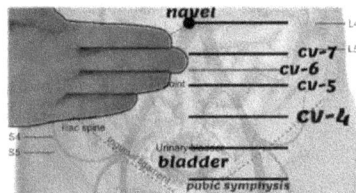

Anatomy 5 - Tanden Height
Based on an anatomy illustration by Dr. Mikael Häggström, M.D.

(089-no)*NOTES AND EXAMPLES* 📖✎ A Dàoist concept.

(095-3t)*THE THREE TEACHINGS* **3ễ**

There are three Tanden: upper Tanden (上丹田), center Tanden (中丹田) and lower Tanden (下丹田). Arguably [97], ˈJō-ˈtan-den (Kami-tanden) is located between the eyebrows, Naˈka-ˈTan-den (Chū Tanden) is in the heart area, and Shiˈmo-ˈtan-den is located below the umbilicus. But usually when we say Tanden, we mean specifically the lower Tanden.

(185-ch)*CHINESE (PINYIN)* 👁📖

dāntián, dantian, dan t'ian, dan tien, tan t'ien

(211-1)丹田

(250-hi)たんでん (hir.)

(256-kat)タンデン (kat.)

(800-tag)*TAGS* ⌨ #dantien, #dantian, dan tian, dan tien, tan-den, tan den, tantien, tan tien

460. Ta ˈni ˈOtoshi

🌢✳ Not to be confused with the Jūdō technique bearing the same name!

(012-k2)*KANJI 2* ☛ Otosu-to drop {落}, p. 193

(055-tt)*THROWING TECHNIQUE* 投技

AKA To Push off a Cliff, Gorge Drop, Valley Drop.

(089-no)*NOTES AND EXAMPLES* 📖✎

The technique does not appear in FUNAKOSHI's 1922 – 1925 editions. The same name is used for a different technique.

(211-1)谷落(250-hi)たにおとし (hir.)

#taniotoshi {{谷落}}##

(056-mt)*FUNAKOSHI MAIN BOOK – THROWING TECHNIQUES* 📕MTT

1935 Suzuki-Johnston 199 (Tani-Otoshi) **1935 Ohshima** 227 (list), 231 (Taniotoshi)

(466-cha)*CHARACTERISTICS* ① A Two-character, which consists of 2 Chinese Logograms and 0 Hiˈra-ga-ˈna Characters.

(185-ch)*CHINESE (PINYIN)* 👁📖 ***Gǔ luò***

(800-tag)*TAGS* ⌨ #tani-otoshi, #tani otoshi

461. ˈTatsu (立)

(000-it)*INCLUDING TERMS (EXAMPLES)* 👁✉ tachi {{立ち}}, p. 228

(077-jg)*GENERAL MEANING (EXAMPLES)* ⚙📖 *verb* ❶ To stand, to stand up, to rise ❷ To erect ❸ To set up.

(185-ch)*CHINESE (PINYIN)* 👁📖 ***lì***

(705-gv)*GODAN VERB* 🐾⑤ **Terminal Form** {u* 🌢✳ but not i*-ru or e*-ru} ˈTatsu [táᐩtsù] (立つ), which means to stand. **Polite Form** {i*-masu} Taˈchimas[u] [tàchímáᐩsù] (立ちます).

(302-kn)*KANJI NOTES* ✎✎ It depicts a man (亠ヽノ) standing on the ground (一)[98]. We should remember that there is no stance (tachi {{立ち}}, p. 228), without a connection to the ground. Can You recognize the Logogram in the ancient Chinese script on page 28?

(830-ik)**IMPORTANT KANJI**

#Tatsu-to stand {立}##

Script 10 – Tatsu-to stand Shang Oracle Bone Script

Script 11 – Tatsu-to stand Western Zhou Bronze Inscriptions

(211-1)立

(250-hi)たつ (hir.)

(275-tō) | た | つ | [táˈtsù] (280-po)pol:TACY

(313-ka)*KANJI* ✎ The Pictogrammatic Radical (Radical 117) ˈTatsu-to stand (立). (313k-cn)**Components** ⚇ No Components – a Simple Logogram; but some say: [大│一] (𡗓) – the inverse of Ten-heaven {天}, p. 240. (313k-ra)**Radical** ✚ 立 stand. (313k-cs)**Composition** ✄ ┼ ⺌ (一 丶 一). (313k-re)**Readings (examples)** ✊ Go-on: りゅう (ryū). Kan-on: りゅう (ryū). Kan'yō-on: りつ (ritsu).

Kun: たつ (tatsu, 立つ); たてる (tateru, 立てる).

462. ˈTe (手)

(000-it)*INCLUDING TERMS (EXAMPLES)*

👁 ✉ hikite {{引き手}}, p. 75; jitte {{十手}}, p. 111; karate {{空手}}, p. 131; kumite {{組手}}, p. 157; maete {{前手}}, p. 162; morote {{諸手}}, p. 172; nahate {{那覇手}}, p. 176; nukite {{貫手}}, p. 185; shutō {{手刀}}, p. 210; shurite {{首里手}}, p. 222; tomarite {{泊手}}, p. 248; torite {{捕手}}, p. 250.

(077-jg)*GENERAL MEANING (EXAMPLES)* ✿📖 *noun* ❶ Hand, arm.

(185-ch)*CHINESE (PINYIN)* ◑📖 *shǒu*

(302-kn)*KANJI NOTES* ✎ ✄ Contains 4 strokes. It depicts all five fingers. #Te-hand {手}##

(189-ok)*OKINAWAN* ● Tī (ティー)

(211-1)手 (211-var)扌 (left)

(250-hi)て (hir.)

(313-ka)*KANJI* ✎ The Pictogrammatic Radical (Radical 64) ˈTe-hand (手). (313k-cn)**Components** ⚇ No components - a Simple Logogram. (313kra)**Radical** ✦ 手 扌 ⺘ hand. (313k-

cs)**Composition** 夆 于 , 一 . (313k-

re)**Readings (examples)** 🗣 Go-on:
しゅ (shu); す (su). Kan-on: しゅう
(shū). Kan'yō-on: ず (zu). Kun: て
(te, 手); た (ta, 手).

(838-su)**SUPER-TERM**

(830-ik)**IMPORTANT KANJI**

463. ˈTe[i] (Chō)

(001-REF-rom) ˈTe[i] ☞ Chō-street { 丁
}, p. 50

#Tei (Chō)##

(002-REF-hi) てい ☞ ちょう

464. ˈTe[i] (Soko)

(001-REF-rom) ˈTe[i] ☞ Soko-bottom
{底}, p. 223

#Tei (Soko)##

(002-REF-hi) てい ☞ そこ

465. ˈTe[i] (Utsu)

(001-REF-rom) ˈTe[i] ☞ Utsu-to hit {打
}, p. 266

#Tei (Utsu)##

(002-REF-hi) てい ☞ うつ (うち 2)

466. ˈTe[i]-ji ˈDachi

(015-w1) *WORD 1* ᵂᵂ ☞ chōji {{丁字}},
p. 51

(016-w2) *WORD 2* ᵂᵂ ☞ tachi {{立ち}},
p. 228

ˈTe[i] (Chō) - ˈTe[i]-ji ˈDachi

(030-st) *STANCES* 立 **AKA** Chō-ji-
dachi, T-shape Stance, Character 丁
Stance, T Stance, Character Tei
Stance, Character Cho Stance **Category** Sidewise high stances

(089-no) *NOTES AND EXAMPLES* 📖✎
Heel in front of the other foot's arch.

(031-ms) *FUNAKOSHI MAIN BOOK -
STANCES* ⟳**MS** 1922 **original** 30.
1925 Ishida 41. **1925 Teramoto** 40.
1935 Suzuki-Johnston 22. **1935
Ohshima** 19 and note 1.

#teijidachi {{丁字立ち}}##

(211-1) 丁字立ち (212-2) 丁字立

(250-hi) ていじだち (hir.)

(280-po) pol:TEEDZIDACI

(466-cha) *CHARACTERISTICS* ⓘ A Four-
character, which consists of 3 Chinese Logograms and 1 Hiˈra-ga-ˈna
Characters.

(483-td) **T⤸d** ⌂ Due to the ˈRen-daku
laws, the unvoiced consonant /T/
may get a Dak[u]-ˈten (゛) and become ~/d/ as a suffix. Example ↯
ˈTachi (たち) turns into Ki-ˈba
Daˈchi (きばだち).

(800-tag)*TAGS* 🖥 #tejidachi, teiji-dachi, teiji dachi, tei ji dachi, #chojidachi, #techidachi

467. ˈTe[i]-ji-ˈgata

(015-w1)*WORD 1* ᵂ ☛ chōji {{丁字}}, p. 51

(013-k3)*KANJI 3* ☛ Kata-shape {形}, p. 134

(070-kt)*KARATE MEANING* ✋📖 *noun*
① T Pattern, T Shape, Character-tei Pattern, Character-cho Pattern, 丁 Pattern, 丁 Character Figure, ⊥ Shape.

(068-me)*FUNAKOSHI MAIN BOOK - ENBUSEN* 🏯**MEN** 1922 **original** 50-51 **1925 Ishida** 58 **1925 Teramoto** 52 **1935 Suzuki-Johnston** 40 **1935 Ohshima** 41

(134-re)*RELATED TERMS* ◎∞ enbusen {{演武線}}, p. 61
#teijigata {{丁字形}}

(211-1)丁字形

(211-al)*ALTERNATIVES OR SEE ALSO*
✐✐ 丁字型

(250-hi)ていじがた (hir.)

(466-cha)*CHARACTERISTICS* ① A Three-character, which consists of 3

Chinese Logograms and 0 Hiˈra-gaˈna Characters.

(482-kg)**K⊃g** 🔔 Due to the ˈRendaku laws, the unvoiced consonant /K/ may get a Dak[u]-ˈten (˚) and become ~/g/ as a suffix. Example 🦵 Keˈri (けり) turns into Maˈe-geˈri (まえげり).

(800-tag)*TAGS* 🖥 #teijigata, teiji-gata, teiji gata, chojigata, chojikata

468. ˈTe[i]-shō

(011-k1)*KANJI 1* ☛ Soko-bottom {底}, p. 223

(012-k2)*KANJI 2* ☛ Tenohira-palm {掌}, p. 244

(040-ul)*UPPER LIMB STRIKE & ANATOMY*
手 **AKA** Soˈko-teˈnohira (底掌), ˈShō-te[i] (掌底), Teˈnohira-soˈko (掌底), Palm-heel, Heel of the Hand, Palm of the Hand (so!) **Category** Hand Anatomy

(185-ch)*CHINESE (PINYIN)* 💬📖 **Dǐ zhǎng**
#teishō {{底掌}}##

(089-no)*NOTES AND EXAMPLES* 📖✐
Sometimes mistakenly written 掌打

or 打掌, since one of Utsu's (打) readings is Tei.

(211-1)底掌 (250-hi)ていしょう (hir.)

(466-cha)*CHARACTERISTICS* ⓘ A Two-character, which consists of 2 Chinese Logograms and 0 Hiˈra-gaˈna Characters.

(800-tag)*TAGS* 🖥 #teisho, #tesho, #tenohirasoko, #shotei

469. ˈTek-ki

(000-it)*INCLUDING TERMS (EXAMPLES)*

👁✉ tekkinidan {{鉄騎二段}}, p. 238; tekkisandan {{鉄騎三段}}, p. 239; tekkishodan {{鉄騎初段}}, p. 239.

(011-k1)*KANJI 1* ☛ Tetsu-iron {鉄}, p. 244

(012-k2)*KANJI 2* ☛ Ki-riding {騎}, p. 143

(060-kg)*KATA GROUP* 形形形 **AKA** Horse Riding, Iron Horse, Iron Knight, Horse-mounting Stance (so! - Kibadachi), Tekki-gata (鉄騎型), Naihanchi (ナイハンチ), Naihanchin (ナイハンチン), Naihanchen (ナイハンチェン), Naifanchi (ナイファンチ), Naifanchin (ナイ

ファンチン), Naifuanchin, Naifanchen (ナイファンチェン), Kibadachi (騎馬立ち), Nai Han Ji, Neh Bo Jin **Style** Shōrei (昭霊) **Number of Kata** Three

(133-sy)*SYNONYMS* 👁= naihanchi {{内歩進}}, p. 177

(134-re)*RELATED TERMS* 👁∞ kibadachi {{騎馬立ち}}, p. 145 #tekki {{鉄騎}}##

(062-mk)*FUNAKOSHI MAIN BOOK - KATA*

🎒**MK 1922 original** 6 (list beginning), 51 (list Enbusen), 93 (Shodan), 227 (Nidan), 232 (Sandan), **1925 Ishida** 20 (list beginning), 58 (list Enbusen), 99 (Shodan), 231 (Nidan), 237 (Sandan) **1925 Teramoto** 26 (list beginning), 52 (list Enbusen), 73 (Shodan), 140 (Nidan), 144 (Sandan) **1935 Suzuki-Johnston** 9 (list styles), 34 (list names), 40-41 (list Enbusen), 91 (Shodan), 101 (Nidan), 107 (Sandan) **1935 Ohshima** 8-9 (list styles), 36 (list names), 120 (Shodan), 129 (Nidan), 136 (Sandan)

(185-ch)*CHINESE (PINYIN)* 👁📖 *Zhíqí*

(211-1)鉄騎

(212-2)鐵騎

(213-3)鉄骑

(250-hi)てっき (hir.)

(466-cha)*CHARACTERISTICS* ⓘ A Two-character, which consists of 2 Chinese Logograms and 0 Hiˈra-ga-ˈna Characters.

(800-tag)*TAGS* ⌨ #teki, #tekkigata

(838-su)**SUPER-TERM**

470. ˈTek-ki ˈNi-dan

(015-w1)*WORD 1* ᵂ/ᵂ ☛ tekki {{鉄騎}}, p. 237

(016-w2)*WORD 2* ᵂ/ᵂ ☛ nidan {{二段}}, p. 184

(061-ka)*KATA* 形 **AKA** Naihanchi Ni-dan (ナイハンチ二段), Tekki Sono Ni, Naihanchi Sono Ni, see other names in Tekki (page 237) **Style** Shōrei (昭霊) **Group** Tekki (鉄騎) **Enbusen** Iˈchi-ji-ˈgata (一字形) - 一 Shape **Number of movements (approximately)** 26 (many say 24)

(185-ch)*CHINESE (PINYIN)* ☯📖 *Zhíqí èr duàn*

(211-1)鉄騎二段

(212-2)鐵騎二段

(213-3)鉄骑二段

#tekkinidan {{鉄騎二段}}##

(062-mk)*FUNAKOSHI MAIN BOOK - KATA*

📖**MK 1922 original** 6 (list beginning), 51 (list Enbusen), 227 **1925 Ishida** 20 (list beginning), 58 (list Enbusen), 231 **1925 Teramoto** 26 (list beginning), 52 (list Enbusen), 140 **1935 Suzuki-Johnston** 9 (list styles), 34 (list names), 40-41 (list Enbusen), 101 **1935 Ohshima** 8-9 (list styles), 36 (list names), 129

(250-hi)てっきにだん (hir.)

(466-cha)*CHARACTERISTICS* ⓘ A Four-character, which consists of 4 Chinese Logograms and 0 Hiˈra-ga-ˈna Characters.

(800-tag)*TAGS* ⌨ #tekinidan, tekki ni-dan

(838-su)**SUPER-TERM**

471. ˈTek-ki ˈSan-dan

(015-w1)*WORD 1* ᵂ/ᵂ ☛ tekki {{鉄騎}}, p. 237

(016-w2)*WORD 2* ᵂ/ᵂ ☛ sandan {{三段}}, p. 204

(061-ka)*KATA* 形 **AKA** Naihanchi Sandan (ナイハンチ三段), Tekki Sono San, Naihanchi Sono San, see other names in Tekki (page 237) **Style** Shōrei (昭霊) **Group** Tekki (鉄騎) **Enbusen** Iˈchi-ji-ˈgata (一字形) - 一 Shape **Number of movements (approximately)** Once 35 (1922, 1925), later 36 (1935, 1958)

(211-1)鉄騎三段

(212-2)鐵騎三段 (213-3)鉄骑三段

(250-hi)てっきさんだん (hir.)

(800-tag)*TAGS* 💻 #tekisandan, tekki sandan

#tekkisandan {{鉄騎三段}}##

(062-mk)*FUNAKOSHI MAIN BOOK - KATA*

📙**MK** **1922 original** 6 (list beginning), 51 (list Enbusen), 93 232 **1925 Ishida** 20 (list beginning), 58 (list Enbusen), 237 **1925 Teramoto** 26 (list beginning), 52 (list Enbusen), 144 **1935 Suzuki-Johnston** 9 (list styles), 34 (list names), 40-41 (list Enbusen), 107 **1935 Ohshima** 8-9 (list styles), 36 (list names), 136

(185-ch)*CHINESE (PINYIN)* 😀📖 *Zhíqí sān duàn*

(466-cha)*CHARACTERISTICS* ① A Four-character, which consists of 4 Chi-

ˈTek-ki-ˈsho-dan - ˈTek-ki-ˈsho-dannese Logograms and 0 Hiˈra-ga-ˈna Characters.

(838-su)**SUPER-TERM**

472. ˈTek-ki-ˈsho-dan

(015-w1)*WORD 1* ʷ☞ tekki {{鉄騎}}, p. 237

(016-w2)*WORD 2* ʷ☞ shodan {{初段}}, p. 217

(061-ka)*KATA* 形 **AKA** Naihanchi Shodan (ナイハンチ初段), Tekki Sono Ichi, Naihanchi Sono Ichi, see other names in Tekki (page 237) **Style** Shōrei (昭霊) **Group** Tekki (鉄騎) **Enbusen** Iˈchi-ji-ˈgata (一字形) - 一 Shape **Number of movements (approximately)** Once 32 (1922, 1925), later 29 (1935, 1958)

(211-1)鉄騎初段

(212-2)鐵騎初段 (213-3)鉄骑初段

(250-hi)てっきしょだん (hir.)

(838-su)**SUPER-TERM**

#tekkishodan {{鉄騎初段}}##

(062-mk)*FUNAKOSHI MAIN BOOK - KATA*

📙**MK** **1922 original** 6 (list beginning), 51 (list Enbusen), 93 **1925 Ishida** 20 (list beginning), 58 (list Enbusen), 99 **1925 Teramoto** 26 (list beginning), 52 (list Enbusen), 73 **1935 Suzuki-Johnston** 9 (list styles), 34 (list names), 40-41 (list Enbusen), 91 **1935 Ohshima** 8-9 (list styles), 36 (list names), 120

(185-ch)*CHINESE (PINYIN)* 🕭📖 ***Zhíqí chūduàn***

(466-cha)*CHARACTERISTICS* ⓘ A Four-character, which consists of 4 Chinese Logograms and 0 Hiˈra-ga-ˈna Characters.

(800-tag)*TAGS* 💻 #tekishodan, tekki shodan

473. ˈTen (天)

(000-it)*INCLUDING TERMS (EXAMPLES)* 👁✉ Tennokata {{天の形}}, p. 241; tennomon {{天の門}}, p. 243.

(077-jg)*GENERAL MEANING (EXAMPLES)* ⚙📖 *noun* ❶ Heaven

(133-sy)*SYNONYMS* 👁= Sora-sky {空}, p. 224

(185-ch)*CHINESE (PINYIN)* 🕭📖 ***tiān*** as in *Tiān'ānmén* (天安門). 💧※ Not to be confused with *tián*, which means field (p. 227)!

(211-1)天

(302-kn)*KANJI NOTES* 🖌🖎 Contains 4 strokes. It depicts a line above a man with outstretched arms and legs.

#Ten-heaven {天}##

(089-no)*NOTES AND EXAMPLES* 📖🖎 ˈTen-ki (天気) means weather.

(250-hi)てん (hir.) (256-kat)テン (kat.)

(313-ka)*KANJI* 🖎 The Compound Ideogram [99] ˈTen-heaven （天）. (313k-cn)**Components** 🗂 [一 ｜ 大] (313k-ra)**Radical** ✦ 大 big (313k-cs)**Composition** ⚔ Top: 一, bottom: 大 (313k-re)**Readings (examples)** 🎤 Go-on: てん (ten). Kan-on: てん (ten). Kun: あま (ama, 天); あめ (ame, 天). Nanori: かみ (kami); そら (sora); た (ta); たか (taka).

(885-tag)*TAGS* 💻 #tian, #tien

(830-ik)**IMPORTANT KANJI**

474. ˈTen no Kaˈta

(000-it)*INCLUDING TERMS (EXAMPLES)* 👁✉ tennokataura {{天の形裏}}, p. 242; tennokataomote {{天の形表}}, p. 242.

(011-k1)*KANJI* 𝟣 ☛ Ten-heaven {天}, p. 240

(012-k2)*KANJI* 𝟤 ☛ Kata-shape {形}, p. 134

(060-kg)*KATA GROUP* 形形形 **AKA** Kuˈmi-te-gaˈta (組手形, 組手型), Kumite-kata, Ki-ˈhon-gaˈta (基本形, 基本型), Kihon-kata, Ki-ˈhon no Gaˈta (基本の形, 基本の型), Kihon no Kata, Heavenly Kata, Celestial Kata, Sparring Kata, Kata of the Universe, Kata of the Heavens, Heaven Sequence **Style** Arguably Shōrei (昭霊) **Number of Kata** Two

(062-mk)*FUNAKOSHI MAIN BOOK - KATA* 🕮**MK** 1935 **Ohshima** 9 (list styles), 35, 37 (list names)

(079-ng)*FUNAKOSHI NYUMON TERAMOTO - GENERALLY* 🕮**NG** 62-63

(211-1)天の形 (212-2)天の型 #Tennokata {{天の形}}##

(089-no)*NOTES AND EXAMPLES* 🕮✎ One may come upon a book called 大日本空手道天の形 or 大日本空手道天之形.

(090-te)*TELL YOUR STUDENTS* 🕮☺ The Ten no Kata and the three Taikyoku Kata were developed by Gigo[100] FUNAKOSHI and his father Gichin[101] FUNAKOSHI.

(134-re)*RELATED TERMS* ◉∞ taikyoku {{太極}}, p. 230

(185-ch)*CHINESE (PINYIN)* ◉🕮 **Tiān xíng**

(250-hi)てんのかた (hir.)

(409-no)*HIRAGANA* ◉ The particle ˈNo (の) is a genitive case marker, which indicates possession: of, -'s.

(466-cha)*CHARACTERISTICS* ⓘ A Three-character, which consists of 2 Chinese Logograms and 1 Hiˈra-gaˈna Characters.

(800-tag)*TAGS* ▤ #tenokata, #tenogata, tenno kata, ten-no kata, ten no kata

(838-su)**SUPER-TERM**

475. ˈTen no Kaˈta Uˈra

(015-w1)*WORD 1* ^W_W ☞ Tennokata {{天の形}}, p. 241

(013-k3)*KANJI 3* ☞ Ura-back {裏}, p. 264

(061-ka)*KATA* 形 **AKA** Back Ten no Kata **Style** Arguably Shōrei (昭霊) **Group** ˈTen no Kaˈta (天の形) **Enbusen** Iˈchi-ji-ˈgata (一字形) - 一 Shape **Number of movements (approximately)** 6 sets

(089-no)*NOTES AND EXAMPLES* 📖✎

Practiced with a partner.

(062-mk)*FUNAKOSHI MAIN BOOK - KATA*

📖**MK 1935 Ohshima** 212

(079-ng)*FUNAKOSHI NYUMON TERAMO-TO - GENERALLY* 📖**NG** 84

#tennokataura {{天の形裏}}##

(134-re)*RELATED TERMS* 👁∞ ippon-kumite {{一本組手}}, p. 106

(185-ch)*CHINESE (PINYIN)* ☯📖 **Tiān**

xíng lǐ

(211-1)天の形裏

(212-2)天の型裏

(213-3)天の形裏

(214-4)天の型裏

(250-hi)てんのかたうら (hir.)

(466-cha)*CHARACTERISTICS* ⓘ A Four-character, which consists of 3 Chinese Logograms and 1 Hiˈra-ga-ˈna Characters.

(838-su)**SUPER-TERM**

476. ˈTen no Kaˈta-ˈomote

(015-w1)*WORD 1* ᵂᵂ ☞ Tennokata {{天の形}}, p. 241

(013-k3)*KANJI 3* ☞ Omote-front {表}, p. 190

(061-ka)*KATA* 形 **AKA** Front Ten no Kata **Style** Arguably Shōrei (昭霊) **Group** ˈTen no Kaˈta（天の形） **Enbusen** Iˈchi-ji-ˈgata（一字形）- 一 Shape **Number of movements (approximately)** 10 sets

(089-no)*NOTES AND EXAMPLES* 📖✎

All moves are forward and practiced without a partner. The first four sets are just Tsuki. The last six sets are blocks followed by a Giakuzuki. #tennokataomote {{天の形表}}##

(062-mk)*FUNAKOSHI MAIN BOOK - KATA*

📖**MK 1935 Ohshima** 202

(079-ng)*FUNAKOSHI NYUMON TERAMO-TO - GENERALLY* 📖**NG** 63

(185-ch)*CHINESE (PINYIN)* ☯📖 **Tiān**

xíng biǎo

(211-1)天の形表 (212-2)天の型表

(213-3)天の形衣 (214-4)天の型衣

(250-hi)てんのかたおもて (hir.)

(466-cha)*CHARACTERISTICS* ⓘ A Four-character, which consists of 3 Chinese Logograms and 1 Hiˈra-ga-ˈna Characters.

(838-su)**SUPER-TERM**

477. ˈTen no ˈMon

List of large photos - p. 10

(011-k1)*KANJI 1* ☛ Ten-heaven {天}, p. 240

(012-k2)*KANJI 2* ☛ Mon-gate {門}, p. 172

(070-kt)*KARATE MEANING* ✋📖 AKA Tokkōzuki (特攻突き), Suicide Attack, Kamikaze Attack, Gates of Heaven *noun phrase* ① At some Dōjō: a special Irimi one-time sparring practice, meant to develop or to test the student's courage.

(133-sy)*SYNONYMS* 👁= tokkōzuki {{特攻突き}}, p. 247

(134-re)*RELATED TERMS* 👁∞ irimi {{入り身}}, p. 107

(466-cha)*CHARACTERISTICS* ① A Three-character, which consists of 2 Chinese Logograms and 1 Hiʹra-gaʹna Characters.

(409-no)*HIRAGANA* ⊙ The particle ʹNo (の) is a genitive case marker, which indicates possession: of, -'s.

(185-ch)*CHINESE (PINYIN)* ☯📖

Tiānmén

#tennomon {{天の門}}##

Masters 21 – Tennomon by Papkin Sensei
List of Sensei Demonstrations next to Values, p. 10
Gal Papkin (right) and Omer Mienis (left) of Israel Shōtōkan demonstrate the Front Shōmen Version Ten no Mon. Photographer: Ohad Shahar.

Masters 22 – Tennomon by Babin Sensei
List of Sensei Demonstrations next to Values, p. 10
Angela Babin (right) and Yael Magnes (left) of Shōtōkan Karate of America (SKA) demonstrate the Side Hanmi Version Ten no Mon. Photographer: Iris Platt.

(211-1)天の門

(250-hi)てんのもん (hir.)

(800-tag)*TAGS* ⌨ #tenomon

478.Teʹnohira (掌)

(000-it)*INCLUDING TERMS (EXAMPLES)* 👁✉ teishō {{底掌}}, p. 236

(077-jg)*GENERAL MEANING (EXAMPLES)* ☼📖 *noun* ❶ Palm, the central region of the palmar (anterior) aspect of the hand

(089-no)*NOTES AND EXAMPLES* 📖✎ Te (手) means hand, no (の) is a possessive particle, and ˈHira (平) means flat – flat of the hand

(134-re)*RELATED TERMS* 👁∞ Hira-calm {平}, p. 98

(185-ch)*CHINESE (PINYIN)* 👁📖 *zhǎng*

(211-1)掌

(212-2)手のひら (213-3)手の平

(800-tag)*TAGS* 🖥 #sho, #shoh, #shoo, #shou

#Tenohira-palm {掌}##

(211-al)*ALTERNATIVES OR SEE ALSO*

✎✎ 爪

(250-hi)てのひら (hir.)

(275-tō)て 𝄀の𝄀ひら [tènóˈhìrà]

(276-tō2)𝄀て𝄀のひら [téˈnòhìrà]

(313-ka)*KANJI* ✎ The Phono-semantic Compound Logogram Teˈnohira-palm (掌). (313k-cn)**Components** 🖧 [phonetic 尚 | semantic 手] (313k-ra)**Radical** ✚ 手扌龵 hand (313k-cs)**Composition** ✂ Top: 尚, bot-

tom: 手 (313k-re)**Readings (examples)**

🎤 Go-on: しょう (shō). Kan-on: しょう (shō). Kun: てのひら (tenohira, 掌).

479.Teˈtsu (鉄)

(000-it)*INCLUDING TERMS (EXAMPLES)* 👁✉ tekki {{鉄騎}}, p. 237; tettsui {{鉄槌}}, p. 245.

(077-jg)*GENERAL MEANING (EXAMPLES)* ☼📖 *noun* ❶ Iron

(185-ch)*CHINESE (PINYIN)* 👁📖 *Zhí*

(211-1)鉄 (212-2)鐵 (211-al)*ALTERNATIVES OR SEE ALSO* ✎✎ 铁

(250-hi)てつ (hir.)

(256-kat)テツ (kat.)

(275-tō)て𝄀つ [tètsú]

(280-po)pol:TETSY

#Tetsu-iron {鉄}##

(313-ka)*KANJI* ✎ The Phono-semantic Compound Logogram ˈTetsu-iron (鉄). (313k-cn)**Components** 🖧 [semantic 金| phonetic 失] (313k-ra)**Radical** ✚ 金釒 metal (313k-cs)**Composition** ✂ Left: 釒, right: 失 (313k-re)**Readings (examples)** 🎤 Go-on:

てち (techi). Kan-on: てつ (tetsu).

Kun: くろがね (kurogane, 鉄); か

ね (kane, 鉄). Nanori: けん (ken);

てつ (tetsu).

(830-ik)**IMPORTANT KANJI**

480. ˈTet-tsui

(011-k1)*KANJI 1* ☞ Tetsu-iron {鉄}, p. 244

(012-k2)*KANJI 2* ☞ Tsuchi-hammer {槌}, p. 252

(070-kt)*KARATE MEANING* 🖐📖 AKA Kentsui (拳槌), Yoko-zuki, Hammer Hand, Hammerfist, Iron Hammer, Side of the Little Finger, Little Finger Side of the Fist *noun* ① Ulnar border of a closed fist ② Ulnar aspect of a fist and the ulna.

(071-dl)💣✳ AA *DOJO LANGUAGE* ⏳📖 *noun* ① Uchikomi (打ち込み), Tettsui-uchi, Tettsui-uke, Soto-ude-uke.

(077-jg)*GENERAL MEANING (EXAMPLES)* ⚙📖 *noun* ❶ Hammer.

(090-te)*TELL YOUR STUDENTS* 📖☺ This term (かなづち or カナヅチ) also means a bad swimmer, striking the water hard. Our Karate should be more harmonious.

(185-ch)*CHINESE (PINYIN)* ☯📖 *Zhíchuí*

(211-1)鉄槌

(212-2)鉄鎚

(250-hi)てっつい (hir.)

#tettsui {{鉄槌}}##

Masters 23 - Tettsui Uchi by Babin Sensei
List of Sensei Demonstrations next to Values, p. 10

Angela Babin of Shotokan Karate of America (SKA) demonstrates Tettsui Uchi. Photographer: Iris Platt.

Anatomy 6 - Tettsui

(134-re)*RELATED TERMS* 👁∞ sotoudeuke {{外腕受け}}, p. 226

(138-co)*COORDINATE TERMS* 👁≈ shutō {{手刀}}, p. 210

(275-tō)て っつい [tèttsúí]

(466-cha)*CHARACTERISTICS* ① A Two-character, which consists of 2 Chinese Logograms and 0 Hiˈra-ga-ˈna Characters.

(800-tag)*TAGS* 🖥 #tetsui, tezui, #kentsui

(838-su)**SUPER-TERM**

481.Toˈbiˈgeˈri

💣☀ Not to be confused with nidan-geri {{二段蹴り}}, p. 184!

(011-k1)*KANJI 1* ☛ Tobu-to fly {飛}, p. 246

(016-w2)*WORD 2* ☛ keri {{蹴り}}, p. 140

(077-jg)*GENERAL MEANING (EXAMPLES)* ☼📖 *noun* ❶ Flying kick, jumping kick.

(134-re)*RELATED TERMS* 👁∞ nidangeri {{二段蹴り}}, p. 184

(185-ch)*CHINESE (PINYIN)* 😊📖 **Fēi cù**

(211-1)飛び蹴り

#tobigeri {{飛び蹴り}}##

(212-2)飛び蹴

(213-3)跳び蹴り

(250-hi)とびげり (hir.)

(466-cha)*CHARACTERISTICS* ① A Four-character, which consists of 2 Chinese Logograms and 2 Hiˈra-ga-ˈna Characters.

(482-kg)**K↻g** ⌂ Due to the ˈRen-daku laws, the unvoiced consonant /K/ may get a Dak[u]-ˈten (゛) and become ~/g/ as a suffix. Example 💧

Keˈri (けり) turns into Maˈe-geˈri (まえげり).

482.Toˈbu (飛)

(000-it)*INCLUDING TERMS (EXAMPLES)* 👁✉ enpi {{燕飛}}, p. 63; tobigeri {{飛び蹴り}}, p. 246

(077-jg)*GENERAL MEANING (EXAMPLES)* ☼📖 *verb* ❶ To fly, to soar ❷ To jump, to leap.

(089-no)*NOTES AND EXAMPLES* 📖✍ H[i]-ˈkō-ki [hɨkó⁺òkì] (飛行機) means airplane.

(185-ch)*CHINESE (PINYIN)* 😊📖 **fēi**[102]

(705-gv)*GODAN VERB* 🏍⑤ **Terminal Form** {u* 💣☀ but not i*-ru or e*-ru} Toˈbu [tòbú] (飛ぶ), which means to fly. **Polite Form** {i*-masu} Toˈbimas[u] [tòbímá⁺sù] (飛びます).

#Tobu-to fly {飛}##

(211-1)飛

(250-hi)とぶ (hir.) (275-tō)と ぶ [tòbú]

(280-po)pol:TOBY

(313-ka)*KANJI* ✒ The Pictogrammatic Radical (Radical 183) Toˈbu-to fly (飛). (313k-cn)**Components** ⛗ No components - a Simple Logogram.

(313k-ra)**Radical** ✦ 飛 fly. (313k-cs)**Composition** 癶 飞 ノ ノ 丨. (313k-re)**Readings (examples)** 🗣 Go-on: ひ (hi). Kan-on: ひ (hi). Kun: とぶ (toˈbu, 飛ぶ); とばす (tobasu, 飛ばす). Nanori: あす (asu); とび (tobi); たか (taka).

(830-ik)**IMPORTANT KANJI**

483.Tok-ˈkō Zuˈki

List of large photos - p. 10

(016-w2)*WORD* 2 W/W ☛ tsuki {{突き}}, p. 253

(070-kt)*KARATE MEANING* 🖐📖 AKA Ten no Mon (天の門), Suicide Attack, Kamikaze Attack, Gates of Heaven *noun phrase* ① At some Dōjō: a special Irimi one-time sparring practice, meant to develop or to test the student's courage.

(089-no)*NOTES AND EXAMPLES* 📖✎ Tokkō stands for Toˈkubets[u] Kōgek[i]-ˈtai (特別攻撃隊), meaning special attack units – the Kaˈmikaˈze units in World War II.

(133-sy)*SYNONYMS* 👁= tennomon {{天の門}}, p. 243

(134-re)*RELATED TERMS* 👁∞ irimi {{入り身}}, p. 107

Tok-ˈkō Zuˈki - Tok-ˈkō Zuˈki

(466-cha)*CHARACTERISTICS* ① A Four-character, which consists of 3 Chinese Logograms and 1 Hiˈra-ga-ˈna Characters.

(185-ch)*CHINESE (PINYIN)* ☯📖 *Tègōng* #tokkōzuki {{特攻突き}}##

Masters 24 – Tokkōzuki by Papkin Sensei
List of Sensei Demonstrations next to Values, p. 10
Gal Papkin (right) and Omer Mienis (left) of Israel Shōtōkan demonstrate the Front Shōmen Version Tokkō-zuki. Photographer: Ohad Shahar.

Masters 25 – Tokkōzuki by Babin Sensei
List of Sensei Demonstrations next to Values, p. 10
Angela Babin (right) and Yael Magnes (left) of Shōtōkan Karate of America (SKA) demonstrate the Hanmi Side Version Tokkō-zuki. Photographer: Iris Platt.
(211-1)特攻突き (212-2)特攻突
(250-hi)とっこうづき (hir.)

Glossary 286•Index 297•Notes 313•Bibliog. abbr. 23•Subscript pharenteses 15•Abbr. 13•Symbols 13 **247**

(800-tag)*TAGS* 🖳 #tokotsuki, #tokko-zuki, #tokozuki, #tokkotsuki

484. ˈTomari (泊)

(000-it)*INCLUDING TERMS (EXAMPLES)*

👁✉ tomarite {{泊手}}, p. 248

(028-pl)*PLACES* 🌐 *name* Historically, the village of ˈTomari played an important part in the development of the Okinawan martial arts. It also served as a significant port. Toˈmaru (泊る) means to be docked. Today, ˈTomari is a neighborhood in Naha.

#Tomari-the village {{泊}}##

(185-ch)*CHINESE (PINYIN)* 👁📖 *Pō*

(189-ok)*OKINAWAN* ● Tomai (トマイ), Tumai

(211-1)泊

(250-hi)とまり (hir.)

(256-kat)トマリ (kat.)

(885-tag)*TAGS* 🖳 #tomai, #tumai

(833-kan)**KANJI**

485. ˈTomari-te

(011-k1)*KANJI 1* ☞ Tomari-the village {{泊}}, p. 248

(012-k2)*KANJI 2* ☞ Te-hand {手}, p. 234

(025-sch)*SCHOOLS* ⛩ *name* Karate styles that are attributed to Tomari. They belong to the ˈShō-rin-ryū (少林流) - the light and long styles, which resemble the northern schools of Chinese martial arts[103].

(133-sy)*SYNONYMS* 👁= shōrinryū {{少林流}}, p. 219; shurite {{首里手}}, p. 222

#tomarite {{泊手}}##

(139-an)*ANTONYMS* 👁↻ nahate {{那覇手}}, p. 176; shōreiryū {{昭霊流}}, p. 218

(185-ch)*CHINESE (PINYIN)* 👁📖 *Pō shǒu*

(189-ok)*OKINAWAN* ● Tomai-di (トマイディ), Tumai-dii

(211-1)泊手

(250-hi)とまりて (hir.)

(466-cha)*CHARACTERISTICS* ⓘ A Two-character, which consists of 2 Chinese Logograms and 0 Hiˈra-ga-ˈna Characters.

486. Toˈra (虎)

(000-it)*INCLUDING TERMS (EXAMPLES)*

👁✉ koshi {{虎趾}}, p. 155

(077-jg)*GENERAL MEANING (EXAMPLES)* ✿📖 *noun* ❶ Tiger.

(089-no)*NOTES AND EXAMPLES* 📖✍

Toˈra-no-Maˈki (虎の巻), created by Hōan KOSUGI (Misai KOSUGI), is Shōtōkan's symbol[104].

(095-3t)*THE THREE TEACHINGS* **3** 🔔 Our Tiger Scroll is a descendent of a Chinese legendary and mysterious creature named The White Tiger (白虎) of the West. A good example of the similarity is an exhibit in the Palace Museum housed in the Forbidden City, called Eave-end Tile with White Tiger.

(136-se)*SEE ALSO* 👁➕ oizuki {{追い突き}}, p. 188

(185-ch)*CHINESE (PINYIN)* 🌐📖 *hǔ*

(203-hi)⏳☉ (206-kata)⏳○

(250-hi)とら (hir.)

(256-kat)トラ (kat.)

#Tora-tiger {虎}##

Figure 4 – The ancient Ancestor of Shōtōkan's tiger

(211-1)虎 (211-al)*ALTERNATIVES OR SEE ALSO* ✑✑乕, 甪, 甫, 虒, 虤

(275-tō)と ら [tòrá]

(313-ka)*KANJI* ✑ The Compound Ideogram Toˈra-tiger (虎). (313k-cn)**Components** ⛙ [虍 | 儿] (313k-ra)**Radical** ✛ 虍 tiger (313k-cs)**Composition** ⚔ Top: 虍, bottom: 儿 (313k-re)**Readings (examples)** 🗣 Go-on: く (ku). Kan-on: こ (ko). Kun: とら (tora, 虎). Nanori: とら (tora).

(302-kn)*KANJI NOTES* ✑✍ 虍 (Radical 141, which also means tiger) depicts the head, and 儿 (Radical 10) depicts the legs and the tail.

(830-ik)**IMPORTANT KANJI**

487. ˈTori

💣※ Do not confuse (both pronounced Torite): 捕手 (p. 250) with 取り手!

(000-it)*INCLUDING TERMS (EXAMPLES)* 👁✉ randori {{乱取り}}, p. 195

(139-an)*ANTONYMS* 👁↺ uke {{受け}}, p. 262

(466-cha)*CHARACTERISTICS* ⓘ A Two-character, which consists of 1 Chi-

nese Logograms and 1 Hi˙ra-ga-˙na Characters.

#tori {{取り}}##

(077-jg)*GENERAL MEANING (EXAMPLES)* ☼📖 *noun* ❶ Taker ❷ Taking ❸ In martial arts: the partner that completes its technique successfully – the practitioner, the "defender" - Ukete. Usually, the role of the ˙Tori is to defend and then to counterattack. The other partner is called U˙ke (受け) (Semete).

(211-1)取り (250-hi)とり (hir.)

(800-tag)*TAGS* 🖥 #dori

488.To˙ri-te

💣✳ Do not confuse (both pronounced Torite): 捕手 with 取り手!

(012-k2)*KANJI* 2 ☛ Te-hand {手}, p. 234

(070-kt)*KARATE MEANING* 🖐📖 AKA Tsukami-waza (掴み技), Tsukami-uke, Tsukami Hiki, Taking Hands, Seizing Hand, Holding Hand, Grasping Hand, Grasping Technique *noun* ① Gripping techniques, grabbing techniques.

(071-dl)💣✳ ᴀᴀ *DOJO LANGUAGE* ⌛📖 *noun* AKA Hazushi-waza (外し技),

Te-hazushi, Releasing Hand, Escape Techniques [105], Freeing Technique, Grab Escapes ① At some Dōjō: Hand-grab release, escaping wrist hold ② At some Dōjō: I-˙ai, sitting together sparring.

(077-jg)*GENERAL MEANING (EXAMPLES)* ☼📖 *noun* ❶ 捕手: Art of capturing with bare hands, arresting techniques. 取り手: receiver, taker.

#torite {{捕手}}##

(089-no)*NOTES AND EXAMPLES* 📖✎ **1** The Hikite of the eighth movement (the one after the open-handed Age-uke) of Heian Shodan is considered a Torite. **2** The concept appears in Ankō Itosu's sixth of Ten Precepts (糸洲十訓)[106].

(090-te)*TELL YOUR STUDENTS* 📖☺ Any Hikite could be a Torite

(185-ch)*CHINESE (PINYIN)* ☯📖

Qŭshŏu

(211-1)捕手

(212-2)捕り手

(213-3)取り手

(214-4)取手

(250-hi)とりて (hir.)

(256-kat)トリテ (kat.)

(466-cha)*CHARACTERISTICS* ⓘ A Two-character, which consists of 2 Chinese Logograms and 0 Hi˙ra-ga-˙na Characters.

489.To˙shi (年)

(021-rb)*RESEARCH (FOR BOOKS)* ✍

noun ❶ Year

(211-1)年

(134-gr-re)*GROUP* 👁(🙀 The following terms are related: shōwa {{昭和}}, p. 221; taisho {{大正}}, p. 230; toshi {年}, p. 251.

#toshi {年}##

(250-hi) と し (hir.) (275-tō) と [し]

[tòshí˙]

(089-no)*NOTES AND EXAMPLES* 📖✍

Examples: 大正 11 年 is the year 1922. And 1907 年 12 月 15 日, for instance, means December 15, 1907.

(833-kan)**KANJI**

490.Ts[u]˙chi (土)

(000-it)*INCLUDING TERMS (EXAMPLES)* 👁✉ dojigata {{土字形}}, p. 58

(077-jg)*GENERAL MEANING (EXAMPLES)* ✿📖 *noun* ❶ Earth.

(185-ch)*CHINESE (PINYIN)* ☯📖 *tǔ*

(211-1)土

(211-al)*ALTERNATIVES OR SEE ALSO* ✒✒ 士, 圡, 圡, 地

(250-hi)つち (hir.)

#Tsuchi-earth {土}##

(275-tō) つ [ち] [tsɵchí˙] (280-po)pol:CCI

(302-kn)*KANJI NOTES* ✒✐ Contains 3 strokes.

(325-kr)*KANJI READINGS* ✒🗣 Go-on: つ (tsu). Kan-on: と (to). Kan'yō-on: ど (do). Kun: つち (tsuchi).

(800-tag)*TAGS* 💻 #zuchi, #tschi

(833-kan)**KANJI**

491.Ts[u]˙chi (槌)

💣 Do not confuse: Tsuchi-hammer {槌}, p. 252 with Tsuchi-hammer {鎚}, p. 252!

(000-it)*INCLUDING TERMS (EXAMPLES)* 👁✉ sakatsuchi {{逆槌}}, p. 200; tettsui {{鉄槌}}, p. 245

(077-jg)*GENERAL MEANING (EXAMPLES)* ✿📖 *noun* ❶ Hammer, mallet

(133-sy)*SYNONYMS* 👁= Tsuchi-hammer {鎚}, p. 252

Ts[u]ˈchi (鎚) - Ts[u]ˈki (月)

(185-ch)*CHINESE (PINYIN)* ◉📖 *chuí, zhuì, duī*

(203-hi)⏳☉

(250-hi)つち (hir.) (211-1)槌

#Tsuchi-hammer {槌}##

(211-al)*ALTERNATIVES OR SEE ALSO*

✎✎ 鎚, 椎

(275-tō)つ|ち [tsùchí˙]

(280-po)pol:CCI

(313-ka)*KANJI* ✎ The Compound Logogram Ts[u]ˈchi-hammer 2 (槌).

(313k-cn)**Components** 🝔 [木 | 追]

(313k-ra)**Radical** ✦ 木 tree (313k-cs)**Composition** ✄ Left: 木, right: 追 (313k-re)**Readings (examples)** 🗣 Go-on: ずい (zui). Kan-on: つい (tsui). Kun: つち (tsuchi, 槌). Nanori: つち (tsuchi); てつ (tetsu).

(830-ik)**IMPORTANT KANJI**

492.Ts[u]ˈchi (鎚)

💣☀ Do not confuse: Tsuchi-hammer {槌}, p. 252 with Tsuchi-hammer {鎚}, p. 252!

(000-it)*INCLUDING TERMS (EXAMPLES)*

◉✉ hizazuchi {{膝鎚}}, p. 101

(077-jg)*GENERAL MEANING (EXAMPLES)* ⚙📖 *noun* ❶ Hammer

(133-sy)*SYNONYMS* 👁= Tsuchi-hammer {槌}, p. 252

(185-ch)*CHINESE (PINYIN)* ◉📖 *chuí*

(211-al)*ALTERNATIVES OR SEE ALSO*

✎✎ 鍾, 锤, 捶, 鏗, 鉖, 錐

#Tsuchi-hammer {鎚}##

(211-1)鎚

(250-hi)つち (hir.)

(275-tō)つ|ち [tsū̄chí˙]

(280-po)pol:CCI

(302-kn)*KANJI NOTES* ✎✍ Contains 18 strokes.

(325-kr)*KANJI READINGS* ✎🗣 Go-on: ずい (zui); て (te). Kan-on: つい (tsui); たい (tai). Kun: つち (tsuchi, 鎚).

(800-tag)*TAGS* 💻 #zchi, #zuchi, #tschi

(833-kan)**KANJI**

493.Ts[u]ˈki (月)

Ð Script 12 - Tsuki-moon Western Zhou Bronze Inscriptions

(000-it)*INCLUDING TERMS (EXAMPLES)*

◉✉ hangetsu {{半月}}, p. 84; mikazuki {{三日月}}, p. 170

(077-jg)*GENERAL MEANING (EXAMPLES)* ✿📖 *noun* ❶ Moon *temporal noun* ❷ Month

(185-ch)*CHINESE (PINYIN)* ☻📖 **yuè**

(302-kn)*KANJI NOTES* ✒✍ Can You recognize the Logogram in the ancient Chinese script on page 28? Gets[u]-ˈyō-bi [gètsúyóˈòbì] (月曜日) (moon day) is Monday, just as Monday (moon-day) in English, Montag in German, Lunes in Spanish, Lundi in French, and Maandag in Dutch.

#Tsuki-moon {月}##

(211-1)月

(250-hi)つき (hir.)

(275-tō) つ き [tsɯ̀kíˈ] (280-po)pol:CKI

(313-ka)*KANJI* ✐ The Pictogrammatic Radical (Radical 74) Ts[u]ˈki-moon (月). (313k-cn)**Components** ⛓ No components - a Simple Logogram. (313k-ra)**Radical** ⚛ 月 moon. (313k-cs)**Composition** ⚔ 冂, 二.

(313k-re)**Readings (examples)** 🖌 Go-on: がち (gachi). Kan-on: げつ (getsu). Kan'yō-on: がつ (gatsu). Kun: つき (tsuki).

(800-tag)*TAGS* 💻 #Tsuki-moon, tski 1, zki 1, zuki 1, suki 1

(830-ik)**IMPORTANT KANJI**

494.Ts[u]˙ki 2

(000-it)*INCLUDING TERMS (EXAMPLES)*

👁✉ agezuki {{上げ突き}}, p. 31; chokuzuki {{直突き}}, p. 52; gyakuzuki {{逆突き}}, p. 73; kagizuki {{鉤突き}}, p. 121; oizuki {{追い突き}}, p. 188; tokkōzuki {{特攻突き}}, p. 247; yamazuki {{山突き}}, p. 270.

(011-k1)*KANJI 1* ☛ Tsuku-to thrust {突}, p. 255

(070-kt)*KARATE MEANING* ✋📖 *noun* ① Thrust.

(077-jg)*GENERAL MEANING (EXAMPLES)* ✿📖 *noun* ❶ Thrust ❷ Stab ❸ Lunge.

#tsuki {{突き}}##

(203-hi)⏳☉

(250-hi)つき (hir.)

(211-sh-2)突き (simp. Jp.)

(Jsh2)突き (simp. Ch.)

(211-ky-1)突き (trad.)

(275-tō)つ|き| [tsùkí] (280-po)pol:CKI

(466-cha)*CHARACTERISTICS* ⓘ A Two-character, which consists of 0 Chinese Logograms and 2 Hiˈra-ga-ˈna Characters.

(800-tag)*TAGS* 💻 #tsuki 2, #zuki 2

(838-su)**SUPER-TERM**

495.Ts[u]ˈku (着)

(000-it)*INCLUDING TERMS (EXAMPLES)*

👁✉ karategi {{空手着}}, p. 131

(070-kt)*KARATE MEANING* ✋📖 *noun* ① Kaˈra-te-gi, training uniform, Kaˈra-te uniform.

(077-jg)*GENERAL MEANING (EXAMPLES)* ☼📖 *verb* ❶ To wear ❷ To arrive *suffix* ❸ Uniform, outfit, clothes.

(089-no)*NOTES AND EXAMPLES* 📖✍ Ki-ˈmono [kìmónó] (着物) is the famous long Japanese robe.

(211-1)着

(250-hi)つく (hir.)

#Tsuku-to wear {着}##

(275-tō)つ|く| [tsùkúˈ]

(276-tō2)|つ|く [tsúˈkù]

(280-po)pol:CKY

(325-kr)*KANJI READINGS* ✒🗣 Go-on: じゃく (jaku). Kan-on: ちゃく (chaku). Kun: つく (tsuku, 着く); つける (tsukeru, 着ける); き (ki, 着); ぎ (gi, 着); きる (kiru, 着る); きせる (kiseru, 着せる).

(833-kan)**KANJI**

(838-su)**SUPER-TERM**

496.Ts[u]ˈku (突)

(000-it)*INCLUDING TERMS (EXAMPLES)*

👁✉ tsuki {{突き}}, p. 253

(077-jg)*GENERAL MEANING (EXAMPLES)* ☼📖 *verb* ❶ To thrust, to poke, to push[107] ❷ To protrude ❸ To stab, to pierce, to prick.

(313-ka.1c)*COMMON* ✒ Some believe the ˈKan-ji depicts a dog bursting out[108] of its kennel (or cave), and some believe it depicts a hound bursting into[109] a hole (to catch a rabbit, for instance). One should think of this charging dog, in every single Oˈi-z[u]ˈki.

(089-no)*NOTES AND EXAMPLES* 📖✍ Taˈma-ts[u]ki (玉突き), for instance, means billiards, pool.

(185-ch)*CHINESE (PINYIN)* ☯📖 ***tū, tú***

(484-tsz)**Tsᴐz** ⌂ Due to the ˈRendaku laws, the unvoiced consonant /Ts/ may get a Dak[u]-ˈten (゙) and become ~/z/ as a suffix. Example ↳ Ts[u]ˈki 2 (つき) turns into Oˈi-z[u]ˈki (おいづき).

(705-gv)*GODAN VERB* 🏍⑤ **Terminal Form** {u* ☀ but not i*-ru or e*-ru} Ts[u]ˈku [tsɯ̈kú] [tsɯ̈ˈkù] (突く), which means to thrust. **Polite Form** {i*-masu} Ts[u]ˈkimas[u] [tsùkímá⁺sù] (突きます).

#Tsuku-to thrust {突}##

(211-sh-2)突 (simp. Jp.)

(Jsh2)突 (simp. Ch.)

(211-ky-1)突 (trad.)

(250-hi)つく (hir.)

(256-kat)ツク (kat.)

(275-tō)つ⟨ [tsɯ̈kú]

(276-tō2)つ‖く [tsɯ̈⁺kù]

(280-po)pol:CKY

(313-ka.1e)**Radical 【common】** ✦ 穴. (313-ka.1r)**Readings 【common】** 🐾 Go-on: どち (dochi). Kan-on: とつ (totsu). Kun: つく (tsuku, 突く).

(313-ka.2s)*SIMPLIFIED (SHINJITAI)* ✒ The Compound Ideogram Ts[u]ˈku-to thrust (突) (simp.). (313-ka.2C)**Components 【simp.】** 🗃 [穴 | 大]. (313-ka.2g)**Building Blocks 【simp.】** � Top: 穴, bottom: 大.

(313-ka.3t)*TRADITIONAL (KYUJITAI)* ✒ The Compound Ideogram Ts[u]ˈku-to thrust (突) (trad.). (313-ka.3c)**Components 【trad.】** 🗃 [穴 | 犬] (313-ka.3g)**Building Blocks 【trad.】** ✗ Top: 穴, bottom: 犬.

(800-tag)*TAGS* 💻 #tsuku 1, tsku, zuku, zku

(830-ik)**IMPORTANT KANJI**

497.Tsuˈbame (燕)

(000-it)*INCLUDING TERMS (EXAMPLES)* 👁✉ enpi {{燕飛}}, p. 63; tsubamegaeshi {{燕返し}}, p. 256

(077-jg)*GENERAL MEANING (EXAMPLES)* ☼📖 *noun* ❶ Swallow ❷ Martin.

(089-no)*NOTES AND EXAMPLES* 📖✎ The Logogram could also mean to relax, to enjoy[110], to be comfortable. In that meaning, it is close to An-calm {安}, p. 33 of heian {{平安}}, p. 90[111].

(302-kn)*KANJI NOTES* ✎ ✍ It depicts a swallow or generally a small bird (head 廿, wings 北, tail 灬). Contains 16 strokes. This Logogram is outside the list of Jō-yō ˈKan-ji, belonging to the Jin-mei-yō ˈKan-ji. #Tsubame-swallow {燕}##

(185-ch)*CHINESE (PINYIN)* ☯📖 *yàn, yān*

(211-1)燕 (250-hi)つばめ (hir.)

(275-tō)つ|ばめ| [tsùbámé]

(313-ka)*KANJI* ✎ The Pictogram Tsuˈbame-swallow (燕). (313k-cn)**Components** 🕸 No components - a Simple Logogram. (313k-ra)**Radical** ✦ 火 灬 fire. (313k-cs)**Composition** 乂 口, 北, 廿, 灬. (313k-re)**Readings (examples)** 🗣 Go-on: えん (en). Kan-on: えん (en). Kun: つばめ (tsubame, 燕); つばくら (tsubakura, 燕); つばくろ (tsubakuro, 燕). Nano-ri: やすし (yasushi).

(830-ik)**IMPORTANT KANJI**

498.Tsuˈbame-ˈgaeshi

(011-k1)*KANJI 1* ☞ Tsubame-swallow { 燕}, p. 256

(015-w1)*WORD 1* W̄w ☞ kaeshi {{返し}}, p. 118

(055-tt)*THROWING TECHNIQUE* 投 技 **AKA** Swallow-return, V-turning Swallow

(056-mt)*FUNAKOSHI MAIN BOOK - THROWING TECHNIQUES* ⚡MTT

1935 Suzuki-Johnston 197 **1935 Ohshima** 227 (list), 230

(185-ch)*CHINESE (PINYIN)* ☯📖 *Yàn fǎn*

(211-1)燕返し (250-hi)つばめがえし (hir.)

#tsubamegaeshi {{燕返し}}##

(466-cha)*CHARACTERISTICS* ① A Three-character, which consists of 2 Chinese Logograms and 1 Hiˈra-ga-ˈna Characters.

(482-kg)**K⤳g** 🔔 Due to the ˈRen-daku laws, the unvoiced consonant /K/ may get a Dak[u]-ˈten (゛) and become ~/g/ as a suffix. Example 🦵 Keˈri (けり) turns into Maˈe-geˈri (まえげり).

(800-tag)*TAGS* 🖥 #tsubame kaeshi, #tsubamegeashi, tsubame geashi

499. Tsuˈranuku (貫)

💧※ Do not confuse: Tsuranuku-to pierce {貫}, p. 257 as in nukite {{貫手}}, p. 185 with Nuku-to extract {抜}, p. 186 as in bassai {{抜塞}}, p. 43 and as in Iai-do's Nuˈkits[u]ˈke (抜き付け)!

(000-it)*INCLUDING TERMS (EXAMPLES)*

👁✉ nukite {{貫手}}, p. 185

(077-jg)*GENERAL MEANING (EXAMPLES)* ✿📖 *verb (transitive)* ❶ To go through, to pierce, to penetrate ❷ To persist, to carry out.

(089-no)*NOTES AND EXAMPLES* 📖✍

Etymology: from Tsura (列) and Nuku (抜)

(134-re)*RELATED TERMS* 👁∞ Nuku-to extract {抜}, p. 186

(185-ch)*CHINESE (PINYIN)* 🌐📖 **guàn**

(211-1)貫 (211-al)*ALTERNATIVES OR SEE ALSO* ✏✏ 貫 (211-ka+hi)貫く

(250-hi)つらぬく (hir.)

#Tsuranuku-to pierce {貫}##

(275-tō) つらぬ く

(313-ka)*KANJI* ✐ The Phono-semantic Compound Logogram Tsuˈranuku-to pierce (貫). (313k-cn)**Components** 🗦 [phonetic 毌 | semantic 貝] (313k-ra)**Radical** ✛ 貝 shell (313k-cs)**Composition** ✖ Top: 毌, bottom: 貝 (313k-re)**Readings (examples)** 🗣 Go-on: かん (kan). Kan-on: かん (kan). Kun: つらぬく (tsuranuku, 貫く) ;ぬき (nuˈki, 貫); ぬく (nuku, 貫く).

(705-gv)*GODAN VERB* 🏍⑤ **Terminal Form** {u* 💧※ but not i*-ru or e*-ru} Tsuˈranuku [tsùránú⁺kù] (貫く), which means to go through. **Polite Form** {i*-masu} Tsuˈranukimas[u] [tsùránúkímá⁺sù] (貫きます).

(800-tag)*TAGS* 🖥 #nuki (ぬき)

(830-ik)**IMPORTANT KANJI**

500. ˈTsuru (鶴)

(000-it)*INCLUDING TERMS (EXAMPLES)*

👁✉ gankaku {{岩鶴}}, p. 68

(077-jg)*GENERAL MEANING (EXAMPLES)* ✿📖 *noun* ❶ Crane

(185-ch)*CHINESE (PINYIN)* 🌐📖 **hè, háo**

(211-1)鶴 (250-hi)つる (hir.)

(275-tō) つ る [tsúˈrù]

#Tsuru-crane {鶴}##

(280-po)pol:CYRY

(325-kr)*KANJI READINGS* ✎🗣 Go-on:

がく (gaku). Kan-on: かく (kaku).

Kun: つる (tsuru, 鶴); たず (tazu,

鶴). Nanori: ず (zu); つ (tsu).

(800-tag)*TAGS* 💻 #zuru

(833-kan)**KANJI**

501.Uˈchi (内)

(000-it)*INCLUDING TERMS (EXAMPLES)*

👁✉ naihanchi {{内歩進}}, p.

177; uchiudeuke {{内腕受け}}, p.

259; uchiuke {{内受け}}, p. 259

(077-jg)*GENERAL MEANING (EXAMPLES)* ⚙📖 *preposition* ❶ Inside

(136-se)*SEE ALSO* 👁➕ Naka-middle {

中}, p. 178

(139-an)*ANTONYMS* 👁↺ Soto-outside

{外}, p. 225

(185-ch)*CHINESE (PINYIN)* 👁📖 *nèi*

#Uchi-inside {内}##

(211-1)内 (211-al)*ALTERNATIVES OR SEE*

ALSO ✎✎ 内

(250-hi)うち (hir.) (275-tō)う ち [ùchí]

(302-kn)*KANJI NOTES* ✎✍ Contains 4

strokes.

(325-kr)*KANJI READINGS* ✎🗣 Go-on:

ない (nai). Kun: うち (uchi, 内); い

れる (ireru, 内れる).

(833-kan)**KANJI**

(838-su)**SUPER-TERM**

502.Uˈchi 2

(000-it)*INCLUDING TERMS (EXAMPLES)*

👁✉ aiuchi {{相打ち}}, p. 31;

shutōuchi {{手刀打ち}}, p. 211

(011-k1)*KANJI 1* ☞ Utsu-to hit {打}, p.

266

(070-kt)*KARATE MEANING* ✋📖 *noun*

① Strike, hit, knock[112].

#uchi {{打ち}}##

(211-1)打ち (250-hi)うち (hir.)

(466-cha)*CHARACTERISTICS* ① A Two-

character, which consists of 1 Chi-

nese Logograms and 1 Hiˈra-ga-ˈna

Characters.

(838-su)**SUPER-TERM**

503.Uˈchi Uˈde Uˈke

(011-k1)*KANJI 1* ☞ Uchi-inside {内}, p.

258

(015-w1)*WORD 1* 𝟣 ᵂ/ᵂ ☞ udeuke {{腕受

け}}, p. 261

(070-kt)*KARATE MEANING* ✋📖 AKA

Uchi-uke, Ude-uke (at some Dōjō) *noun phrase* ① Inside arm block, inside forearm block, inner arm block, internal arm block ② From inside arm block, inside to outside arm block, outward arm block

(133-sy)*SYNONYMS* 👁= uchiuke {{内受け}}, p. 259

(139-an)*ANTONYMS* 👁↺ sotoudeuke {{外腕受け}}, p. 226

(185-ch)*CHINESE (PINYIN)* ☯📖 *Nèi wàn shòu*

(211-1)内腕受け

(212-2)内腕受

#uchiudeuke {{内腕受け}}##

(250-hi)うちうでうけ (hir.)

(089-no)*NOTES AND EXAMPLES* 📖✎

Any of the adjectives "inner" or "outer", can be interpreted as centrifugal (outward) or centripetal (inward). Different schools give opposite meanings to Soto-ude-uke and to Uchi-ude-uke. Outer can mean coming from outside or going to outside. In this dictionary, the name goes after the origin of the movement - Uchi means centrifugal (beginning inside), and Soto means centripetal (beginning outside).

(466-cha)*CHARACTERISTICS* ⓘ A Four-character, which consists of 3 Chinese Logograms and 1 Hi˙ra-ga-˙na Characters.

(838-su)**SUPER-TERM**

504.U˙chi U˙ke

(011-k1)*KANJI 1* ☛ Uchi-inside {内}, p. 258

(015-w1)*WORD 1* $^{W}_{W}$ ☛ uke {{受け}}, p. 262

(070-kt)*KARATE MEANING* ✋📖 AKA

Uchi-ude-uke, Ude-uke (at some Dōjō) *noun phrase* Inside block, internal block ② From inside block, inside to outside block, outward block ③ Uchi Ude Uke, inside arm block, inside forearm block, internal arm block.

(133-sy)*SYNONYMS* 👁= uchiudeuke {{内腕受け}}, p. 259

(139-an)*ANTONYMS* 👁↺ sotouke {{外受け}}, p. 225

(185-ch)*CHINESE (PINYIN)* ☯📖 *Nèi shòu*

(211-1)内受け

#uchiuke {{内受け}}##

(089-no) *NOTES AND EXAMPLES* 📖✎

Any of the adjectives "inner" or "outer", can be interpreted as centrifugal (outward) or centripetal (inward). Different schools give opposite meanings to Soto-ude-uke and to Uchi-ude-uke. Outer can mean coming from outside or going to outside. In this dictionary, the name goes after the origin of the movement - Uchi means centrifugal (beginning inside), and Soto means centripetal (beginning outside).

(212-2) 内受

(250-hi) うちうけ (hir.)

(466-cha) *CHARACTERISTICS* ⓘ A

Three-character, which consists of 2 Chinese Logograms and 1 Hi˙ra-ga-˙na Characters.

505.U˙de (腕)

(000-it) *INCLUDING TERMS (EXAMPLES)*

👁✉ haiwanuke {{背腕受け}}, p. 79; jōwan {{上腕}}, p. 114; udeuke {{腕受け}}, p. 261; udewa {{腕輪}}, p. 261

(077-jg) *GENERAL MEANING (EXAMPLES)* ⚙📖 *noun* ❶ Arm.

(089-no) *NOTES AND EXAMPLES* 📖✎

U˙dewa [ùdéwá] (腕 輪) means bracelet.

#Ude-arm {腕}##

(185-ch) *CHINESE (PINYIN)* 👁📖 **wàn**

(211-1) 腕

(250-hi) うで (hir.)

(275-tō) う 　で　 [ùdé⁺]

(325-kr) *KANJI READINGS* ✒🗣 Go-on: わん (wan). Kan-on: わん (wan). Kun: うで (ude, 腕); かいな (kaina, 腕).

(833-kan) **KANJI**

(838-su) **SUPER-TERM**

506.U˙de U˙ke

(000-it) *INCLUDING TERMS (EXAMPLES)*

👁✉ sotoudeuke {{外腕受け}}, p. 226; uchiudeuke {{内腕受け}}, p. 259.

(011-k1) *KANJI 1* ☞ Ude-arm {腕}, p. 260

(015-w1) *WORD 1* ☞ uke {{受け}}, p. 262

(070-kt) *KARATE MEANING* 🖐📖 *noun phrase* ① Forearm block, arm block.

(185-ch)*CHINESE (PINYIN)* ☯📖 ***Wàn shòu***

#udeuke {{腕受け}}##

(089-no)*NOTES AND EXAMPLES* 📖✎ At some Dōjō, Ude Uke means specifically Uchi-ude-uke – inside forearm block, since Soto-ude-uke is not practiced.

(211-1)腕受け (212-2)腕受

(250-hi)うでうけ (hir.)

(466-cha)*CHARACTERISTICS* ⓘ A Three-character, which consists of 2 Chinese Logograms and 1 Hi'ra-ga-'na Characters.

(838-su)**SUPER-TERM**

507.U'de-wa

(011-k1)*KANJI 1* ☛ Ude-arm {腕}, p. 260

(012-k2)*KANJI 2* ☛ Wa-ring {輪}, p. 267

(055-tt)*THROWING TECHNIQUE* 投技

Old Name K[u]'sari-wa (鎖環, 鎖環) **AKA** Mo'ro-te-ga'ri (諸手刈り), Chain Ring, Arm Ring, To Encircle with the Arm, Two Handed Reap, Open Arms Reaping

(077-jg)*GENERAL MEANING (EXAMPLES)* ✿📖 *noun* ❶ Bracelet.

(134-re)*RELATED TERMS* ◉∞ kubiwa {{首輪}}, p. 156

(185-ch)*CHINESE (PINYIN)* ☯📖

Wànlún

(250-hi)うでわ (hir.)

#udewa {{腕輪}}##

(056-mt)*FUNAKOSHI MAIN BOOK - THROWING TECHNIQUES* 📚**MTT**

1922 original 54 （鎖環） **1925 Ishida** 61 **1925 Teramoto** 53 (Kusariwa), 54 (鎖環) **1935 Suzuki-Johnston** 200 (Udewa) **1935 Ohshima** 227 (list), 231-232 (Udewa).

(211-1)腕輪

(212-2)腕環

(275-tō)う[でわ] [ùdéwá]

(466-cha)*CHARACTERISTICS* ⓘ A Two-character, which consists of 2 Chinese Logograms and 0 Hi'ra-ga-'na Characters.

508.U'e (上)

(000-it)*INCLUDING TERMS (EXAMPLES)* ◉✉ age {{上げ}}, p. 30; jōdan

{{上段}}, p. 114; jōwan {{上腕}}, p. 114; ***Kami Ichidan Verb** (p. 290).*

(077-jg)GENERAL MEANING (EXAMPLES) ☼📖 *noun* ❶ Top. *preposition* ❷ Up, above, over.

(302-kn)KANJI NOTES 🖋✍ 二 is the historic [113] version of the Simple Ideogram U'e-top (上).

(185-ch)CHINESE (PINYIN) ☯📖 ***shàng***

(711-sh)SHIMO ICHIDAN VERB 🏍①❶

Terminal Form {e*-ru} A'geru [àgérú] (上げる), which means to raise. **Polite Form {-masu}** A'gemas[u] [àgémá⁺sù] (上げます).

#Ue-top {上}##

(139-an)ANTONYMS 👁↺ Shimo-bottom {下}, p. 213

(211-1)上 (250-hi)うえ (hir.)

(275-tō)う[え] [ùé]

(313-ka)KANJI 🖋 The Simple Ideogram [114] U'e-top (上). (313k-cn)**Components** 🖧 No components - a Simple Logogram. (313k-ra)**Radical** ✦ 一 one. (313k-cs)**Composition** ⚒ ⺊, 一. (313k-re)**Readings (examples)** 🗣 Go-on: じょう (jō). Kan-on: しょう (shō). Kun: うえ (ue); かみ (kami); あげる (ageru); あがる (agaru); あがり (agari). Nanori: あげ (age).

(830-ik)**IMPORTANT KANJI**

509.U'ke

(000-it)INCLUDING TERMS (EXAMPLES)

👁✉ ageuke {{上げ受け}}, p. 30; haiwanuke {{背腕受け}}, p. 79; jūjiuke {{十字受け}}, p. 116; manjiuke {{卍受け}}, p. 164; osaeuke {{押え受け}}, p. 191; shutōuke {{手刀受け}}, p. 211; sotouke {{外受け}}, p. 225; uchiuke {{内受け}}, p. 259; udeuke {{腕受け}}, p. 261

(011-k1)KANJI 1 ☛ Ukeru-to receive {受}, p. 263

(077-jg)GENERAL MEANING (EXAMPLES) ☼📖 *noun* ❶ Defense ❷ Reception, popularity ❸ Agreement.

(211-1)受け (212-2)受

(250-hi) うけ (hir.) (275-tō) う[け] [ùké⁺]

#uke {{受け}}##

(070-kt)*KARATE MEANING* ✋📖 *noun*
① Block[115] ② In pair training: Receiver of the technique, opponent, attacker, aggressor, assailant, partner [116] (Semete). The partner that trains the other, the teaching side. Usually, the Uke's role is to attack. The practitioner that gets to complete its technique successfully ("defender") is called 'Tori (取り) (Ukete).

(139-an)*ANTONYMS* 👁↻ tori {{取り}}, p. 250 (for ②)

(466-cha)*CHARACTERISTICS* ⓘ A Two-character, which consists of 1 Chinese Logograms and 1 Hi'ra-ga-'na Characters.

(838-su)**SUPER-TERM**

510.U'keru (受)

(000-it)*INCLUDING TERMS (EXAMPLES)*
👁✉ uke {{受け}}, p. 262

(077-jg)*GENERAL MEANING (EXAMPLES)* ✿📖 *verb* ❶ To receive, to get, to accept.

(185-ch)*CHINESE (PINYIN)* 👁📖 **shòu**
verb ❶ To receive, to accept, to get ❷ To bear, to endure[117], to stand

(302-kn)*KANJI NOTES* ✎✐ It arguably depicts a hand (又) receiving something[118] (冖) (凡) from another hand (爫) (爪)[119].

(711-sh)*SHIMO ICHIDAN VERB* 🏍①☝

Terminal Form {e*-ru} U'keru [ùké⁺rù] (受ける), which means to receive. **Polite Form** {-masu} U'kemas[u] [ùkémá⁺sù] (受けます).

(250-hi)うける (hir.)
#Ukeru-to receive {受}##

(211-1)受

(211-ka+hi)受ける

(275-tō)う|け|る [ùké⁺rù]

(313-ka)*KANJI* ✎ The Compound Ideogram U'keru-to receive (受). (313k-cn)**Components** ⛏ [爪 | 凡 | 又].
(313k-ra)**Radical** ⊹ The Radical in this Compound Logogram is Radical 'Mata (又) [120] (Radical 29), which used to mean right hand[121], and today means again. (313k-re)**Readings (examples)** 🌿 Go-on: ず (zu). Kan-on: しゅう (shū). Kan'yō-on: じゅ (ju). Kun: うかる

(ukaru, 受かる); うける (ukeru, 受ける); うけ (uke, 受け).

511.Uˈma (馬)

(000-it)*INCLUDING TERMS (EXAMPLES)*

👁✉ kiba {{騎馬}}, p. 144

(077-jg)*GENERAL MEANING (EXAMPLES)* ☼📖 *noun* ❶ Horse.

(185-ch)*CHINESE (PINYIN)* ☯📖 *mǎ*

(211-1)馬

(211-al)*ALTERNATIVES OR SEE ALSO*

✎✐ 马, 馬, 傌, 骂, 騳, 騳, 騳

(250-hi)うま (hir.) (256-kat)ウマ (kat.)

(302-kn)*KANJI NOTES* ✎✐ It depicts a horse running to the reader's left. The horse's mane is blowing to the right. Can You recognize the horse Logogram in the ancient Chinese script on page 28?

#Uma-horse {馬}##

Script 13 - Uma-horse Shang Oracle Bone Script

Script 14 – Uma-horse Shuowen Jiezi Small Seal Script

(275-tō)う ま [ùmá ˙]

(313-ka)*KANJI* ✐ The Pictogrammatic [122] Radical (Radical 187) Uˈma-

horse (馬). (313k-cn)**Components** ⬒
No components (313k-ra)**Radical** ✛
馬 horse (313k-cs)**Composition** ✗ ⌐
三 | 灬 (313k-re)**Readings (examples)**
🎐 Go-on: め (me). Kan-on: ば (ba). Kan'yō-on: ま (ma). Kun: うま (uma, 馬); ま (ma, 馬).

512.Uˈra (裏)

(000-it)*INCLUDING TERMS (EXAMPLES)*

👁✉ tennokataura {{天の形裏}}, p. 242; uraken {{裏拳}}, p. 265

(077-jg)*GENERAL MEANING (EXAMPLES)* ☼📖 *adjective* ❶ Back

(185-ch)*CHINESE (PINYIN)* ☯📖 *Lǐ* (裡)

#Ura-back {裏}##

(139-an)*ANTONYMS* 👁↺ Omote-front {表}, p. 190

(211-1)裏 (250-hi)うら (hir.)

(275-tō)う ら [ùrá ˙]

(833-kan)**KANJI**

513.Uˈra-ken

(011-k1)*KANJI 1* ☛ Ura-back {裏}, p. 264

(012-k2)*KANJI 2* ☛ Ken-fist {拳}, p. 140

(040-ul) *UPPER LIMB STRIKE & ANATOMY*

手 **AKA** Urachen, Backfist, Back Fist, Back of the Fist **Category** Hand Anatomy

(089-no) *NOTES AND EXAMPLES* 📖✍

The impact area is the proximal side of MCP (metacarpophalangeal joints) II and III

(041-mu) *FUNAKOSHI MAIN BOOK – UPPER LIMB* 📖**MUL** 1935 **Suzuki-Johnston** 24 (list), 25 **1935 Ohshima** 17, 21 (list), 21.

#uraken {{裏拳}}##

Anatomy 7 - Uraken

(042-nu) *FUNAKOSHI NYUMON TERAMO-TO – UPPER LIMB* 📖**NUL** 48 (list), 55.

(185-ch) *CHINESE (PINYIN)* ☯📖 ***Lǐ quán***

(211-1) 裏拳

(250-hi) うらけん (hir.)

(466-cha) *CHARACTERISTICS* ⓘ A Two-character, which consists of 2 Chinese Logograms and 0 Hiʹraʹ-gaʹ-ʹna Characters.

(838-su) **SUPER-TERM**

514.Uʹshiro (Ato)

Uʹshiro (Ato) - Uʹshiro-geʹri

(001-REF-rom) Uʹshiro ☞ Ato-behind {後}, p. 41

(250-hi) うしろ (hir.)

(211-1) 後ろ

#Ushiro (Ato)##

(002-REF-hi) うしろ ☞ あと

(009-REF-kan) 後ろ ☞ 後

(275-tō) う し ろ [ùshíró]

515.Uʹshiro-geʹri

(011-k1) *KANJI 1* ☞ Ato-behind {後}, p. 41

(015-w1) *WORD 1* 🆆 ☞ keri {{蹴り}}, p. 140

(070-kt) *KARATE MEANING* 🖐📖 *noun*

① Back kick, turning back kick, rear kick, backwards kick.

(185-ch) *CHINESE (PINYIN)* ☯📖 ***Hòu cù***

(211-1) 後ろ蹴り

(212-2) 後ろ蹴

(213-3) 後蹴

(466-cha) *CHARACTERISTICS* ⓘ A Four-character, which consists of 2 Chinese Logograms and 2 Hiʹraʹ-gaʹ-ʹna Characters.

#ushirogeri {{後ろ蹴り}}##

(250-hi) うしろげり (hir.)

(482-kg)**K➲g** 🔔 Due to the 'Rendaku laws, the unvoiced consonant /K/ may get a Dak[u]-'ten (゛) and become ~/g/ as a suffix. Example Ke'ri (けり) turns into Ma'e-ge'ri (まえげり).

(493-g)**G** 🔔👂 Sometimes, /g/ may be pronounced differently than [g]. /g/ in the middle of a word, especially when pronounced by the older generation, may sound [ŋ]. Example Ma'e-ge'ri may be pronounced [Ma'e-ne'ri].

(800-tag)*TAGS* 💻 #ushirokeri

516. 'Utsu (打)

(000-it)*INCLUDING TERMS (EXAMPLES)*

👁✉ uchi {{打ち}}, p. 258

(077-jg)*GENERAL MEANING (EXAMPLES)* ☼📖 *verb* ❶ To hit, to strike, to beat.

(185-ch)*CHINESE (PINYIN)* ☯📖 ***dǎ*** *verb* ❶ To strike[123], to hit a blow[124], to knock, to pound, to beat ❷ To fight[125]

(705-gv)*GODAN VERB* 🏍⑤ **Terminal Form** {u* 💣 but not i*-ru or e*-ru} 'Utsu [ú✦tsù] (打つ), which means to hit. **Polite Form** {i*-masu} U'chimas[u] [ùchímá✦sù] (打ちます).

(211-1)打 (250-hi)うつ (hir.)

#Utsu-to hit {打}##

(275-tō)うつ [ú✦tsù]

(280-po)pol:UCY

(313-ka)*KANJI* 🖌 The Phono-semantic Compound Logogram 'Utsu-to hit (打). (313k-cn)**Components** [semantic 扌 | phonetic 丁]. (313k-ra)**Radical** 手 扌 龵 hand. (313k-cs)**Composition** ⚒ Left: 扌 (abbreviated form of 手), right: 丁. (313k-re)**Readings (examples)** 🗣 Go-on: ちょう (chō). Kan-on: てい (tei). Kun: うち (uchi, 打ち); うつ (utsu, 打つ); ぶつ (butsu, 打つ); ダース (dāsu, 打).

(830-ik)**IMPORTANT KANJI**

517. 'Wa (輪)

(000-it)*INCLUDING TERMS (EXAMPLES)*

👁✉ katawa {{片輪}}, p. 137; kubiwa {{首輪}}, p. 156; udewa {{腕輪}}, p. 261

(077-jg)*GENERAL MEANING (EXAMPLES)* ☼📖 *noun* ❶ Ring, circle, loop ❷ Wheel

(185-ch)*CHINESE (PINYIN)* 😊📖 *lún*

(211-1)輪 (211-al)*ALTERNATIVES OR SEE ALSO* ✏✏ 轮, 環

(250-hi)わ (hir.)

#Wa-ring {輪}##

(302-kn)*KANJI NOTES* ✏✍ Contains 15 strokes.

(313-ka)*KANJI* ✏ The Phono-semantic Compound Logogram ˈWa-ring (輪). (313k-cn)**Components** 🖧 [semantic 車 | phonetic 侖] (313k-ra)**Radical** ✦ 車 car (313k-cs)**Composition** ✗ Left: 車, right: 侖 (313k-re)**Readings (examples)** 🎋 Go-on: りん (rin). Kan-on: りん (rin). Kun: わ (wa, 輪).

(830-ik)**IMPORTANT KANJI**

518.ˈWan-shū (enpi)

(001-REF-rom)ˈWan-shū ☞ enpi {{燕飛}}, p. 63

(009-REF-kan)汪輯 ☞ 燕飛

(009-REF-kan)腕秀 ☞ 燕飛

#wanshū (enpi)##

(002-REF-hi)わんしゅう ☞ えんぴ

(256-kat)ワンシュー (kat.)

(800-tag)*TAGS* 💻 #wanshu, #wangshu, wang shu, wangshū, yun bi

519.Waˈza (技)

(000-it)*INCLUDING TERMS (EXAMPLES)* 👁✉ ashiwaza {{足技}}, p. 39; keriwaza {{蹴り技}}, p. 141; nagewaza {{投げ技}}, p. 175; wazaari {{技有り}}, p. 268

(077-jg)*GENERAL MEANING (EXAMPLES)* ☼📖 *noun* ❶ Technique, art, skill ❷ Trick ❸ Move.

(136-se)*SEE ALSO* 👁➕ Jutsu-art {術}, p. 116

(185-ch)*CHINESE (PINYIN)* 😊📖 *jì*

(211-1)技 (250-hi)わざ (hir.)

(830-ik)**IMPORTANT KANJI**

#Waza-technique {技}##

(275-tō)わ ざ [wàzá˩]

(313-ka)*KANJI* ✏ The Phono-semantic Compound Logogram Waˈza-technique (技). (313k-cn)**Components** 🖧 [semantic 扌 | phonetic 支]. (313k-ra)**Radical** ✦ 手 扌 龵 hand. (313k-cs)**Composition** ✗ Left: 扌 (abbreviated form of 手), right: 支. (313k-re)**Readings (examples)** 🎋 Go-on:

ぎ (gi). Kan-on: き (ki). Kun: わざ (waza).

(838-su)**SUPER-TERM**

520.Waˈza-aˈri

(011-k1)*KANJI 1* ☛ Waza-technique {技}, p. 267

(015-w1)*WORD 1* ^W_W ☛ ari {{有り}}, p. 34

(077-jg)*GENERAL MEANING (EXAMPLES)* ⚙📖 *noun* ❶ Wazaari, half-point, second highest score.

(134-re)*RELATED TERMS* ◉∞ ippon {{一本}}, p. 105

(185-ch)*CHINESE (PINYIN)* ◐📖 *Jì yǒu*

#wazaari {{技有り}}##

(211-1) 技有り

(212-2) 技あり

(250-hi) わざあり (hir.)

(275-tō) わざあり [wàzáárí]

(466-cha)*CHARACTERISTICS* ⓘ A Three-character, which consists of 2 Chinese Logograms and 1 Hiˈra-gaˈna Characters.

(800-tag)*TAGS* ⌨ #wazari

521.Yaˈma (山)

(000-it)*INCLUDING TERMS (EXAMPLES)* ◉✉ yamadachi {{山立ち}}, p. 269; yamazuki {{山突き}}, p. 270

(077-jg)*GENERAL MEANING (EXAMPLES)* ⚙📖 *noun* ❶ Mountain.

(089-no)*NOTES AND EXAMPLES* 📖✎ This is the same Yaˈma as in Admiral Yaˈma-moˈto (山本).

(185-ch)*CHINESE (PINYIN)* ◔📖 *shān*

(211-1) 山

(211-al)*ALTERNATIVES OR SEE ALSO* ✎✎ 屾, 峀

(302-kn)*KANJI NOTES* ✎✎ Contains 3 strokes. It depicts three mountain peaks.

#Yama-mountain {山}##

Script 15 – Yama-mountain Shang Oracle Bone Script

List of large photos - p. 10

(250-hi) やま (hir.) (256-kat) ヤマ (kat.)

(275-tō) や ま [yàmá⁺]

(313-ka)*KANJI* ✎ The Pictogrammatic Radical (Radical 46) Yaˈma-mountain (山). (313k-cn)**Components** 🖧 No components - a Simple Logogram (313k-ra)**Radical** ✦ 山 mountain (313k-cs)**Composition** ✗ 凵 丨

(313k-re)**Readings (examples)** 🗣 Go-on: せん (sen). Kan-on: さん (san). Kun: やま (yama, 山).

(830-ik)**IMPORTANT KANJI**

522.Yaˈma-daˈchi

Figure 5 – Yama-dachi (Ohshima 95)

(011-k1)*KANJI 1* ☞ Yama-mountain { 山}, p. 268

(015-w1)*WORD 1* W/W ☞ tachi {{立ち}}, p. 228

(070-kt)*KARATE MEANING* ✋📖 AKA Yama-gamae *noun* ① Mountain stance, mountain position, mountain posture, mountain Kamae.

(077-jg)*GENERAL MEANING (EXAMPLES)* ☼📖 *noun* ❶ Bandit ❷ Hunter.

(090-te)*TELL YOUR STUDENTS* 📖☺ Appears in Bassai-dai (movement 23) and in Jitte. Some do not consider the Bassai example as a Yama-dachi.

(089-no)*NOTES AND EXAMPLES* 📖✎ The Character Yaˈma-mountain (山), contains three vertical lines based on a horizontal line.

(185-ch)*CHINESE (PINYIN)* 💬📖 *Shān lì*

(211-1)山立ち

#yamadachi {{山立ち}}##

Script 16 –Yama-mountain Regular Script

Masters 26 - Yamadachi by Pavlović Sensei
List of Sensei Demonstrations next to Values, p. 10
List of large photos - p. 10

Maria Anette Pavlović of Sweden Kase-ha demonstrates Yama-dachi. Photographer: Denis Sopovic.

(212-2)山立

(250-hi)やまだち (hir.)

(466-cha)*CHARACTERISTICS* ⓘ A Three-character, which consists of 2 Chinese Logograms and 1 Hiˈra-gaˈna Characters.

(483-td)**T⊃d** 😀 Due to the ˈRen-daku laws, the unvoiced consonant /T/ may get a Dak[u]-ˈten (゛) and become ~/d/ as a suffix. Example ↳ ˈTachi (た ち) turns into Ki-ˈba Daˈchi (きばだち).

523.Yaˈma-zuˈki

(011-k1)*KANJI 1* ☛ Yama-mountain { 山}, p. 268

(015-w1)*WORD 1* ^W_W ☛ tsuki {{突き}}, p. 253

(070-kt)*KARATE MEANING* ✋📖 AKA Aˈwase Zuˈki (合せ突き), Morote-zuki *noun* ① Mountain thrust, U-punch, C-punch, overhand punch, overcut punch, double fist punch, narrow double fisted strike, double handed punch, double u punch, vertical Morote zuki.

(466-cha)*CHARACTERISTICS* ⓘ A Three-character, which consists of 2 Chinese Logograms and 1 Hiˈra-ga-ˈna Characters.

(185-ch)*CHINESE (PINYIN)* 🌐📖 ***Shān tū***

#yamazuki {{山突き}}##

Figure 6 - Yama-zuki Evolution

Funakoshi's Bassai-dai, right to left: 1922[126], 1925[127] and 1935[128] (flipped horizontally)

(090-te)*TELL YOUR STUDENTS* 📖☻ Which of the three versions looks most like Yama-mountain (山)?

QR Code 8 - Yamazuki, Awasezuki & Morotezuki
List of QR Codes (Video), p. 11

(211-1)山突き

(212-2)山突

(250-hi)やまとづき (hir.)

(800-tag)*TAGS* 💻 #yamatsuki, #morotezuki, #awasezuki

524.Yaˈme

List of large photos - p. 10

(018-imp)*IMPERATIVE FORM OF* ❗ ☛ Ya-mu-to stop {止}, p. 272

(019-ste)*STEM FORM OF* ❗ ☛ yameru {{止める}}, p. 271

(070-kt)*KARATE MEANING* ✋📖 *verb (imperative mood)* ① Stop! finish! ② Go back to Ready Stance! return to Yō-i Position!

See
List of Commands, p. 25

(139-an)*ANTONYMS* 👁↺ hajime {{始め}}, p. 81

(134-gr-re)*GROUP* 👁(⌒) The following terms are related: hajime {{始め}}, p. 81; kamae {{構え}}, p. 123; kamaete {{構えて}}, p. 125; naore {{直れ}}, p. 180; yame {{止め}},

p. 271; yasume {{休め}}, p. 274;

yōi {{用意}}, p. 277

#yame {{止め}}##

QR Code 9 – Yame, Yasume & Naore Lily (wJ7a_kGZ2GQ)
List of QR Codes (Video), p. 11

(211-1)止め

(250-hi)やめ (hir.)

(256-kat)ヤメ (kat.)

(275-tō)や め [yàmé]

(610-In-Tr)*VERB PAIR* 👁◑ The Intransitive Verb is Yamu-to stop {止}, p. 272. The Transitive verb is yameru {{止める}}, p. 271.

(466-cha)*CHARACTERISTICS* ① A Two-character, which consists of 1 Chinese Logograms and 1 Hi˙ra-ga-˙na Characters.

(885-tag)*TAGS* 🖥 #stop

(838-su)**SUPER-TERM**

525.Ya˙meru

(011-k1)*KANJI 1* ☛ Yamu-to stop {止}, p. 272

(077-jg)*GENERAL MEANING (EXAMPLES)* ⚙📖 *verb (transitive)* ❶ To stop.

(135-ge)*GERUND* 👁⏩ yame {{止め}}, p. 271

(610-In-Tr)*VERB PAIR* 👁◑ The Intransitive Verb is Yamu-to stop {止}, p. 272. The Transitive verb is yameru {{止める}}, p. 271.

(203-hi)⏳⊙

(250-hi)やめる (hir.)

(211-1)止める (212-2)廃める

(256-kat)ヤメル (kat.)

(275-tō)や める [yàmérú]

#yameru {{止める}}##

(600-vt)**Form**	**Shimo Ichidan Transitive (~eru)**
Terminal	yàmérú
Plain ~te Request	yàmété
Polite ~te Request	yàmété kuda˙sai
Plain Imperative	yàméró
Stem	ya˙me
Polite Imperative	ya˙me na˙sai
Formal	yàmémá⁺s[ù]

See

List of Commands, p. 25

(466-cha)*CHARACTERISTICS* ① A Three-character, which consists of 1 Chinese Logograms and 2 Hi˙ra-ga-˙na Characters.

(810-vpTr)**VERB PAIR – TRANSITIVE PART**

526.Ya˙mu (止)

(000-it)*INCLUDING TERMS (EXAMPLES)*

👁✉ yameru {{止める}}, p. 271; yame {{止め}}, p. 271.

(077-jg)*GENERAL MEANING (EXAMPLES)* ⚙📖 *verb (intransitive)* ❶ To stop.

(185-ch)*CHINESE (PINYIN)* 🌐📖 ***zhǐ***

(211-1)止

(211-ka+hi)止む

(211-var)𣥂 (bottom)

(212-2)罷む

(213-3)已む

(250-hi)やむ (hir.)

(256-kat)ヤム (kat.)

(275-tō)や[む] [yàmú]

(280-po)pol:JAMY

(610-In-Tr)*VERB PAIR* 👁◐ The Intransitive Verb is Yamu-to stop {止}, p. 272. The Transitive verb is yameru {{止める}}, p. 271.

(800-tag)*TAGS* 💻 #tomaru, #tomeru

(811-vpIn)**VERB PAIR – INTRANSITIVE PART**

(830-ik)**IMPORTANT KANJI**

#Yamu-to stop {止}##

(600-vt)**Form**   **Godan Intransitive**

~mu

Terminal	yàmú
Plain ~te Request	yàńdé
Polite ~te Request	yàńdé kudaˈsai
Plain Imperative	yàmé
Stem	yaˈmi
Polite Imperative	yaˈmi naˈsai
Formal	yàmímá⁺s[ù]

See
List of Commands, p. 25

(313-ka)*KANJI* ✒ The Pictogrammatic Radical (Radical 77) Yaˈmu-to stop (止). (313k-cn)**Components** 🔗 No components - a Simple Logogram. (313k-ra)**Radical** ⯌ 止 stop. (313k-cs)**Composition** 🗡 丨 卜 一 .

(313k-re)**Readings (examples)** ✊ とまる (tomaru, 止まる); とめる (tomeru, 止める); とどまる (todomaru, 止まる); とどめる (todomeru, 止める); やむ (yamu, 止む); やめる (yameru, 止める); よす (yosu, 止す).

527.Yaˈri (槍)

(000-it)*INCLUDING TERMS (EXAMPLES)*

👁✉ yaridama {{槍玉}}, p. 273

(077-jg)*GENERAL MEANING (EXAMPLES)* ✿📖 *noun* ❶ Spear, lance.

(185-ch)*CHINESE (PINYIN)* ☯📖 **qiāng**

(203-hi)⌛☉

#Yari-spear {槍}##

(250-hi)やり (hir.)

(211-1)槍 (211-al)*ALTERNATIVES OR SEE ALSO* 🖌🖊 鎗, 枪, 鑓

(275-tō) や|り [yàrí]

(833-kan)**KANJI**

528.Yaˈri-daˈma

(011-k1)*KANJI 1* ☛ Yari-spear {槍}, p. 273

(012-k2)*KANJI 2* ☛ Tama-ball {玉}, p. 231

(055-tt)*THROWING TECHNIQUE* 投技

AKA Yari-tama, Spearing a Ball, To Spear a Ball, Spearing Through.

(056-mt)*FUNAKOSHI MAIN BOOK - THROWING TECHNIQUES* 📚**MT̈**

1922 original 56 **1925 Ishida** 63 **1925 Teramoto** 53 (list), 55 **1935 Suzuki-Johnston** 198 **1935 Ohshima** 227 (list), 230-231

(077-jg)*GENERAL MEANING (EXAMPLES)* ✿📖 *noun* ❶ Victim, scapegoat, someone singled out

#yaridama {{槍玉}}##

(185-ch)*CHINESE (PINYIN)* ☯📖

Qiāngyù

(211-1)槍玉 (250-hi)やりだま (hir.)

(466-cha)*CHARACTERISTICS* ① A Two-character, which consists of 2 Chinese Logograms and 0 Hiˈra-ga-ˈna Characters.

(483-td)**T↻d** 🔔 Due to the ˈRen-daku laws, the unvoiced consonant /T/ may get a Dak[u]-ˈten (゛) and become ~/d/ as a suffix. Example ↲ ˈTachi (たち) turns into Ki-ˈba Daˈchi (きばだち).

(800-tag)*TAGS* 💻 #yaritama

529.yaˈsumaru

(011-k1)*KANJI 1* ☛ Yasumu-to rest {休}, p. 276

(077-jg)*GENERAL MEANING (EXAMPLES)* ✿📖 *verb (intransitive)* ❶ To be rested. ❷ To feel at ease.

(211-1)休まる

(212-2)安まる

(250-hi)やすまる (hir.)

(256-kat)ヤスマル (kat.)

(466-cha)*CHARACTERISTICS* ① A Three-character, which consists of 1

Chinese Logograms and 2 Hiˈra-ga-ˈna Characters.

(813-vpIn-2)**VERB PAIR – INTRANSITIVE PART 2**

#yasumaru {{休まる}}##

(600-vt)**Form**	**Godan Intransitive ~aru**
Terminal	yaˈsumaru
Plain ~te Request	yaˈsumatte
Polite ~te Request	yaˈsumatte kudaˈsai
Plain Imperative	yaˈsumare
Stem	yaˈsumari
Polite Imperative	yaˈsumari naˈsai
Formal	yasuˈmarimas[u]

See

List of Commands, p. 25

(611-1Tr2In)*VERB PAIRS (INTRANSITIVE x2)* 👁◖◗ The first Intransitive Verb is Yasumu-to rest {休}, p. 276. The second Intransitive Verb is yasumaru {{休まる}}, p. 274. The Transitive verb is yasumeru {{休める}}, p. 275.

530.Yaˈsume

(018-imp)*IMPERATIVE FORM OF* ! ☛ Yasumu-to rest {休}, p. 276

(019-ste)*STEM FORM OF* ! ☛ yasumeru {{休める}}, p. 275

(070-kt)*KARATE MEANING* ✋📖 AKA Yasumi (休み) *verb (imperative mood)* ① Rest!, relax! ② Recover to Natural Stance!, return to Natural Position!

See

List of Commands, p. 25

(077-jg)*GENERAL MEANING (EXAMPLES)* ☼📖 *verb (imperative mood)* ❶ At ease!, stand at ease!

(089-no)*NOTES AND EXAMPLES* 📖✎ O-ˈyasuminaˈsai (お休みなさい) means good night

(134-gr-re)*GROUP* 👁(◠‿◠) The following terms are related: hajime {{始め}}, p. 81; kamae {{構え}}, p. 123; kamaete {{構えて}}, p. 125; naore {{直れ}}, p. 180; yame {{止め}}, p. 271; yasume {{休め}}, p. 274; yōi {{用意}}, p. 277

#yasume {{休め}}##

QR Code 10 – Yame, Yasume & Naore Lily (wJ7a_kGZ2GQ)
List of QR Codes (Video), p. 11

(133-sy)*SYNONYMS* 👁= naore {{直れ}}, p. 180

(611-1Tr2In)*VERB PAIRS (INTRANSITIVE x2)* 👁◖◗ The first Intransitive Verb is Yasumu-to rest {休}, p.

276. The second Intransitive Verb is yasumaru {{休まる}}, p. 274. The Transitive verb is yasumeru {{休める}}, p. 275.

(211-1)休め

(250-hi)やすめ (hir.)

(256-kat)ヤスメ (kat.)

(280-po)pol:JASYME

(466-cha)*CHARACTERISTICS* ⓘ A Two-character, which consists of 1 Chinese Logograms and 1 Hiˈra-ga-ˈna Characters.

(800-tag)*TAGS* 💻 #yasme

(838-su)**SUPER-TERM**

531.yaˈsumeru

(011-k1)*KANJI 1* ☞ Yasumu-to rest {休}, p. 276

(077-jg)*GENERAL MEANING (EXAMPLES)* ✿ 📖 *verb (transitive)* ❶ To rest.

(135-ge)*GERUND* 👁 ▶▶ yasume {{休め}}, p. 274

(211-1)休める

(250-hi)やすめる (hir.)

(256-kat)ヤスメル (kat.)

(275-tō)や すめ る [yàsúmé⁺rù]

(466-cha)*CHARACTERISTICS* ⓘ A Three-character, which consists of 1 Chinese Logograms and 2 Hiˈra-ga-ˈna Characters.

(810-vpTr)**VERB PAIR – TRANSITIVE PART**

#yasumeru {{休める}}##

(600-vt)**Form**	**Shimo Ichidan Transitive (~eru)**
Terminal	yàsúmé⁺rù
Plain ~te Request	yàsú⁺mètè
Polite ~te Request	yàsú⁺mètè kudaˈsai
Plain Imperative	yàsúmé⁺rò
Stem	yaˈsume
Polite Imperative	yaˈsume naˈsai
Formal	yàsúmémá⁺s[ù]

See

List of Commands, p. 25

(611-1Tr2In)*VERB PAIRS (INTRANSITIVE x2)* 👁 ◀❙❙▶ The first Intransitive Verb is Yasumu-to rest {休}, p. 276. The second Intransitive Verb is yasumaru {{休まる}}, p. 274. The Transitive verb is yasumeru {{休める}}, p. 275.

532.Yaˈsumu (休)

(000-it)*INCLUDING TERMS (EXAMPLES)* 👁 ✉ yasumaru {{休まる}}, p. 274; yasume {{休め}}, p. 274; yasumeru {{休める}}, p. 275.

(077-jg)*GENERAL MEANING (EXAMPLES)* ✿📖 *verb (intransitive)* ❶ To rest, to have a break. ❷ To stop doing some ongoing activity for a time.

(090-te)*TELL YOUR STUDENTS* 📖☺ The Polite Imperative Form (Strong Request Form) Yasumi nasai (休みなさい) means good night.

(611-1Tr2In)*VERB PAIRS (INTRANSITIVE x2)* 👁◀❚❚▶ The first Intransitive Verb is Yasumu-to rest {休}, p. 276. The second Intransitive Verb is yasumaru {{休まる}}, p. 274. The Transitive verb is yasumeru {{休める}}, p. 275.

(185-ch)*CHINESE (PINYIN)* ☻📖 *xiū*

(211-1)休

(211-ka+hi)休む

(250-hi)やすむ (hir.)

(256-kat)ヤスム(kat.)

(275-tō)や[す]む [yàsúˑmù]

#Yasumu-to rest {休}##

(600-vt)**Form**	**Godan Intransitive ~mu**
Terminal	yaˈsumu
Plain ~te Request	yaˈsunde
Polite ~te Request	yaˈsunde kudaˈsai
Plain Imperative	yaˈsume
Stem	yaˈsumi
Polite Imperative	yaˈsumi naˈsai
Formal	yaˈsumimas[u]

See

List of Commands, p. 25

(302-kn)*KANJI NOTES* 🖌✎ It depicts a man (イ) leaning against a tree (木)[129]. 休 is a Radical-Radical Compound.

(313-ka)*KANJI* 🖌 The Compound Ideogram Yaˈsumu-to rest (休). (313k-cn)**Components** ⛓ [人 man | 木 tree] (313k-ra)**Radical** ✢ 人 man. (313k-cs)**Composition** ✖ Left: イ, right: 木.

(325-kr)*KANJI READINGS* 🖌🗣 Go-on: く (ku). Kan-on: きゅう (kyū). Kun: やすまる (yasumaru, 休まる); やすむ (yasumu, 休む); やすめる (yasumeru, 休める). Nanori: やすみ (yasumi).

(812-vpIn-1)**VERB PAIR – INTRANSITIVE PART 1**

(830-ik)**IMPORTANT KANJI**

533. ˈYo-dan

(000-it)*INCLUDING TERMS (EXAMPLES)*

◉✉ heianyodan {{平安四段}}, p. 94

(011-k1)*KANJI 1* ☛ Yon-four {四}, p. 280

(012-k2)*KANJI 2* ☛ Dan-level {段}, p. 56

(070-kt)*KARATE MEANING* ✋📖 *noun* ① Fourth Level ② Fourth dan, fourth degree black belt ③ Four.

(211-1)四段 (250-hi)よだん (hir.) #yodan {{四段}}##

(077-jg)*GENERAL MEANING (EXAMPLES)* ☼📖 *noun* ❶ Fourth grade, level four, fourth rank, fourth-degree.

(466-cha)*CHARACTERISTICS* ⓘ A Two-character, which consists of 2 Chinese Logograms and 0 Hiˈra-ga-ˈna Characters.

(800-tag)*TAGS* 💻 #yo-dan, yo dan, #yondan

(838-su)**SUPER-TERM**

534.ˈYō-i

See

List of Commands, p. 25: List of large photos - p. 10

💣※ Not to be confused with Yoi (良い).

(012-k2)*KANJI 2* ☛ I-meaning {意}, p. 102

(070-kt)*KARATE MEANING* ✋📖 AKA Yoi-dachi, Yoi-gamae (用意構え) *noun* ① Ready position [130], ready posture, preparatory position, Yoi position *verb (imperative mood) et al.* ② Ready! [131] Get ready!, prepare! attention! *adjective* ③ Ready [132], prepared, set

(089-no)*NOTES AND EXAMPLES* 📖✍ Arguably, each technique [133] and each Kata has its own Yō-i – its own ready position. But at some schools, the word Yō-i is mainly used for Heiko-dachi (p. 95) or Hachiji-dachi.

(800-tag)*TAGS* 💻 #yoi #yōi {{用意}}##

(077-jg)*GENERAL MEANING (EXAMPLES)* ☼📖 *noun* ❶ Preparation, getting ready, arrangements

(134-gr-re)*GROUP* ◉(👥 The following terms are related: hajime {{始め}}, p. 81; kamae {{構え}}, p. 123; kamaete {{構えて}}, p. 125; naore

{{直れ}}, p. 180; yame {{止め}},
p. 271; yasume {{休め}}, p. 274;
yōi {{用意}}, p. 277

(185-ch)*CHINESE (PINYIN)* 👁📖 **yòngyì**

(211-1)用意

(250-hi)**よう い** (hir.)

(275-tō) よ — い [yóˑòì]

(280-po)pol:JOOI

(466-cha)*CHARACTERISTICS* ⓘ A Two-
character, which consists of 2 Chinese Logograms and 0 HiꞋra-ga-Ꞌna
Characters.

(838-su)**SUPER-TERM**

535.YoꞋko (横)

(000-it)*INCLUDING TERMS (EXAMPLES)*

👁✉ yokogeri {{横蹴り}}, p. 279

(077-jg)*GENERAL MEANING (EXAM-
PLES)* ⚙📖 *adjective* ❶ Horizontal
❷ Side to side

(185-ch)*CHINESE (PINYIN)* 👁📖 **héng,
hèng, guāng, huáng, huàng**

(211-1)横

(212-2)横

(250-hi)**よ こ** (hir.)

(275-tō) よ こ [yòkó]

(830-ik)**IMPORTANT KANJI**

#Yoko-horizontal {横}##

(302-kn)*KANJI NOTES* ✎✍ Contains 15
strokes.

(313-ka)*KANJI* ✎ The Phono-semantic
Compound Logogram YoꞋko-
horizontal (横). (313k-cn)**Components**
🖧 [semantic 木 | phonetic 黄] (313k-
ra)**Radical** ✦ 木 tree (313k-
cs)**Composition** ✗ Left: 木, right:
黄 (313k-re)**Readings (examples)** 👄
Go-on: おう (ō). Kan-on: こう (kō).
Kun: よこ (yoko, 横).

(838-su)**SUPER-TERM**

536.YoꞋko-geꞋri

(000-it)*INCLUDING TERMS (EXAMPLES)*

👁✉ yokogerikeage {{横蹴り蹴上
げ}}, p. 279; yokogerikekomi {{横
蹴り蹴込み}}, p. 280

(011-k1)*KANJI* 𝟷 ☛ Yoko-horizontal {
横}, p. 278

(015-w1)*WORD 𝟷* ᵂ/ᵂ ☛ keri {{蹴り}}, p.
140

(070-kt)*KARATE MEANING* ✋📖 *noun*
① Side kick

(185-ch)*CHINESE (PINYIN)* 👁📖 **Héng
cù**

(211-1)横蹴り (212-2)横蹴

(466-cha)*CHARACTERISTICS* ⓘ A

Three-character, which consists of 2 Chinese Logograms and 1 Hiˈra-ga-ˈna Characters.

#yokogeri {{横蹴り}}##

(250-hi)よこげり (hir.)

(482-kg)**Kↄg** 🔔 Due to the ˈRen-daku laws, the unvoiced consonant /K/ may get a Dak[u]-ˈten (゙) and become ~/g/ as a suffix. Example ↳ Keˈri (けり) turns into Maˈe-geˈri (まえげり).

(493-g)**G** 🔔🖋 Sometimes, /g/ may be pronounced differently than [g]. /g/ in the middle of a word, especially when pronounced by the older generation, may sound [ŋ]. Example ↳ Maˈe-geˈri may be pronounced [Maˈe-neˈri].

(800-tag)*TAGS* 🖥 #yokokeri, yoko-geri, yoko geri, yoko keri

(838-su)**SUPER-TERM**

537.Yoˈko-geˈri ˈKe-age

(015-w1)*WORD 1* ᵂ⁄W ☞ yokogeri {{横蹴り}}, p. 279

(016-w2)*WORD 2* ᵂ⁄W ☞ keage {{蹴上げ}}, p. 139

(070-kt)*KARATE MEANING* ✋📖 AKA

Yoˈko-keˈˈage (横蹴上げ) *noun phrase* ① Side snap kick, quick snapping side kick, side flick kick, side rising kick, side up kick

(185-ch)*CHINESE (PINYIN)* 🌐📖 *Héng cù cù shàng*

(211-1)横蹴り蹴上げ

(212-2)横蹴蹴上

(250-hi)よこげりけあげ (hir.)

#yokogerikeage {{横蹴り蹴上げ}}##

(090-te)*TELL YOUR STUDENTS* 📖☺ In this term, the Kanji ˈKeru (蹴) (page 142) appears twice.

(466-cha)*CHARACTERISTICS* ⓘ A Six-character, which consists of 4 Chinese Logograms and 2 Hiˈra-ga-ˈna Characters.

(482-kg)**Kↄg** 🔔 Due to the ˈRen-daku laws, the unvoiced consonant /K/ may get a Dak[u]-ˈten (゙) and become ~/g/ as a suffix. Example ↳ Keˈri (けり) turns into Maˈe-geˈri (まえげり).

(838-su)**SUPER-TERM**

538.Yoˈko-geˈri ˈKe-komi

(015-w1)*WORD 1* ᵂ⁄ᵂ ☞ yokogeri {{横蹴り}}, p. 279

(016-w2)*WORD 2* ᵂ⁄ᵂ ☞ kekomi {{蹴込み}}, p. 140

(070-kt)*KARATE MEANING* ✋ 📖 AKA Yoˈko ˈKe-komi (横蹴込み) *noun phrase* ① Side thrust kick, horizontal kick, side direct kick, foot-blade kick

(089-no)*NOTES AND EXAMPLES* 📖✎ 込 is a Japanese-coined character.

(090-te)*TELL YOUR STUDENTS* 📖☺ In this term, the Kanji ˈKeru (蹴) (page 142) appears twice.
#yokogerikekomi {{横蹴り蹴込み}}##

(211-1)横蹴り蹴込み (212-2)横蹴蹴込 (250-hi)よこげりけこみ (hir.)

(466-cha)*CHARACTERISTICS* ① A Six-character, which consists of 4 Chinese Logograms and 2 Hiˈra-ga-ˈna Characters.

(482-kg)**K⊃g** ⌂ Due to the ˈRen-daku laws, the unvoiced consonant /K/ may get a Dak[u]-ˈten (゛) and become ~/g/ as a suffix. Example ↳

Keˈri (けり) turns into Maˈe-geˈri (まえげり).

(838-su)**SUPER-TERM**

539. ˈYon (四)

(000-it)*INCLUDING TERMS (EXAMPLES)* 👁✉ yodan {{四段}}, p. 277; shi-kodachi {{四股立ち}}, p. 209.

(077-jg)*GENERAL MEANING (EXAMPLES)* ✿📖 *noun* ❶ Four

(185-ch)*CHINESE (PINYIN)* ☯📖 *sì*

(211-1)四 (211-al)*ALTERNATIVES OR SEE ALSO* ✐✐ 肆 (250-hi)よん (hir.)

(800-tag)*TAGS* 💻 #4

(833-kan)**KANJI**

#Yon-four {四}##

(089-no)*NOTES AND EXAMPLES* 📖✎ In both Chinese and Japanese, *sì* and ˈShi (respectively) also mean death (死). Many times, people refrain from using the ˈShi On-reading.

(325-kr)*KANJI READINGS* ✐🗣 Go-on: し (shi). Kan-on: し (shi). Kun: よ (yo, 四); よん (yon, 四).

(838-su)**SUPER-TERM**

540. ˈYon-dan (yodan)

(001-REF-rom) ˈYon-dan ☞ yodan {{四段}}, p. 277

#yondan (yodan)##

(002-REF-hi)よんだん ☞ よだん

541.Yoˈri

(000-it)*INCLUDING TERMS (EXAMPLES)*

👁✉ yoriashi {{寄り足}}, p. 281

(011-k1)*KANJI 1* ☛ Yoru-to approach {寄}, p. 281

(077-jg)*GENERAL MEANING (EXAMPLES)* ✿📖 *noun, suffix* ❶ Leaning towards, tending towards ❷ Proximity, nearness, being close.

#yori {{寄り}}##

(211-1)寄り (250-hi)より (hir.)

(275-tō)より [yòrí]

(466-cha)*CHARACTERISTICS* ⓘ A Two-character, which consists of 1 Chinese Logograms and 1 Hiˈra-ga-ˈna Characters.

(885-tag)*TAGS* 🖳 #iori, #yore

542.Yoˈri Aˈshi

(015-w1)*WORD 1* ᵂ/ᵂ ☛ yori {{寄り}}, p. 281

(012-k2)*KANJI 2* ☛ Ashi-foot {足}, p. 37

(070-kt)*KARATE MEANING* ✋📖 AKA Suˈri-aˈshi (摺足) *noun phrase* ① Sliding step, simultaneous sliding, slide stepping, sending foot slide, sliding feet, dragging step, dragged step, gliding footwork.

#yoriashi {{寄り足}}##

(185-ch)*CHINESE (PINYIN)* 💬📖 *Jì zú*

(211-1)寄り足 (250-hi)よりあし (hir.)

(466-cha)*CHARACTERISTICS* ⓘ A Three-character, which consists of 2 Chinese Logograms and 1 Hiˈra-ga-ˈna Characters.

(800-tag)*TAGS* 🖳 #yoreashi, yore-ashi, #suriashi, suri-ashi

543.Yoˈru (寄)

(000-it)*INCLUDING TERMS (EXAMPLES)*

👁✉ yori {{寄り}}, p. 281

(077-jg)*GENERAL MEANING (EXAMPLES)* ✿📖 *verb (intransitive)* ❶ To draw near, to get near, to come close, to approach.

(185-ch)*CHINESE (PINYIN)* 💬📖 *jì*

(203-hi)⌛☉

#Yoru-to approach {寄}##

(250-hi)よる (hir.)

(211-1)寄

(211-ka+hi)寄る

(325-kr)*KANJI READINGS* ✒🎋 Go-on: き (ki). Kan-on: き (ki). Kun: よる (yoru, 寄る).

(833-kan)**KANJI**

544. ˈYū (有)

(000-it)*INCLUDING TERMS (EXAMPLES)*

👁✉ ari {{有り}}, p. 34; arigato {{有難う}}, p. 35; cho-sakukenshoyū {{著作權所有}}, p. 53; dōmoarigatō {{どうも有難う}}, p. 59

(077-jg)*GENERAL MEANING (EXAMPLES)* ✿📖 *noun* ❶ Existence ❷ Possession, having.

(705.1-ir)*IRREGULAR GODAN VERB* 🏍⑤☠ **Terminal Form** {u* 💣 but not i*-ru or e*-ru} ˈAru [áˉrù] (ある), which means to exist. **Polite Form** {i*-masu} Aˈrimas[u] [àrí-máˉsù] (あります).

(731-vn)*VERB NOTES* 🏍✍ The existential verb ˈAri is the Classical Japanese form of ˈAru [áˉrù] (ある)[134]. #Yū-existence {有}##

(211-1)有

(250-hi)ゆう (hir.)

(275-tō)ゆ|う [yúˉù]

(313-ka)*KANJI* ✎ The Phono-semantic Compound Pictogram ˈYū-existence

(有). (313k-cn)**Components** 🗂 [又 | 月 (abbreviated form of 肉, not to be confused with 月)]. (313k-cs)**Composition** ✖ Top: ナ, bottom: 月. (313k-re)**Readings (examples)** 🗣 Go-on: う (u). Kan-on: ゆう (yū). Kun: ある (aru); あり (ari). Nanori: あ (a); あら (ara); あり (ari); ある (aru).

(800-tag)*TAGS* 💻 #yu, #yuu

(830-ik)**IMPORTANT KANJI**

545. Yuˈbi (指)

(000-it)*INCLUDING TERMS (EXAMPLES)*

👁✉ ashiyubi {{足指}}, p. 39

(077-jg)*GENERAL MEANING (EXAMPLES)* ✿📖 *noun* ❶ Finger, toe, digit

(089-no)*NOTES AND EXAMPLES* 📖✍ Yuˈbi-ˈwa [yùbíwá] (指輪), for instance, is a finger ring.

(185-ch)*CHINESE (PINYIN)* ☯📖 *zhǐ*

(211-1)指 (250-hi)ゆび (hir.)

(275-tō)ゆ|び [yùbíˉ]

#Yubi-finger {指}##

(313-ka)*KANJI* ✎ The Phono-semantic Compound Logogram Yuˈbi-finger

(指). (313k-cn)**Components** ⛬ [semantic 手 | phonetic 旨]. (313k-ra)**Radical** ✦ 手扌⺘ hand. (313k-cs)**Composition** ⚔ Left: 扌 (abbreviated form of 手), right: 旨. (313k-re)**Readings (examples)** 🗣 Go-on: し (shi). Kan-on: し (shi). Kun: ゆび (yubi).

546. ˈZa (座)

(000-it)*INCLUDING TERMS (EXAMPLES)*

👁️✉️ arigatogozaimashita {{有難う御座いました}}, p. 36; seiza {{正座}}, p. 207; zazen {{座禅}}, p. 283

(077-jg)*GENERAL MEANING (EXAMPLES)* ✲📖 *noun* ❶ Seat ❷ Position ❸ Status ❹ Place

(089-no)*NOTES AND EXAMPLES* 📖✍️

Go-zaimas[u] (御座います) means to be, to exist.

#Za-seat {座}##

(185-ch)*CHINESE (PINYIN)* ☯️📖 *zuò*

(211-1)座

(211-al)*ALTERNATIVES OR SEE ALSO*

✍️✍️ 坐

(250-hi)ざ (hir.)

(325-kr)*KANJI READINGS* ✒️🗣 Go-on: ざ (za). Kan-on: さ (sa). Kun: すわる (suwaru, 座る).

(833-kan)**KANJI**

547. Za-ˈzen

(011-k1)*KANJI 1* ☞ Za-seat {座}, p. 283

(012-k2)*KANJI 2* ☞ Zen-dhyāna {禅}, p. 284

(077-jg)*GENERAL MEANING (EXAMPLES)* ✲📖 *noun* ❶ Seated meditation, sitting meditation in Zen Buddhism, Zen meditation.

(134-gr-re)*GROUP* 👁️(🗣) The following terms are related: iai {{居合}}, p. 103, mokusō {{黙想}}, p. 171, seiza {{正座}}, p. 207, zazen {{座禅}}, p. 283

#zazen {{座禅}}##

(185-ch)*CHINESE (PINYIN)* ☯️📖

Zuòchán

(211-1)座禅

(212-2)座禪 (213-3)坐禅

(250-hi)ざぜん (hir.)

(275-tō)ざ⟨ぜん⟩ [zàzéń]

(276-tō2)ざ⟨ぜん⟩ [zàzé⁺ǹ]

(466-cha)*CHARACTERISTICS* ⓘ A Two-character, which consists of 2 Chinese Logograms and 0 Hiˈra-ga-ˈna Characters.

548. ˈZen (Mae)

(001-REF-rom)ˈZen ☞ Mae-front {前}, p. 160

#Zen (Mae)##

(002-REF-hi)ぜん ☞ まえ

549. ˈZen (禅)

(000-it)*INCLUDING TERMS (EXAMPLES)* 👁✉ zazen {{座禅}}, p. 283

(077-jg)*GENERAL MEANING (EXAMPLES)* ⚙📖 *noun* ❶ Profound meditation, Dhyāna (ध्यान) ❷ Zen, *Chánzōng*, school of Mahāyāna Buddhism.

#Zen-dhyāna {禅}##

(185-ch)*CHINESE (PINYIN)* 👁📖 *chán*

(203-hi)⌛☉

(250-hi)ぜん (hir.)

(211-1)禅

(212-2)禪

(833-kan)**KANJI**

550. ˈZen-kutsu

(000-it)*INCLUDING TERMS (EXAMPLES)* 👁✉ zenkutsudachi {{前屈立ち}}, p. 285

(011-k1)*KANJI 1* ☞ Mae-front {前}, p. 160

(012-k2)*KANJI 2* ☞ Kagamu-to stoop {屈}, p. 120

(070-kt)*KARATE MEANING* ✋📖 *noun* ① ˈZen-kutsu-ˈdachi (前屈立ち)

(077-jg)*GENERAL MEANING (EXAMPLES)* ⚙📖 *noun, verb* ❶ Anteflexion, forward bend, bending forward.

#zenkutsu {{前屈}}##

(139-an)*ANTONYMS* 👁↻ kōkutsu {{後屈}}, p. 150

(185-ch)*CHINESE (PINYIN)* 👁📖 *Qián qū*

(211-1)前屈

(250-hi)ぜんくつ (hir.)

(280-po)pol:DZENKYCY

(466-cha)*CHARACTERISTICS* ⓘ A Two-character, which consists of 2 Chinese Logograms and 0 Hiˈra-ga-ˈna Characters.

(838-su)**SUPER-TERM**

551. ˈZen-kutsu-ˈdachi

(015-w1)*WORD 1* ☝Ｗ ☞ zenkutsu {{前屈}}, p. 284

(016-w2)*WORD 2* Ｗ ☞ tachi {{立ち}}, p. 228

(030-st)*STANCE* 立 **AKA** ˈZen-kutsu, ˈZen-kutsu ˈShi-se[i] （前屈姿勢）, ˈZen-kutsu Shitsu （前屈膝）, Zenkutsu Stance, Front stance, Forward Stance, Front Long Stance, Long Frontal Stance, Forward-bending, Front-leg-bent Stance, Front Knee Bent Stance, Front Knee Flexion Stance, Front Bending **Category** Low frontal stances.

(139-an)*ANTONYMS* ☉↻ kōkutsudachi {{後屈立ち}}, p. 150

(211-1)前屈立ち

(212-2)前屈立

(466-cha)*CHARACTERISTICS* ① A Four-character, which consists of 3 Chinese Logograms and 1 Hiˈra-ga-ˈna Characters.

#zenkutsudachi {{前屈立ち}}##

(031-ms)*FUNAKOSHI MAIN BOOK - STANCES* ⛩**MS** 1922 original 30 (list), 32 （前屈姿勢） **1925 Ishida** 41 (list), 43 **1925 Teramoto** 40 (list), 41 **1935 Suzuki-Johnston** 22 (list), 22 **1935 Ohshima** 19 (list), 20 End of values

(032-ns)*FUNAKOSHI NYUMON TERAMOTO - STANCES* ⛩**NS** 59 (list), 59-60

(185-ch)*CHINESE (PINYIN)* ☯📖 **Qián qū lì**

(190-kf)*KUNG FU TERMINOLOGY* ☯⚲ *Gōng bù* （弓步）

(250-hi)ぜんくつだち (hir.)

(483-td)**T⊃d** ⌂ Due to the ˈRen-daku laws, the unvoiced consonant /T/ may get a Dak[u]-ˈten (゛) and become ~/d/ as a suffix. Example ↰ ˈTachi （たち） turns into Ki-ˈba Daˈchi （きばだち）.

(800-tag)*TAGS* 💻 #zenkutsutachi

(838-su)**SUPER-TERM**

552.Zuˈki (tsuki)

(001-REF-rom)tsuki {{突き}}, p. 253 #zuki (tsuki)##

(002-REF-hi)づき ☞ つき

553.Zuˈki (Tsuki)

(001-REF-rom)Zuˈki ☞ Tsuki-moon {月}, p. 253 #Zuki (Tsuki)##

(002-REF-hi)づき ☞ つき

(800-tag)*TAGS* 💻 #zki 1

Glossary of Linguistic Terms

💣 The following glossary includes some of the linguistic terms we use in this dictionary. Note that other sources may interpret them differently!

Examples of our own terminology:

✂ Potential Radical *(p. 292)*

✂ Off-duty Radical *(p. 292)*

✂ Real Radical *(p. 293)*

✂ On-duty Radical *(p. 293)*

#*Character* 📖 A written Character is the smallest unit of a writing system[135]. Hence, concerning the Characters that appear in this dictionary, Hi'ra-ga-'na (p. 99) and Ka'ta-ka-'na (p. 136) syllabary are Characters too - and not only Chinese Logograms *(p. 286)*. However, in many relevant sources, Character means specifically a Chinese Logogram *(p. 286)*. **Example** 🔩 ageuke {{上げ受け}} (p. 30), which consists of 2 Chinese Logograms *(p. 286)* and 2 Hi'ra-ga-'na (p. 99) characters. **See** 👁 *Logogram (p. 290)*.

#*Chinese Character* (Ch. *hànzì*, Jp. 'Kan-ji)] 📖 A Chinese Logogram *(p. 286)*[136]. **Synonyms in this dictionary =**✂ Kanji (p. 127), *Logogram (p. 290)*, Logograph, *Chinese Character (p. 286)*, *Chinese Logogram (p. 286),* Chinese Logograph

#*Chinese Logogram* 📖 Logograms *(p. 290)* that were developed for the Chinese writing. They are usually[137] square-shaped[138]. Thousands of Chinese Logograms are used in the Japanese writing system. **Examples** 🔩 ❶ Kata-shape {形} (p. 134) – Kata (form). ❷ Kata-shoulder {肩} (p. 135) - shoulder. **Synonyms in this dictionary =**✂ Kanji (p. 127), *Logogram (p. 290)*, Logograph, *Chinese Character (p. 286)*, *Chinese Logogram (p. 286),* Chinese Logograph

#Chinese Logograph ☞ *Chinese Logogram (p. 286)*

#*Component* (部件) [AKA Constituent, Unit, Character Component, Element] 📖 A Chinese Logogram *(p. 286)* that is part of a Compound Logogram *(p. 287)*. ✂ In many sources, the term Component serves to describe a Structural Component[139].

#*Compound* ☞ *Compound Logogram* *(p. 287)*

#**Compound Character** ☞ *Compound Logogram* *(p. 287)*

#*Compound Ideogram* (会意字) [AKA Associative Compound, Combined Ideogram, Combined Pictorgram, Compound Ideogram, Compound Pictogram, Compound Pictograph, Etymonic Compound, Form Compound, Iconic Compound, Ideogrammatic Compound, Ideogrammic Compound, Logical Aggregates, Logical Aggregates, Pictogrammatic Compound, Pictogrammic Compound] 📖 A *Compound Logogram* *(p. 287)* that represents an idea. **Antonyms or coordinate terms** ↻**/-** *Simple Ideogram* *(p. 294)*

#**Compound Ideograph** ☞ *Compound Ideogram* *(p. 287)*

#*Compound Logogram* (合体字) [AKA Compound, Compound Character, Composite Character, Complex Character, Multi-component Character] 📖 A Chinese Logogram *(p. 286)* that consists of two Components *(p. 287)* or more – usually a Semantic Component (indicating a meaning) and a Phonetic Component (indicating a pronunciation). **Example** ↳ Ki-riding {騎} (p.143) – riding on horseback, which includes Semantic Component 馬 and Phonetic Component 奇. **Antonyms or coordinate terms** ↻**/-** *Simple Logogram (p. 294)*. **See** 👁 ❶ *Radical 3 –* ✂ *On-duty Radical (p. 293)* ❷ *Stem (p. 295)*.

#**Compound Logograph** ☞ *Compound Logogram* *(p. 287)*

#**Compound Pictogram** ☞ *Compound Ideogram* *(p. 287)*

#Compound Pictograph ☞ *Compound Ideogram (p. 287)*

#*Compound Word* [AKA Compound, Multi-logogram, Poly-logogram, Multi-kanji, Combination of Kanji] 📖 To put it simply, a Compound Word is made up of two or more words. In our case – of two or more Chinese Logograms *(p. 286).* **Synonyms = *Multi-logogram** (p. 291).*

#Five-character A word or a phrase containing five Characters *(p. 286).* In this dictionary ✄ These can be Chinese Logograms *(p. 286),* Hiˈra-ga-ˈna (p. 99) Characters and Kaˈta-ka-ˈna *(p. 136)* Characters. **Example** ↳ gyakumawashi-geri {{逆回し蹴り}} (p. 74), which consists of 3 Chinese Logograms *(p. 286)* and 2 Hiˈra-ga-ˈna (p. 99) characters.

#Five-kanji ☞ *Five-logogram (p. 288)*

#*Five-logogram* 📖 A word or a phrase containing Five Chinese Logograms *(p. 286),* and possibly additional Ka-ˈna (p. 126) as well. **Example** ↳ naka-dakaipponken {{中高一本拳}} (p. 179) , which consists of 5 Chinese Logograms *(p. 286)* and 0 Hiˈra-ga-ˈna (p. 99) characters.

#Four-character 📖 A word or a phrase containing four Characters *(p. 286).* In this dictionary ✄ These can be Chinese Logograms *(p. 286),* Hiˈra-ga-ˈna (p. 99) Characters and Kaˈta-ka-ˈna *(p. 136)* Characters. **Example** ↳ ageuke {{上げ受け}} (p. 30), which consists of 2 Chinese Logograms *(p. 286)* and 2 Hiˈra-ga-ˈna (p. 99) characters.

#Four-kanji ☞ *Four-logogram (p. 288)*

#*Four-logogram* 📖 A word or a phrase containing four Chinese Logograms *(p. 286),* and possibly additional Ka-ˈna (p. 126) as well. **Example** ↳ The Six-character yokogerikeage {{横蹴り蹴上げ}} (p. 279), which consists of 4 Chinese Logograms *(p. 286)* and 2 Hiˈra-ga-ˈna (p. 99) characters.

#*Godan Verb* (ˈGo-dan Verb) **(五段活用)** [AKA U-verb, U-dropping Conjugation, Group 1, V1 Verb, Five-form Verb, 5-row Verb, v5r, Qadri-grade] 📖 A verbal conjugation class. Most of the verbs that do NOT end in i*-ru or e*-ru. **Antonyms or coordinate terms** ↻/- **#*Ichidan Verb*** *(p. 289)*

#*Hiragana* (Hiˈra-ga-ˈna) ☞ hiragana {{平仮名}}, p. 99

#*Ichidan Verb* (Iˈchi-dan Verb) **(一段活用)** [AKA Ru-verb, Ru-dropping Conjugation, Group 2, V2, One-form Verb, One-row Verb, v1r, Unigrade] 📖 Most of the verbs that end in i*-ru or e*-ru. **Antonyms or coordinate terms** ↻/- *Godan Verb (p. 289).* **See** 👁 *Kami Ichidan Verb (p. 290), Shimo Ichidan Verb (p. 294).*

#*Ideogram* (指事) [AKA Associative Character, Iconic Character, Form Character, Indicative[140]] 📖 A Logogram *(p. 290)* that represents an idea. **Example** ↳ Ue-top {上} (p. 262). **Antonyms or coordinate terms** ↻/- *Pictogram (p. 292).*

#*Ideogrammatic* [AKA Ideogrammic] ☞ *Ideogram (p. 289)*

#*Ideogrammatic Compound* ☞ *Ideogrammatic Compound (p. 289)*

#*Ideogrammic* ☞ *Ideogram (p. 289)*

#*Ideogrammic Compound* ☞ *Ideogrammatic Compound (p. 289)*

#*Ideograph* ☞ *Ideogram (p. 289)*

#*Indexing Component* [AKA Radical, Lexical Component, Lexicographic[141] Component] The Component *(p. 287)* under which the Compound Logogram *(p. 287)* is listed in a traditional dictionary[142]. **Synonyms = *Radical 3* – ✂ *On-duty Radical (p. 293).* **See** 👁 *Kangxi (p. 290).*

#***Kami Ichidan Verb*** i (Kaˈmi-ˈichi-dan Verb) (上一段活用) [AKA Upper 1-row, Group 2a, Unigrade i] 📖 A verbal conjugation class. Upper monograde conjugation. Most of the verbs that end in i*-ru. **Antonyms or co-ordinate terms** ↻/-*Shimo Ichidan Verb (p. 294)*. **See** 👁 ❶ ***Ichidan Verb** (p. 289)* ❷ Ue-top {上} (p. 262)

#**Kana** (Ka-ˈna) ☞ kana {{仮名}} (p. 126)

#***Kangxi*** 📖 The Chinese *Kāngxī* Dictionary from the 18th century (*Kāngxī zìdiǎn*), containing 214 Potential Radicals *(p. 292)* ordered by stroke count (*Kāngxī bùshǒu*) **See** 👁 ❶ ***Radical 1 - Generally** (p. 292)* ❷ ***Compound Logogram** (p. 287)* ❸ ***Component** (p. 287)* ❹ ***Indexing Component** (p. 289)*

#**Kanji** ☞ kanji {{漢字}}, p. 127. **Synonyms in this Dictionary** =✂ Kanji (p. 127), ***Logogram** (p. 290)*, Logograph, ***Chinese Character** (p. 286)*, ***Chinese Logogram** (p. 286)*, Chinese Logograph

#**Katakana** (Kaˈta-ka-ˈna) ☞ katakana {{片仮名}}, p. 136

#**Lexical Component** ☞ ***Indexing Component** (p. 289)*

#***Logogram*** [AKA Logograph, Lexigraph, Grapheme] 📖 A Character *(p. 286)* symbolizing the meaning of a Morpheme *(p. 290)* or a word. The difference between a word and a Morpheme is, that a word necessarily can stand alone[143], and a Morpheme is not always independent[144] - it may be bound. In this dictionary ✂ Logogram means specifically a Chinese Logogram *(p. 286)*. **Synonyms in this Dictionary** =✂ Kanji (p. 127), ***Logogram** (p. 290)*, Logograph, ***Chinese Character** (p. 286)*, ***Chinese Logogram** (p. 286),* Chinese Logograph

#**Logograph** ☞ ***Logogram** (p. 290)*

#***Morpheme*** 📖 The smallest linguistic unit that has a meaning. It cannot be divided without losing its specific meaning.

#Multi-character [AKA Poly-character] 📖 A word or a phrase containing several Characters *(p. 286)*. In this dictionary ✂ These can be Chinese Logograms *(p. 286)*, Hi'ra-ga-'na (p. 99) Characters and Ka'ta-ka-'na *(p. 136)* Characters. **Example** ↳ ageuke {{上げ受け}} (p. 30), which consists of 2 Chinese Logograms *(p. 286)* and 2 Hi'ra-ga-'na (p. 99) characters.

#Multi-kanji ☞ *Multi-logogram (p. 291)*

#Multi-logogram [AKA Multi-kanji, Poly-kanji, Poly-logogram, Poly-logograph] 📖 In this dictionary ✂ A word or a phrase containing several Chinese Logograms *(p. 286)*, and possibly additional Ka-'na (p. 126) as well. **Example** ↳ yokogerikeage {{横蹴り蹴上げ}} (p. 279), which consists of 4 Chinese Logograms *(p. 286)* and 2 Hi'ra-ga-'na (p. 99) characters. **Synonyms =** *Compound Word (p. 288)*

#Multi-logograph ☞ *Multi-logogram (p. 291)*

#Off-duty Radical ✂ ☞ *Radical 2 –* ✂ *Off-duty Radical (p. 292)*

#On-duty Radical ✂ ☞ *Radical 3 –* ✂ *On-duty Radical (p. 293)*

#One-character [AKA Single-character] 📖 A word or a phrase containing one Character *(p. 286)*. In this dictionary ✂ It can be Chinese Logogram *(p. 286)*, Hi'ra-ga-'na (p. 99) Character or Ka'ta-ka-'na *(p. 136)* Character. **Example** ↳ Ukeru-to receive {受} (p. 263)

#One-logogram [AKA Single-logogram] 📖 A word or a phrase containing one Chinese Logogram *(p. 286)*, and possibly additional Ka-'na (p. 126) as well. **Example** ↳ mawashi {{回し}}, p. 166, which consists of 1 Chinese Logograms *(p. 286)* and 1 Hi'ra-ga-'na (p. 99) Characters.

#Phono-semantic Compound (形聲) [AKA Signific-phonetic Compound, Phonetic Compound, Phonetic-semantic Compound, Radical-phonetic

Compound] 📖 The most common type of Chinese Logogram *(p. 286)*. Includes a Semantic Component *(p. 287)* and a Phonetic Component.

#*Pictogram* (象形) [AKA Pictograph, Pictogramme, Picto, Associative Character, Iconic Character, Form Character] 📖 A Logogram *(p. 290)* that represents a physical object. **Example** ⅄ Ashi-foot {足}, p. 37. **Antonyms or coordinate terms** ↻/- *Ideogram (p. 289)*.

#Pictogrammatic ☞ ***Pictogram** (p. 292)*

#Pictogrammatic Compound ☞ ***Compound Ideogram** (p. 287)*

#Pictogrammic ☞ ***Pictogram** (p. 292)*

#Pictograph ☞ ***Pictogram** (p. 292)*

#*Potential Radical* ✄ ☞ ***Radical 2 – ✄ Off-duty Radical** (p. 292)*

#*Radical 1 - Generally* (部首) [AKA Indexing Component, Indexing Chinese Character Component, Lexical Component, The Radical of a Compound, Classifier, Key, Significs] 📖 A Chinese Logogram *(p. 286)* that either serves (✄On-duty Radical *(p. 293)*) or can serve (✄Off-duty Radical *(p. 292)*) as an Indexing Component *(p. 289)* in a Compound Logogram *(p. 287)*. According to the Traditional Radical System *(p. 290)*, there are 214 Radicals. A Radical can be also a Compound Logogram *(p. 287)*[145] - e.g. Ao-blue {青} (p. 34). Some Radicals are structurally complicated Chinese Logograms *(p. 286)*, and contain up to seventeen (!) Strokes *(p. 295)* – e.g. Uma-horse {馬} (p. 264). By the way, in Japan Radical Horse (馬) is taught in second grade. **See** 👁 ***Compound Logogram** (p. 287),* ***Component** (p. 287),* ***Indexing Component** (p. 289),* ***Kangxi** (p. 290).*

#*Radical 2 – ✄ Off-duty Radical* (✄ Potential Radical) [AKA Radical] 📖 A "Radical" outside a Compound Logogram *(p. 287)* (Free Radical), or a "Radical" in a Compound Logogram that does not serve as a its Indexing Component *(p. 289).* In other words, an Off-duty Radical - or a Potential Radical - is a Chinese Logogram *(p. 286)* that can potentially serve as a Radical in a Compound Logogram. Let us emphasize: if a Radical appears in a specific Compound Logogram *(p. 287)* and does not serve as its Indexing Component *(p. 289)*, it will not be called a Radical – at least not a real Radical. Potential Radicals are not real Radicals[146].

#*Radical 3 –* ✂ *On-duty Radical* (Radical, ✂Real Radical) [AKA Radical, Lexical Component, Lexicographic [147] Component] 📖 A Chinese Logogram *(p. 286)* that serves as the Indexing Component *(p. 289)* of a Compound Logogram *(p. 287)*. Indexing Components *(p. 289)* are real Radicals[148]; thus, may be called simply *Radicals*. Usually, the left-hand Component *(p. 287)* of the Compound Logogram *(p. 287)* is the Radical. In a Phono-semantic Compound *(p. 291)*, the Radical is usually the Semantic Compound Logogram and not the Phonetic Compound Logogram. ✂ Here we assume that a Radical is the Chinese Logogram *(p. 286)* that practically serves as the Compound Logogram's *(p. 287)* Indexing Component *(p. 289)*. Nevertheless, in many sources one can find different meanings of the term Radical: A. The Semantic[149] Component. B. every Chinese Logogram *(p. 286)* inside a Compound Logogram *(p. 287)* - Radical is equivalent to Component *(p. 287)*. C. And of course, a Radical outside a Compound Logogram *(p. 287)* - a Potential Radical *(p. 292)*. **Synonyms = *Indexing Component** (p. 289)*. **See** 👁 ❶ *Kangxi (p. 290).* ❷ *Stem (p. 295).*

#*Real Radical* ✂ ☞ *Radical 3 –* ✂ *On-duty Radical (p. 293)*

#Same-compound Pictogram [AKA Same-compound Character[150], Duplication] 📖 A Pictogram *(p. 292)* that consists of identical Chinese Logograms *(p. 286)*. **Examples** 🔱 ❶ Mawaru-to turn {回}, p. 165 (Outside: 囗, center: 口) ❷ Hayashi-grove {林} (p. 89) (Left: 木, right: 木). 👁 **Antonyms or coordinate terms** ↺/- Different-compound Pictogram.

#*Shimo Ichidan Verb* e (Shiˈmo-ˈichi-dan Verb) (下一段活用) [AKA Lower 1-row, Group 2b, Unigrade e] 📖 A verbal conjugation class. Lower monograde conjugation. Most of the verbs that end in e*-ru. **Antonyms or co-ordinate terms** ↺/- *Kami Ichidan Verb* (p. 290). **See** 👁 *#Ichidan Verb* (p. 289), Shimo-bottom {下} (p. 213).

#Simple Character ☞ *Simple Logogram* (p. 294)

#*Simple Ideogram* 📖 [AKA Simple Ideograph, Single-unit Ideogram, Single Component Ideogram, Distinct Ideogram, Unbreakable Ideogram] An Ideogram (p. 289) that cannot be divided (or can be divided only structurally). **Examples** ↳ ❶ San-three {三} (p. 201). ❷ Ue-top {上}, p. 262. **Antonyms or coordinate terms** ↺/- *Compound Ideogram* (p. 287)

#*Simple Logogram* (独体字) [AKA Simple Character, Single Body Logogram, Single Unit Character, Single Component Character, Distinct Character, Unbreakable Character, Primary Character, Basic Character, Integral Character] 📖 A Chinese Logogram (p. 286) that cannot be divided (or can be divided only structurally). A Simple Logogram has only one Logogram inside it, although the Logogram may have some Strokes (p. 295) attached to it. A Simple Logogram may be graphically complicated. A good example of a graphically complicated Simple Logograms is the Pictogrammatic Radical (Radical 187) Uˈma-horse (馬) (p. 264). The Simple Logograms are but a small percentage of the total Chinese Characters[151]. **Examples** ↳ Ue-top {上} (p. 262). **Antonyms or coordinate terms** ↺/- *Compound Logogram* (p. 287).

#Simple Pictogram [AKA Simple Pictograph, Single-unit Pictogram, Single Component Pictogram, Distinct Pictogram, Unbreakable Pictogram] ☞ *Pictogram* (p. 292)

#*Simplified Character* [AKA ˈShin-ji-ˈtai, New Character Form] 📖 A Chinese Logogram *(p. 286)* that has undergone reforms, such as a reduction in the number of Strokes *(p. 295)*. **Example** ✂ The Pictogrammatic Radical (Radical 187) Uˈma (馬) (p. 264): 騎 (trad.) as opposed to 骑 (simp.). **Antonyms or coordinate terms** ↻/- *Traditional Character (p. 296)*.

#Six-character 📖 A word or a phrase containing six Characters *(p. 286)*. In this dictionary ✂ These can be Chinese Logograms *(p. 286)*, Hiˈra-ga-ˈna (p. 99) Characters and Kaˈta-ka-ˈna *(p. 136)* Characters. **Example** ✂ yoko-gerikeage {{横蹴り蹴上げ}} (p. 279), which consists of 4 Chinese Logograms *(p. 286)* and 2 Hiˈra-ga-ˈna (p. 99) characters.

#Six-kanji ☞ *Six-logogram*

#Six-logogram 📖 A word or a phrase containing six Chinese Logograms *(p. 286)*, and possibly additional Ka-ˈna (p. 126) as well. **Example** ✂ jiyūippon-kumite {{自由一本組手}}, p. 113, which consists of 6 Chinese Logograms and 0 Hiˈra-ga-ˈna Characters.

#*Stem* 📖 ✂ Most Chinese Logograms *(p. 286)* consist of one Radical *(p. 293)* and one Stem. That is to say, a Stem is the non-Radical Component *(p. 287)* in a Compound Logogram *(p. 287)*.

#*Stroke* 📖 Any continuous brushstroke, until the writing instrument is lifted off the paper[152]. **Example** ✂ The Pictogrammatic Radical (Radical 187) Uˈma-horse (馬) (p. 264), contains ten Strokes.

#Three-character 📖 A word or a phrase containing three Characters *(p. 286)*. In this dictionary ✂ These can be Chinese Logograms *(p. 286)*, Hiˈra-ga-ˈna (p. 99) Characters and Kaˈta-ka-ˈna *(p. 136)* Characters. **Examples** ✂ ❶ Tennokata {{天の形}}, p. 241, which consists of 2 Chinese Logograms *(p. 286)* and 1

Hiˈra-ga-ˈna (p. 99) Character. ❷ aiuchi {{相打ち}}, p. 31, which consists of 2 Chinese Logograms *(p. 286)* and 1 Hiˈra-ga-ˈna (p. 99) Characters.

#Three-kanji ☞ *Three-logogram*

#Three-logogram 📖 A word or a phrase containing three Chinese Logograms *(p. 286)*, and possibly additional Ka-ˈna (p. 126) as well. **Example** ⚡ bassaidai {{抜塞大}}, p. 44, which consists of 3 Chinese Logograms and 0 Hiˈra-ga-ˈna Characters.

#*Traditional Character* [AKA ˈKyū-ji-ˈtai, Old Character Form] 📖 An unreformed Chinese Logogram *(p. 286)*. **Example** ⚡ The Pictogrammatic Radical (Radical 187) Uˈma (馬) (p. 264): 騎 (trad.) as opposed to 骑 (simp.). **Antonyms or coordinate terms** ↺/- *Simplified Character (p. 295)*.

#Traditional Radical System ☞ *Kangxi (p. 290)*

#Two-character 📖 A word or a phrase containing two Characters *(p. 286)*. In this dictionary ✂ These can be Chinese Logograms *(p. 286)*, Hiˈra-ga-ˈna (p. 99) Characters and Kaˈta-ka-ˈna *(p. 136)* Characters. **Examples** ❶ mawashi {{回し}}, p. 166, which consists of 1 Chinese Logograms *(p. 286)* and 1 Hiˈra-ga-ˈna (p. 99) Characters. ❷ kaiten {{回転}}, p. 121, which consists of 2 Chinese Logograms *(p. 286)* and 0 Hiˈra-ga-ˈna (p. 99) characters.

#Two-kanji ☞ *Two-logogram (p. 296)*

#*Two-logogram* 📖 A word or a phrase containing two Chinese Logograms *(p. 286)*, and possibly additional Ka-ˈna (p. 126) as well. **Examples** ❶ ageuke {{上げ受け}}, p. 30, which consists of 2 Chinese Logograms *(p. 286)* and 2 Hiˈra-ga-ˈna (p. 99) Characters. ❷ hangetsu {{半月}}, p. 84, which consists of 2 Chinese Logograms *(p. 286)* and 0 Hiˈra-ga-ˈna (p. 99) characters.

Index

This index case sensitive, diacritic sensitive, etc. It includes the notes, and that is one of the reasons we have put the notes at the end of the book. If You are looking for "eyes", for instance, You will find that many of the entries are located in the very end of the book, since one of the popular sources is Adam Dobrzynski **Heian Shodan in Daoist Eyes (Shotokan Katas 1)** (2021). See Technical Remarks on page 24.

O

P

R

'

R

'

S

T

U

V

W

卍

卍 163

卍受け 163, 164, 262

受

受 25, 262, 263, 291

型

型 25, 132, 133, 134

大

大 25, 28, 44, 55, 129, 188, 215, 230, 233, 240, 255

天

天 25, 224, 233, 239, 240, 242

天の形 25, 133, 229, 239, 240, 241, 242, 295

天安門 33, 171, 240

太

太 63, 228, 229

太極 25, 63, 148, 229, 241

小

小 55, 214, 215

少

少 214, 215, 218

少林 ... 25, 42, 44, 62, 67, 88, 89, 90, 91, 92, 93, 111, 127, 128, 215, 218, 229

居

居 102

居合 102, 171, 206, 283

山

山 25, 28, 267, 268, 269

山突き 25, 253, 268, 269, 270

山立ち 25, 28, 227, 268, 269

平

平 33, 89, 94, 97, 98, 99, 243

平仮名 97, 98, 126, 135, 289

平安 33, 90, 91, 92, 93, 97, 98, 194, 255

平拳 25, 97, 99, 139

平行 74, 94, 97

引

引 75, 76, 192

引き分け 75

引き手 75, 234

形

形 15, 17, 44, 57, 62, 67, 68, 83, 90, 91, 92, 93, 103, 109, 111, 115, 128, 132, 133, 134, 148, 235, 237, 238, 239, 240, 241, 242, 286

手

手 15, 17, 75, 87, 88, 99, 106, 111, 120, 130, 140, 157, 162, 172, 175, 179, 184, 187, 198, 205, 209, 222, 234, 236, 243, 244, 248, 249, 264, 266, 267, 282

日

日 96, 159, 170

月

月 28, 34, 70, 83, 86, 97, 99, 138, 154, 169, 252, 253, 282, 285

木

木 55, 89, 101, 124, 148, 251, 276, 278, 293

松

松 164, 219

    松濤 67, 164, 220

林

林 88, 89, 196, 218, 293

止

止 9, 26, 45, 46, 270, 271, 272

    止め 9, 26, 29, 81, 123, 125, 180, 270, 271, 274, 277

武

武 9, 25, 29, 45, 46, 47, 48, 60, 201, 211

    武侠社 45, 47

    武士 45, 48, 201, 211

    武術 45, 47, 116

    武道 45, 46, 57

気

気 25, 69, 141, 142, 143, 146, 187, 231

    気合 25, 41, 141, 143

空

空 126, 129, 130, 223, 224, 239

    空手 129, 130, 131, 132, 223, 234

突

突 25, 187, 253, 254, 255

立

立 16, 25, 28, 64, 78, 84, 85, 94, 95, 144, 150, 153, 173, 182, 195, 202, 227, 233, 235, 284

    立ち..... 55, 64, 78, 84, 85, 94, 95, 144, 150, 153, 173, 182, 195, 202, 209, 227, 233, 235, 268, 284

身

身 72, 85, 107, 168, 228

道

道 46, 48, 57, 58, 131

End of index

Notes

For the reader's convenience, we did not follow the common referencing rules as to repeated references. Instead, all footnotes provide full citations.

---

[1] Adam Dobrzynski **Heian Shodan in Daoist Eyes (Shotokan Katas 1)** (2021) 10.

[2] Ruthie Kotek **What is so Japanese about Shotokan Karate-Do? : Protection of Cultural Identity and Economic Rights in the Global Sphere (M.A. Thesis, University of Haifa)** (2016) 38.

[3] 論語, 子路, 三 (Lúnyǔ, 13, 3).

אמירה כץ **מאמרות קונפוציוס** (2006) 406.

[4] Fung Yu-lan **A History of Chinese Philosophy 1: The Period of the Philosophers (from the beginnings to circa 100 B. C.)** (2nd ed. 1952) 60.

[5] Ruthie Kotek **What is so Japanese about Shotokan Karate-Do? : Protection of Cultural Identity and Economic Rights in the Global Sphere (M.A. Thesis, University of Haifa)** (2016) 66.

[6] Lera Boroditsky "Does Language Shape Thought?: Mandarin and English Speakers' Conceptions of Time" 43(1) **Cognitive Psychology** (2001) 1, 2, 20.

[7] "Dong Zhongshu, "An In-Depth Investigation into Names and Designations" From Luxuriant Dew of the Spring and Autumn Annals 35 translation by Mark Csikszentmihalyi and Bryan W. Van Norden" **Readings in Later Chinese Philosophy: Han Dynasty to the 20th Century** (Justin Tiwald and Bryan W. Van Norden ed., 2014) 10, 11.

[8] Sunny Y. Auyang **The Dragon and the Eagle: The Rise and Fall of the Chinese and Roman Empires** (2014) 98. Anne Schmiedl **Chinese Character Manipulation in Literature and Divination: The Zichu by Zhou Lianggong (1612-1672)** (2020) 79 and note 43.

[9] 左傳, 宣公,十二年 (*Zuǒ Chuán, Xuān Gong*, 12).

[10] Likutei Moharan, Part II 48:2:7.

[11] Adam Dobrzynski **Heian Shodan in Daoist Eyes (Shotokan Katas 1)** (2021) 8-10.

[12] L. Wieger **Chinese Characters: Their Origin, Etymology, History, Classification and Signification - A Thorough Study from Chinese Documents** (2nd ed. 1927) 169 lesson 67 A.

[13] Alison Matthews & Laurence Matthews **Tuttle Learning Chinese Characters (HSK Level A): A Revolutionary New Way to Learn and Remember the 800 Most Basic Chinese Characters** (2007) 75 value 91.

[14] <u>Wood-East</u>: Adam Dobrzynski **Heian Shodan in Daoist Eyes (Shotokan Katas 1)** (2021) 17.

[15] <u>Wood-Beginning</u>: Adam Dobrzynski **Heian Shodan in Daoist Eyes (Shotokan Katas 1)** (2021) 14 around reference 20.

[16] University of Tokyo Kanji Research Group **Essential Japanese Kanji 2: Learn the Essential Kanji Characters Needed for Everyday Interactions in Japan (JLPT Level N4)** (2016) 193.

[17] United States War Department **Japanese-English Glossary: Technical Communication Terms** (1943) 146.

[18] Zhang Yu Huan & Nigel Wiseman **Chinese Medical Characters 2: Acupoint Vocabulary** (2005) 210 (orange book).

[19] Zhang Yu Huan & Nigel Wiseman **Chinese Medical Characters 4: Diagnostic Vocabulary** (2009) 70 value 332 (blue book).

[20] Andrew Ellis, Nigel Wiseman & Ken Boss **Grasping the Wind: An Exploration into the Meaning of Chinese Acupuncture Point Names** (1989) 369.

[21] Sunny Y. Auyang **The Dragon and the Eagle: The Rise and Fall of the Chinese and Roman Empires** (2014) 98. Anne Schmiedl **Chinese Character Manipulation in Literature and Divination: The Zichu by Zhou Lianggong (1612-1672)** (2020) 79 and note 43.

[22] 左傳, 宣公,十二年 (*Zuŏ Chuán*, *Xuān Gong*, 12).

[23] Masaya Shimokusu "Hirai Teiichi, the Japanese Translator of *Dracula* and Literary Shape-shifter" **Multiple Translation Communities in Contemporary Japan** (Routledge Advances in Translation and Interpreting Studies 10) (Beverley Curran, Nana Sato-Rossberg & Kikuko Tanabe ed., 2015) 169, 171.

[24] Andrew Ellis, Nigel Wiseman & Ken Boss **Grasping the Wind: An Exploration into the Meaning of Chinese Acupuncture Point Names** (1989) 359.

[25] Adam Dobrzynski **Heian Shodan in Daoist Eyes (Shotokan Katas 1)** (2021) 24-26.

[26] Christopher Seely & Kenneth G. Henshall **The Complete Guide to Japanese Kanji: Remembering and Understanding the 2,136 Standard Characters** (1998) 290 value 944.

[27] Adam Dobrzynski **Heian Shodan in Daoist Eyes (Shotokan Katas 1)** (2021) 32.

[28] Adam Dobrzynski **Heian Shodan in Daoist Eyes (Shotokan Katas 1)** (2021) 46.

[29] Gichin Funakoshi **Karate Jutsu – the Original Teachings of Master Funakoshi** (John Teramoto trans., 2001) 50.

[30] Claude Larre, Jean Schatz & Elisabeth Rochat de la Valle **Survey of Traditional Chinese Medicine** (1986) 112 – 114.

[31] Adam Dobrzynski **Heian Shodan in Daoist Eyes (Shotokan Katas 1)** (2021) 12 – 14.

[32] Andrew Ellis, Nigel Wiseman & Ken Boss **Grasping the Wind: An Exploration into the Meaning of Chinese Acupuncture Point Names** (1989) 403.

[33] Adam Dobrzynski **Heian Shodan in Daoist Eyes (Shotokan Katas 1)** (2021) 13 around note 18.

[34] José Erasmo de Oliveira Júnior **Karate-Dō Shōtōkan: História, Princípios e Conceitos Básicos** (edición revisada 2016) 116.

[35] Yukio Tono, Makoto Yamazaki & Kikuo Maekawa **A Frequency Dictionary of Japanese: Core Vocabulary for Learners** (2013) 75 value 1372.

[36] Sochin-Sochin Dachi: Hirokazu Kanazawa **Shotokan Karate International Kata 1** (1981) 187.

[37] Tsutomu Ohshima **Notes on Training** (1998) 61 chapter 3.6.

[38] 江上茂『空手道　専門家に贈る』[Egami Shigeru **Karatedō: Senmonka ni Okuru**] (1970 年) 67.

[39] Christopher Seely & Kenneth G. Henshall **The Complete Guide to Japanese Kanji: Remembering and Understanding the 2,136 Standard Characters** (1998) 576 value 1925.

[40] Adam Dobrzynski **Heian Shodan in Daoist Eyes (Shotokan Katas 1)** (2021) 8–10.

[41] Christopher Seely & Kenneth G. Henshall **The Complete Guide to Japanese Kanji: Remembering and Understanding the 2,136 Standard Characters** (1998) 565 value 1892.

[42] Adam Dobrzynski **Heian Shodan in Daoist Eyes (Shotokan Katas 1)** (2021) 9-10.

[43] Andrew Ellis, Nigel Wiseman & Ken Boss **Grasping the Wind: An Exploration into the Meaning of Chinese Acupuncture Point Names** (1989) 354.

[44] Alan Hoenig **Chinese Characters: Learn & Remember 2,178 Characters and Their Meanings** (Simplified Character ed. 2009) 240 §1191.

[45] Arthur Cooper **The Other Greek: An Introduction to Chinese and Japanese Characters, Their History and Influence** (2018) 55.

[46] L. Wieger **Chinese Characters: Their Origin, Etymology, History, Classification and Signification - A Thorough Study from Chinese Documents** (2nd ed. 1927) 50 lesson 15 A.

[47] Mark Edward Cody **Wado Ryu Karate/Jujutsu** (2008) 277.

[48] Ferol Arce & Patrick McDermott **Mind Body Spirit: The Triangle of Life**

(2007) 30.

[49] Wolfgang Hadamitzky & Mark Spahn **Tuttle Japanese Kanji & Kana: A Complete Guide to the Japanese Writing System** (3rd ed. 2011) 134 value 448.

[50] Wolfgang Hadamitzky & Mark Spahn **Tuttle Japanese Kanji & Kana: A Complete Guide to the Japanese Writing System** (3rd ed. 2011) 133 value 439.

[51] Kevin Vandeyck **Ninja's Handbook: Shin-Tengu-Ryu Ninjutsu** (3rd ed. 2017) 87.

[52] Kosho Uchiyama **Deepest Practice, Deepest Wisdom: Three Fascicles from** *Shobogenzo* **with Commentary** (2018) 20.

[53] Gichin Funakoshi **Karate-Dō Kyōhan: The Master Text** (Tsutomu Ohshima trans., 1973) 103.

[54] Gichin Funakoshi **Karate Dō Kyōhan: Master Text for the Way of the Empty-Hand** (Harumi Suzuki-Johnston trans., 2nd ed. 2012) 80.

[55] Christopher Seely & Kenneth G. Henshall **The Complete Guide to Japanese Kanji: Remembering and Understanding the 2,136 Standard Characters** (1998) 432 value 1458.

[56] Haruo Shirane **Classical Japanese: A Grammar** (2005) 31.

[57] Andrew Ellis, Nigel Wiseman & Ken Boss **Grasping the Wind: An Exploration into the Meaning of Chinese Acupuncture Point Names** (1989) 385.

[58] John Harrington Gubbins **A Dictionary of Chinese-Japanese Words in the Japanese Language 2** (1889) 435.

[59] Ki Chiu Kwong **An English and Chinese Dictionary: Compiled from the Latest and Best Authorities, and Containing All Words in Common Use, With Many Examples of Their Use** (1887) 300. Alison Matthews & Laurence Matthews **Tuttle Learning Chinese Characters (HSK Level A): A Revolutionary New Way to Learn and Remember the 800 Most Basic Chinese Characters** (2007) 332 value 740.

[60] Andrew Ellis, Nigel Wiseman & Ken Boss **Grasping the Wind: An Explo-**

ration into the Meaning of Chinese Acupuncture Point Names** (1989) 402.

[61] Christopher Seely & Kenneth G. Henshall **The Complete Guide to Japanese Kanji: Remembering and Understanding the 2,136 Standard Characters** (1998) 137 value 375.

[62] Christopher Seely & Kenneth G. Henshall **The Complete Guide to Japanese Kanji: Remembering and Understanding the 2,136 Standard Characters** (1998) 90 value 178.

[63] Yukio Tono, Makoto Yamazaki & Kikuo Maekawa **A Frequency Dictionary of Japanese: Core Vocabulary for Learners** (2013) 21 value 209.

[64] Sandra L. Beckett **Crossover Picturebooks: A Genre for All Ages** (2012) 101.

[65] Tomie Hahn **Sensational Knowledge: Embodying Culture Through Japanese Dance** (2007) 53.

[66] Pradeep Kumar Yadav **Shotokan Karate- Easiest way to get Black Belt** (2021) 26-27.

[67] Adam Dobrzynski **Heian Shodan in Daoist Eyes (Shotokan Katas 1)** (2021) 24-25.

[68] Yamaguchi Momoo & Steven Bates **A Japanese-English Dictionary of Culture, Tourism and History of Japan** (2014) 409.

[69] Masayuki Shimabukuro & Leonard J. Pellman **Karate as the Art of Killing: A Study of Its Deadly Origins, Ideology of Peace, and the Techniques of Shito-Ryu** (2022) 363.

[70] Yukio Tono, Makoto Yamazaki & Kikuo Maekawa **A Frequency Dictionary of Japanese: Core Vocabulary for Learners** (2013) 43 value 731.

[71] Adam Dobrzynski **Heian Shodan in Daoist Eyes (Shotokan Katas 1)** (2021) 45 around reference 118.

[72] Andrew Ellis, Nigel Wiseman & Ken Boss **Grasping the Wind: An Exploration into the Meaning of Chinese Acupuncture Point Names** (1989) 409.

[73] Adam Dobrzynski **Heian Shodan in Daoist Eyes (Shotokan Katas 1)** (2021) 40.

[74] Chris Denwood **Naihanchi (Tekki) Kata: The Seed of Shuri Karate 1 – Framework, Structure & Dynamics** (2013) 22.

[75] Chris Denwood **Naihanchi (Tekki) Kata: The Seed of Shuri Karate 1 – Framework, Structure & Dynamics** (2013) 21.

[76] Christopher Seely & Kenneth G. Henshall **The Complete Guide to Japanese Kanji: Remembering and Understanding the 2,136 Standard Characters** (1998) 409 value 1379.

[77] Bruce D. Clayton **Shotokan's Secret: The Hidden Truth Behind Karate's Fighting Origins** (2004) 157.

[78] Ernest Mason Satow & Ishibashi Masakata **An English-Japanese Dictionary of the Spoken Language** (3rd ed. 1904) 734.

[79] 孟子, 告子上, 二 (Mèngzǐ, Gào zi shàng, 2).

[80] Adam Dobrzynski **Heian Shodan in Daoist Eyes (Shotokan Katas 1)** (2021) 40.

[81] Adam Dobrzynski **Heian Shodan in Daoist Eyes (Shotokan Katas 1)** (2021) 40.

[82] Brandon W. Maynard **From Dawn to Dan: The Journey of Karate Masters (Ph. D. Thesis, Antioch University Santa Barbara)** (2017) x.

[83] Adam Dobrzynski **Heian Shodan in Daoist Eyes (Shotokan Katas 1)** (2021) 40.

[84] Adam Dobrzynski **Heian Shodan in Daoist Eyes (Shotokan Katas 1)** (2021) 23.

[85] Adam Dobrzynski **Heian Shodan in Daoist Eyes (Shotokan Katas 1)** (2021) 32.

[86] Gichin Funakoshi & Genwa Nakasone **The Twenty Guiding Principles of**

Karate: The Spiritual Legacy of the Master (2003) 125-126. Bruce D. Clayton **Shotokan's Secret: The Hidden Truth Behind Karate's Fighting Origins** (2004)103 note 171.

[87] Gichin Funakoshi **Karate-Dō Kyōhan: The Master Text** (Tsutomu Ohshima trans., 1973) 9, 37.

[88] 朱子語類, 理氣上 (*Zhūzi yǔ lèi, Lǐqì shàng*). Gichin Funakoshi **Karate-Dō Kyōhan: The Master Text** (Tsutomu Ohshima trans., 1973) 42 note 2.

[89] Wm. Theodore De Bary & Irene Bloom **Sources of Chinese Tradition 1: From Earliest Times to 1600** (2nd ed. 1999) 673-674. Joseph A. Adler **Reconstructing the Confucian Dao: Zhu Xi's Appropriation of Zhou Dunyi** (2014) 113.

[90] 道德经, 四十二 (*Dàodé Jīng*, 42).

[91] Koo Dong Yun **The Holy Spirit and Ch'i (Qi): A Chiological Approach to Pneumatology** (2012) 53. Justin Tiwald & Bryan W. Van Norden **Readings in Later Chinese Philosophy: Han Dynasty to the 20th Century** (2014) 136.

[92] Peter Deadman, Mazin Al-Khafaji & Kevin Baker **A Manual of Acupuncture** (2001) 502.

[93] Andrew Ellis, Nigel Wiseman & Ken Boss **Grasping the Wind: An Exploration into the Meaning of Chinese Acupuncture Point Names** (1989) 432. Richard Bertschinger **The Great Intent: Acupuncture Odes, Songs and Rhymes** (2013) 291 Ren-7.

[94] Peter Deadman, Mazin Al-Khafaji & Kevin Baker **A Manual of Acupuncture** (2001) 505.

[95] Huang-fu Mi **The Systematic Classic of Acupuncture & Moxibustion** (1994) 94. Wang Shu-he **The Pulse Classic: A Translation of the Mai Jing** (1997) 53.

[96] Giovanni Maciocia **Obstetrics and Gynecology in Chinese Medicine** (2nd ed. 2011) 173 REN-4. Richard Bertschinger **The Great Intent: Acupuncture**

Odes, Songs and Rhymes (2013) 291 Ren-4. Bede Benjamin Bidlack **In Good Company: The Body and Divinization in Pierre Teilhard De Chardin, SJ and Daoist Xiao Yingsou (East Asian Comparative Literature and Culture 5)** (2015) 160 note 42.

[97] Shōji Kobayashi **Acupuncture Core Therapy: Shakujyū Chiryō** (2008) viii.

[98] Alan Hoenig **Chinese Characters: Learn & Remember 2,178 Characters and Their Meanings** (Simplified Character ed. 2009) 238 value 1179.

[99] Andrew Ellis, Nigel Wiseman & Ken Boss **Grasping the Wind: An Exploration into the Meaning of Chinese Acupuncture Point Names** (1989) 396.

[100] Gichin Funakoshi & Genwa Nakasone **The Twenty Guiding Principles of Karate: The Spiritual Legacy of the Master** (2003) 125-126. Bruce D. Clayton **Shotokan's Secret: The Hidden Truth Behind Karate's Fighting Origins** (2004)103 note 171.

[101] Gichin Funakoshi **Karate-Dō Kyōhan: The Master Text** (Tsutomu Ohshima trans., 1973) 9, 37.

[102] Andrew Ellis, Nigel Wiseman & Ken Boss **Grasping the Wind: An Exploration into the Meaning of Chinese Acupuncture Point Names** (1989) 362.

[103] Adam Dobrzynski **Heian Shodan in Daoist Eyes (Shotokan Katas 1)** (2021) 40.

[104] Pradeep Kumar Yadav **Shotokan Karate- Easiest way to get Black Belt** (2021) 26-27.

[105] Gichin Funakoshi **Karate-Dō Kyōhan: The Master Text** (Tsutomu Ohshima trans., 1973) 235.

[106] Lee Taylor Ananko **Kata Form & Function** (2014) 46.

[107] Yukio Tono, Makoto Yamazaki & Kikuo Maekawa **A Frequency Dictionary of Japanese: Core Vocabulary for Learners** (2013) 139 value 2747.

[108] Andrew Ellis, Nigel Wiseman & Ken Boss **Grasping the Wind: An Exploration into the Meaning of Chinese Acupuncture Point Names** (1989) 398.

[109] Christopher Seely & Kenneth G. Henshall **The Complete Guide to Japanese Kanji: Remembering and Understanding the 2,136 Standard Characters** (1998) 538 – 539 value 1805.

[110] Bernhard Karlgren **Analytic Dictionary of Chinese and Sino-Japanese** (1923) 97 value 245.

[111] Hongkyung Kim **The Analects of Dasan 2: A Korean Syncretic Reading** (2nd ed. 2018) 199.

[112] William McClure **Using Japanese: A Guide to Contemporary Usage** (2000) 66.

[113] Andrew Ellis, Nigel Wiseman & Ken Boss **Grasping the Wind: An Exploration into the Meaning of Chinese Acupuncture Point Names** (1989) 409.

[114] Giorgio Francesco Arcodia & Bianca Basciano **Chinese Linguistics: An Introduction** (2021) 65.

[115] **Japanese English Bilingual Visual Dictionary** (Angela Wilkes ed., 2011) 237.

[116] Luke A. Archer **From Conflict to Conversation: A Verbal Aikido™ Practitioner's Guide** (2020) 6.

[117] Li Dong **Tuttle Learner's Chinese-English Dictionary** (2nd ed. 2015) 168.

[118] University of Tokyo Kanji Research Group **Essential Japanese Kanji 1: Learn the Essential Kanji Characters Needed for Everyday Interactions in Japan (JLPT Level N5)** (2015) 169 value 213. Alex Adler **The World of Kanji: Learn 2136 Japanese Characters through Real Etymology** (2018) 353 value 1424.

[119] But see: Robert Morrison **A Dictionary of The Chinese Language in Three Parts 1** (1815) 342 (Radical 29).

[120] John Young & Kimiko Nakajima-Okano **Learn Japanese: New College Text IV** (1985) 127 value 7.6.8. Ian Low **Dictionary of 10,000 Chinese Characters (Traditional): With Fast Look-up Combined Strokecount-Radical**

Main Index and Cantonese and Mandarin Common Phonetic Spelling Indexes (2012) 44 value 1305.

[121] Alison Matthews & Laurence Matthews **Tuttle Learning Chinese Characters: (HSK Level A) A Revolutionary New Way to Learn and Remember the 800 Most Basic Chinese Characters** (2007) 53 value 52.

[122] Victor H. Mair "Language and Script" **The Columbia History of Chinese Literature** (Victor H. Mair ed., 2010) 19, 39-40.

[123] United States War Department **Dictionary of Spoken Chinese: Chinese-English, English-Chinese** (1945) 69.

[124] Robert Morrison **A Dictionary of The Chinese Language in Three Parts 3.6** (1822) 413 (STR).

[125] Ian Low **Chinese to English Dictionary (Simplified Characters): With Fast Look-up Combined Strokecount-Radical Index** (2012) 74.

[126] 船越義珍『琉球拳法 唐手』(大正 11 年) [Funakoshi Gichin **Ryūkyū Kenpō Tō-te** (1922)] 246 illustration 182.

[127] 船越義珍『錬膽護身 唐手術』(大正 14 年) [Funakoshi Gichin **Rentan Goshin Tō-te Jutsu** (1925)] 246 photograph 193.

[128] 船越義珍『空手道教範』(昭和 10 年) [Funakoshi Gichin **Karate-dō Kyōhan** (1935)] 91 photograph 69.

[129] Kent Sisco **Finding Rest** (2016) 90.

[130] Gichin Funakoshi **Karate-Dō Kyōhan: The Master Text** (Tsutomu Ohshima trans., 1973) 30, 42, 43 note 3.

[131] Gichin Funakoshi **Karate-Dō Kyōhan: The Master Text** (Tsutomu Ohshima trans., 1973) 31.

[132] Gichin Funakoshi **Karate-Dō Kyōhan: The Master Text** (Tsutomu Ohshima trans., 1973) 43 note 3.

[133] Gichin Funakoshi **Karate-Dō Kyōhan: The Master Text** (Tsutomu Ohshima trans., 1973) 30.

[134] Yoko Hasegawa **Japanese: A Linguistic Introduction** (2015) 116 note 2.

[135] Andrew Deitsch & David Czarnecki **Java Internationalization** (2001) 421. Masato Hagiwara **Real-World Natural Language Processing** (2021) 52.

[136] Jian Wang, Albrecht W. Inhoff & Hsuan-Chih Chen **Reading Chinese Script: A Cognitive Analysis** (1999) 116.

[137] Mary C. Dyson & Ching Y. Suen **Digital Fonts and Reading (Language Processing, Pattern Recognition, and Intelligent Systems 1)** (2016) 120-121.

[138] Hartmut Walravens, Oliver Corff & Barbara Kellner-Heinkele **Statehood in the Altaic World: Proceedings of the 59th Annual Meeting of the Permanent International Altaistic Conference (PIAC), Ardahan, Turkey, June 26-July 1, 2016** (2018) 107.

[139] Shouhui Zhao & Richard B. Baldauf, Jr. **Planning Chinese Characters: Reaction, Evolution or Revolution? (Language Policy 9)** (2008) 14.

[140] Giorgio Francesco Arcodia & Bianca Basciano **Chinese Linguistics: An Introduction** (2021) 65.

[141] James Myers **The Grammar of Chinese Characters: Productive Knowledge of Formal Patterns in an Orthographic System** (2019) 53.

[142] Alison Matthews & Laurence Matthews **Tuttle Learning Chinese Characters: (HSK Level A) A Revolutionary New Way to Learn and Remember the 800 Most Basic Chinese Characters** (2007) 12.

[143] Chu-Ren Huang & Dingxu Shi **A Reference Grammar of Chinese** (2016) 9.

[144] Eliane Segers & Paul van den Broek **Developmental Perspectives in Written Language and Literacy: In Honor of Ludo Verhoeven** (2017) 220.

[145] Hsuan Chih Chen & Ovid J.L. Tzeng **Language Processing in Chinese** (1992) 5.

[146] Shouhui Zhao & Richard B. Baldauf, Jr. **Planning Chinese Characters: Reaction, Evolution or Revolution? (Language Policy 9)** (2008) 13.

[147] James Myers **The Grammar of Chinese Characters: Productive**

Knowledge of Formal Patterns in an Orthographic System (2019) 53.

[148] Shouhui Zhao & Richard B. Baldauf, Jr. **Planning Chinese Characters: Reaction, Evolution or Revolution? (Language Policy 9)** (2008) 13.

[149] Fritz Pasierbsky "Adaptation Processes in Chinese: Word Formation" **Language Adaptation** (Florian Coulmas ed.,1989) 90, 95.

[150] Han Jiantang **Chinese Characters** (2012) 62.

[151] Shouhui Zhao & Richard B. Baldauf, Jr. **Planning Chinese Characters: Reaction, Evolution or Revolution? (Language Policy 9)** (2008) 13.

[152] Jian Wang, Hsuan-Chih Chen, Ralph Radach & Albrecht Inhoff **Reading Chinese Script: A Cognitive Analysis** (1999) 190.

www.ingramcontent.com/pod-product-compliance
Lightning Source LLC
Chambersburg PA
CBHW081130090426
42737CB00018B/3283